Contents

Acknowledgments

HUNDREDS OF PEOPLE in the outdoor community in Denver and Boulder, and throughout the Front Range and beyond, contributed to the making of this book. The guide came to be a collective sharing of local outdoor knowledge earned over lifetimes of experience. Thanks to you all. People here value and love the hills and rivers and mountains around them with a profound respect, and I was constantly moved by everyone's willingness to entrust favorite places to the readers of this book. I hope that we can repay them by being excellent stewards and guardians of these resources.

I use the pronoun "we" a lot in this book, because I worked very closely with my researcher,

Sarah Knopp, to create it. We explored a lot of the trails together and she had thoughtful, fun input every step of the way. She's a Denver native and knew a lot about the area that I never could have known, and her enthusiasm and careful, conscientious work made the book happen.

Thanks also to Colorado State Parks; Jefferson County Open Space; Denver Water; and city parks in Denver, Boulder, Golden, and other towns for carving out and protecting so many beautiful areas—and for fielding hours and hours of questions. The U.S. Forest Service and the U.S. Park Service were also immensely helpful.

Special thanks to Ardis Rohwer, Barbara Evert, Andy Arnold, and John Jaycox, Senior Backcountry Consultants, for sharing their extensive knowledge.

Several companies gave strong support and sponsorship. Thanks to Specialized Bicycles for the fine blue Rockhopper that Sarah rode all over the Front Range; Verizon Wireless for the generous use of cell phones, which were extremely handy in our explorations and research; Gaia Paddlesports of Athens, Tennessee, for some of the best dry bags and waterproof map and GPS cases we've seen; and Wildwasser Sports in Boulder, for unrelenting generosity in sharing Prijon boats and paddles, and their own top-of-line sprayskirts and dry bags.

This book would not have happened without all of you who patiently, generously, and enthusiastically shared your experience and knowledge. You made the project fun, and I am extremely grateful.

Introduction

WHEN I FIRST came to Colorado's Front Range I lived fifteen minutes up Boulder Canyon on a hill called Sugarloaf. The house was in the pines. The air was redolent with their scent, and they combed the wind night and day with a rush like spectral surf. I could look over their tops, downcanyon, through the V of the shouldering ridges, and see the city on the high plain. Farther out, at night, were the lights of the suburbs north of Denver.

My housemate, John Mattson, was crazy. He was a successful design/build contractor, well loved by his friends and generally sweet to pets and children. But he was possessed. I'm not sure I've ever met a more passionate outdoorsman and

adventurer. In the evening he'd challenge me to a game of pool and then, as I leaned over the break, he'd say, "Let's go paddle Upper Upper Boulder Creek tomorrow."

"I don't think anybody's ever done it, and besides, there's no water in it."

Silence. I'd let my eyes stray upward, and he'd be grinning, his eyes sparking with a demonic light, and he'd say, "Aw, c'mon Pete, there's a little water in it." And the next afternoon I'd find myself following his kayak over a barely wet ledge, grabbing rocks to do pivot moves through ten-inch-wide channels. It was the same, months later, with skiing: "There's not enough snow." "Use your rock skis." "I don't have rock skis." "I'll lend you some." And we'd be crashing through the woods behind his house on threadbare strips of white, down into the canyon, and by the end of the run I owned a pair of rock skis.

John, among others, showed me the ropes. In the afternoon we drove ten minutes up to the Switzerland Trail and mountain biked an hour-and-a-half loop on rough dirt road and singletrack that contoured past views of the Indian Peaks, and descended steeply to a little stream and a grove of aspen. It was early fall. As the days progressed the aspen yellowed, and the leaves spun and trembled with a drier rattle, and they littered the trail along the creek.

Some evenings we met friends in town and paddled kayaks in the whitewater park on Boulder Creek, or headed out to the reservoir for long flatwater paddles. Sometimes I fly-fished on the rocky bends just upstream of the electric station. John was a fanatic rock climber, and he spent a lot of his free time climbing difficult routes in famed Eldorado Canyon just south of town, or on the cliffs in Boulder Canyon. When he was down on the Colorado University campus studying engineering, he bouldered on the engineering building. (The practice is now illegal.) He hauled dates up the easier climbs on the Flatirons.

Personally, I drew the line at rock climbing. Every time he suggested I accompany him on a climb I had a previous engagement. Finally I said, "I'm afraid of heights." He said, "It's an acquired phobia." "Well, I acquired it." He looked at me as if he were trying to assess how much work it would be to make me inquire it, then he smiled and asked if I wanted an oatmeal stout.

Another friend was a leading marathon runner. She trained on the rolling dirt trails that skirted the foothills north of town, or on the wooded runs out of Chautauqua Park, above the center of the city. Another was a paraglider who jumped off the same hills.

It dawned on me that while I was essentially living in a city, I was also living in an outdoorsperson's paradise. Anything I wanted to do, and a lot I hadn't yet become interested in, like windsurfing and in-line skating, was minutes away—often within the city limits—as were all the restaurants, music, films, and fancy coffee of a small, extremely self-respecting metropolis.

Years later, when I moved to Denver from Colorado's Western Slope, I was surprised again. I found myself paddling more whitewater than I had in years. I'd drive seven minutes to the rapids at Confluence on the South Platte, a paddle-throw from Union Station, and surf my head off. At high water, I'd go twenty minutes south to a prime play spot called Union Chutes, or half an hour west to Golden and the brilliant whitewater park on Clear Creek, right in the middle of town. Just upstream, in Clear Creek Canyon, are classic river-runs that range from Class III to Class V. I discovered the technical mountain biking at Mathews Winters Park, fifteen minutes from Denver, and the High Line Canal, a lovely, tree-shaded ride or run accessible from downtown; also the stunning steep rides up in White Ranch and Golden Gate Canyon State Park and Waterton Canyon, all about thirty-five minutes from the city. Within forty-five minutes are a dozen good trout streams. Within an hour and a quarter is all the skiing, both backcountry and resort downhill, a knee would ever want to handle.

There's so much adventuring to do within and just outside of Denver and Boulder it can make an enthusiast giddy. And because these are cities, there are a lot of people doing everything, from casual funsters to competitive champions and extreme rad envelope-pushers. It's never hard to connect with people, and it makes for an exciting adventure culture. You can adventure during lunch hour, you can adventure after work, and with a little more time, you have thousands of square miles of some of the most exquisite terrain anywhere. And because these are cities, you can, thank God, do city things after you come off the hill. Denver and Boulder are getting increasingly sophisticated, with world-class dance, music, and theater including excellent local drama companies doing original work; blues and bluegrass festivals; natural history museums; and aquariums and zoos. The area's cultural life is no longer limited to the annual visit of *Phantom of the Opera.*

But it took a long time, and a lot of advice from outdoor devotees, to suss out the best places to explore. The purpose of this book is to spare you months and years of research. A guide like this, covering a score of activities, can only be highly selective, and makes no claim to being a comprehensive or definitive source. The book covers the possibilities of Urban, and Barely Extra-Urban, and Decidedly Un-Urban Adventure. My hope is that it will serve as a useful and encouraging signpost on your own unfolding path of exploration. I've included classic routes and areas, and some sleepers—spots that are less well known and that can handle more use. And for the novice or less experienced, I've listed instruction and guide services, and clubs and specialty shops where a person can hook up. Also, some basic tips from the experts, such as Don't get Dehydrated, and Bring a Hat.

I didn't include my favorite fishing hole or mountain bike ride in this book. There are intimacies and loves and secrets. And for all of us, the excitement of finding our own.

How to Use This Book

This is a guidebook for adventurous people.

All mileage is approximate—meaning pretty close. Elevations are reasonably accurate, and elevation gain is calculated from the lowest elevation on a route to the highest, and does not include all the ups and downs in between. Descriptions of routes are brief, briefer than in most guidebooks, and probably won't include every landmark and every distance to every turn. The idea is to point you toward the best places to go and to try to keep you from getting lost. Good judgment, a sense of humor, and a decent sense of direction can be extremely helpful. Companions with these qualities are also a wonderful resource.

Except for very technical activities, such as rock climbing, where you really need a comprehensive guidebook, the route descriptions found here, along with the recommended map, should get you there and back. (Often, as is the case with trails in state parks and city and county Open Spaces, the maps are on handy brochures right at the trailhead.) But the very best thing to do, should you get excited about any activity, is to get the guidebooks referred to in each chapter. No one can tell you better how to fish the area's streams, or give you more ideas on new creeks than fly-fishing writers Marty Bartholomew and Todd Hosman.

Jack Roberts, Richard Rossiter, Stewart M. Green, and Phillip Benningfield will tell you how to climb the area's best rock, ice, and boulder routes. The authors of all guides, in all the sports, are passionate and wise, and will suggest many other route options in any area, and give a lot of great background, history, safety, and technical advice. I couldn't have written this book without them.

Also, for an overview of all the areas and the best help in getting to them, pick up the *Colorado Atlas and Gazetteer.* It covers the entire state in 1:160,000 topos, with roads of all sizes and a lot of trails. It's superb for getting around the state and for a general idea of how the country ties together.

A few words on how the chapters are organized. Most of the routes are divided into *City Limits* and *Backyard* for either Denver or Boulder. *City Limits* means very close to downtown. *Backyard* means, loosely, routes within an easy hour's drive. I say "loosely," because some routes, like the kayak runs on the South Platte near its confluence with the North Fork, are frequented so often by Denverites that they have to be considered in a Denver kayaker's Spiritual Backyard, even if they take over an hour to get to. Driving miles and directions are given to these backyard spots from their respective cities. Then there are the *Short Hops.* These are, generally, within an hour-and-a-half drive. Usually they lie west in the mountains, and so directions begin at the junction of US 6 and I-70, confident that the reader can get to that point, or find the best access from home. The town of Golden, west of Denver and south of Boulder, lies roughly equidistant from each city. In and around it is a lot of beautiful country. For routes outside of Golden, directions from both Denver and Boulder are given.

As for the stats at the beginning of most route descriptions, here's what they mean:

Location: Provides the driving miles and general direction from the intersection of I-25 and 6th Avenue (US 6) in Denver; or the intersection of 28th Street (US 36) and Canyon Boulevard (CO 119) in Boulder. *Short Hop* distances are measured from the junction of US 6 and I-25 west of Denver.

Length: The total length of the trail, route, or paddle. Each is designated as either a loop or an out-and-back.

Difficulty: Easy, moderate, or difficult. Take these with a grain of salt and a gulp of Gatorade. This is a very general rating designation. I didn't get more specific because I realize that these are often subjective distinctions, and because I feel that much of the sense of adventure in exploring new terrain is not knowing beforehand exactly what to expect.

Terrain: The character of the ground over which you'll be walking, running, pedaling, or riding.

Elevation gain: Calculated from the lowest point on a route to the highest. All the in-between ups and downs are extra.

Highest elevation: Highest elevation on a trail. Used only on trails in the high country.

Maps and books: Many guidebooks recommend a list of relevant maps for each route. For the purposes of concision, I usually recommend just the one I found easiest to use and most useful in completing the route. Often this can be the simple sketch found in the brochure at an Open Space trailhead—it works and it's free.

Dogs: Yes or no. Allowed or not. More specific regulations can be found at trailheads. Some places require that a dog be on a leash; others simply stipulate that he or she be under voice and sight control.

Heads up: Highlights, things to look out for, or hazards worth emphasizing.

Description: A general description of the place, the terrain, and the route to give you a feel for what you're in for.

Route: On-trail or on-river route directions. Distances to turn-offs, trail junctions, and so forth are usually rounded off to the nearest mile, so stay aware and use good judgment.

Directions: Driving directions to the trailhead or river put-in. Directions for routes in Denver *City Limits* and *Backyard* are from the intersection of I-25 and 6th Avenue (US 6) in Denver; for Boulder *City Limits* and *Backyard* routes, directions are given from the intersection of 28th Street (US 36) and Canyon Boulevard (CO 119) in Boulder. Directions to *Short Hops* begin at the junction of US 6 and I-70 west of Denver.

One other important concept to note: The book can best be used by creatively combining trails in different chapters. The "Hiking" chapter, for instance, describes only a dozen routes. However, just about every trail in the book can be a great hike. Check out trails in "Mountain Biking," "Running," "Snowshoing," and "Cross-Country Skiing." The same holds true for many of the other activities. As long as there's enough snow on the ground, a lot of the hikes or runs make great snowshoe routes. So don't limit yourself to the trails in any one chapter when you're looking for new places to explore.

Writing this book was a labor of love. The luck of living in this place, and the beauty of it, informed the entire process. This is our home—the rugged mountains looming to the west, and the expansive sweep of high plains unrolling to the east. The creeks and canyons and rivers. We're so lucky. Have fun and take care of each other.

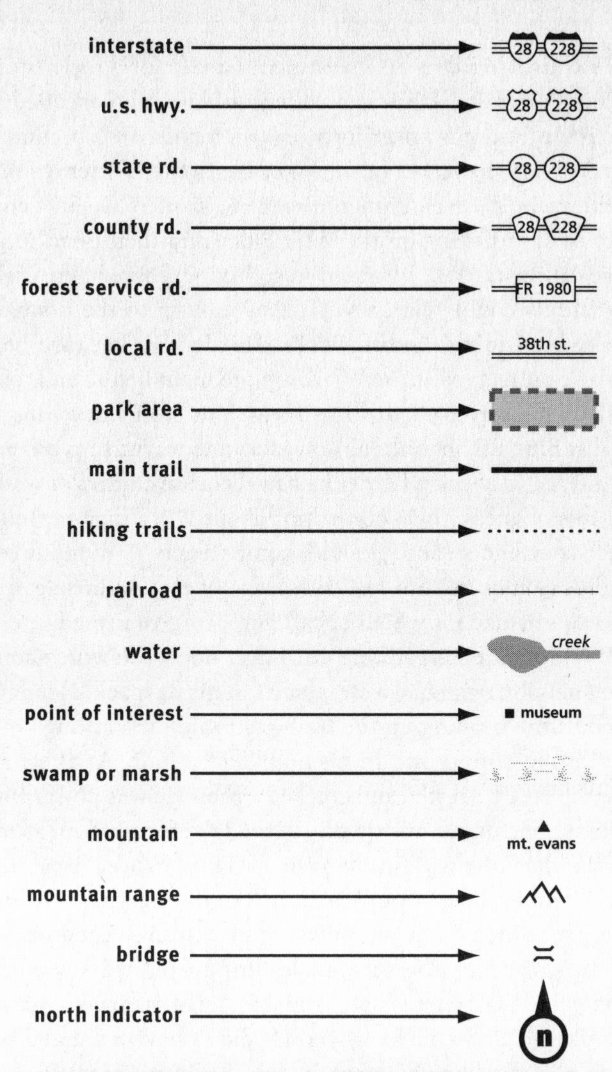
interstate
28
228
u.s. hwy.
28
228
state rd.
28
228
county rd.
28
228
forest service rd.
FR 1980
local rd.
38th st.
park area
main trail
hiking trails
railroad
water
creek
point of interest
museum
swamp or marsh
mountain
mt. evans
mountain range
bridge
north indicator
n
Legend

Mountain Safety

My cousin Willy is an investment banker for a top firm in New York City. He was a college athlete who excelled at lacrosse, and now, near forty, enjoys tennis. He's become a little overweight, but has the constitution and strength of a Brahma bull. Last summer he came to visit. We spent a couple of days fishing on the West Slope and then I had to go back to work. Willy wanted to go hiking, somewhere high, where he could "eat snow." I sent him up to the Brainard Lake area in the Indian Peaks. He slept in because he'd drunk quite a lot at the Wynkoop the night before and took off from Denver about nine; I saw him stuff three cans of Pabst Blue Ribbon into his daypack, and waved him off, not thinking to check whether he had adequate clothes or water or food. I guess it was something about Will's high-powered self-confidence and general competence—I didn't even think to inquire into his knowledge of mountain safety. It was a mistake for which I shall never forgive myself.

Will didn't start hiking until near noon. He wore shorts and a T-shirt and had a sweatshirt in his daypack. He made good time heading up the trail—as I said, he's strong—and he broke timberline in an hour and a half. At the first alpine lake he rested and cracked a beer. He was powerfully thirsty. He drank a little out of the lake for good measure. With that one icy sip, months of Third World fiscal and credit static lifted from his brain like morning fog. He was a little chilled, so he put on his thick cotton sweatshirt and then started up the rockfall leading to the ridge. He felt dizzy, a little nauseous, and his head banged, but he chalked it up to his hangover. He didn't have a hat and the sun hammered on his nose; he felt the burn already. By the time he got to the snow, he felt quite ill. Some sort of food would be great right now, he thought, but he didn't have any, and anyway, he was fast losing his appetite—a result of the onset of altitude sickness. He thought he could salvage his day by making the top of the ridge and getting the big view. It was then about 3:00.

Will didn't notice the dark thunderheads gathering quickly in the southwest, or the stiffening wind. He humped up to the ridge, and just as he made the top was blasted by driving rain and hail. He hugged himself. The cotton sweat- and T-shirts were soaked immediately and afforded no warmth or protection. The wintry wind sheared through them as if they were gauze. Will panicked. He began to shiver uncontrollably. He started down the steep talus field, but couldn't maintain his footing on the jumble of rocks, so he headed across and down a steep gully of old snow. . . .

You get the picture, an ugly one at that. And it brings to mind the simple litany of mountain safety precautions that Will so blithely violeted. First, and most obviously, he could have avoided a lot of pain by bringing some:

Basic Equipment

Sunglasses, sunscreen, and a brimmed hat (the sun's ultraviolet rays increase in intensity approximately 5 percent for every 1,000 feet in elevation gain)
Food and plenty of water
Headlamp and batteries
First-aid kit
Map and compass
Fire starter paste
Matches
Knife
Emergency blanket
Warm clothes (wool or fleece hat; gloves; sweater; waterproof, windproof shell; *no cotton*)

An experienced outdoorsperson in Colorado reflexively throws all of this stuff into a daypack or dry bag for any kind of jaunt into the mountains that will take her any distance from a trailhead.

Basic Safety

Altitude Sickness

Altitude sickness is an overall feeling of malaise brought on by not allowing enough time to acclimate to the lower concentrations of atmospheric oxygen that occur at higher elevations. Symptoms include nausea, dizziness, headache, and loss of appetite. Severe cases can result in high-altitude pulmonary and cerebral edema death. Your best defense is to stop and rest, go slower, and drink plenty of water. Make sure you are getting enough sodium, either in food or in tablets. If this advice doesn't seem to help, descend to a lower elevation.

Giardiasis

Do not drink untreated water from Colorado's lakes and streams. The mean little protozoan *Giardia lamblia* is ubiquitous. You do not want to get what it can give you within days or weeks of ingestion: diarrhea, loss of appetite, weight loss, cramps, fatigue. Take easy-to-use iodine crystal systems, such as Polar Pure, or one of the many personal water purification pumps now on the market. Make sure the pore size of the filter is 5 microns or less.

Mountain Weather

Colorado weather changes quickly. Precipitation amounts increase with elevation. Temperature decreases—dropping 3.5°F with every 1,000 feet of elevation gain. Generally, storms sweep across the mountains from the west.

To prepare yourself for all weather conditions, dress in layers. The first layer, next to the skin, should be a wicking layer made from lightweight, noncotton materials, such as Capiline, polypropylene, and bergaline. The next layer insulates. It should be made from wool or a synthetic material such as pile. The shell or top layer should be made of windproof, waterproof, and breathable materials such as Gore-Tex. The shell is the most important layer! It keeps rain or snow away from the body and allows the insulating layer to retain heat that would otherwise blow away in the wind.

Never wear cotton while hiking Fourteeners. It absorbs water, including sweat, and does not dry fast enough. Moisture next to the skin results in rapid heat loss.

Lightning

In June through August the Colorado mountains experience regular daily thunderstorms that include heavy rain, hail, and lightning. If you are caught on a ridge or the summit during a thunderstorm descend quickly, stash any metal gear, and crouch down with your feet together and fingers laced over the back of your neck. If available, place an insulating layer, such as a foam pad, between your feet and the ground. *Do not crouch next to large boulders or tall trees, and stay out of standing water.*

The best way to deal with lightning is to avoid it entirely. Always begin your adventure early—be at the summit before noon to avoid thunderstorms. This means that if you're climbing a Fourteener you need to start before dawn.

Hypothermia

Hypothermia is a rapid loss of body temperature that leads to mental and physical collapse and possibly death. It is caused by exposure to cold and aggravated by water, wind, and exhaustion. Most cases of hypothermia occur when the air temperature is between 30 and 50°F.

The first stage is exposure: the body starts to lose heat faster than it can produce it. In response, the body makes involuntary adjustments to preserve normal temperature in its vital organs.

The second stage is hypothermia. If exposure lasts until the body runs out of energy, cold reaches the brain, taking away judgment and reasoning power. The victim will not know this is happening, will lose control of his hands, and become drowsy. Defense: Stay dry. Choose raingear that covers the head, neck, body, and legs and provides good protection against wind.

Symptoms of hypothermia include uncontrollable shivering; vague, slow, slurred speech; memory lapses; lurching gate; drowsiness; apparent exhaustion; and the inability to get up after rest.

To treat hypothermia, get the patient out of the wind and rain and strip off all wet clothes. Give him warm drinks if he can swallow. Get him into warm clothes and a warm sleeping bag. If he is badly impaired, attempt to keep him awake, strip his clothes off, and put him in a sleeping bag with another naked person. Start a fire.

Avalanche

Traveling in avalanche terrain can be dangerous any time there's a snowpack. Learn how to recognize avalanche terrain—slopes between 30 and 45°F, leeward aspects, avalanche paths and chutes. Learn how to move through it safely and make wise decisions about when not to and carry safety gear, such as beacons and shovels, and know how to use them. *The best thing to do is to take an avalanche safety course.* Check for course offerings at REI (303-756-3100); they offer classes with the Colorado Avalanche Information Center (CAIC). For daily snowpack conditions around the state call the Avalanche Hotline (303-275-5360). Also check skicountryusa.com for snow and avalanche reports from all the ski areas in Colorado. The CAIC publishes a great booklet called *Avalanche Wise* by Knox Williams and Dale Atkins. Write the CAIC at 325 Broadway, WS1, Boulder, CO 80303. They have a tremendous Web site that includes avalanche reports, books, and course offerings at www.caic.state.co.us

Ice Safety

Two inches of clear, solid ice can support one fisherman on foot; 4 inches can support ice fishing; 8 inches, a passenger car (2 tons); 10 inches, a medium truck (3.5 tons). New ice is generally stronger than old ice.

These are only guidelines, not guarantees; ice thickness varies throughout reservoirs and streams and is affected by many things including weather, underwater currents, and water-level fluctuation. Indicators of weak ice include different colored ice, surface water on the ice, cracks, porous-looking ice, pressure ridges, and open water or bubbles.

If your companion falls through the ice, get her out of water immediately, being careful not to end up in the water yourself. Remove all wet clothing and wrap her in a warm blanket or sleeping bag. Place her in a heated automobile and transport to the nearest medical facility. Do not rub or massage skin tissue, give alcoholic beverages, or allow her to walk around or expend energy. If she is not breathing or has no pulse, begin CPR.

Wildlife

The top-of-the-food-chain kind, specifically mountain lions and bears, can cause you harm. Wesley Massey, an Outdoor Recreation Specialist for the U.S. Forest Service, has the following tips.

For bear: If you see one in Colorado there's a 99 percent chance that it *won't* be a grizzly. So you're dealing with black bears, which are much less dangerous. Eighty percent of bear–human contacts occur in campgrounds. Store food properly and don't bring any into your tent. If a bear comes into camp, yell, bang pots, wave your arms, and scare it away. The same applies in the backcountry. Do *not* get in between a sow and her cubs. If attacked, fight back.

For mountain lion: These are very elusive creatures. They travel a large territory, up to one hundred square miles, and are very shy. If you see one they probably don't care—not a good sign. Don't run or climb a tree. Grab anything you can use as a weapon—rock, stick, knife, .357 magnum—and prepare to fight. Back away slowly. If attacked, there's not a damn thing good about it—the lion is stressed and hungry—so fight like hell.

In general, don't let your children run ahead down the trail. If in known bear or lion territory, leash your dogs. Massey says that it's common for contacts to occur because a dog spooked the animal, then ran back to camp, bringing the enraged guest with it.

Archery and black powder hunting seasons begin in late August, and big game rifle season starts in early October and runs into November. If you plan to be in the back country during these times, it's a good idea to wear a vest and hat of Universal orange. Call the Colorado Division of Wildlife at (303) 297-1192 for more information on safety.

HUNTING SEASON

Archery and black powder hunting seasons begin in late August, and big game rifle season starts in early October and runs into November. If you plan to be in the backcountry during these times, it is a good idea to wear a vest and hat of Universal orange. Call the Colorado Division of Wildlife at (303) 297-1192 for more information.

Some basic tenets apply to all adventuring: Don't go alone if you can help it. Leave early. Be prepared—bring proper equipment and a knowledge of the hazards you may face. And if you do go alone, file a flight plan of your route and schedule with someone before you leave.

Leave No Trace

The backcountry is fragile. With all the people recreating in the mountains and valleys of Colorado, it's imperative that we take care of them and be as careful as we can to leave the country as we found it. It's our most fundamental ethic and the simplest way to honor the land that is giving us so much beauty and joy. The idea is to tread lightly and leave no lasting mark of your visit. Some basic minimum impact techniques are

- Plan ahead. Don't take an overlarge group into a wilderness or fragile area, generally, no more than eight to ten people. Plan on even smaller group sizes when going off-trail. Avoid creating new trails.
- Camp where the damage has already been done—on ground that's been trampled and compacted. If the area is not well used, select a fresh site rather than one that is just beginning to be impacted. In pristine areas, select a site on resistant ground, such as sandy terrain or forest floor.
- Camp at least 200 feet from water sources and trails.
- Use a camp stove. If you have to make a fire, use already established fire rings. Burn small sticks.
- Bring a light trowel and bury human waste in a 6–8″ cat hole. Burn toilet paper before you bury it. Pack out tampons and sanitary napkins—so far, there's no danger from grizzlies in Colorado.
- Pack animals: Hobble stock, or use temporary electric fences, rather than picketing or tying them to one place for an extended period. Water stock on gravel stream banks where possible, rather than on lake shores or soft meadows. Use lightweight camping gear to reduce number of stock.

- Be quiet as the southwest wind. Whistles, shouts, and radios shatter and pollute the backcountry silences.
- Tread carefully on alpine tundra. Avoid stepping on fragile plants, or "skiing" down scree slopes.
- Respect wildlife. Act like an honored guest in their generous house. Don't feed the animals, and pick up every bit of food and trash.

Thanks to John Fielder and Mark Pearson and their *Complete Guide to Colorado's Wilderness Areas* for a comprehensive and concise review of minimum impact techniques and for most of the information given above.

Outdoor Recreation Information Center (ORIC)

You've just moved to Denver—or Boulder—and you've read this book. You've read other guidebooks. You want to get outside next weekend on your bike, your feet, your skis. You want to get farther out than a Short Hop; you want to camp and fish or climb . . . and yet all of Colorado west of that wall of mountains still seems like a jumble of humps, a tangle of trails and confusing back roads, a blur of Wilderness camping regulations. You're getting paralyzed and overwrought. You don't want to read another guidebook. You want to see a real person, face to face, fall at his feet, hug his thick hiker's ankles, and cry out, "Where, where the heck should I go with my long weekend?"

The folks at ORIC, the Public Lands Outdoor Recreation Trip Planning Center at the REI flagship store, can tell you. That's their job. They are cheerful and knowledgeable, experienced in the Colorado backcountry; they're backed up by a huge archive of all kinds of maps—and guidebooks—and their services are free. But mostly, they've been there. Set up as a central, walk-in location for trip planning on public lands in Colorado and a way to encourage good land-use ethics, ORIC is staffed by volunteer outdoorspeople. It's a remarkable service. The map kiosk provides a point-and-zoom screen that will zero in on any place in the state and render it in a colorful USGS topo map (there's a fee to print the map). There's also a big map table with a lot of the Front Range topos. There are stacks of information on any activity you can think of, and the volunteers will help you plan a trip of any length. You can buy any kind of state or federal pass here, from Golden Age federal recreation passports to Colorado hunting and fishing licenses to firewood and Christmas-tree cutting permits.

ORIC was put together with involvement from many government agencies and nonprofit organizations—U.S. Forest Service, U.S. Geological Survey, Colorado Division of Wildlife, the Rocky Mountain Nature Association and the Colorado Mountain Club, and REI—to name a few.

Walk-in service only. The REI flagship store is at 1416 Platte Street. You're welcome to call to make sure the ORIC desk is open (303-756-3100). ORIC's hours are 10:30–7:00 Monday, Thursday, and Friday; 10:30–4:30 Saturday and Sunday; closed Tuesday and Wednesday.

Mountain Biking

THE FAT TIRE biking within easy reach of Denver and Boulder has to be some of the best in the world. For one thing, there's not much mud, and in a lot of places, where there's good southern exposure, you can bike all winter. The terrain ranges from rolling to epic, from open meadow to pine woods, ridge-top to ravine, dirt road to mine-field singletrack. Minutes from the city you can be having the ride of your life in a remote drainage fragrant with juniper while the resident mountain lion looks you over. I guess it's the reason so many mountain bike champions grow up and train here.

That's the other great thing about biking in this area: there are so many superb, elite riders tearing

around. They're all over the place, chugging out of draws, whipping around switchbacks, and they tend to be extremely generous to the less accomplished rider. On too many occasions to count I've met a competition-level rider on the trail or in the parking lot and received spirited advice on trail conditions, technique, gear, and rides I should definitely try when I recover from the current epic. The same is true in all the small bike shops. The energy is less about making sales than about sharing the excitement of riding. It's a tremendous environment for the growing mountain biker—there could not be a better time, or place, to be in the sport.

There may not be a city better suited than Denver to a mountain bike. Wide streets, a web of bike lanes, smooth bike paths along the rivers, and dirt singletrack in the middle of town make Denver a godsend for an urban biker. Some outstanding neighborhood bike shops offer all kinds of camaraderie and support—places like SingleTrack Cyclery in Wash Park, where you can take solace in the Wall of Pain, a photographic tribute to hematoma and human frailty. The mountain biking just outside of town, up on the foothills, is world class. Because so many of the best trails just out of town start at the base of these foothills, many have a similar character: long tough climbs rewarded by stunning views and a bit of flatter respite, followed by exciting descents. Mathews Winters, Mt. Falcon, Apex, and Deer Creek Canyon all follow this pattern. Or you can drive thirty-five minutes out of midtown and be biking on adrenaline-pumping singletrack through cool pine forest and glades of aspen, or on a dirt road along a winding blackwater river.

Boulder, unlike Denver, is smack against the foothills. The mountains hover over it like a great wave about to break. Mountains lions regularly come into neighborhoods like Sunshine Canyon and eat house pets. Mountain men with exuberant beards and musk of woodsmoke come down from Nederland and read hearty poetry at Penny Lane. The advantage of the mountains' proximity is that you can take a ride at lunch hour that includes some dirt singletrack and views of the high plains washing against the hills. Included here are some classic rides in Boulder's backyard and one loop from town that includes the Boulder Creek Trail, the Foothills Trail, and Boulder Reservoir. All of these can be done in shorter legs for quick workouts.

The Boulder Creek Bike Path speaks for itself. It's a gentle urban ride on smooth concrete along a stream. From Eben Fine Park at the mouth of the canyon it rolls east for 8.5 miles and connects up with several other trails. It's also crowded. The abundance of mountain rides possible from the middle of the city is fantastic, if you don't mind doing some riding on the road. You can crank out of Eben Fine Park on the bike path heading up Boulder Canyon, turn up Fourmile Canyon Road, then in a few miles ride up Logan Mill Road. From there you can loop back through Betasso Preserve, or continue on to the Switzerland Trail and all the riding up off the Peak to Peak Highway. There's a multitude of options. Get ahold of the Zia Designs' Boulder County Mountain Bike Map and go nuts. Also, talk to the folks at University Bicycles on Pearl Street. They're knowledgeable and nice. On Sunday mornings they lead a woman's mountain bike ride for all abilities.

In the following chapter you'll find rides to do on your lunch break in the center of the city, rides to hit after work, longer day-rides, easy rides (we've made a special effort to include some close-in routes with a more easy-going, rolling character), and terrifying rides. In each locale are often other options for great routes, which are left for you to discover; they usually suggest themselves. Or check out the bike-specific guidebooks listed at the end of the chapter. There's also info on shops and festivals, races, clubs, and one or two places to get iced coffee along the way.

Thanks to Tom Barnhart and all the great info in his superb guide, *Front Range Single Tracks.*

Song of the Night Rider

GARRET MILLER IS a normal Joe. That is, he's married and works as a bike mechanic at REI during the day, and at UPS most nights, sorting packages until 10:30 P.M. He's also a passionate mountain biker. He resolves the demands of this love with one powerful light mounted to his handlebars, another fixed to his helmet. He drives out of town to Buffalo Creek or Apex or Mount Falcon, and he starts riding just after midnight.

"The neatest thing is the spiders. You've got blue spiders that glow like snowflakes. They're everywhere. If you ride Apex at night—the main trail—it's kind of in a draw. You climb out of the draw and you start to see the city lights. It's amazing how big the city is. I remember when the lights of Stapleton—the old airport—disappeared. The fear is something you get used to. I know mountain lions are more active at night. When your card is ready to be punched it's ready to be punched. It's cooler at night. I never see anybody on the trails. I do it alone. None of my friends will go. The Green Mountain Loop at Buffalo Creek takes about two and a half hours. That's usually how long your lights last. The smallest sound—a little animal like a squirrel—is amplified. Everything seems faster at night. The sound of your tires is like running water, very soothing. It's wonderful. You don't get bugs in your eyes. Full moon rides—on the climb you turn off your lights, let your eyes adjust, and work with the moon. Then the nights when there is no light, a rainy night when the ground is wet—the night just soaks up your light like a sponge. I'm glad I'm a mechanic. You want to watch your lines so you don't get a pinch flat—the rock crests don't look as sharp. That's when it sets on you—the fear—when you're working on your bike at night. Night riding is a passion. That's all I love to do. I should grow up but it gets worse with age—you kind of go through your life as a child. I can function on four hours of sleep. Fun is my income. Thank God my wife is the same way or she would have left me. I've been married since '84 and she understands when I go camping and riding at night."

Denver City Limits

HIGH LINE CANAL

Location: Downtown

Length: 39 miles one-way

Physical difficulty: Moderate—flat but long

Technical difficulty: Easy

Terrain: Smooth paved surface, graded dirt

Elevation gain: Minimal

Map and book: Bicycling Metro Denver Route Map; *Guide to the High Line Canal*

Dogs: Yes

Heads up: Country lane in the city.

Description: Riverine forest, huge cottonwoods, gentle meadow, and open wetland; genteel horse farms, nouveau Italianate villa developments with names like The Reserve, and the cool breath of moving water. And a wide, flat, generally smooth, mostly dirt bike and foot path that passes close to downtown and runs for over 50 miles. It's easy to believe that the High Line Canal was constructed just so a third-millennium Denverite could hop on a bike and get a

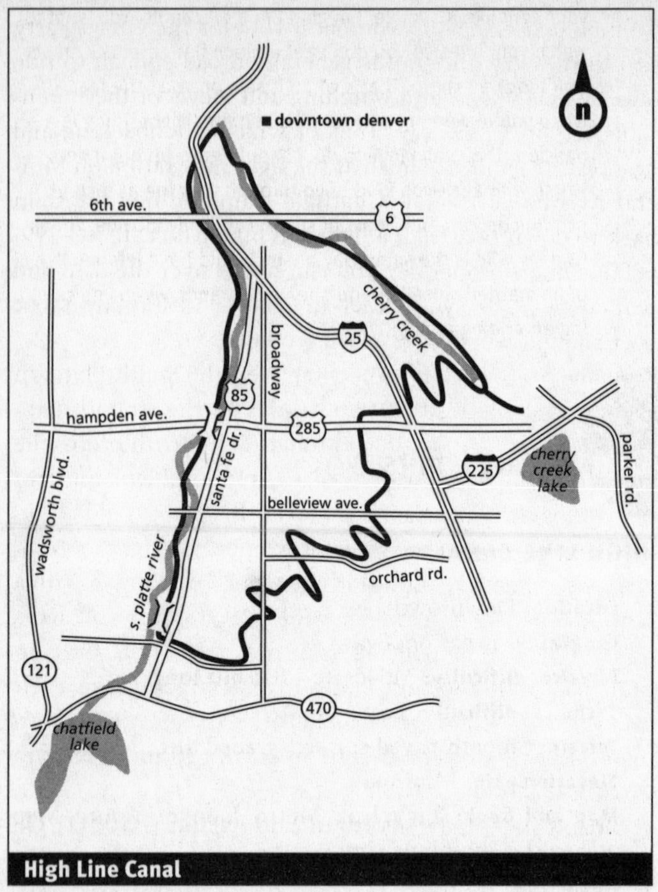

High Line Canal

quick respite from the city on a shaded cruiser ride. The canal, built for the purposes of drinking water and irrigation, was completed in 1883. It runs from Waterton Canyon above the southern end of Chatfield Lake all the way out to the neighborhood of Denver International Airport. The section described below is a fun, relaxing day-ride that starts from downtown. Great for the discursive biker, 4-hour conversations about meaningful relationships, and

10 mph debates about whether a vote for the Green Party is a throwaway, the trail is generally broad enough to ride side by side. Good bird-watching and views of the mountains all along the way. Tons of wide switchbacking and aggravating oxbows. Finish at the light rail station on Mineral Avenue, just below Chatfield Dam and hop the train back to downtown. (For a light rail bike pass call 303-299-6000.) On a summer day you can hump over the dam and tear down to the Swim Beach in Chatfield Park, buy a root beer and bratwurst, and splash around.

Route: Start at Confluence Rapid on the South Platte in the shadow of REI. Point your bike up the smooth path along Cherry Creek. Ride through downtown along the creek, a lovely ride at water's edge. At mile 12 look for right turn onto High Line Canal, which at this point is old blacktop. Proceed 25 miles to Mineral Avenue. Go right on Mineral—use sidewalk south side of avenue—and finish with a 2-mile coast to light rail station. Be grateful you have remembered your light rail bike pass and $1.25. Or continue 0.25 mile to South Platte River Trail and take a left over the dam road into Chatfield Park. An epic option: turn right on the South Platte Trail and crank 18 miles back to Confluence Rapid.

Directions: Take I-25 north to 23rd Avenue (exit 211). Go east on 23rd, which becomes Water Street as it turns north. The parking lot is located on the east side (right), just south of the Speer Boulevard overpass.

CITY PARKS

Location: Slightly southeast of downtown
Length: 12 miles out and back
Physical difficulty: Easy
Technical difficulty: Easy

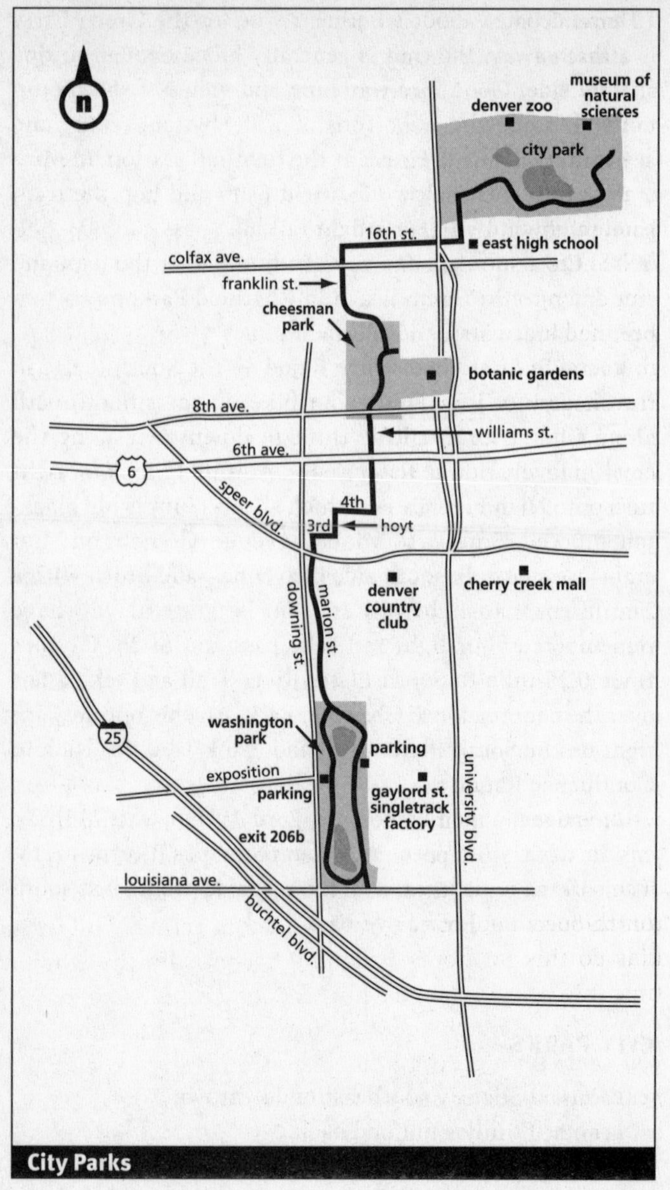

n
museum of natural sciences
denver zoo
city park
16th st.
east high school
colfax ave.
franklin st.
cheesman park
botanic gardens
8th ave.
williams st.
6th ave.
6
speer blvd.
4th
3rd
hoyt
cherry creek mall
denver country club
downing st.
marion st.
washington park
25
parking
exposition
parking
gaylord st. singletrack factory
university blvd.
exit 206b
louisiana ave.
buchtel blvd.
City Parks

Terrain: Bike lanes on wide streets, paved park paths

Elevation gain: Minimal

Map: Bicycling Metro Denver Route Map

Dogs: Not recommended

Heads up: Great Sunday brunch and family ride.

Description: Every city west of Burlington, Vermont, has a neighborhood where graduates of Eastern prep schools feel comfortable hanging out. That's Wash Park. Five minutes among the formal flowerbeds and lakes and rec center parking lots and you know that the density of fit folks jogging around you who have read an entire book by Annie Proulx and at least know someone who summers on Martha's Vineyard is abnormally high. The ride starts with a circumnavigation of this peaceful gem of city parks, then proceeds north through prosperous, quiet streets on established bike lanes into Cheesman Park, past the Botanic Gardens, and on into City Park, another example of stunning urban landscaping. Circle the park and end at the Museum of Nature and Sciences and the zoo. The highlights of this ride may be the cries of peacocks that waft over the zoo fence and the fountain behind the museum. This is my favorite fountain on earth. The green park, the lake, the skyline of the city rolls out below you. Dozens of water jets set in a pink stone circle fire off at random intervals in whimsical patterns, with a glug and thump like drums. Sometimes they all fire off at once. The game is to run through the hot zone and see if you get nailed. Little kids do this for hours, laughing hysterically the whole time. Riding across it on a bike is not permitted, but make sure no one is watching and do it anyway. Go back the way you came for a great 12-mile urban tour, and eat brunch near Wash Park at one of the many eateries on Gaylord between Mississippi and Arizona.

Route: Start in Wash Park. The Exposition Street parking lot by the rec center is a good place to meet. Ride out of the north end of the park onto Marion Street. Follow Bike Lane D-11 north, which doglegs east on 3rd Avenue just after the Denver Country Club, and continues north up Hoyt for a one-block dogleg east again on 4th. North again up Williams to Cheesman Park. Follow Park Road and exit north up Franklin Street. Leave the path here to go east on 16th to Esplanade, in front of the brick monolith of East High School. Peddle on into City Park and circle the south side of the lake to the museum at the east end. To return, bike around the north side of City Park and backtrack to Wash Park.

Directions: Take I-25 south to Washington Street/Emerson Street (exit 206B). Merge onto Buchtel Boulevard going north to Louisiana Avenue. Turn left (east) onto Louisiana, then left (north) onto Downing Street. Parking is located on the street or in the parking lot, toward the north side of park.

The Wall of Pain

JUST OFF WASH Park on the corner of Gaylord and Mississippi is a small, excellent bike shop called The SingleTrack Factory. Everyone who works there is obsessed with bikes in one way or another and is willing to go a long way toward helping you become obsessed too. On a wooden ceiling beam that bisects the shop is an evolving testimonial to the Wipe Out. A crushed helmet (the head inside it remained intact), photographs of grinning riders with collarbones sticking through skin. It's a little reminiscent of the grotto at Lourdes—bedecked with the crutches and orthopedic devices of the cured faithful—except in reverse. Reeves Macdonald, with intense blue eyes and blonde mutton-chop sideburns, is a mechanic there. He's a fanatic commuter—goes everywhere, does everything, on his bike. Sometimes when he rides he wears a gas mask he got from the Institute of Sociometry; he wears it to make drivers more aware of the pollution they're causing. He says that most clear days in winter and early spring are Red Pollution Days, which means that in an hour a bike commuter is breathing in the equivalent of about a pack and a half of cigarettes. Reeves and a few of his buddies are cannibalizing scores of old bikes and building choppers in a shack behind Reeves' apartment. They have four-foot forks, little front wheels, and high handlebars. The Triclops is their next project. Reeves sketched it on a napkin at the Coffee Nut across the street from the bike shop. It's a side-by-side tandem chopper. The two peddlers sit beside each other over the rear axle. "It's actually a three-person bike," Reeves said. "The rider in front doesn't actually peddle. He just steers."

Denver Backyard

DAKOTA RIDGE AND MATHEWS WINTERS

Location: 11 miles west of Denver

Length: 7-mile loop with a less technical 4.6-mile option

Physical difficulty: Strenuous

Technical difficulty: Difficult

Terrain: Hardpack, loose rocks, boulders, waterbars, steps

Elevation gain: 970′

Maps and book: Jefferson County Open Space brochure—Mathews Winters Park; USGS Morrison (7.5 minute); *Front Range Single Tracks*

Dogs: Yes

Heads up: Technical steeps, red rocks, and hogbacks 15 minutes from town.

Description: You couldn't dream this any better. Fifteen

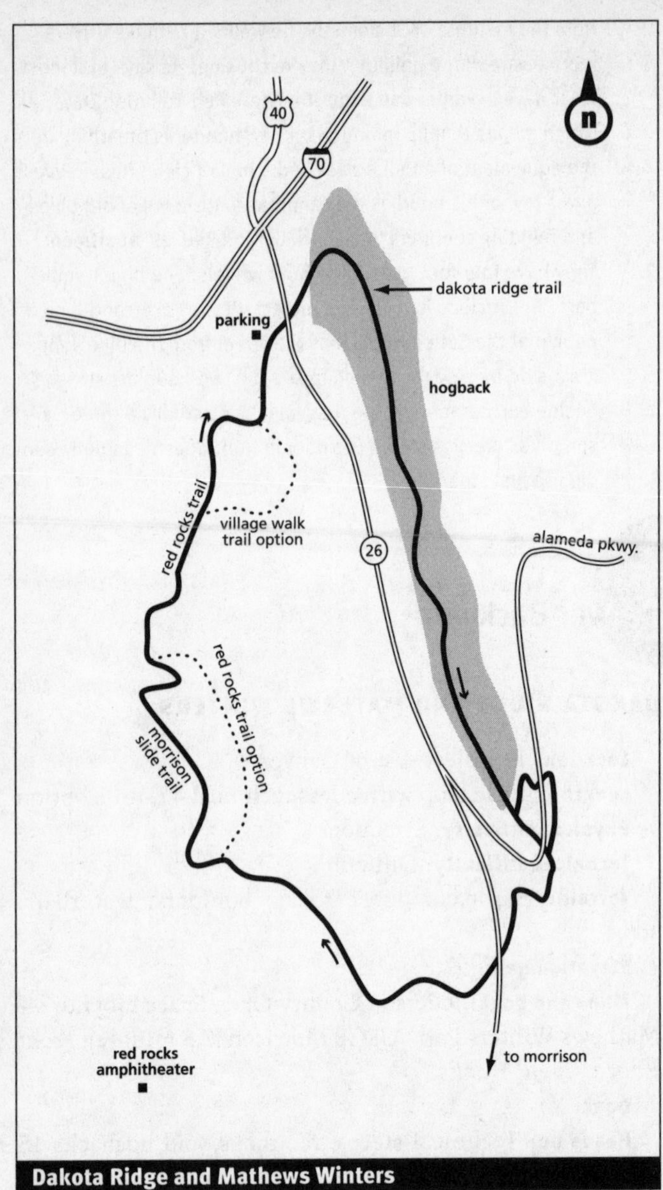

Dakota Ridge and Mathews Winters

minutes from town is a gonzo, strenuous loop in the gorgeous, swooping, hogback ridge country around Red Rocks. A long, knifelike ridge following an open, descending valley, grassy slopes with scattered juniper forest, and red sandstone rock formations define this area. The route has a steep rocky descent that will raise the hair off the most proficient rider. For those who want an easier loop, there's a 4.6-mile option that skips Dakota Ridge. Tremendous after-work riding.

Route: From parking lot ride east across CO 26 and climb the obvious doubletrack to the top of Dakota Ridge. Follow the singletrack south and descend tough rocky sections to the Alameda Parkway, dismounting as needed. Cross the parkway and ride south to Red Rocks Trail. Climb the steep, rocky trail to the top of the hogback and continue down fast, fun singletrack to the road. Cross the road and enter Red Rocks Park. Turn right onto Red Rocks Trail and climb to the intersection with Morrison Slide Trail. Turn right, staying on Red Rocks Trail. Fast smooth singletrack leads to Village Walk Trail. Turn right and swoop back down into the parking lot.

Option: For a fun, considerably less technical, but still demanding 4.6-mile loop, skip Dakota Ridge. From the parking lot take Village Walk Trail south to Red Rocks Trail and go left. Cross Cherry Gulch and climb on the Morrison Slide Trail to the top of the bench (great views of the whole valley), and descend the switchbacks to the Red Rocks Trail. Follow the trail back to the parking lot.

Directions: Drive west on I-70 to Morrison/Golden (exit 259). Go south on CO 26 and turn right (west) almost immediately into Mathews Winters parking lot. Dakotoa Ridge is across the street to the east.

WATERTON CANYON

Location: 14 miles southwest of Denver

Length: 17-mile cherry-stem loop

Physical difficulty: Moderate

Technical difficulty: Easy to difficult

Terrain: Hardpack gravel road, loose sand, rocks

Elevation gain: 1,600′

Map and book: Trails Illustrated map 135—Deckers/Rampart Range; *Front Range Single Tracks*

Dogs: No

Heads up: Bighorn sheep, gorgeous secluded river canyon.

Description: The charm of a canyon that has been allowed to keep any of its wildness is that once you enter it the rest of the world seems to fall away. As you climb the smooth dirt road up into Waterton, following the South Platte as it spills through rocky drops and black pools, it's hard to believe that Denver swarms a few miles to the north. Big ponderosas lean over the bends, glossy oak brush crowds the shoulder of the road, and steep grassy slopes climb to broken rimrock. If you bring your rod, there's excellent trout fishing. A herd of bighorn sheep lives along the river—in the heat of summer they hang out in the cool spray below Strontia Dam. A beautiful 6-mile, steady warm-up climb on the road breaks into a fine, technical 4.5-mile singletrack loop at the top. The descent on the road back to the car is sheer rush. The only motor vehicles allowed in the canyon are those of the Denver Water Board, but the road is popular with runners and hikers, so be careful flying back down.

Route: Ride 6.5 miles up the dirt road to where the Colorado Trail comes in from the left. Follow it past the big sign onto singletrack. Climb through pine forest to the ridgetop where Carpenter Peak Trail heads off to the left. Follow Carpenter up through scrub oak and down through

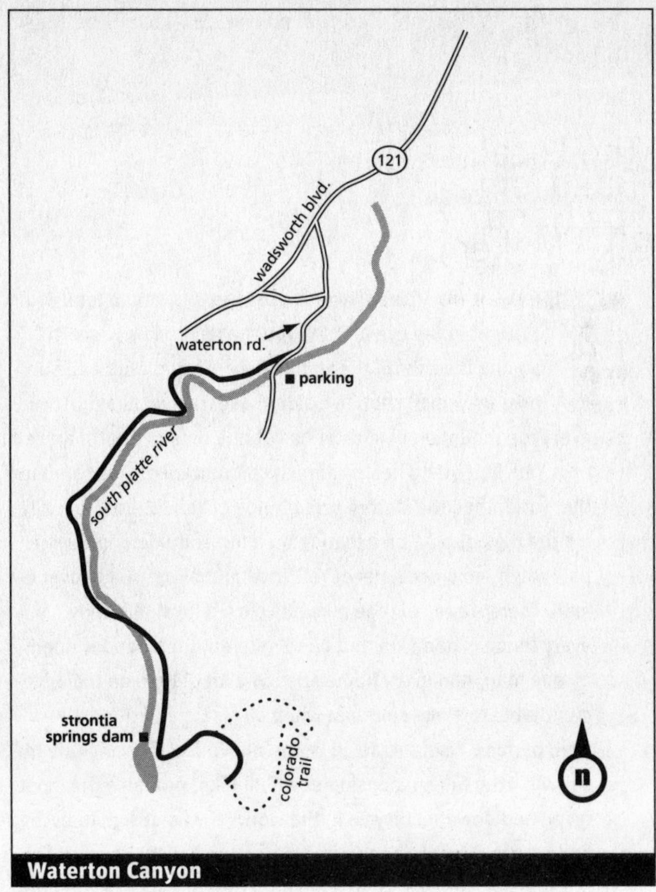

Waterton Canyon

pines. Follow the creek, crossing it twice. Climb a small ridge and descend to an intersection with an unnamed trail. Turn left and descend back to the dam. Be careful of the ledge dropoff on this last leg; it has surprised and tumbled many a rider.

Directions: Go west on 6th Avenue (US 6) to I-70 westbound, stay in the right lane and merge onto CO 470. Take it to South Platte Canyon Road (CO 121), and go south 4 miles to the Waterton Canyon entrance. Turn left (east) into parking lot.

The Local, Build 'em by Hand Bike Maker

THERE'S NO HONEST woman or man that would look you straight in the eye and tell you that Yeti bikes weren't among the best in the world. They're hand built at a surprisingly small shop in Golden; over the years almost every top mountain bike racer has at one time or another raced on a Yeti. The brand has an almost cult following. From around the world, the little factory gets photos of Yeti tattoos—usually a hairy bigfoot on a bike tearing up a tan shoulder, or down a pale thigh—and accounts of Yeti Tribe gatherings roll in over e-mail. There's a reason the bike has such a loyal following: every frame is hand cut and hand mitered, then hand welded by one man, and every frame spends a lot of time on the alignment table to make sure that when all's said and done it's, well, perfect. Also, the designs are innovative. They include the Lawwill DH-9 full-suspension downhill bike, probably the most respected downhill bicycle in the world. It was designed by motorcycle racer Mert Lawwill, who brought suspension to flat-track racing. "He was almost laughed off the track," a Yeti rider said. "And he won everything." Yeti's full-suspension ASR mountain bike, twenty-two pounds of viciously nimble technology, is cutting edge. The man who hand welds each and every Yeti frame is Roberto Vega. He started welding for Yeti when he was sixteen. Bike makers know a Vega frame just by looking at the welds. It's a signature "stack of dimes," a perfectly even, scalloped line of overlapping circles that is envied throughout the industry. The folks at Yeti, all of whom are passionate riders, feel lucky to be tucked against the Golden foothills. "We do a lot of lunch ride product testing," manager Joe Hendrickson said. "Between Mathews Winters—Dakota Ridge, and Apex, and Green Mountain—we're pretty lucky to have the riding that we do right out the door."

Yeti tribespeople take regular after-work factory rides every first and third Tuesday. Meet at the shop at about 5:30 in-season. Call ahead to make sure. Also, Yeti encourages riders to visit the factory. They're proud of what they do and enjoy taking people through the shop. Contact Yeti, 600 Corporate Circle, Unit D, Golden, CO 80401; (303) 278-6909; www.yeticycles.com.

Heads up: My researcher Sarah says that I have to add: "*Girls!* Go take the shop tour. Yeti is full of cute, in-shape guys happy to show their stuff." All right, I said it.

MOUNT FALCON

Location: 15 miles southwest of Denver

Length: 7 miles out and back with loop options at the top

Physical difficulty: Strenuous

Technical difficulty: Moderate

Terrain: Hardpack with occasional small, loose rock. Steps and waterbars

Elevation gain: 1,620′

Map and book: Jefferson County Open Space Park brochure—Mount Falcon Park; *Front Range Single Tracks*

Dogs: Yes

Heads up: Tough climb with a pine forest and ruined castle at the top.

Description: Another up-the-face-of-the-foothills classic. Climb, climb, climb. Views, views, views (Red Rocks Amphitheater, Bear Creek Reservoir, Denver). Waterbars and a lot of open slope. One runner described it as the best place around to see charismatic megafauna and the city at

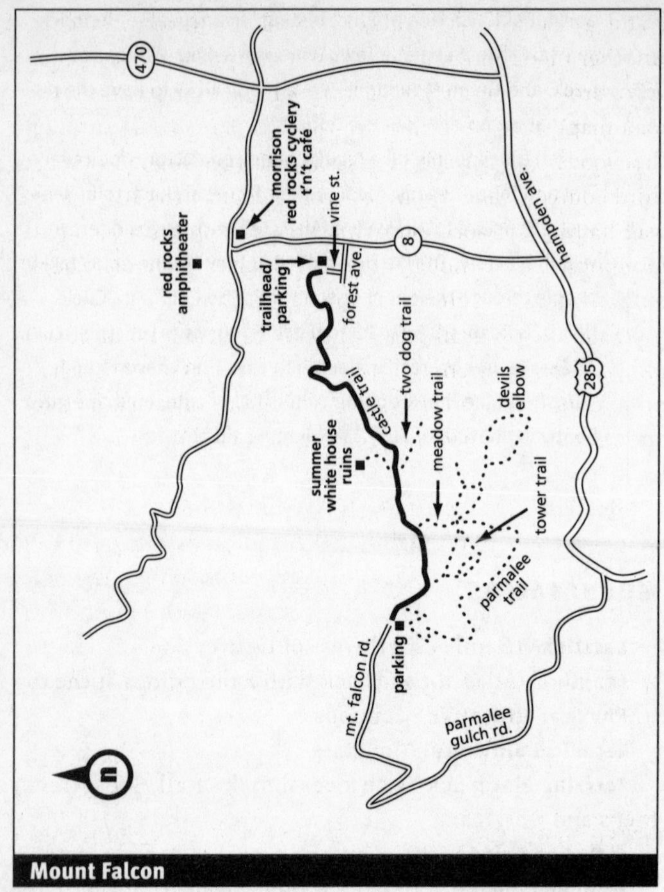

Mount Falcon

the same time. Lots of deer and the occasional big cat. He'd actually seen a couple of mountain lions. (See wildlife cautions, pp. 27–28.) The nice thing about this ride is that you top out on a rolling, wooded plateau at a ruined castle, which is always pleasant. The castle is actually the remnant of John Brisben Walker's rock house, which burned in 1918. Walker planned to build a summer White House for presidents just to the east, but World War

I and a "waning of Walker's good fortunes" nixed it. Another nice thing is that if you're feeling wimpy you can drive around the back side through Kittredge (check the road map) straight to the top, ride the short trails through the woods, and get the views without breaking a sweat. A third bonus is that you access this ride near the little gateway hamlet of Morrison, which has the charm of a small mountain town, though it's next door to Denver. Check out Red Rocks Cyclery and the T'n'T Café.

Route: Castle Trail pretty much straight up for almost 3 miles. The trail then mellows and widens; it's another half mile to Walker's Dream ruins. Check out many short loop options through the woods at the top. Then point yourself back downhill.

Directions: Go west on 6th Avenue (US 6) to I-70 westbound and stay in the right lane so you can merge onto CO 470. Drive south on CO 470 to the Morrison (CO 8) exit and turn west onto CO 8. CO 8 turns south before Bear Creek Canyon; take it to Forest Avenue and turn right (west). Take this to Vine Street and turn right (north). Continue to the trailhead.

THREE SISTERS

Location: 27 miles southwest of Denver

Length: 6-mile loop

Physical difficulty: Moderate

Technical difficulty: Moderate

Terrain: Hardpack, a few waterbars and a few rocky sections on the climb to the saddle between the Three Sisters and on the final descent.

Elevation gain: 820′

Map and book: Jefferson County Open Space Park brochure—Alderfer; *Front Range Single Tracks*

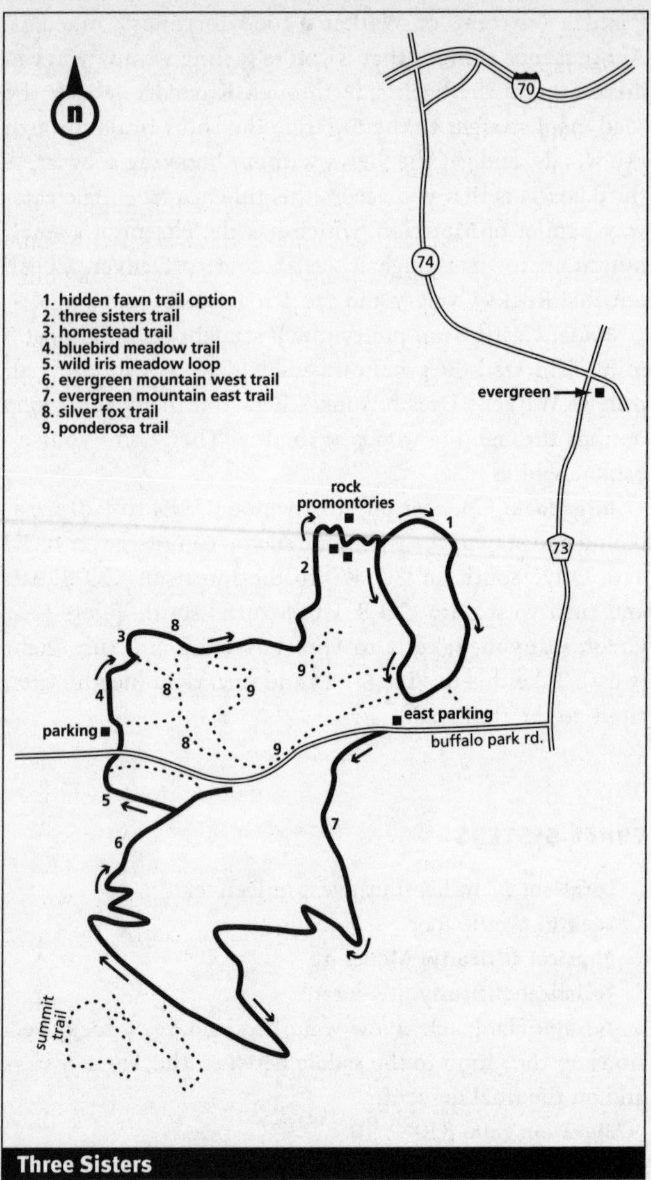

Three Sisters

Dogs: Yes

Heads up: Pines and shade and rolling trails with fun technical sections.

Description: The great thing about this ride is that it begins and ends in the woods—the pines above Evergreen. An excellent choice for a hot summer afternoon, as it is shaded and fragrant. Mostly smooth hardpack, with some challenging rocky sections, and a few big views of the hills, especially if you park your bike and scramble up one of the rock promontories for which the park is named. A great area to explore, as there are many loops and route options for all abilities.

Route: From the east parking lot, cross Buffalo Park Road and climb on wide singletrack. Turn left on the Evergreen Mountain East Trail, with smooth doubletrack switchbacks to a great overlook. Continue climbing past the trail to the top of Evergreen Mountain. Descend Evergreen Mountain West Trail to the Wild Iris Meadow Loop. Turn left and ride to the west parking lot. At the west end of the lot, take Bluebird Meadow Trail to Homestead Trail. Turn left and climb over a short hill to Silver Fox Trail. Turn left and pedal to Three Sisters Trail, which enters on the left. Climb up Three Sisters Trail through a more technical, rockier section to a saddle between two of the Sisters. (Park your bike and scramble up the rocks to great views.) Continue down a steep, rocky descent with some tight switchbacks and waterbars. Go left on Hidden Fawn Trail and back to the east parking lot.

Directions: Head west on 6th Avenue (US 6) to westbound I-70 about 17 miles to Evergreen Parkway (CO 74, exit 252). Go south 7 miles on CO 74 to Evergreen. In the middle of town turn right (south) onto 73 RD and go about a mile to Buffalo Park Road (88 RD). Turn right (west) and follow the signs 1.3 miles to the east parking lot.

Red Rocks Cyclery—and Café

MORRISON IS A little mountain town just below Red Rocks Park. It sits at the mouth of a canyon. Bear Creek runs out of the canyon and flows behind the shops on the south side of the main drag. Fly fishermen often park behind the stores and fish right in town. At the top of the street looms Mt. Morrison. The town was established during gold mining fever, and many of the little frame houses of those days, along with the old stone courthouse, still stand. Though Morrison is minutes from Denver, it always seems cooler and wetter and calmer. One of the best breakfast joints in this part of the state is the T'n'T Café on the main drag, Bear Creek Road. Red Rocks Cyclery is a block down the street in a clapboard storefront. The first thing I noticed when I walked into the cyclery was not the racks of high-quality bikes, but the coffee mug framed behind glass over one end of the espresso counter. It appears to be full of coffee—black. John Colson, part owner, says that the cup belonged to his mother. "For the past twenty years Mom nuked her coffee in it, so it's pretty blown up," he explains. "We kids threw it out again and again, but she dug it out of the garbage. Two decades of frigging explosive coffee." When he says this he sounds a little awed. The shop has become a gathering place for bikers of every ilk. Some of the best riding on the Front Range is just above town, and you can come in after a ride and order a latte and pastry and sit in a comfortable chair and tell horror stories and brag and talk shop. Every Sunday morning between December and April, fifty to seventy riders meet at the store and take a fifty-mile foothills road ride en masse. The shop also sponsors Red Rocks Velo, a racing team with riders in all categories—beginner to expert—in mountain bike, road, and cyclo-cross competitions. Their riders, who train on some of the most demanding terrain anywhere, tend to be highly competitive. The store does custom fits and custom builds. They specialize in cyclo-cross and road bikes, but most of their sales are mountain bikes, which they also rent.

ELK MEADOWS

Location: 23 miles southwest of Denver

Length: 6-mile loop

Physical difficulty: Easy

Technical difficulty: Easy

Terrain: Smooth hardpack, occasional rocks, waterbars

Elevation gain: 700′

Maps and book: Jefferson County Open Space brochure—Elk Meadow Park; USGS Evergreen (7.5 minute); *Front Range Single Tracks*

Dogs: Yes

Heads up: Perfect, pretty, start-of-the-season ride.

Description: Touted as maybe the best beginner ride on the Front Range, this is a wonderful season-starter through pine woods and fields. Great workout on easy, mostly smooth singletrack, with a wildly fun descent through the big meadow. Also, a killer climb option up Bergen Peak for the advanced rider.

Route: From the parking lot head up the Meadow Trail to Meadow View Trail. Turn left. Pass the Bergen Peak Trail (don't take it unless you want an unmerciful climb!) and veer left at the junction with Elk Ridge Trail. Staying on Meadow View, continue past Too Long Trail to Painter's Pause Trail. Turn right onto Painter's Pause and continue to the junction with Sleepy S Trail and turn right. Go past Elk Ridge Trail to Meadow Trail, and turn left. Ride back to the car.

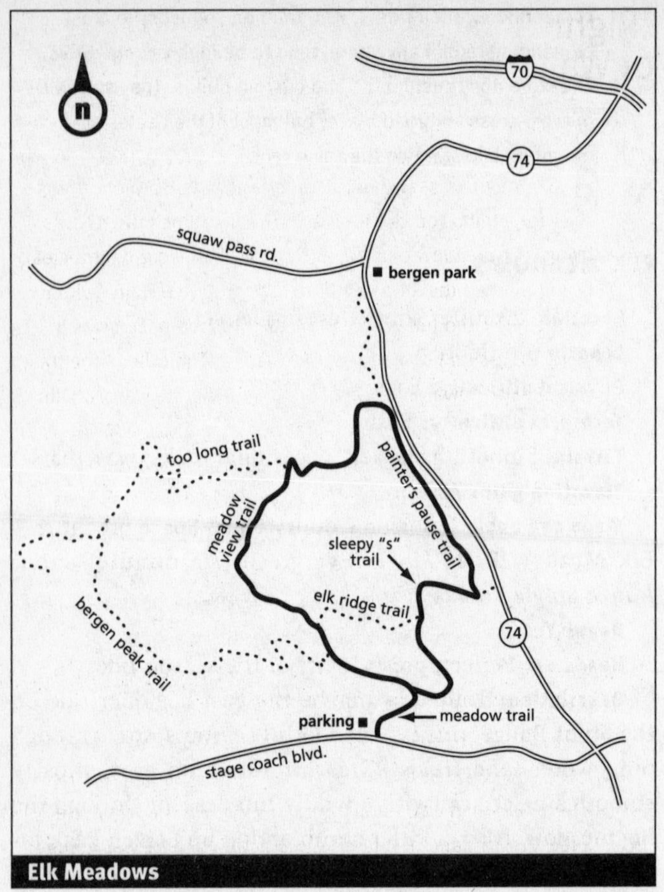

Elk Meadows

Directions: Head west on 6th Avenue (US 6) to westbound I-70 about 17 miles to Evergreen Parkway (CO 74, exit 252). Drive 5 miles south to Stage Coach Boulevard (476 RD) and turn right (west). Go about 1 mile to the south parking lot.

Right of Way

THE LOOP AROUND Elk Meadow, outside of Evergreen, has a marvelous descent. It's a smooth straight singletrack through grass with occasional small steps, and it drops for a mile. You can haul ass. The first time I did it I was flying. The meadow blurred, and the trail ahead got ultra-clear. I caught air on the steps and the tires grabbed. Hands vibrated on the grips and the wind cooled as it rushed past. I was in a zone. Up ahead I saw a man. He was in the middle of the trail, was walking toward me, and I could see that he was watching me. He must have been a quarter of a mile away. As I got closer I kept expecting him to take a simple half step to the side, but he didn't. His posture changed, stiffened. He was an old man, and he found my eyes and held them, frowned and kept walking, completely resolute. "Oh, shit!" I thought as I squeezed the brakes, skidded, and swerved. I hopped out of the groove, kept my balance in the grass, and jounced past the man and back on to the trail. I didn't look back but I was pissed. So easy to step off. At the end of the ride, as I pedaled toward the parking lot, I saw the sign—BIKERS YIELD TO PEDESTRIANS. Suddenly I felt ashamed. I knew he had seen it too. He was an old man who had earned his place in the world. He knew the law, and at total risk to life and limb he was going to observe it. There was no way he was going to abrogate his right for some punk in Lycra. I admired him. I imagined him just then, walking slowly up into the pines, feeling that the world still had some pride and some order.

DEER CREEK CANYON PARK—PLYMOUTH CREEK TRAIL TO RED MESA LOOP

Location: 19 miles southwest of Denver

Length: 8-mile cherry-stem loop

Physical difficulty: Strenuous

Technical difficulty: Moderate

Terrain: Hardpack

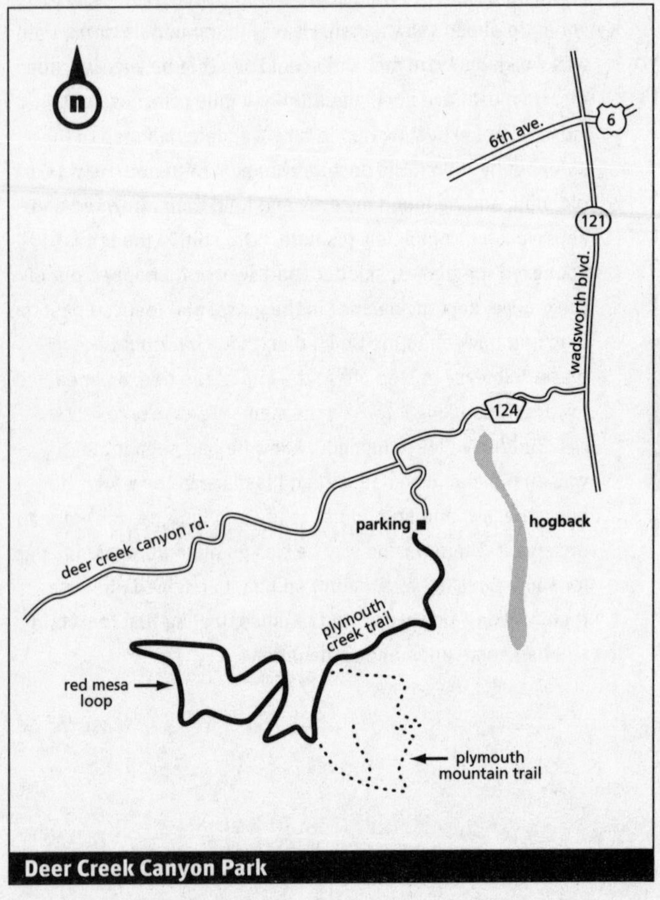

Deer Creek Canyon Park

Elevation gain: 1,600′

Map and book: Jefferson County Open Space Park brochure—Deer Creek Canyon Park; *Front Range Single Tracks*

Dogs: Yes

Heads up: Best view of the hogback.

Description: Just 19 miles south of town, this canyon has a remote feel, rigorous climbs, and superb views of the Hogback with its soft grass slopes and pastel bands of stratified sandstone.

Route: From the parking lot go past the restrooms on your right to the Plymouth Creek Trail. After 2 miles, join the Red Mesa Loop. Go right or left, the choice is yours. Return the same way.

Directions: Go west on 6th Avenue (US 6) 3.5 miles to Wadsworth Boulevard (CO 121) and turn left (south). Continue about 12 miles to Deer Creek Canyon Road (124 RD). Turn right and in about 3 miles turn left (south) on Grizzly Drive. The parking lot is on the right (west).

Boulder City Limits

FOOTHILLS TRAIL TO BOULDER RESERVOIR

Location: Just west of Boulder

Length: About 20 miles, with a shorter, 7.4-mile option

Physical difficulty: Easy to moderate

Technical difficulty: Easy

Terrain: Hardpack, occasional loose rocks, waterbars, pavement

Elevation gain: 560′

Map: Zia Designs' Boulder County Mountain Bike Map

Dogs: Yes

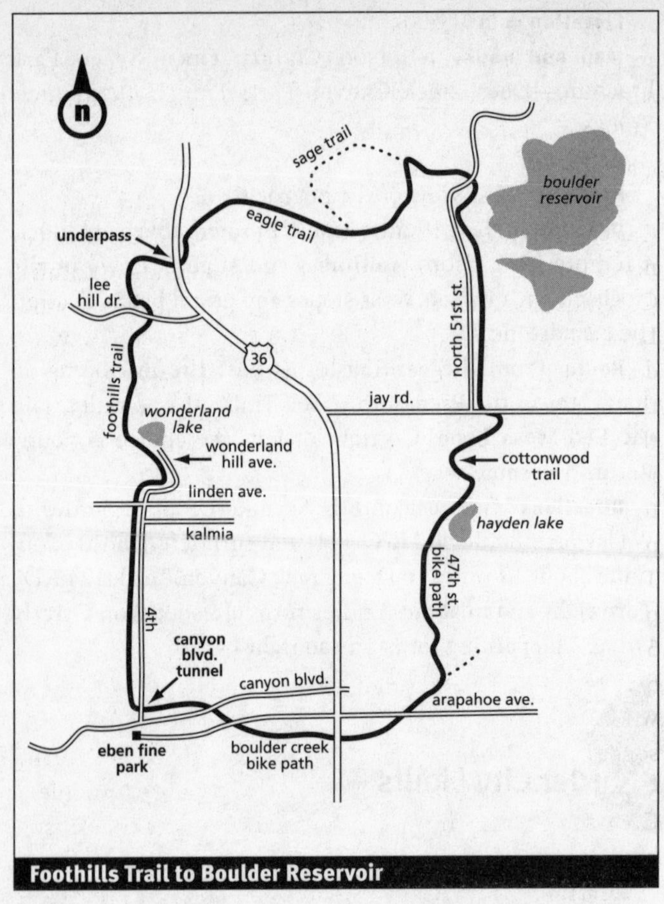

Foothills Trail to Boulder Reservoir

Heads up: Rolling high plains with green fields and a swim on the way.

Description: I love this ride. It's rolling, nontechnical, starts and ends downtown, and is absolutely beautiful. In the warm months, as you pedal east out toward the reservoir, you can glance back at the Flatirons across the plain and the soft foothills. Then you get to the edge of the plateau and look down on rich green pastures, the horses and big cottonwoods and lake. It's stunning. On a hot day, stop at the reservoir and take a swim. With the windsurfers, waterskiers, and sunbathers it's like Little Malibu. A shorter option (7.4 miles) is to circle Wonderland Lake and return.

Route: Eben Fine Park to Settler's Park through the Canyon Boulevard Tunnel. Take Pearl Street to 4th. Go north on 4th, and dogleg left at the dead end to Kalmia. Continue north on the bike path, crossing Linden. Follow Linden east to Wonderland Hill Avenue. Turn north. Wonderland Hill curves right. A paved bike path takes off left in the middle of the curve. Take it to Wonderland Lake and the Foothills Trail. Follow the gravel trail north. Cross Lee Hill Drive. Climb to a short, steep descent over waterbars to US 36. Go through the underpass and turn left out of the parking area onto a dirt road. Follow this road to Eagle Trail. Take Eagle Trail down a second steep descent off the plateau and out toward the reservoir to 51st Street. Take 51st south 1 mile to the reservoir entrance. Continue on 51st to Jay Road. Turn right (east) onto Jay to the Cottonwood Trail, which takes off south. Follow Cottonwood south, cross Independence, and pass Hayden Lake to the 47th Street Bike Path. Follow the path south to the Boulder Creek Bike Path. Turn west and follow Boulder Creek back home.

Directions: Take Canyon Boulevard west to 9th Street and turn left. Turn right on Arapahoe Avenue to 3rd Street and the Eben Fine Park entrance on the right.

WALKER RANCH LOOP

Location: 9 miles southwest of town

Length: 7 miles

Physical difficulty: Strenuous

Technical difficulty: Difficult

Terrain: Rocks! Loose stuff, tight switchbacks

Elevation gain: 1,740′

Maps and book: Boulder County Open Space brochure—Walker Ranch; Zia Designs' Boulder County Mountain Bike Map; *Front Range Single Tracks*

Dogs: Yes

Heads up: Beautiful and very tough, like your favorite professional wrestlers.

Description: Be expert or be terrified. Maybe even cry. This is outstanding, beautiful technical riding where the less proficient can get used to carrying their bikes. Definitely dismount on the steps down to South Boulder Creek. A very popular loop with every species of recreationalist, so yield to those walking erect, and hit the trail on off hours.

Route: Take the South Boulder Creek Trail down to South Boulder Creek. Cross over the bridge to the Crescent Meadows Trail. Climb to the Walker Ranch Loop Trail sign, take Gross Dam Road on the left to the Crescent Meadows parking lot. Descend on singletrack (as the trail nears the creek you might want to walk down the steps). Climbing again on the Eldorado Canyon Trail, take a left onto Columbine Gulch Trail to the top of the ridge and finally descend into parking lot.

Directions: Take Canyon Boulevard (CO 119) to Broadway (CO 93), and turn left (south). Continue on Broadway to Baseline Road, turn right (west) onto Baseline. Go about

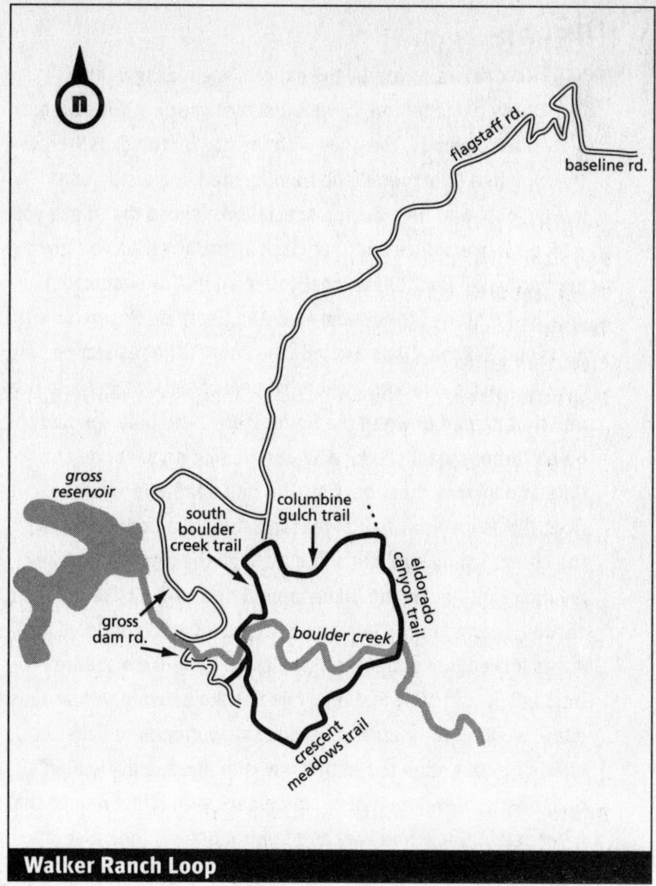

Walker Ranch Loop

8 miles to Walker Ranch. The South Boulder Trailhead parking lot. *Note:* For those coming from Denver, it's a much shorter drive to start at the Crescent Meadows Trailhead. From CO 93 turn west up the Coal Creek Canyon Road (CO 72) and go right at the turn to Gross Reservoir.

Clipless

THE CLAIMS MADE by the experts seem exaggerated: thirty percent more power, just by swapping out your old plastic pedals, the ones with the basket toe clips, screwing in a little metal stub framing the female side of a locking clip, and then buying special bike shoes that make you walk a bit like a duck and that clack aggressively as you divot the hardwood floor of the local coffee shop. Thirty percent is a lot. The first time I tried them I went to Chatfield Reservoir with my friend Sascha. I was excited. The sound, the resistance, and click as the cleat locked in were all deeply satisfying. We took a trail that looped down to the South Platte. The bike seemed to be on turbo. I practiced kicking out, freeing my feet one at a time and locking them back in. The trail dead-ended at the river. It was lovely. A pair of teal splashed in an eddy across the creek. Spring sunlight sifted through the poplars. I kicked my right foot free as the bike stopped and said, "I like it," then casually leaned to the left. I went to put my left foot down but it was locked in. I struggled. I panicked. I felt like a snared rabbit. I fell over in slow motion while Sascha laughed. A few days later I went up to Boulder and rode the Wonderland Lake Loop. I hadn't even gotten to the trail. I was in pizza delivery man's hell, a fancy development of cul-de-sacs with street names that all ended in Circle and Way and Court. I bravely took a shortcut over a bank of river rocks, pinched, and stalled. Two high school girls were on the sidewalk just below me. I smiled, wriggled desperately to kick out, and fell over. This one really hurt. When I blinked my eyes open the girls were leaning over me saying, "Sir? Sir? Are you okay?" I hate being called sir. I was beginning to feel real aversion to my new shoes. After many rides I have never grown to love them, but I could never go back.

BETASSO PRESERVE—CANYON LOOP TRAIL

Location: 7 miles west of Boulder

Length: 3-mile loop

Physical difficulty: Easy

Technical difficulty: Easy

Terrain: Smooth, hardpacked singletrack

Elevation gain: 490′

Maps and book: Boulder County Parks and Open Space brochure—Betasso Preserve; Zia Designs' Boulder County Mountain Bike Map; *Front Range Single Tracks*

Dogs: Yes

Heads up: Gentle, swooping trail in the ponderosa pines.

Description: Betasso is the little rollercoaster. Gentle, kind singletrack through glades of ponderosa and meadows, but still a thrill, with some short steep climbs and swoop-

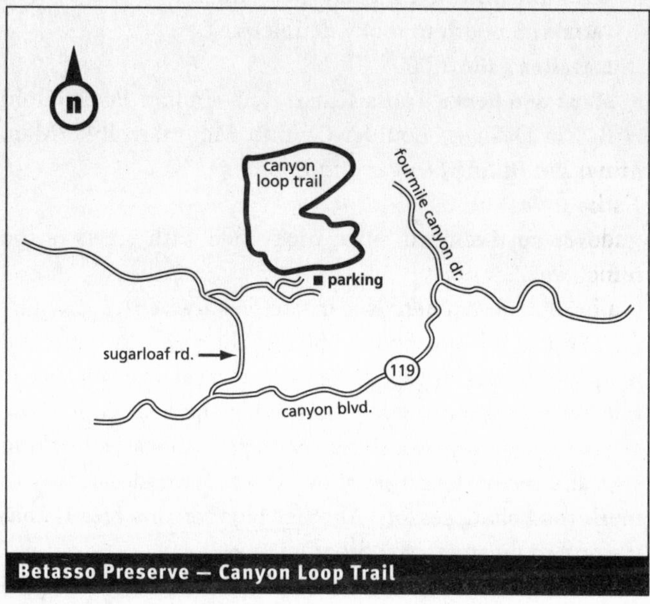

Betasso Preserve – Canyon Loop Trail

ing descents. A great ride to build confidence for the big screamers. Only minutes from Boulder, with deer, the dark tuft-eared Abert's squirrel, and plenty of hikers and dog walkers. Go clockwise; it's the law.

Route: Roll north out of the parking lot and take the Canyon Loop Trail. Again, go clockwise.

Directions: Head west up Canyon Boulevard (CO 119) 6 miles to Sugarloaf Road (122 RD) and turn right (north). Continue about 1 mile to a Betasso Preserve sign and turn right (east). The parking lot is on the left.

PENNSYLVANIA GULCH—SWITZERLAND TRAIL

Location: 12 miles west of Boulder

Length: 10-mile loop; Bean Gulch is a 7-mile option

Physical difficulty: Easy to moderate

Technical difficulty: Moderate to difficult

Terrain: Smooth to rocky doubletrack

Elevation gain: 1,000′

Maps and book: Trails Illustrated—Indian Peaks/Gold Hill; Zia Designs' Boulder County Mountain Bike Map; *Mountain Biking Denver and Boulder*

Dogs: Yes

Heads up: Secluded, high, rocky ride with views of the Indian Peaks.

Description: Up here it starts to feel alpine. A rocky dirt road descends from about 8,500 feet through spruce, fir and pine, and groves of aspen. The Indian Peaks jag across the northwest. I spent a whole fall doing the Bear Gulch ride almost every day, watching the aspen leaves yellow and spin and the peaks gather snow. It was a wonderful way to mark the ebbing season. Another plus for this area is that it's rare to meet another biker on a weekday.

Route: From the dirt parking area follow rough dirt road

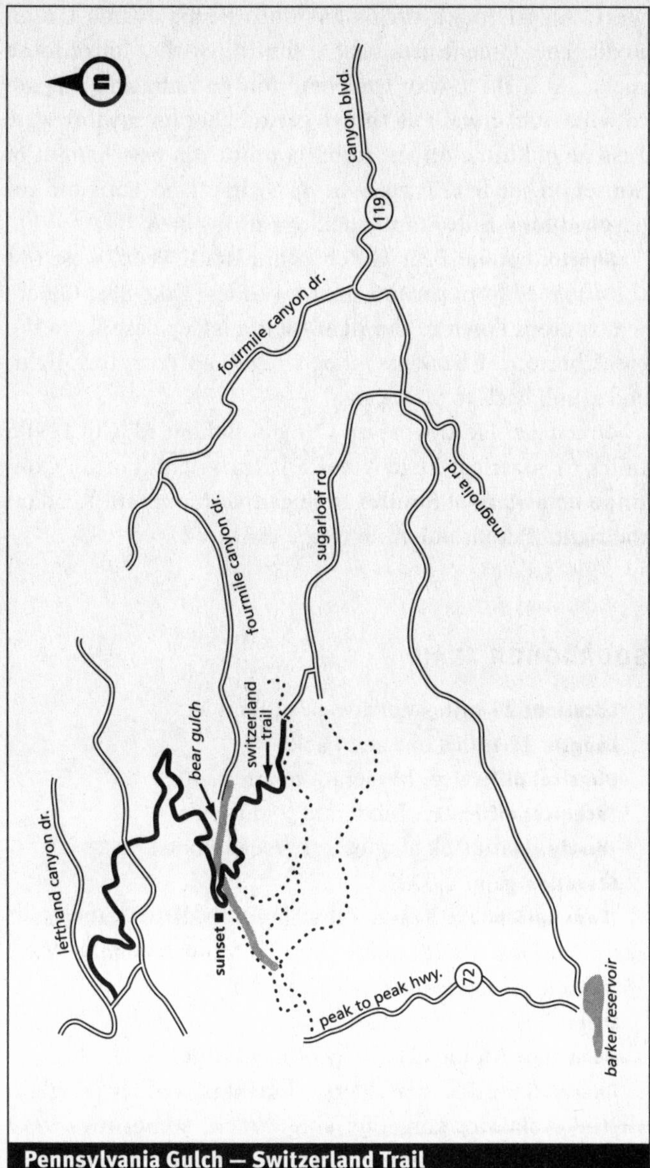

Pennsylvania Gulch — Switzerland Trail

west. At 4.1 miles turn right onto Pennsylvania Gulch Road. The descent gets very technical, with a lot of loose rocks. At a three-way trail junction go right and prepare to wipe out or walk as things get rougher for a short way. Pass an old mine on the right; continue on past hamlet of Sunset on the left. Turn right up Switzerland Trail and get psyched for 4-mile crank back to parking area.

Shorter option: Bear Gulch. Same start. Pedal west out the dirt road from parking area 2.4 miles. Take Bear Gulch, which drops down to the right—a fun, steep descent to the creek bottom. T back into the Switzerland Trail, turn right, and climb back to your car.

Directions: Head west up Canyon Boulevard (CO 119) 6 miles to Sugarloaf Road (122 RD). Turn right (north). Continue up Sugarloaf 5 miles to Sugarloaf Mountain Road on the right. Take it one mile to the trailhead.

SOURDOUGH TRAIL

Location: 24 miles northwest of Boulder

Length: 12 miles out and back

Physical difficulty: Moderate to strenuous

Technical difficulty: Moderate to difficult

Terrain: Hardpack singletrack, rocks, roots

Elevation gain: 1,000′

Maps and book: Trails Illustrated—Indian Peaks/Gold Hill; Zia Designs' Boulder County Mountain Bike Map; *Mountain Biking Denver and Boulder*

Dogs: Yes

Heads up: Alpine classic, cool in summer.

Description: Boulder riders adore this trail. It's a high-altitude, classic, gorgeous singletrack, sometimes very technical, through pine forest. It crosses little bridges, skirts a bog. An excellent choice in summer when it's broil-

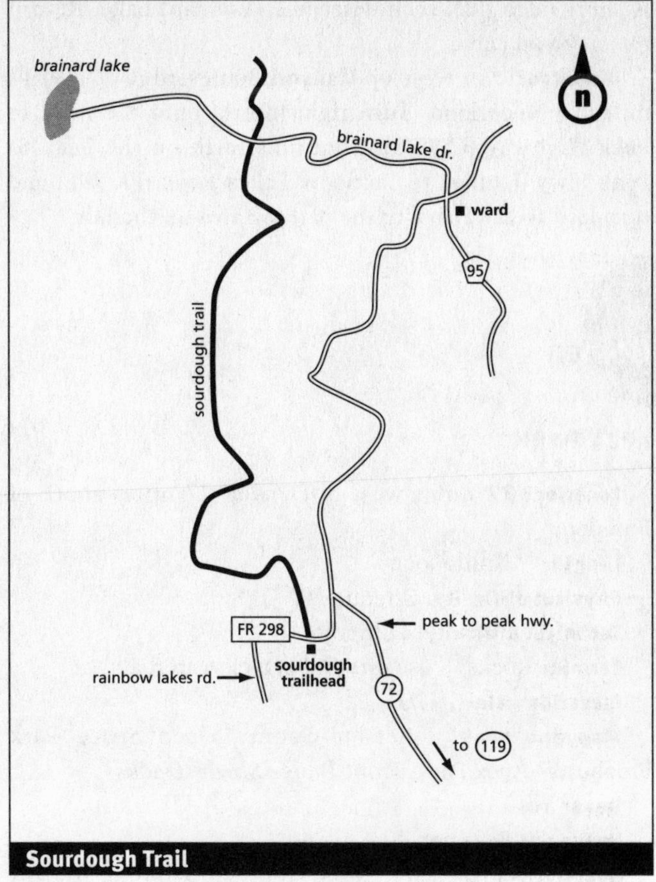

Sourdough Trail

ing in the lowlands. The ride starts above 9,000 feet and gains a thousand more, so be acclimated. Careful screaming back into the parking lot; the last hundred feet is loose gravel.

Route: Head north on the Sourdough Trail, climbing as you turn west and then north. Watch for a cross-country ski sign. There is a series of climbs and descents leading to Peace Memorial Bridge. Here is where you start climbing!

A short ridge ride, then descend to Brainard Lake. Return the way you came.

Directions: Go west up Canyon Boulevard (CO 119) 17 miles to Nederland. Turn right (north) onto the Peak to Peak Highway (CO 72). Continue north on the Peak to Peak Hwy 7 miles to Rainbow Lakes Road (FR 298) and turn left (west). Drive to the parking area on the left.

Golden

APEX PARK

Location: 12 miles west of Denver, 27 miles south of Boulder

Length: 5.3-mile loop

Physical difficulty: Strenuous

Technical difficulty: Difficult

Terrain: Rocks, loose dirt and gravel, waterbars

Elevation gain: 1,120′

Map and book: Jefferson County Open Space Park brochure—Apex Park; *Front Range Single Tracks*

Dogs: Yes

Heads up: Be tough.

Description: Apex is a classic Front Range hump. Straight up the face of the foothills with the vastness of the high plains pressing at your back. The first time we went to do this ride we took one look at the climb and drove into Morrison and had breakfast. The trail ascends through grassy slopes and patches of evergreen woods. Over a 1,000 feet of gain. Inspiring views of Gomorrah simmering on the flats. Steep descent with some tight turns, waterbars, and rocky sections.

Route: Get ready to get Western with these evocative

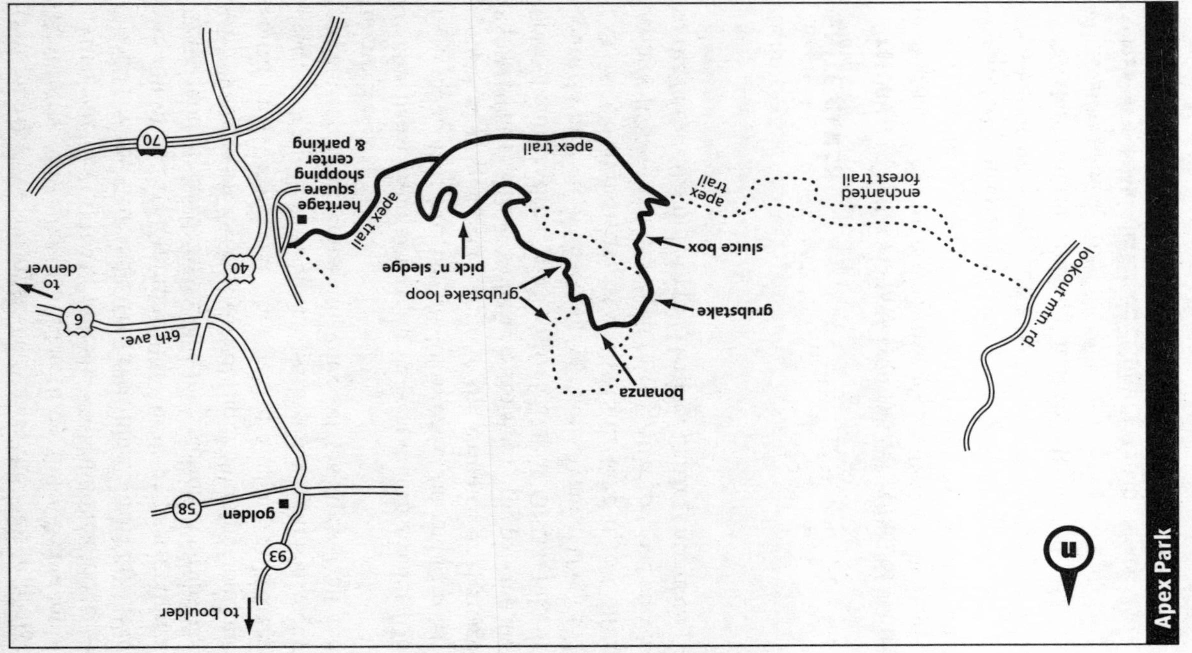
Apex Park
to boulder
93
golden
58
6th ave.
6
to
denver
40
70
heritage
square
shopping
center
& parking
apex trail
pick n' sledge
grubstake loop
apex trail
bonanza
grubstake
sluice box
apex
trail
enchanted
forest trail
lookout mtn. rd.
n

trail names. West on Apex Trail, past the Pick 'n Sledge Trail to the Sluice Box Trail. North up Sluice Box (a lot of loose switchbacks) to the junction with the Pick 'n Sledge Trail. Here the Grubstake Trail continues north. Take it to the top of Indian Mountain. Fast descent past Bonanza Trail, another short climb to the intersection of Grubstake with Bonanza on the east side of the mountain. Continue south on Grubstake to the Pick 'n Sledge Trail. Steep descent down Pick 'n Sledge, with some technical rocky sections and enlivening drop-offs. Left on Apex Trail and home. Eureka.

Directions: From Denver, drive west on 6th Avenue (US 6) to the Colfax Avenue (US 40) intersection and turn left (south). Continue over 1 mile to the entrance to Heritage Square. The trailhead is on the north side of the parking lot. From Boulder, drive west to Broadway (CO 93). Take it south 23 miles to intersection with 6th Avenue (US 6) and CO 58. Continue straight onto US 6. Take it to Colfax Avenue (US 40) and turn right (west). After the road curves to the left it's 0.5 mile to the Heritage Square entrance.

WHITE RANCH

Location: 22 miles northwest of Denver, 30 miles south of Boulder

Length: 10-mile loop

Physical difficulty: Strenuous

Technical difficulty: Difficult

Terrain: Hardpack, rocks, waterbars, steps

Elevation gain: 1,170′

Map and book: Jefferson County Open Space Park brochure—White Ranch; *Front Range Single Tracks*

Dogs: Yes

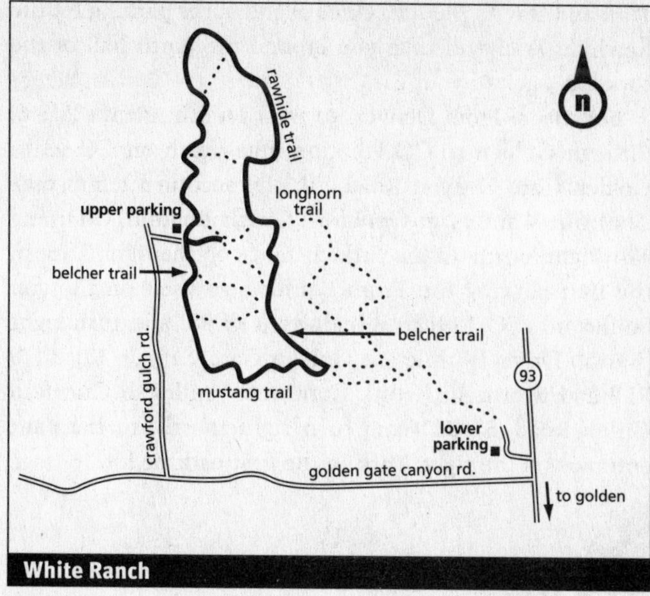

White Ranch

Heads up: Steep woods and swooping meadows looking over the plains.

Description: This is one of the first areas I ever rode on the Front Range and it made a deep impression—the remoteness and quiet, the smooth singletrack cutting through the meadow, the views of the plains, and the steep climbs over waterbars. I also remember being confused by all the trail options. They are myriad, long and short, moderate and very tough. It's a great place to explore. If you want to start with a real grunt, begin riding at the lower parking lot just off CO 93 near the bottom of Golden Gate Canyon Road.

Route: Take the Belcher Trail across from the upper parking lot. Climb up over waterbars and steps to the Mustang Trail. Turn left on Belcher Trail, climbing to Maverick Trail, then turn left on Longhorn Trail. Climb to Rawhide

Trail and stay to the left. Once at the upper parking lot the Rawhide Trail will take you around the north half of the park and back to your car.

Directions: From Denver, go west on 6th Avenue (US 6) through Golden to CO 93. Continue north on CO 93 to Golden Gate Canyon Road (70 RD) and turn left (west). Continue 4 miles to Crawford Gulch Road (57 RD) and turn right (north) to the park entrance on the right. Park in the first parking lot. From Boulder, go west on Canyon Boulevard (CO 119) to Broadway (CO 93) and turn right (south). Drive 19 miles to Golden Gate Canyon Road (70 RD) and turn right (west). Continue 4 miles to Crawford Gulch Road (57 RD) and turn right (north) to the park entrance on the right. Park in the first parking lot.

Short Hops

I have this dream: Mozart calls me on one of the new cell phones that access the internet as well as wrinkles in the time-space continuum. He says, "Pete, I have heard about this thing called rock 'n' roll. To which two songs must I listen?" Vermeer asks about Impressionism—two paintings. Dante is curious about Blake. A friend from Dubuque wants to know a single Indian restaurant in New York. In the dream I move my lips like a fish and realize that I'm swimming in a nightmare. You get the picture: There is so much superb mountain biking within an hour and a half of Denver and Boulder . . . Here are two well-loved rides worth the drive. There are scores and scores of others.

WINTER PARK'S TIPPERARY CREEK LOOP

Location: 55 miles northwest of Denver

Length: 23-mile loop

Physical difficulty: Strenuous

Technical difficulty: Moderate

Terrain: Gravel road, doubletrack, singletrack, some rocks

Elevation gain: 1200′

Maps and book: Winter Park and the Fraser Valley Trail Guide; Trails Illustrated #503 Winter Park/Grand Lake Bike map; *Front Range Single Tracks*

Dogs: Yes

Heads up: Best of the mountains. For more fun riding and trails that connect with the Tipperary Creek Loop check the maps.

Description: This is a classic mountain ride—high meadows, pine woods, creeks, a tough uphill grunt, and cool thin air. Worth the drive.

Route: From Winter Park ride north on Fraser River Trail along US 40 (in town, it's the sidewalk on the west side of the street) to Fraser and turn left on 4-Bar-4 Road (5 RD). Cross the railroad tracks. Within 1/4 mile turn left on 50 RD (Church Park Road). You'll pass the Tally Ho Lodge just before entering Arapaho National Forest. Watch for cattleguards. Once you have reached the Tipperary Creek Trail veer right and cross Tipperary Creek, following switchbacks to a stream—you're about halfway! You'll climb to 10,200′ and descend down to St. Louis Creek. Turn left on the St. Louis Creek Road. Follow the road across cattleguards and past John Work Rodeo Arena as you re-enter Fraser. Turn right at Fraser Parkway, then left on County Road 72 (Elk Creek Road) and right again on the Fraser River Trail and US 40 to Winter Park.

Directions: Drive west on I-70 28 miles to Empire (US 40)

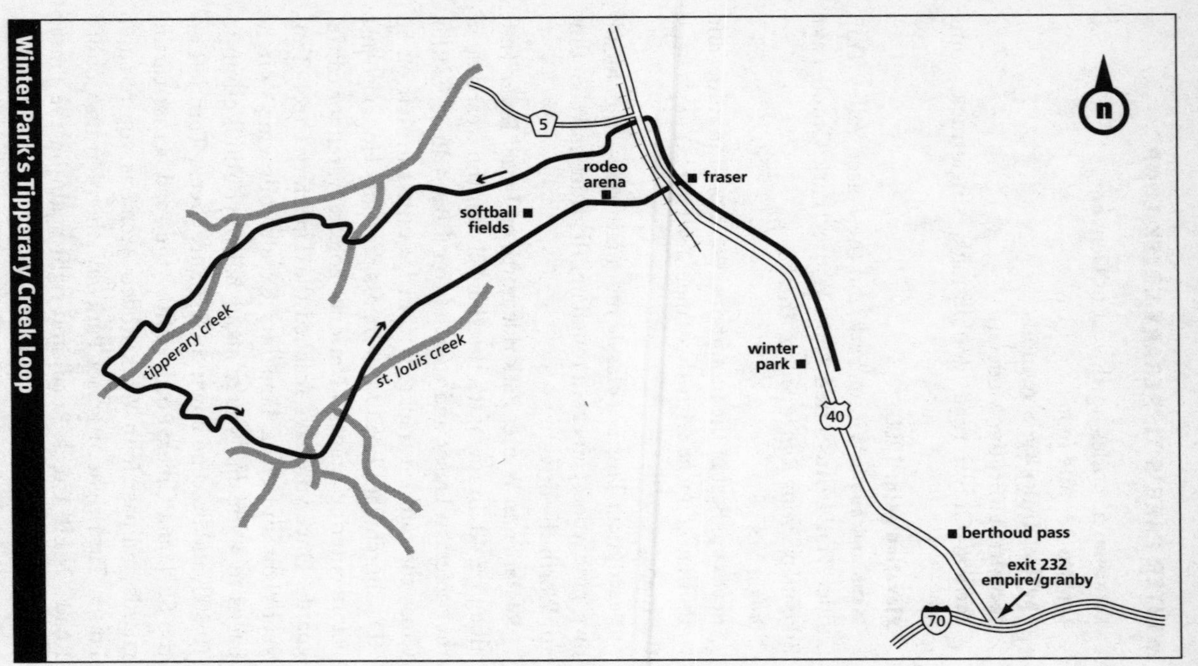
Winter Park's Tipperary Creek Loop
n
5
rodeo arena
fraser
softball fields
tipperary creek
st. louis creek
winter park
40
berthoud pass
exit 232 empire/granby
70

(exit 232). Exit on US 40 and drive through Empire, 26 miles to the heart of Winter Park.

BUFFALO CREEK BIG RIDE

Location: 35 miles southwest of Denver

Length: 20-mile loop

Physical difficulty: Moderate to difficult

Technical difficulty: Moderate

Terrain: Gravel and sandy hardpack. Some dirt road

Elevation gain: 2,600′

Map and book: Trails Illustrated $35 Deckers/Rampart Range; *Front Range Single Tracks*

Dogs: Yes

Heads up: Everything you want in a long ride away from town: creek, rocky sections, woods in a challenging loop.

Description: The Hi Meadow fire in the summer of 2000 significantly changed the character of this ride. While definitely smoother and faster than before the fire, it still is one of the premier gallops in the Buffalo Creek mountain biking trail system. The Strawberry Jack Trail has been relocated and rebuilt in several sections and there is much more gravel and sand now. Most of the ride is through partially to completely burned areas. The Big Ride really only has two hills to climb, but both are long and extended. And of course, there are two long, stellar downhills. The best part of this ride is the Charlie's Cutoff trail section as you snake your way over and around slick rock. It is an absolute kick and something of a rarity around Denver.

Route: Find the Narrow Gauge Trail on the north side of the river and take it to the North Fork View Trail at 0.3 mile and turn left. Cross the river, pick up the Buck Gulch Trail, and begin climbing on the wide, roadlike trail. The trail switchbacks to the right at 0.8 mile and steepens on loose gravel. Climb steadily on this loose surface to the junction with the Skipper Trail, just as you meet Forest Road 552 and an information kiosk at 3.2 miles. Turn left at the kiosk and fly down on the frequently sandy and rutted Skipper Trail before climbing out of Buck Gulch to a four-way intersection (4.5 miles). Turn right and continue climbing. At the crest of the next hill, find Charlie's Cutoff on your left at 5.1 miles and take it as you generally drop to the unmarked Homestead Trail, riding some cool slickrock along the way. Turn right on Homestead and continue downhill. Just as you pop out next to a large meadow, the trail veers left and becomes the Sandy Wash Trail (6.9 miles). Follow Sandy Wash to a stream crossing then a quick climb in a severely burned section of the forest. Sandy Wash will soon start the long drop to Buffalo Creek. Watch your speed as the trail is loose gravel for most of the way down. As you spy the road below and as Sandy Wash veers left, take the short spur down to Forest Road 543, at 9.8 miles. As an option, you can continue to take Sandy Wash for about 1 mile as the trail parallels the road and ultimately unites with Forest Road 543. Turn right on the road and start the second long climb, this one to the Baldy Trail/Gashouse Trail signs at mile 12.5. Climb a short distance, turn right on the Baldy Trail, and climb back to a ridge, but not before finding yet another fine piece of slickrock on which to practice your Moab skills. Descend off the ridge to the Gashouse Gulch Trail (15.7 miles) and turn right onto Gashouse. Descend to Miller Gulch Road (16.3 miles) and turn right after a short distance to the Homestead Trail, which can be found on your left. A quick climb puts you at Charlie's Cutoff. (If you want to do Charlie's again, do it, but turn left at the Homestead Trail, which will swing you back to the familiar four-way trail intersection.) Drop off the ridge and fly back to the four-way trail intersection. Continue straight, now on the relocated

Strawberry Jack Trail and get some wonderful air while descending all the way back to Pine Valley.

Option: Many riders prefer to climb out of the Buffalo Creek drainage via the Gashouse Gulch Trail instead of Baldy. It is a bit longer, but there is less climbing. To reach the Gashouse Trail, continue on Forest Road 543 past the Baldy/Gashouse Trail sign and turn right on Forest Road 550. After about a mile of easy climbing, spot the Gashouse Trail sign at a dirt road and start climbing. The road becomes singletrack and connects on the ridgetop with the Baldy Trail.

Directions: Take I-25 south to Santa Fe Drive (US 85). Take US 85 south to Hampden Avenue (US 285). Go west on Hampden to Pine Junction, and turn left (south) on Pine Valley Road (126 RD). Drive for 6 miles to Pine Valley Ranch. Turn right at the park entrance and follow the signs to the parking lot.

Mecca

A mountain bike mecca worth the trip.

WINTER PARK

Location: 55 miles northwest of Denver

Why we mention it again: Because it's got 600 more miles of trails!

Someone in Tabernash, a few miles down the Fraser River Valley from Winter Park, once told me that the growing season up there was 18 days. I'm not sure if that's mountain swagger, but I wouldn't doubt the claim. Winter Park is alpine. On summer nights when it's 80°F in Denver it can be 20°F up there. The lodgepole forests and the meadows of wheatgrass and sagebrush, the creeks cutting through them crowded by purple-stemmed willows, the moose and elk, and the high snowy ridges of the Divide, all give the valley a *Northern Exposure* feel and a sere beauty. Winter Park's made a name for itself as a top ski area, and now, with over 600 miles of trails and some of the best singletrack anywhere, the area is becoming a mountain bike mecca. For a fat tire aficionado living in Denver or Boulder, Winter Park is a no-brainer. You've got to go. Since it is a resort, the town has all the restaurants, bars, and sport shops you'd ever want, twice over—all piled on top of each other along US 40. I like to R-and-R in Fraser, a few miles down the road, where the wood paneling is real and the pool tables are warped. See *The Very Best of Winter Park: Dirt Mountain Bike Guide* for excellent, detailed info. Or contact Winter Park FATS, P.O. Box 1337, Winter Park, CO 80482, (970) 726-4118. They are an extraordinary local mountain bike club that has had a lot to do with the opening of the extensive trail system.

Where to Connect

Books

Front Range Single Tracks: The Best Single-Track Trails Near Denver and Boulder, by Tom Barnhart (Littleton, Colo.: Fat Tire Press, 1999).

Mountain Biking Denver and Boulder, by Bob D'Antonio (Helena, Mont.: Falcon Publishing, 1997).

Dirt: The Very Best of Winter Park and East Grand County, Colorado by Fernan DeLeon (Hood River, Oreg.: Hood River Publishing, 1999).

Guide to the High Line Canal (Denver, Colo.:

Denver Water Community Relations Office, 1999).

Shops

Denver

The SingleTrack Factory
1005 South Gaylord Street
Denver, CO 80209
(303) 733-3334
Home of Reeves Macdonald and the Wall of Pain.

Mojo Wheels
5970 West Dartmouth Avenue
Denver, CO 80227
(303) 985-4487
Best singletrack testing area for buying a new bike.

Wheat Ridge Cyclery
7085 West 38th Avenue
Wheat Ridge, CO 80033
(303) 424-3221
Great store on west side of town.

Boulder

University Cycles
839 Pearl Street
Boulder, CO 80302
(303) 444-4196
One of the friendliest and most helpful shops around. Sunday morning all-women mountain bike rides.

Morrison

Red Rocks Cyclery
300 Bear Creek Avenue
Morrison, CO 80465
(303) 697-8833
The place to get an early repair and a cup of coffee. The folks are as handy with an espresso as with a tune-up.

Clubs and Organizations

Denver

Denver Bicycle Touring Club
P.O. Box 260517
Lakewood, CO 80226-0517
(303) 756-7240

Rocky Mountain Cycling Club
P.O. Box 101473
Denver, CO 80250-1473
www.rmccrides.com

Boulder

International Mountain Bicycling Association
P.O. Box 7578
Boulder, CO 80306
888-442-IMBA

Boulder Bicycle Commuters
3239 9th Street
Boulder, CO 80304
(303) 499-7466

Boulder Seniors on Bikes
2431 Mapleton Avenue
Boulder, CO 80304
(303) 443-7623

Boulder Women's Cycling Team
(303) 497-8427

FARTHER AFIELD:

Clear Creek Bicycle Club
P.O. Box 496
Idaho Springs, CO 80452
(303) 569-2729

Winter Park Mountain Bike Hot Line
(800) 903-7275

Winter Park Sport Shop
P.O .Box 55
Winter Park, CO 80482
(970) 726-5593

Events

Elephant Rock Cycling Adventure

A huge cycling event. Offering road and off-road rides from 10 to 100 miles, the Elephant Rock attracts 6,500 riders from all over Colorado and surrounding states. After the ride, cyclists relax with a barbecue lunch, music, kid's bike races, liquid refreshments, and demos by sponsors' cycling teams. June.

Moonlight Classic

Thousands of cyclists pedal through Denver on a warm summer night by the light of the full moon. Good-night clocks, good-night shocks . . . Midnight in August.

Moonlight Classic Hotline:
(303) 282-9020

Denver Critical Mass

The San Francisco bike movement/protest ride lives in Denver. Pedal for more bike lanes, increase bicycle awareness. Meet at Civic Center Park (across from the capitol building, near the seal fountain pool on the Colfax Avenue side of the park). The ride begins at 6:00 P.M., proceeds through downtown Denver, and ends at Auraria Campus. Last Friday of every month, 6 P.M., at Civic Center Park.

American Red Cross Fat Tire Classic

One of the largest mountain bike events in Colorado—close to 2,000 participants! Raises money for the American Red Cross. Music, food, and fantastic mountain riding. In Winter Park, mid-summer.

Road Riding

Chris Osgood of Putney, Vermont, came into my family when he married my cousin, Mary. He has always been a wonderful athlete and outdoorsman. He's a great cross-country skier, and cyclist, runner, wood chopper, and a dyed-in-the-wool New Englander. Once when I was back East he told me something I'll never forget: He said he sometimes dreams of coming out to Colorado and just riding his road bike "up those long inclines." He extended his hand slowly on a rising glide path, and followed it with his eyes, squinting as he met the sun high over the old barn. Not that there aren't inclines in Vermont, but I knew what he meant. From Denver or Boulder you can head upcanyon through a cleft in the Front

Range, crank all the way to the top of Mt. Evans, and top out at 14,624′ after a seven thousand–foot gain. Or start from the Boulder–Golden Road (CO 93) and ride fifteen hundred feet into the pine-covered hills of Golden Gate Canyon State Park. If you love a good, sustained climb on a bike, there's almost no better place to live. If you just like to spin and take in some spectacular country as you ride rolling loops at the edge of the foothills, you can do that too. Both kinds of rides are included here, short and long. This is, of course, a very limited selection—it's fun to take out a road map and put together loops convenient to where you live, and with the right mix of distance and elevation.

It's worth noting, in addition to all the amazing rides in the Boulder vicinity, that night riders and hellions tearing down Boulder Canyon have reaped their harvest of accident victims. Ride with a very good light at night in Boulder or you're likely to get pulled over and ticketed. Also, be careful coming down Canyon Boulevard (CO 119) and keep your speed down.

A ton of cycling enthusiasts live in the area, so there are a lot of good resources, from full-service shops to clubs to weekly rides. From outside Red Rocks Cyclery in Morrison scores of riders take a fifty miler every Sunday morning from January to April. There's even a restaurant not far from Washington Park called the Handlebar Grill whose soul, whose whole *raison d'etre*, is to cycling, from the clientele to the racing jerseys framed on the walls. If you live here and you don't own a road bike, you might consider getting one. The terrain is unbeatable and you can ride almost year-round—barring snowstorms—when the mountain bike trails in the hills are snowed covered or wet. A growing number of business people are commuting on bikes—saving fuel and getting a workout in the bargain. The trend is encouraging more corporate showers and locker rooms, and spawning innovative, bike-friendly centers such as the Bike Depot.

Thanks to Burt and Terry Struthers for the details in their fine book, *The Guide to Bicycling the Roads Out of Boulder*.

Denver City Limits

BELOW BEAR CREEK LAKE TO CHERRY CREEK LAKE

Location: 10 miles southwest of Denver
Length: 52 miles out and back
Difficulty: Easy
Elevation gain: Minimal
Map: Bicycling Metro Denver Route Map
Heads up: Long ride all on a paved path, no cars. Park in Morrison to avoid paying the park fee. Bring a swimsuit. *Note:* If you do this ride at night, use a strong light as homeless people often sleep right in the path.

Description: The Denver urban classic from one side of the city to the other, surprisingly pretty and along flowing water the whole way. Starting at Bear Creek Lake Park in the foothills on the west side of town, you get a great look at all of Denver. Nice not to contend with cars, but there's plenty of pedestrian and skating traffic along Cherry Creek, especially on evenings and weekends, so be considerate. On a hot day you can take a swim at the midpoint in Cherry Creek Lake.

Route: Go east on the Bear Creek Bike Path to the junction with the South Platte Path. Turn left (north) and ride to Confluence Park, where the South Platte River meets Cherry Creek. Turn right (southeast) on the Cherry Creek

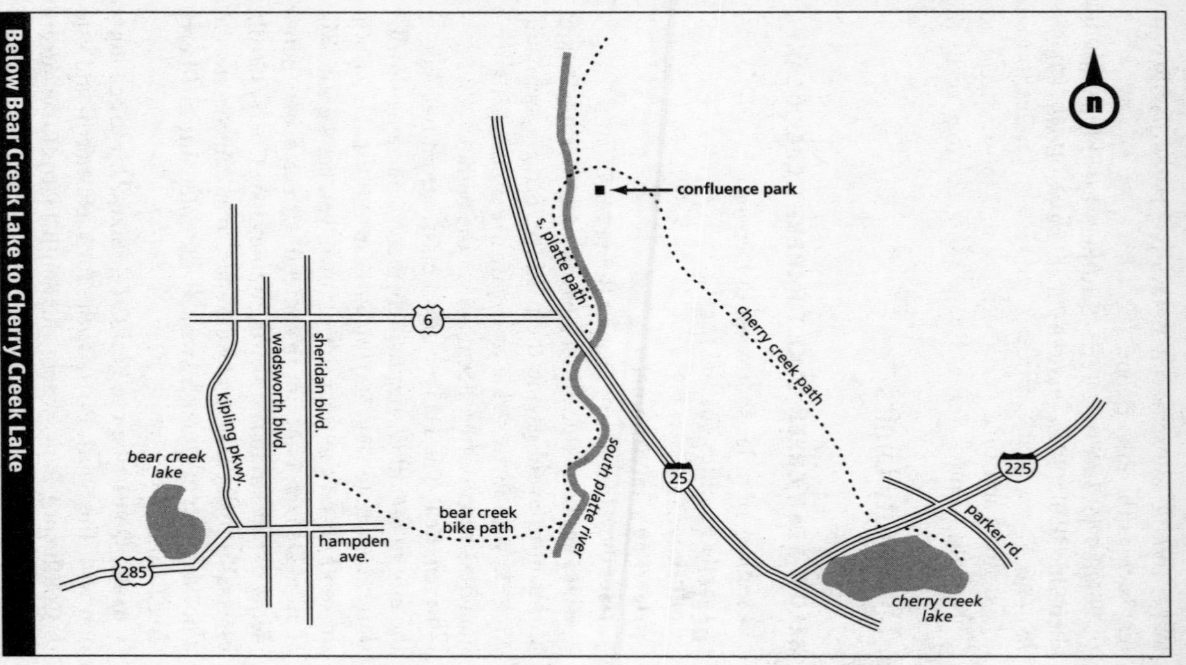
Below Bear Creek Lake to Cherry Creek Lake
n
confluence park
s. platte path
cherry creek path
south platte river
bear creek
bike path
6
25
225
285
parker rd.
cherry creek
lake
bear creek
lake
kipling pkwy.
wadsworth blvd.
sheridan blvd.
hampden
ave.

Bike Path. Follow it to Cherry Creek Lake. Return the same way.

Directions: Drive west on 6th Avenue (US 6) to Kipling Street. Turn south on Kipling. (Kipling Street becomes Kipling Parkway at Alameda Avenue.) Go 4 miles to Morrison Road and turn left (east). Go to Kipling Street and turn right (south). You can park along the road or in the parking lots.

Denver Backyard

DEER CREEK CANYON LOOP

Location: 19 miles southwest of Denver

Length: 50-mile loop

Difficulty: Moderate to difficult

Elevation gain: 3,000′

Maps: *Colorado Atlas and Gazetteer*

Heads up: A very popular, beautiful ride that avoids US 285.

Description: Tough climbing in gorgeous foothills. The last 10 miles are steep and winding downhill . . . Yeeeeeee.

Route: Ride west up Deer Creek Canyon Road (124 RD). At Twin Forks turn left (west) onto North Turkey Creek Road (64 RD). Climb to 73 RD and turn right (north); descend into downtown Evergreen. Turn right (east) on CO 74 and descend into Kittredge. Turn right (south) onto Meyer's Gulch Road (120 RD). (After a tough climb it becomes Parmalee Gulch Road.) Cross US 285. You are now on Turkey Creek (122 RD) which becomes Deer Creek Canyon Road. Ride southeast and then east to Wadsworth Boulevard.

Directions: Drive west on 6th Avenue (US 6), to

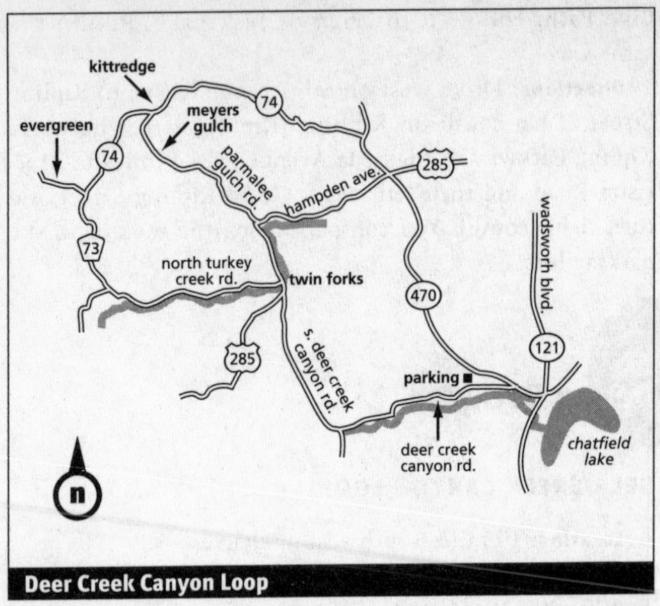

Deer Creek Canyon Loop

Wadsworth Boulevard (CO 121). Turn left (south) and go about 12 miles to Deer Creek Canyon Road (124 RD). Park along the north side of the road.

SEDALIA TO PALMER LAKE, PERRY PARK ROAD

Location: 22 miles south of Denver

Length: 46 miles out and back

Difficulty: Moderate

Elevation gain: 1,000′

Maps: *Colorado Atlas and Gazetteer*

Heads up: This ride will make you want to ride more and more.

Description: Great ride on a sunny winter day. A long, winding road and rolling hills with a nice rhythm. Waterfowl, eagles, and herons fly over and land on the shores of

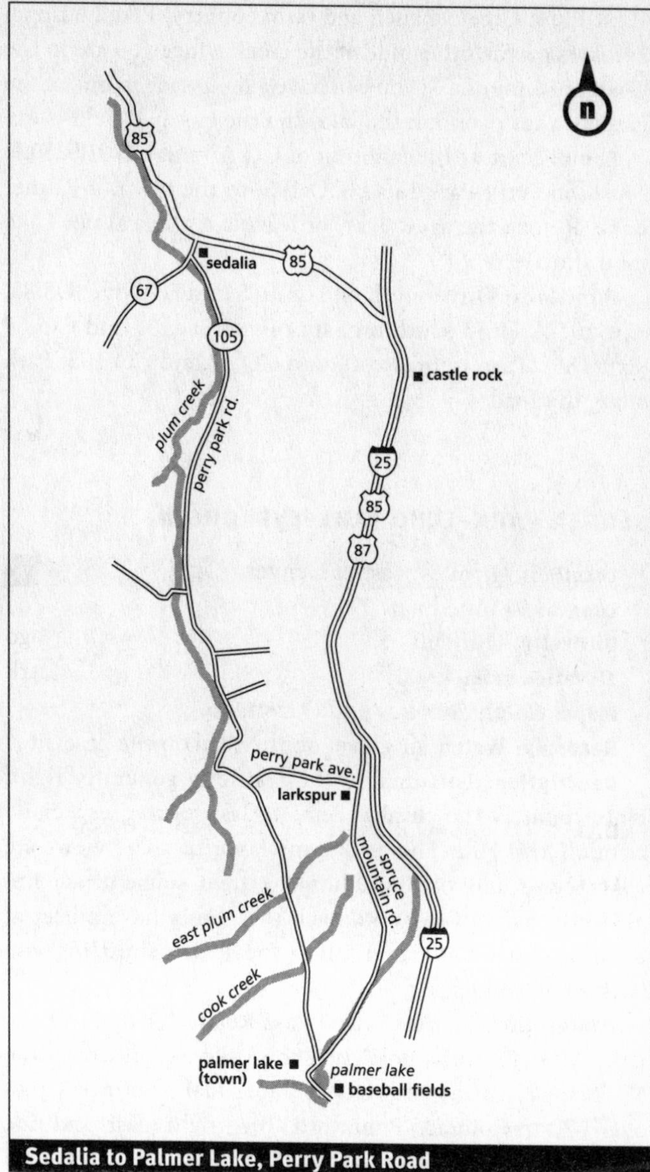

Sedalia to Palmer Lake, Perry Park Road

West Plum Creek. Ranch and farm country; Pike National Forest is on the other side of the creek. Once you are in the town of Palmer Lake you can have a lemonade in one of the gazebos that overlook the lake and the baseball field.

Route: Start at the junction of CO 67 and CO 105. Ride south on Perry Park Road (CO 105) to the town of Palmer Lake. Return the same way, or leave a car in Palmer Lake for a shuttle.

Directions: Drive south on I-25 to Santa Fe Drive (US 85, exit 207B). Head south on Santa Fe to Sedalia and CO 67 (exit 183). Turn right (west) onto CO 67 and CO 105. Park along the road.

BERGEN PARK–ECHO LAKE–EVERGREEN

Location: 21 miles west of Denver

Length: 64-mile loop

Difficulty: Difficult

Elevation gain: 4,600′

Maps: *Colorado Atlas and Gazetteer*

Heads up: Watch for gravel on the road on the descent.

Description: Fortunately the traffic is generally light. Unfortunately the climbs seems to last forever, especially 2-mile Floyd Hill. This is one my favorites. The views are spectacular and you take home a great sense of accomplishment. If you can't stomach the climb, have a beer at Kermit's Roadhouse and talk a local into shuttling you back to Bergen Park.

Route: Ride west up Squaw Pass Road (CO 103) to Echo Lake. CO 103 turns north at Echo Lake and descends the Mt Evans Highway (still CO 103) into Idaho Springs. Cross over I-70 to Colorado Boulevard. Turn right (east) and ride through Idaho Springs. Cross back over I-70 and head toward the baseball field on 314 RD (south side on I-70).

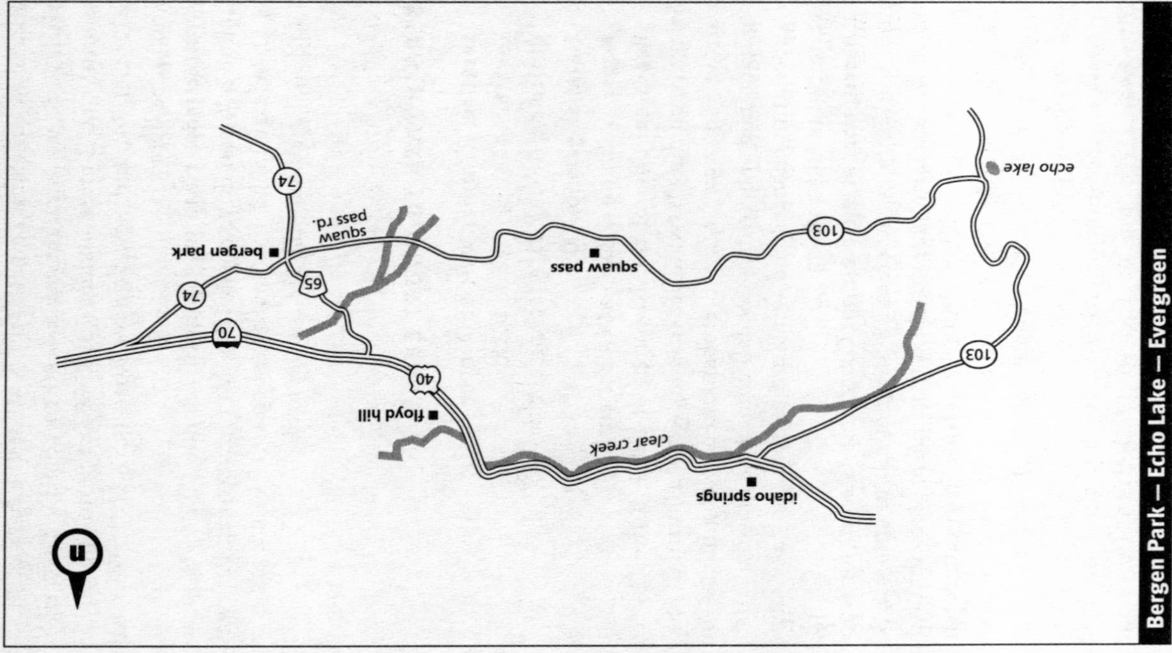

Bergen Park — Echo Lake — Evergreen

Ride east on the bike path to US 40 at the base of Floyd Hill. Ride up, straight up, US 40 to 65 RD. Turn right (south); you'll cross under I-70. Ride to the junction of 65 RD, CO 74, and Squaw Pass Road (CO 103). Your car should be here.

Directions: Head west on 6th Avenue (US 6) to westbound I-70 and drive about 17 miles to Evergreen Parkway (CO 74, exit 252). Drive southwest on CO 74 for 2 miles to CO 103. Park along the side of the road.

BERGEN PARK TO MOUNT EVANS

Location: 21 miles west of Denver

Length: 64 miles out and back

Difficulty: Advanced, a technical ride

Elevation gain: 6,900′

Maps: *Colorado Atlas and Gazetteer*

Heads up: One of the 10 toughest rides in the United States (including Hawaii). Take along a few aspirin. CO 5 is narrow and tricky. Stay to embankment side (unless you are not afraid of heights)—the fall could be a long one. Also, temperature changes and wind are extreme so take along warm tights and a jacket.

Description: A huge climb. Okay, this is word for word from Carl Shipley, a veteran: "Steep climb to summit, 32 miles, yeah, take an aspirin, find that magic place that balances heart rate with breathing, keep your heart rate down, start slow, slowly speed up incrementally, and be your strongest at the end. It's a combination of cadence, heart rate, and breathing."

Route: Go west on CO 103 to CO 5 and the summit of Mt. Evans, the top of the world. Return the same wayyyyyyyyy . . .

Directions: Head west on 6th Avenue (US 6) to west-

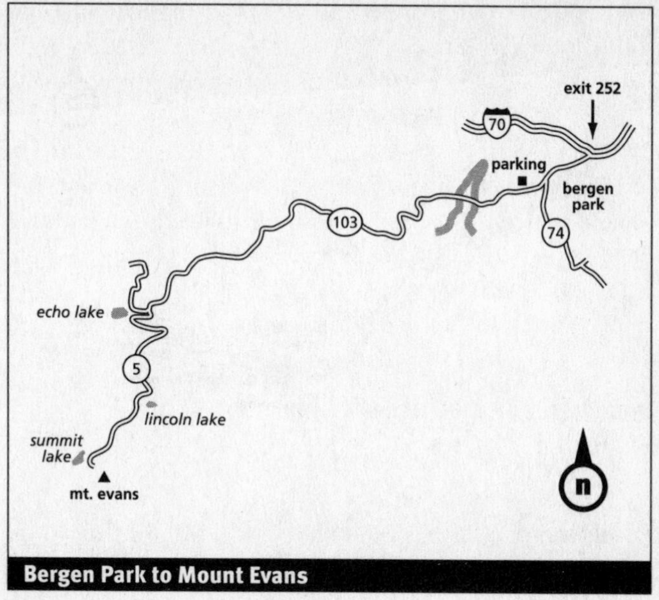

Bergen Park to Mount Evans

bound I-70 and drive about 17 miles to Evergreen Parkway (CO 74, exit 252). Drive south on CO 74 for 2 miles to CO 103. Park along the side of the road.

Boulder City Limits

SALINA VIA FOURMILE CANYON

Location: West side of Boulder
Length: 13 miles out and back
Difficulty: Moderate
Elevation gain: 1,130′
Maps and book: *Colorado Atlas and Gazetteer; The Guide to Bicycling the Roads Out of Boulder*

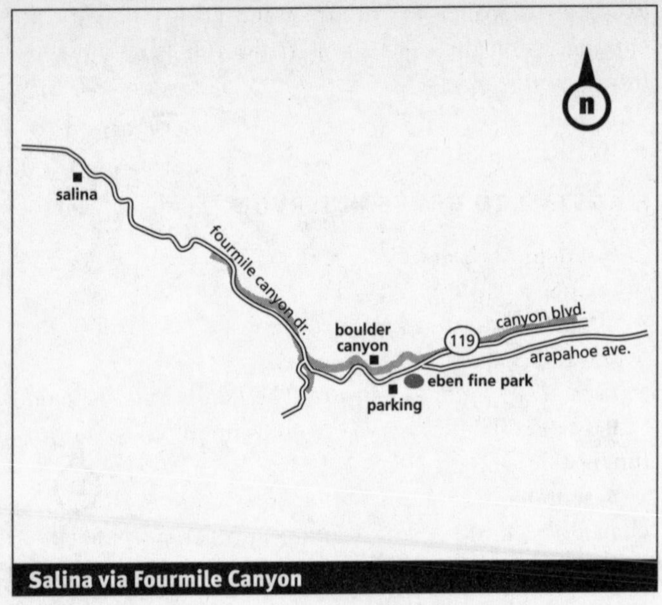

Salina via Fourmile Canyon

Heads up: Considerably less traffic than on Canyon Boulevard (CO 119), but wear your helmet—there's no shoulder.

Description: Pretty good straight climb to Salina in pretty good curvy canyon. The descent is fun. It would be a wise idea to obey the speed limit, because cops have been known to ticket cyclists.

Route: Start at Eben Fine Park. Ride west on the Boulder Creek Bike Path to its end at Fourmile Canyon. Cross CO 119 and continue riding northwest on Fourmile Canyon Drive, ascending to Salina. Return the same way.

Option: Since there is a lot of gravel on the bike path, you could ride west on Canyon Boulevard (CO 119) from Boulder to Fourmile Canyon.

Directions: Take Canyon Boulevard (CO 119) west to 9th Street. Turn left (south) to Arapahoe Avenue. Turn right (west) on Arapahoe to 3rd Street and Eben Fine Park; the entrance is on the right. Or start the ride from anywhere from town.

FLAGSTAFF TO GROSS RESERVOIR

Location: Boulder
Length: 19 miles
Difficulty: Moderate
Elevation gain: 1,750′
Book: *The Guide to Bicycling the Roads Out of Boulder*
Heads up: Traffic, curves, and climbing all make for a fun, fast descent.

Description: All uphill, for a mere 8.5 miles. This is your chance to crank out of Boulder and get up behind the

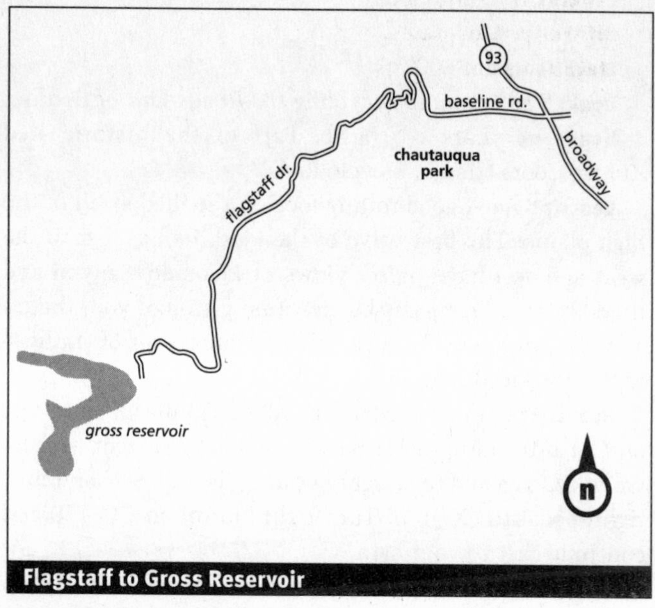

Flagstaff to Gross Reservoir

Flatirons. Beautiful views of Gregory Canyon, Flagstaff Mountain to the north, and Green Mountain to the south. Huge sweep of the plains on the way back.

Route: Ride west up Baseline Road, which becomes Flagstaff Drive, to Gross Reservoir. Return the same way.

Directions: Take Canyon Boulevard (CO 119) west to Broadway (CO 93) and turn left (south). Continue on Broadway to Baseline Road. Turn right (west) onto Baseline to 9th Street. Turn left (south) into the Chautauqua parking lot.

Boulder Backyard

MORGUL–BISMARK

Location: 7 miles south of Boulder

Length: 13.2-mile loop

Difficulty: Moderate

Elevation gain: 400′

Book: *The Guide to Bicycling the Roads Out of Boulder*

Heads up: Lots of traffic. Part of the historic Red Zinger/Coors Classic Bicycle Race.

Description: A good rolling loop on the final swell of the high plains. The first wave of the foothills lies just to the west and you have pretty views of Eldorado Canyon and the Flatirons. Don't let the elevation gain fool you; there's a lot of climbing. There can also be quite a bit of traffic—watch for speeding cars.

Route: Begin at the Marshall Mesa Trailhead. Ride east on CO 170 to McCaslin Boulevard and turn right (south). Go to CO 128 and turn right (west); pedal to US 93 and turn right; pedal to CO 170. Turn right (north) on CO 170 and continue east to your car.

Directions: Go west on Canyon Boulevard (CO 119) to

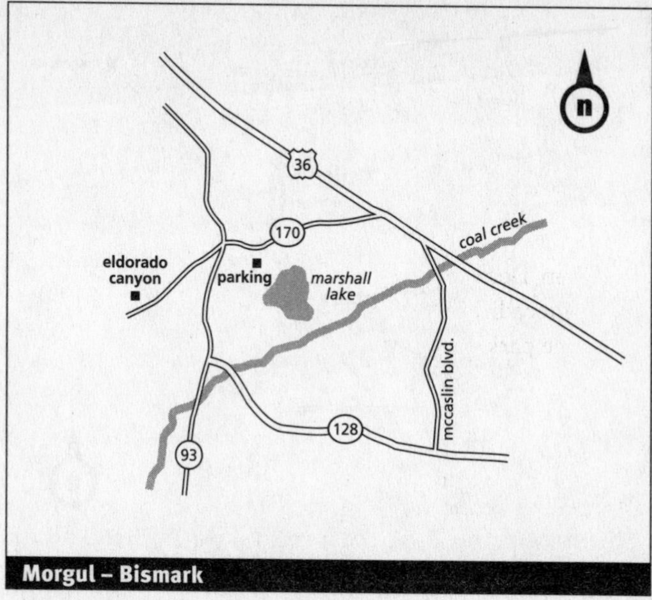

Morgul – Bismark

Broadway (CO 93) and turn left (south). Drive 5 miles to the Eldorado Springs (CO 170) exit. Turn left (east) on CO 170 and drive about 1 mile to the Marshall Mesa Trailhead on the right (south) side.

NELSON ROAD LOOP

Location: 2 miles northeast of Boulder

Length: 23-mile loop, also a 22-mile out-and-back option

Difficulty: Easy

Elevation gain: 250′

Maps and book: *Colorado Atlas and Gazetteer; The Guide to Bicycling Roads Out of Boulder*

Heads up: More climbing than is represented in the elevation gain.

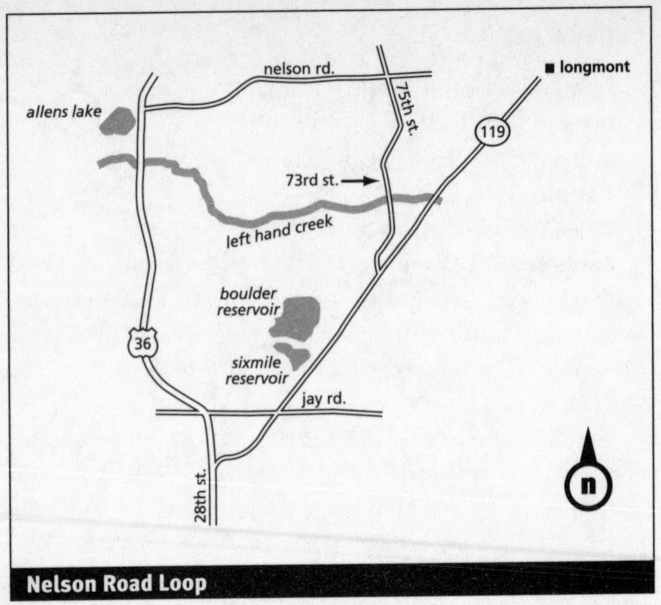

Description: Rolling plains and man-made lakes below the grassy crests of the foothills. Wide views across the plains to the Flatirons on the way back. If you're hot, when you get back to Jay Road hang a hard right up 51st Street and detour to the Boulder Reservoir for a swim.

Route: Ride north on US 36 to Nelson Road (20 RD). Turn right onto Nelson Road and pedal to 75th Street. Go south, right on 75th, which becomes 73rd, to CO 119. Go southwest, right on CO 119, to Jay Road. Turn west on Jay Road to US 36.

Option: The Diagonal, CO 119, from Boulder to Longmont and back is a popular ride that has a wide shoulder in both directions. It's 11 miles one way.

Directions: Drive north on 28th Street (US 36) to Jay Road. Park along the side of the road.

CARTER LAKE

Location: 26 miles north of Boulder

Length: 17 miles

Difficulty: Moderate to difficult

Elevation gain: 630′

Maps: *Colorado Atlas and Gazetteer*

Heads up: Just another pretty Front Range ride.

Description: Get into the country north of Boulder and Longmont. Killer climb, fun descents, woodlands. Blue Mountain rises directly west, keeping careful watch of you and the lake.

Route: Ride west on 8E RD. At 31 RD turn right and ride along the east side of the reservoir to 18E RD. Turn right (east) and peddle to 29 RD. Turn right. You will be traveling south, then east; 29 RD becomes 12 RD. Continue east until 23 RD and turn right, south. Turn right to 8E RD where your car is parked.

Directions: Drive north on 28th Street (US 36) to the Longmont Diagonal (CO 119) and turn right (northeast). Go to 95th Street and turn left (north); 95th jogs to the right at Crystal Lake. Turn left at Yellowstone Road, then an immediate right onto 95th Street. Continue to 10 RD and turn left (west). You'll reach a T intersection with 23 RD; turn left (south) and drive to 8E RD. Turn right. Park along the side of the road.

PEAK TO PEAK HIGHWAY

Location: 8 miles north of Boulder

Length: 82-mile loop; there is a 55.5-mile-loop option

Difficulty: Difficult. Option is moderate

Elevation gain: 3,800′; elevation gain on the option is 2,100′

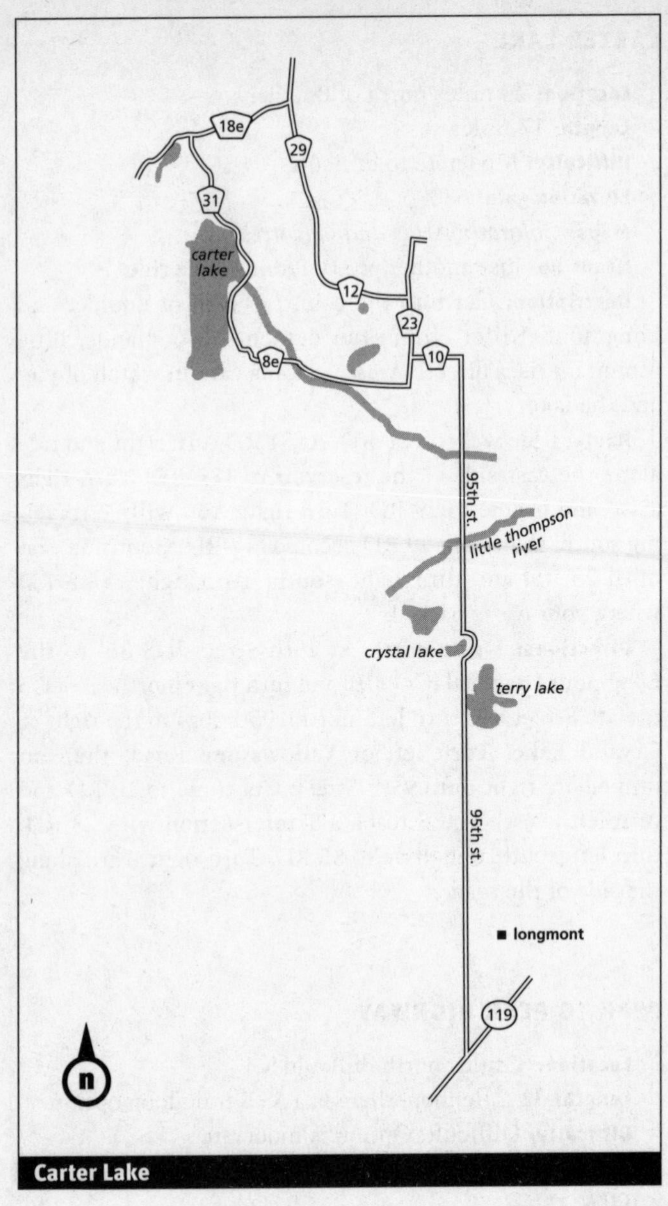
18e
29
31
carter lake
12
23
10
8e
95th st.
little thompson river
crystal lake
terry lake
95th st.
longmont
119
n
Carter Lake

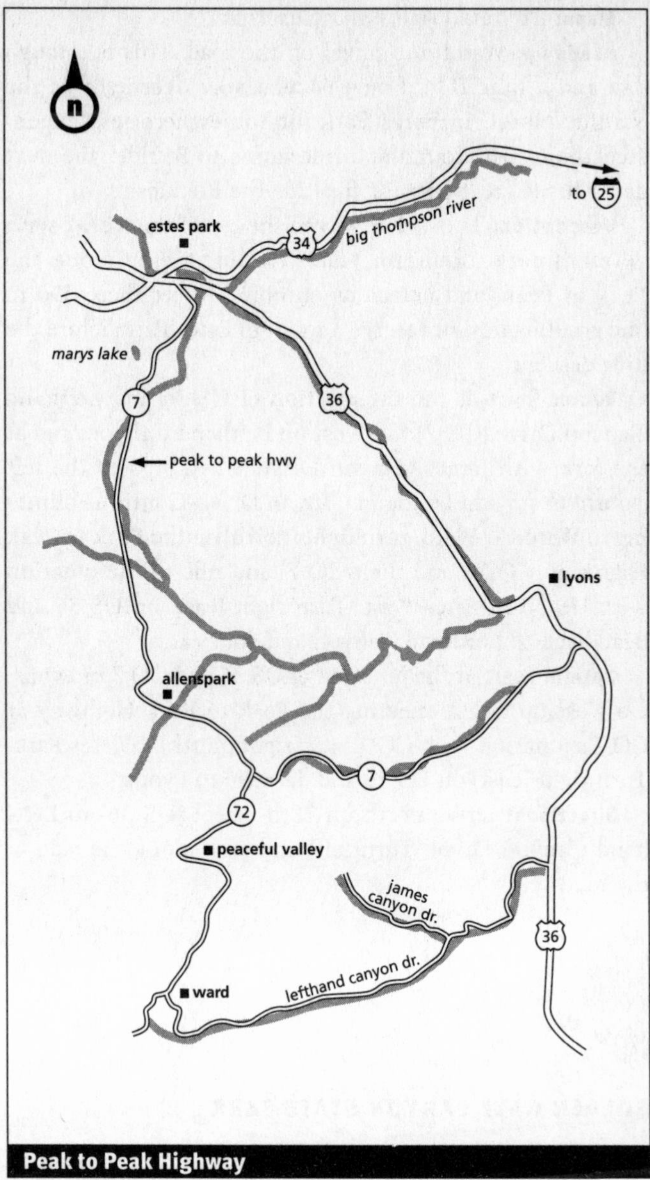

Peak to Peak Highway

Maps: *Colorado Atlas and Gazetteer*

Heads up: Watch for gravel on the road. This is a tough day and a long ride. I suggest you stay overnight at the Stanley Hotel, in Estes Park (or somewhere less expensive),then turn around and ride home to Boulder the next day. This is great training for Ride the Rockies.

Description: This is halfway to the top of the world, with extraordinary mountain vistas, rolling riding along the Peak to Peak, and helacious climbing to get there. Do in one grueling day, or reserve a room in Estes Park before the long descent.

Route: Start at the intersection of US 36 and Lefthand Canyon Drive (CO 7). Go west up Lefthand Canyon, and at the fork with James Canyon Drive (94 RD) go to the left (south) to stay on Lefthand Canyon Drive. Continue climbing to Ward. At Ward, turn right (north) on the Peak to Peak Highway (CO 72 and then CO 7) and ride to the junction with US 36 in Estes Park. Turn right (east) on US 36 and head back to Lefthand Canyon and your car.

Option: Start at the junction of US 36 and CO 7 in Lyons. Go west up CO 7, meeting the Peak to Peak Highway at CO 7's junction with CO 72. Go right (north) to Estes Park. Turn right (east) on US 36 and descend to Lyons.

Directions: Drive north on 28th Street (US 36) to Lefthand Canyon Drive. Turn left, and park along the side of the road.

Golden

GOLDEN GATE CANYON STATE PARK

Location: 22 miles northwest of Denver; 30 miles south of Boulder

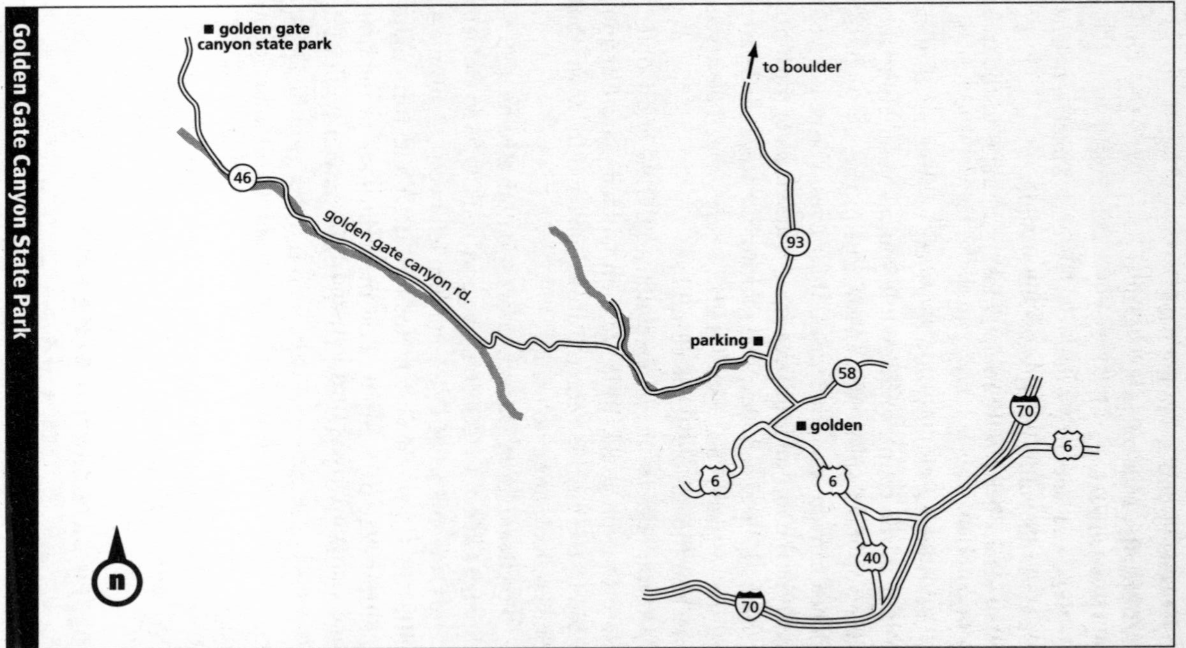

Golden Gate Canyon State Park

Length: 26 miles out and back

Difficulty: Moderate to difficult

Elevation gain: 1,530′

Maps and book: *Colorado Atlas and Gazetteer; The Guide to Bicycling the Roads Out of Boulder*

Heads up: Narrow shoulder, most of riding is in the traffic lane.

Description: The loveliest, curviest of grueling climbs. You're in the country now. While you ask your legs to forgive you, take spiritual nourishment in the steep, grass-sloped canyon, the ponderosas, the groves of aspen as you get near the top, and the occasional wide views of the pine-covered hills ahead. Best done during the week, and early on the weekends because of traffic. There's a well-deserved break in the middle of the climb.

Route: Start at the intersection of CO 93 and Golden Gate Canyon Road. Ride west on Golden Gate Canyon Road to the visitors center. Turn around and fly down the canyon, look mom no brains . . .

Directions: From Denver, go west on 6th Avenue (US 6) through Golden to CO 93. Drive north on CO 93 to Golden Gate Canyon Road (CO 46) and turn left (west). Continue 4 miles to Crawford Gulch Road (57 RD) and turn right (north) to the park entrance on the right. Park in the first parking lot. From Boulder, go west on Canyon Boulevard (CO 119) to Broadway (CO 93) and turn left (south). Drive 19 miles to Golden Gate Canyon Road (CO 46) and turn right (west). Continue 4 miles to Crawford Gulch Road (57 RD) and turn right (north) to the park entrance on the right. Park in the first parking lot.

Where to Connect

Book and Link

The Guide to Bicycling the Roads Out of Boulder, 3rd edition, by Burt and Terry Struthers (Boulder, Colo.: Published by the authors, 1998).

www.active.com
Tons of events every week listed in all classes of cycling.

Restaurant

The Handlebar Grill
305 South Downing
Denver, CO 80209
(303) 778-6761
A must-eat for serious riders. This is not a kitchy theme restaurant—it's a joint that lives, breathes, eats, even drinks cycling and racing. Race jerseys on the walls, photos, bike frames, and burgers with names like the Tour of the Rockies (cheddar and BBQ) and the Pearl Izumi (crisp bacon and cheddar cheese). Real cyclists hang here—the racers are the ones that aren't drinking.

Shops

Denver

Turin Bicycles, LTD
700 Lincoln
Denver, CO 80203
(303) 837-1857
www.turinbikes.com

Campus Cycles
2102 South Washington Street
Denver, CO 80210
(303) 698-2811
www.campuscycles.com

Schwabb Cycles
1565 Pierce Street
Lakewood, CO 80214
(303) 238-0243
www.schwabbcycles.com

Wheat Ridge Cyclery
7085 West 38th Avenue
Wheat Ridge, CO 80033
(303) 424-3221
www.ridewrc.com
Owned by Ron Kiefel, who raced the Tour de France seven times.

Tandem Cycle Works
1084 South Gaylord Street
Denver, CO 80209

(303) 715-9690
www.tandemsOnline.com

An entire shop devoted to tandem bicycles—both road bikes and mountain bikes!

Boulder

University Cycles
839 Pearl Street
Boulder, CO 80302
(303) 444-4196
www.ubikes.com

Morrison

Red Rocks Cyclery
300 Bear Creek Avenue
Morrison, CO 80465
(303) 697-8833

The place to get an early repair and a cup of coffee. The staff is as handy with an espresso as a tune-up. Also, 50-mile group rides, on Sunday, January through April. Call them—the slowest they go is 17 mph.

Clubs and Organizations

Denver

Rocky Mountain Cycling Club
P.O. Box 101473
Denver, CO 80250-1473
www.rmccrides.com

Colorado Bicycle Racing Association for Seniors, Inc. (COBRAS)
621 17th Street, Suite 1550
Denver, CO 80293
(303) 320-4413

Team in training. Raising money for the Leukemia Society of America.

Sunburst Cycle Club

Training rides leave Sundays from downtown Denver at 10:30 A.M. Helmets are required. For exact location and more information call: (303) 790-5258.

Boulder

The Bolder Bicycle Commuters
3239 9th Street
Boulder, CO 80304
(303) 499-7466, (303) 449-7439

Evergreen

Team Evergreen Bicycle Club Inc.
P.O. Box 3804
Evergreen, CO 80437
(303) 674-6048
www.teamevergreen.org

Sponsors the Triple Bypass race—see "Events."

Events

Ride the Rockies

A classic and a total gas. Put on by the Denver Post *each June, the tour takes 2,000 cyclists on a 6-to-7-day ride on paved roads through the mountains. The route is different each year, but always climbs some mountain passes and showcases the Rockies. Daily rides can be as short as 35 miles or as long as 100, but generally average 60–65 miles. The 2001 registration fee was $235 and included camping space, restrooms and showers, transportation of one bag during the tour, a Ride the Rockies cycling jersey, water bottle, tour map book, shuttle transportation in host communities, aid stations, bike repair vans, sag vehicles, and medical support. For more information, call (303) 820-1338, e-mail rtr@denverpost.com, or visit www.ridetherockies.com.*

The Triple Bypass

A 1-day, 117-mile ride from Evergreen to Eagle and Vail over Squaw (11,140'), Loveland (11,990'), and Vail (10,560') Passes. Over 10,000 feet of elevation gain. The name of this race is no joke. visit www.teamevergreen.org/triplebypass.htm for more info.

The Handlebar Grill and Bob Cook Memorial Mount Evans Hill Climb

Each July over 600 riders compete in this grueling climb. The race pays tribute to Bob Cook, a local rider and 1980 Olympian who won the race five times in the 1970s. Cook lost his battle with cancer at the age of 23 in 1981. The race continues as a memorial to him offering races in 11 categories for varying age groups and abilities. Visit www.bicyclerace.com for info.

Kayaking

ONE STEAMY, LATE afternoon in July, my old friend Adam drove into Denver with a rodeo boat in the back of his truck and we decided to go paddling. We drove into the center of the city and parked in the little lot just north of the aquarium, crossed the railroad tracks and the bike path, and set the kayaks on the top of the high grass bank above the South Platte. Across the river, the downtown skyscrapers offered the precipitous relief of a canyon wall. Screams, foreshortened by the Doppler effect, surged like gusts of wind from the rollercoaster at Elitch's Amusement Park. We could hear the bells at the 15th Street crossing as the Amtrak Sunset Limited pulled out of Union Station, and sirens, and the gush of the river sluicing through the Confluence Rapids just downstream. We squeezed into the boats, seal-launched down the bank, and hit the water, which smelled a little of ammonia. We paddled under the deep shade of two bridges and into the funnel of the first drop and whipped into an eddy. Adam threw down a couple of cartwheels in the little hydraulic. From the footbridge some gangsta kids whistled and gave each other props. At the next two drops we spun tailstands; in the bottom hole we practiced flat spins. A little blue heron who had been a regular for weeks stood one-legged on the rock, guarding the eddy, watching us with a jaundiced eye. It seemed interested but not impressed. The air got grainy with dusk, and streetlights on the Cherry Creek bike path came on and lit the water. An old man sat on the rocks and drank out of a paper bag. A couple on mountain bikes watched from the top of the wall. When I slid off my nose plugs I smelled pot. There were only three paddlers left: Adam and I, and a serious, polite young hot-dogger who jostled against us in the eddy and rode the hole and never said a word. I was riding the white pile in the middle of the current when Adam started yelling. I braced against the bucking foam, looked over my shoulder, and saw him pointing at the biggest beaver I've ever seen. It sat in a half hunch just above the heron. The streetlights glistened off his rough fur and it looked at me, at everyone, with a malevolent, city-hardened beaver glare. It scared me. Maybe it was the strange light. He looked like a rodent grizzly with a toothache. Then he dropped off the rock and swam unhurriedly upstream through a pool of dark gleams. I powered into the eddy. I had broken up with my girlfriend in February, and I said, "Man, that's the first beaver I've seen in months!" The straight-faced kid burst into laughter. It was like a bark. He couldn't help himself. It was the only sound he made all night. He was embarrassed, and peeled out into the current. An hour later, we were eating burgers in My Brother's Bar a block up the street and Adam said, "You made him laugh, the Silent American."

Denver and Boulder are paddling towns. Between the two cities and Golden there are four superb whitewater play parks: Confluence and Union Chutes in Denver, Boulder Creek in Boulder, and the lively freestyle circus on Clear Creek next to the Golden Rec Center. They are fine places for an expert to hone play skills, as well as for the paddler just getting started—if you end up out of your boat, several hotshots who have Been There are likely to break formation and swoop down on you and your gear. I know people who learned to kayak in Denver, in the heart of the city, and in Boulder, downtown, and you could almost have an entire paddling career without ever leaving the city. A wildwater paddler haunts the slick water below Denver's Zuni power plant, training on cold winter nights when steam shrouds the arc lights. Slalom racers have set up gates in the moving water above Confluence and trained all year. It's not uncommon to see freestylers throwing vertical moves in the holes in the Boulder Creek Park at all hours and seasons. Sometimes, when there's a call for power on a winter night, a surge of water is released for the electric station. Enthusiasts will boat the lower Boulder Creek run with flashlights inside their bows; they glow like crazy party sconces.

Within an hour of both cities are whitewater runs for every ability. I've included the most obvious: the sequence of great Class III to V paddles on Clear Creek, from Dumont to Golden; Boulder Creek; some of the runs on the Upper South Platte; and a few fun runs for the beginner that are lovely enough to be interesting for any paddler. Also described are a couple of classic steep creek runs for the expert who has just arrived in town. There are many, many more.

Flatwater touring is becoming increasingly popular. Touring and sea kayaks that once ranged almost exclusively on the coasts are now being seen on lakes and rivers across the country. I do a flatwater paddle almost every night within the city limits of Denver. It's a great workout, and as soon as I am buoyant and push off from shore, there's a sudden and dramatic respite from the city-as-we-know-it and from the day's concerns. It's as if, once afloat, I get a special dispensation to observe and feel—geese and cormorants, the southwest wind, the scents of Russian olive, the hues of the sky as weather piles in over the mountains.

To find out what is hot and information on river access and prime water levels, check out *Colorado Rivers and Creeks*; it may be the best guidebook ever assembled, bar none. Also, stop in and see the folks at Confluence Kayaks on Platte Street, a block north of the big REI store and just across from the rapids in Denver. They have a huge selection of boats and a bounty of expertise, goodwill, and information. The Boulder Outdoor Center in Boulder and Alpenglow in Golden are also good places to stop.

Note: For daily river flows call Watertalk at (303) 831-7135. Then press the number-and-asterisk sequence given in the *Gauge* section in each run description. Or check kayakingcolorado.com/flows.

Thanks again to Gordon Banks and Dave Eckardt and their brilliant *Colorado Rivers and Creeks* for much of the good information provided.

Denver City Limits

Get ready to play your tail off. The claim has been made that Denver offers more whitewater paddling than any other major city in America. It's probably true. The South Platte runs through the middle of town, and when it has water in it, and even when it doesn't, you can have a hoot. One paddler I know practiced flat spins and tailstands all winter long in the hole and strong eddy line to the left of the 16th Street bridge abutment just below Confluence.

While you could probably have a boating career without ever leaving the city, it would probably be a career heavy on the antibiotics and gamma globulin, which is the only real drawback to boating the South Platte. Locals sometimes call the drops at Confluence Hepatitis A, B, and C. Water quality can be pretty gross, especially in summer at low flows, when everything is concentrated and the water is warm and smells like Ajax. Then again, just after rain or melting snow, when the current surges, is not the best time either: most of the street gutters in Denver wash into the river untreated. It's not fun to imagine the result. Despite this impediment, brave regulars swear that you build up an immunity over time, and I can attest that I've never suffered more than itchy eyes, even after gulping some large draughts. Enough said. Here's where to play.

CONFLUENCE RAPIDS

Location: Denver central

Difficulty: Class III

Gauge: Call Watertalk, (303) 831-7135 1*41*; South Platte at Denver

Heads up: Downtown urban playground.

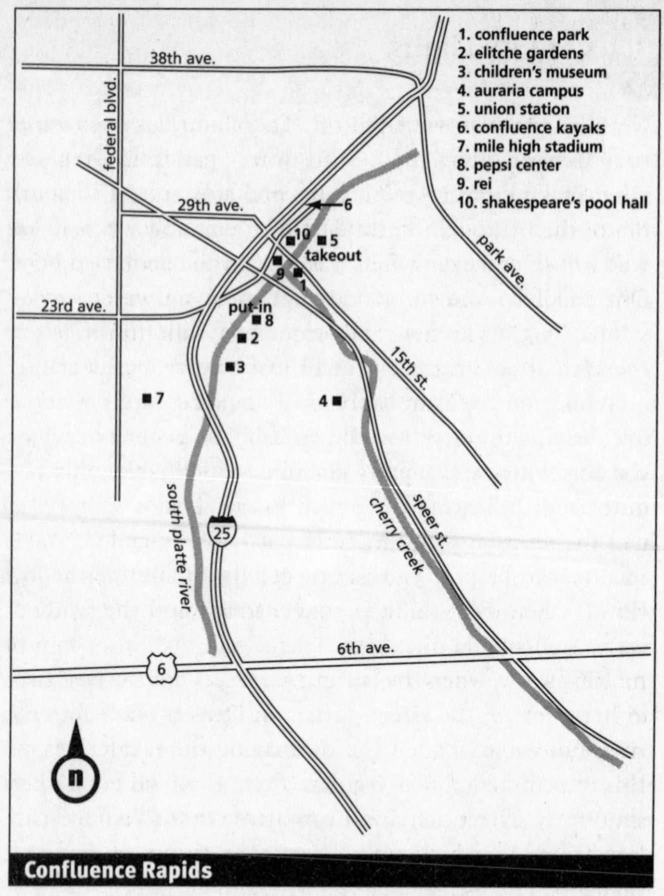

Confluence Rapids

Description: Confluence Rapids is about as urban a surf as you'll ever get. It flows through a series of man-made constrictions and drops at the junction of the South Platte River and Cherry Creek. It feels like the pulsing heart of Denver. Lower Downtown (LODO), Union Station, the Tattered Cover, and Elitch's Amusement Park lie off the right bank. On the left are several venerable drinking and eating establishments, among them My Brother's Bar and

Shakespeare's Pool Hall. Confluence Kayaks, a tremendous resource for the paddler, and the REI superstore—Temple Mount for outdoor gear, are also on the left. It's festive. The two bike trails that parallel the river and the creek come together here, so there's always a flow of passersby, an audience of bikers and in-line skaters and runners. At the bottom of the rapid, in summer, there are usually a few folks with a buzz on wading and splashing in the pool.

You can find decent playing here at most water levels. The best way to scout Confluence is to walk into REI, get a frappucino from the Starbucks at the river end of the building, and stroll out to the deck perched over the drop. You'll notice a rocky weir shredding the water river-left, which is where you don't want to go. You'll also probably notice a lot of guys in tiny, planing-hull boats doing tricks in every one of the five short stair-step drops along the right side. Ready to try it? You're probably parked in the REI lot, which is not where the company wants you to stay. If you feel bad, consider buying a tent, or drive up Platte Street to the pull-out parking lot just upstream. It's probably full, so drive downriver, again on Platte, go through the light, and park in the free dirt lot on the left, on the other side of Confluence Kayaks and Paris on the Platte—which is another great place to get caffeine if you don't mind listening to Pearl Jam or watching poets at work. From this lot you can walk across the street, through the court between the new condos, and down the steps to the wave and hole at the 16th Street bridge abutment. Good flat spinning and tailstands are possible here, even at low water. I generally start here, even if the hole isn't in shape, because it's easy to paddle upstream to the main rapid.

As mentioned above, the biggest mistake at Confluence may be forgetting to wear nose plugs. Or ear plugs. Or goggles. It's a tragedy for Denver that such a wonderful recreational and visual resource is marred by terrible water quality. After an evening at Confluence, I've woken up with my eyes stuck together. Friends have developed strange rashes and spots. *Do not* paddle here right after new rain raises the water level—many Denver streets drain untreated into the river. Despite the hygienic challenges, most paddlers feel that the fun of playing in the heart of the city is worth the risk.

Directions: From its intersection with 6th Avenue (US 6), take I-25 north to the 23rd Avenue exit. Turn right (east) off the exit and drive past the aquarium to the first pull-out parking lot. From downtown, drive west on 15th and you'll see the rapid as you cross the bridge.

UNION CHUTES

Location: 6 road miles south of Denver

Difficulty: Class III

Gauge: Call Watertalk, (303) 831-7135 1*62*; Platte River at Union Avenue

Heads up: Best urban playing.

Description: Brilliant, city-side whoop-ass playing. I love this place. Half a dozen artificial drops are spaced over a third of a mile of river. The top drop is a cushy, low-head hole great for flat spins and breaking paddles. A hundred yards below is a tight little gnashing pocket ideal for fast vertical moves and turning your eyelids inside-out. Then comes a long, easy pile perfect for the less experienced to get used to hole riding. Below all that are a couple of big honking glassy waves. All within 2 minutes of trucking company lots and topless sports bars. Catch the Chutes at good flows-above 1,300 cfs and the bigger the better. This is urban-industrial paddling, so use nose plugs and keep up on your hepatitis vaccine.

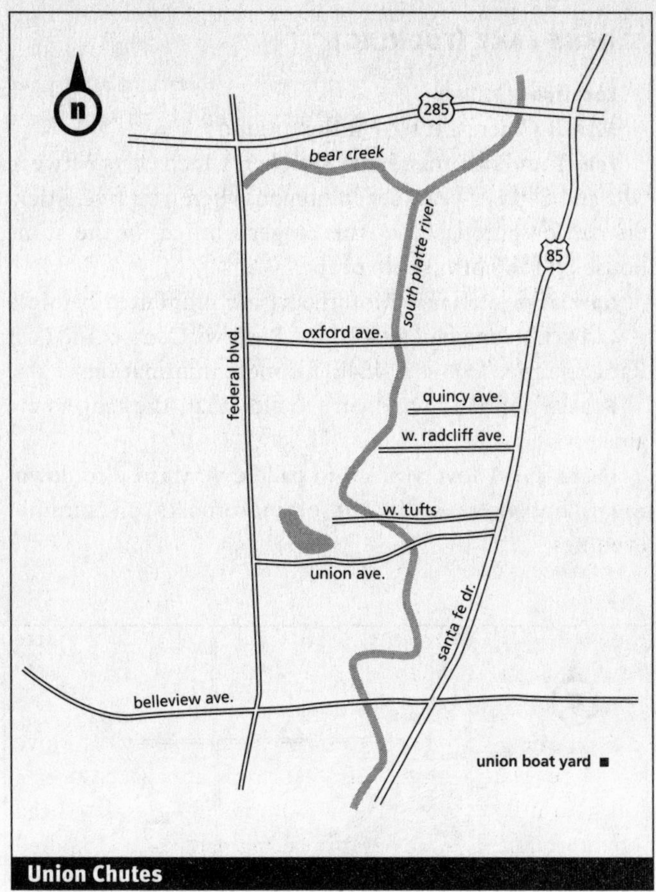

Union Chutes

Note: Check out the Union Boat Yard on the right bank, Confluence Kayaks' new outpost.

Directions: From its intersection with 6th Avenue (US 6), take I-25 south to the Santa Fe Drive (US 85) exit. Take Santa Fe Drive south about 5 miles to Union Avenue. Turn right (west) and look for the parking across the river on the right.

SLOANS LAKE (TOURING)

Location: Denver

Size: 177 acres; it's 2.7 miles around

Fee: Your boat must have a sticker, which costs between $20 and $40 per year, depending on where you live. Stickers can be purchased at the ranger's office, in the stone house on the north shore of the lake.

Special regulations: Motorboats are prohibited before 9 A.M.! Do not land on Duck Island Reserve. Contact the Boat Rangers office (303-458-4840) for more information.

Season: April to October. Outside that, the rangers are gone, so . . .

Heads up: A lovely place to paddle very close to downtown, but there are a lot of motorboats on summer evenings.

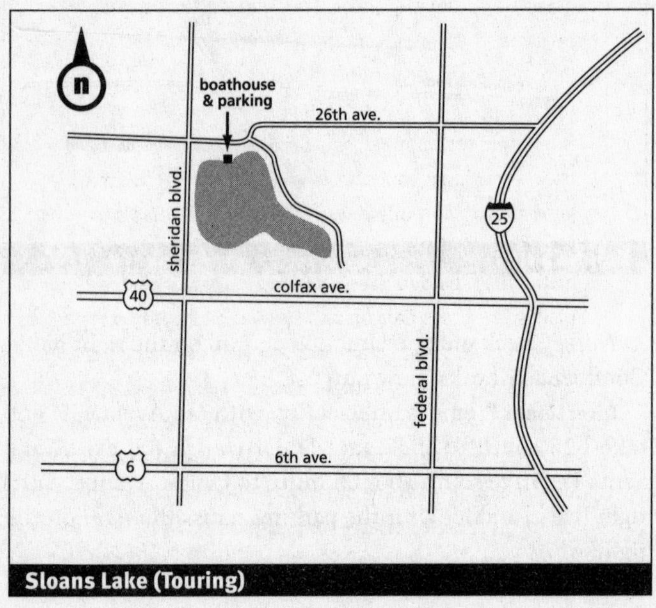

Sloans Lake (Touring)

Description: Beloved by anglers and bird-watchers-and wakeboarders. Paddle early in the morning, or at dusk for a glassy, beautiful workout.

Directions: West on 6th Avenue to Sheridan Boulevard. North on Sheridan to Byron on north side of lake. (Byron is approximately 25th Avenue. Take a right on Byron and park.)

Confluence Kayaks

ONE OF THE best resources for the paddler in Denver is Confluence Kayaks down by the South Platte. John Kahn, a young kayak instructor, saw a need and started the shop in 1995. It's a block from the Confluence Whitewater Park, on historic Platte Street, just north of the REI and the 15th Street bridge. The shop has the largest selection of kayaks in Denver, and it's run and staffed by avid, expert boaters, which makes all the difference when you're seeking information on local paddles, water conditions, and gear. Because it's so close to the rapids and the wave at the 16th Street bridge abutment, you can borrow a hot new demo rodeo boat, throw it on your shoulder, and paddle it five minutes later after a short urban walk. The store also has a top-notch kayak school, with group classes on weekends, private lessons all the time, guided river trips, and multiday teaching trips at places like Grays Canyon and Desolation Canyon on the Green River. A great way to start paddling is to attend one of their pool rolling and basic stroke clinics. They're held in the fall and winter on regular evenings at area pools. The cost is $30, $20 with your own equipment. Call for details and general information. In spring 2001 the store opened an outpost right at the Union Chutes Whitewater Park—the Union Boat Yard. Squeegee in for a new paddle after you break yours against the concrete floor of the first hole, or get nose plugs when you're tired of attempting self-vaccination against Denver viruses. Confluence sells sea kayaks as well, and has a sea kayak instruction and trips program. These are great folks, and the shop gets my highest rating for an outdoor resource in Denver.

Denver Backyard

On the Upper South Platte, in the area where the North Fork and the South Fork meet, are a lot of opportunities for beginner and intermediate boaters. There's also a wild advanced run called Bailey.

WATERTON CANYON

Location: 40-odd miles southwest of Denver

Length: 1.3 miles

Difficulty: Class III+ when water levels are less than 900 cfs; Class IV at water levels greater than 900 cfs

Put-in: 14.2 miles southeast of US 285 at Conifer

Takeout: Strontia Springs Reservoir

Gauge: Call Watertalk, (303) 831-7135 1*50*; South Platte at South Platte

Heads up: Summer standby.

Description: Short and sweet intermediate after-work run that is usually up for a good time when every other run is showing its bones from lack of water. A lovely canyon paddle, rudely interrupted by Strontia Springs Reservoir; you can imagine how beautiful it must have been before the dam. A lot of good playing with an infamous hole called Vertical Blender that gets extremely sticky above 1,000 cfs. Also watch for Green Bridge rapid (Class IV–) above the

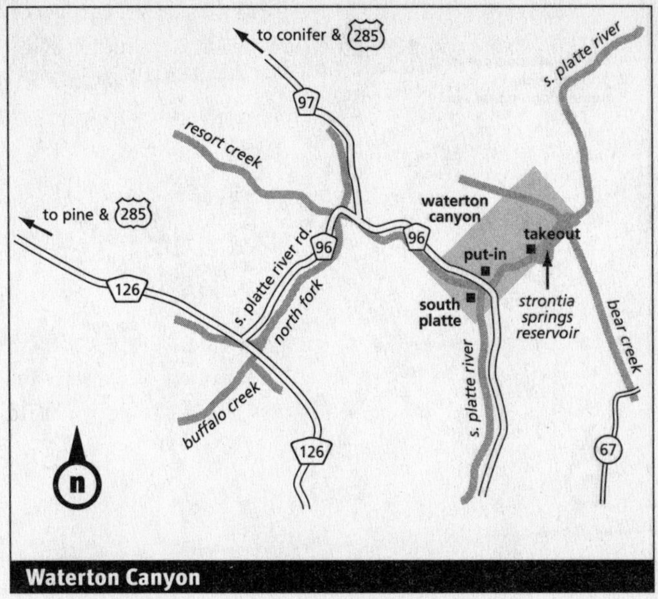

Waterton Canyon

broken bridge pieces. The shuttle is a drag, literally: drag or hump your boat the 1.3 miles back from the lake.

Directions: Take I-25 south to Santa Fe Drive (US 85) exit. Take US 85 south to US 285 west. Turn off US 285 just south of the town of Conifer onto South Foxton Road (97 RD); you'll be heading south. Continue to South Platte River Road (96 RD). Turn left onto it and continue to the confluence of the South Platte and the North Fork of the South Platte.

FOXTON

Location: About 35 miles southwest of Denver

Length: 4.5 miles

Difficulty: Class III when water levels are less than 600

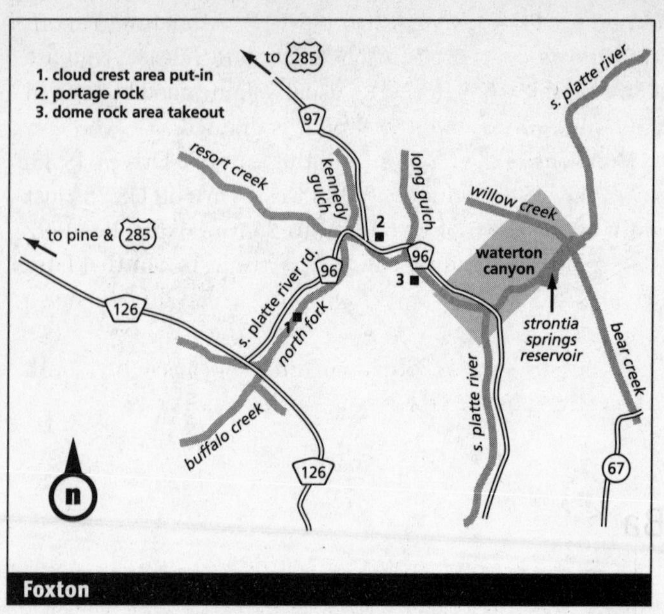

Foxton

cfs; Class IV– at water levels greater than 600 cfs, possible portage

Put-in: Cloud Crest Bridge area

Takeout: Dome Rock area

Gauge: Call Watertalk, (303) 831-7135 1*42*; North Fork of South Platte at Grant

Heads up: Gorgeous country.

Description: Beautiful intermediate run on the North Fork of the South Platte. Wooded hills, granite domes and spires, fun eddy hopping through boulder gardens and tight rapids. Spend a couple of days up here: camp out and explore an abundance of mountain bike, fly-fishing, and rock-climbing options.

Note: There's a mandatory portage around a low bridge just after the intersection of South Foxton Road (97 RD)

and South Platte River Road (96 RD). After June runoff, water flows depend on unscheduled dam releases and are unpredictable, though there's usually some good boating in September when Dillon Reservoir is drained.

Directions: Take I-25 south to the Santa Fe Drive (US 85) exit. Take US 85 south to US 285 west. Turn off US 285 just south of the town of Conifer onto South Foxton Road (97 RD), you'll be heading south. Continue to South Platte River Road (96 RD). Turn right onto it and drive about a mile to the put-in.

To get to the takeout, continue southeast on South Platte River Road to the Dome Rock area.

Bailey

SINCE WE'RE IN the area, I've got to mention this 10-mile, Class IV+-with-a couple-of-Vs-and-a-gnarly-ClassVI-drop classic. I won't go into it, because you need to go out and buy *Colorado Rivers and Creeks* anyway. If you're good enough to run Bailey you need to own this book.

CO 470 TO SOUTH PLATTE GRILL

Location: 12 miles south of Denver

Length: About 6 miles

Difficulty: Class II–III

Put-in: Little park where CO 470 crosses river

Takeout: Union Chutes at Union Avenue

Gauge: Call Watertalk, (303) 831-7135 1*62*, Platte River at Union Avenue

Heads up: Teaching run made in heaven.

Description: This sweet teaching and beginner run is a perfect outing for the first few times on moving water

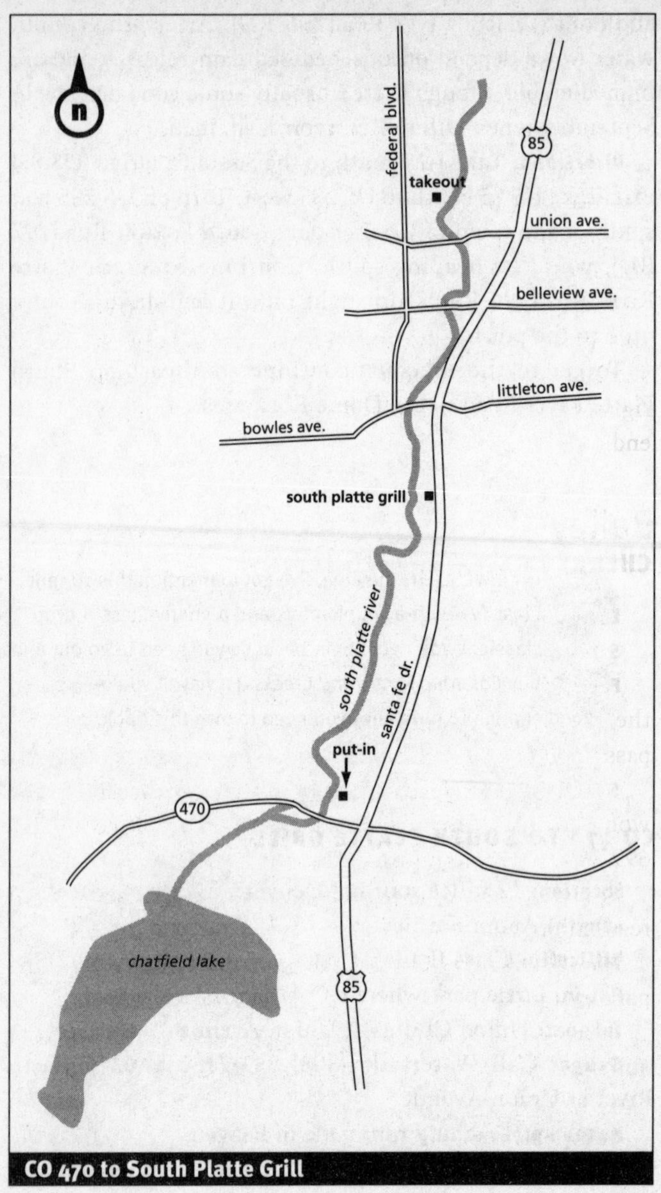

CO 470 to South Platte Grill

with a good teacher. It's pretty, there's a lot of wildlife—herons and ducks and kingfishers—and there are three Class III drops toward the end that are easy to scout and have plenty of room below for fishing out swimmers and gear. You can take out early at the South Platte Grill, or continue on for another mile or so of flat water to the Union Chutes playground and finish off with a hole ride and a rebel yell.

Directions: Take I-25 south to the Santa Fe Drive (US 85) exit. Take US 85 south to CO 470. Turn right (west) on CO 470 and drive less than a mile to the first little road on the right. Turn right and follow this to the parking area at its end.

CHERRY CREEK LAKE (TOURING)

Location: 10 miles southeast of Denver

Size: 880 acres

Fee: $5 for a daily vehicle pass (includes $1 collected for the Water Basin Authority) or $43 for an annual vehicle pass (includes $3 collected for the Water Basin Authority).

Special regulations: If there's any ice on the lake, they won't let any boats on. Contact the reservoir office at (303) 699-3860 for more information.

Season: The gate is manned year-round, but see Special regulations.

Map: The Cherry Creek Lake brochure is available at the park entrance.

Heads up: This state park was the site of the prayer vigil and papal mass with Pope John Paul II during World Youth Day 1993.

Description: A big lake close to town. The happenin' party lake. Bikinis, drunk boaters, the sound of the skeet

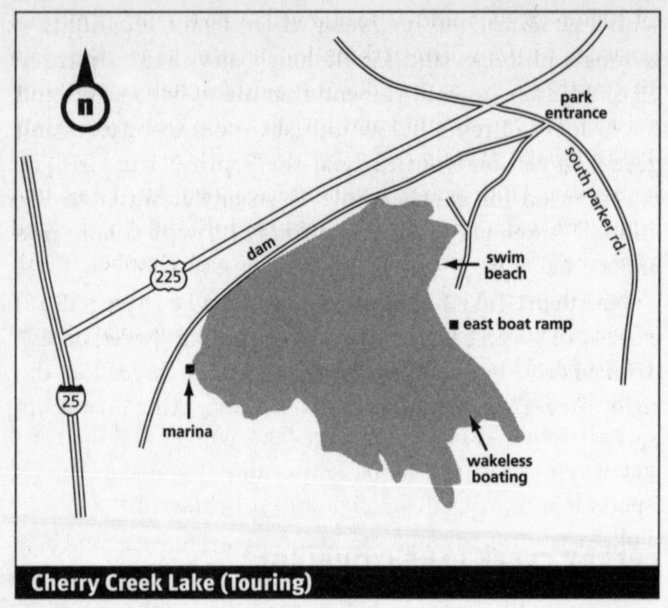

Cherry Creek Lake (Touring)

range. A great place for a kayaker to get killed on a weekend afternoon.

Directions: Take I-25 south to I-225. Take I-225 east to South Parker Road. Turn right and go 1 mile south on South Parker to the park entrance.

BARR LAKE (TOURING)

Location: About 25 miles northeast of Denver

Size: When the lake is full, nearly 1,000 acres are available for boating. The entire lake is 1,918 acres.

Fee: A state parks pass costs $4 per day per vehicle or $40 per year.

Special regulations: Only sailboats, hand-propelled craft, and boats with electric trolling motors or gasoline motors of 10 horsepower or less are allowed. A boat ramp is located adjacent to the north parking lot. Boating is restricted to the northern half of the lake; the southern half is a wildlife refuge. For more information, contact Colorado State Parks, (303) 659-6005.

Season: High water levels are reached April through June. The water level drops quickly in July and August, and the lake can be closed in September and October. Refill occurs in late October or November.

Map: The Barr Lake State Park brochure is available at the park entrance.

Heads up: Great bird-watching.

Description: A beautiful, large lake, perfect for a half-day getaway tour. In the 1880s it was an elite outing area for sportsmen from Denver: "The finest fishing in the West." Pollution almost ruined the lake, but strong laws and con-

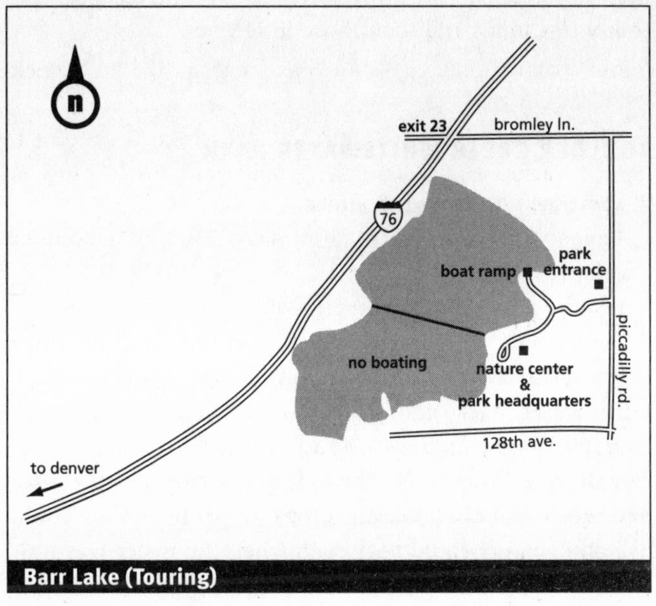

Barr Lake (Touring)

trols instituted in the 1960s helped stop the flow of toxins. What makes it special now is that it's edged by huge old cottonwoods and marshes; the south half of the lake is a wildlife refuge. Three hundred and thirty species of birds have been spotted here, giving it an international reputation. Regular visitors include herons, pelicans, grebes, and other waterfowl. It also hosts one of the few successful bald eagle nests on the Front Range.

Directions: Take I-76 northeast from Denver, exit onto Bromley Lane (exit 23). Go east to Piccadilly Road (17N RD). Turn right (south) and drive to the park entrance.

Boulder City Limits

Throw away your ear plugs and Visine. Boulder Creek is nearly drinkable. This whitewater playground feels considerably less industrial than those in Denver.

BOULDER CREEK WHITEWATER PARK

Location: Downtown Boulder

Gauge: Call Watertalk, (303) 831-7135 1*9*; Boulder Creek at Orodell

Heads up: Local urban staple.

Description: The best thing to happen to Boulder since Allen Ginsberg and shiatsu may be the Boulder Creek Whitewater Park and Bike Path. Thank Gary Lacey, hydraulic engineer and whitewater paddler extraordinaire, who designed the thing. The idea of the river element was to create a series of pools and drops so that fishermen could fish and boaters could boat even when the water was low. It worked. The whitewater is raced, played on, and floated

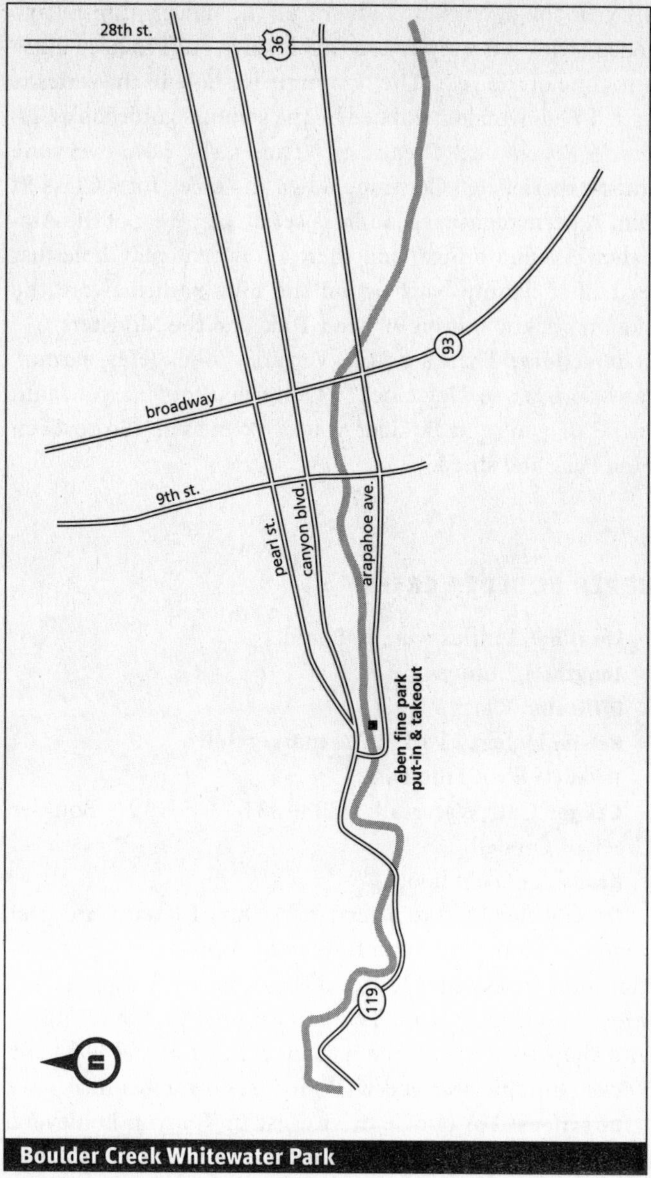

Boulder Creek Whitewater Park

all year long. With the advent of the newer, diminutive rodeo boats, a freestyler can find enough stuff to keep dizzy any time of the year. The bottom ledge-hole in the series is called Widowmaker, dubbed by the seminal guidebook *Colorado Rivers and Creeks* as "The trashy hole everyone must experience." Continue down the creek for a Class III run. A permanent racecourse is set up just west of the Arapahoe Avenue bridge, and there's a decent play hole just east of it. Hump back up on the bike path; beware the skaters rockin' out on Bighead Todd and the Monsters.

Directions: There's an old Vermont joke: "Hey, farmer, how do I get to Newfane?" "Don't you move a goddamn inch." If you're in Boulder you can't miss it. Go to Eben Fine Park and shred.

UPPER BOULDER CREEK

Location: 3 miles west of Boulder

Length: 3.2 miles

Difficulty: Class IV

Put-in: Doherty Park (mile marker 38)

Takeout: Eben Fine Park

Gauge: Call Watertalk, (303) 831-7135 1*9*; Boulder Creek at Orodell

Heads up: Local hoot.

Description: A fine after-work Class IV with nonstop action and some tight rapids. Watch for the Sleeping Policeman pipe just below Bridge 38148 about 0.2 mile downstream from the put-in. The hardest drop is about 2 miles into the run. You can scout it by parking at the Elephant Rocks climbing area and walking just downstream.

Directions: For put-in, drive west up Canyon Boulevard (CO 119) from its intersection with 28th Street (US 36) into Boulder Canyon. Park at Doherty Park, mile marker 38.

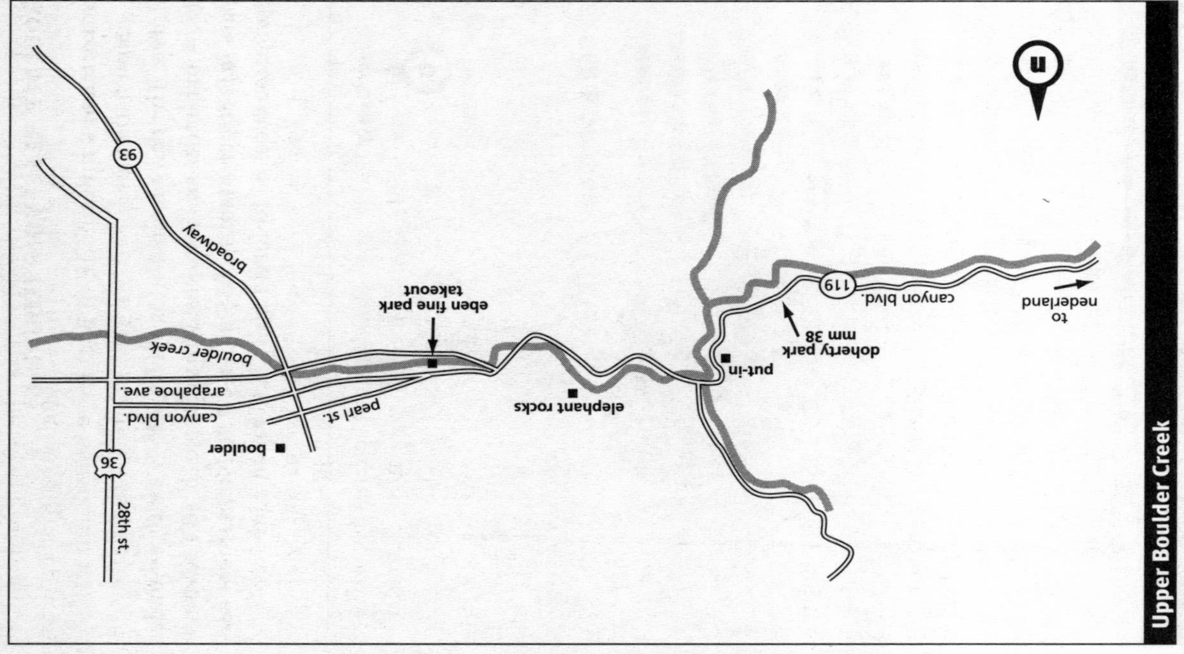
Upper Boulder Creek
28th st.
36
93
broadway
boulder
canyon blvd.
arapahoe ave.
boulder creek
pearl st.
eben fine park
takeout
elephant rocks
put-in
doherty park
mm 38
119
canyon blvd.
to
nederland
n

BOULDER RESERVOIR (TOURING)

Location: 4 miles north of Boulder

Size: 540 acres

Fee: The daily fee is $4 for adults, $1.75 for those under 18, 4 and under are free. Residents can purchase a seasonal pass for $80 for a family, $35 for an adult. Nonresident season passes cost $110 for a family, $50 for an adult.

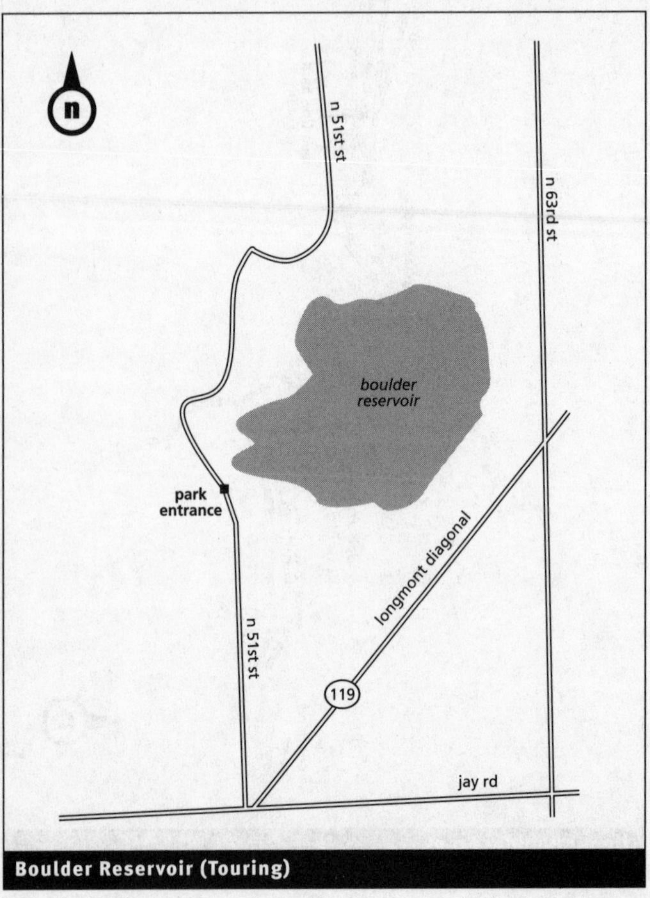

Boulder Reservoir (Touring)

Special regulations: Motorboats must have a city permit; nonmotorized boats need no permit. Contact Boulder Parks and Recreation (303-413-7201), or the park's gate (303-441-3468), boathouse (303-441-3456), or guard shack (303-441-3469) for more information.

Season: After Labor Day and before Memorial Day the gate is open, but no one's home, so have at it!

Heads up: No fees Labor Day to Memorial Day; Boulder Reservoir brochure available at park entrance.

Description: One fall I paddled around the lake almost every evening. Sometimes I hammered into very stiff winds, and I was a little awed by the athletic windsurfers tearing around on their short boards, especially when the weather got really cold. It's a beautiful, fair-sized reservoir, with the mountains cresting to the west and a lot of bird life including ospreys; northern harriers; American pelicans; white-faced ibises; least bitterns; and, in spring and fall, flocks of geese and duck V-ing down, squadron after squadron, for a night's rest.

Directions: Go north on US 36 to the Longmont Diagonal (CO 119) and turn northeast. At Jay Road (44 RD) turn west and then north almost immediately onto 51st Street.

Sick Bird

GORDON BANKS WROTE the book on kayaking in Colorado. As coauthor of *Colorado Rivers and Creeks* he has researched—paddled—most of the runnable whitewater in the state. The first time I met him was at Upper Clear Creek in the mid-80s. We were in a group running the Narrows and Gordon was wearing an old football helmet. It had a faceguard, and this was long before steep creekers were so armored they looked like motocross riders in boats. I thought, "This guy must be serious." I was right. Gordon is constitutionally modest, and says he's not a particularly great boater, nor responsible for putting down a lot of first descents. But he, coauthor Dave Eckardt, and their cohorts made a habit of regularly paddling runs that were considered high adrenaline, breakthrough hairball. They cleaned out the dangerous wood, and by advertising rivers in their book turned many fringe paddles into classics.

For the past few years Gordon and a handful of sick birds have met at dawn on a morning in late June and conducted the Sick Bird Loop. Water levels and cliff-face access have to be synchronized, so it's kind of spontaneous. It starts at Eldorado Springs with a two-and-a-half-hour, 5.11 climb up the Naked Edge. Some years the climb has had to be clandestine, as the Red Garden Wall was closed due to nesting peregrine falcons. Next is a long road-bike ride, which includes a steep, eleven-mile hill, to the put-in of Upper South Boulder Creek. Then into kayaks for miles of Class IV, V, and V+ boating, culminating with the Class VI Harmon Falls back in Eldorado Springs. Gordon said, "The boating part's last. The ones who've already climbed and biked, they're kind of frazzled and drained. You need kind of a safety boater hanging around." He added that last year they had to stop and give first aid to a safety boater who needed stitches. "This is definitely not a sanctioned event," he said.

Boulder Backyard

SOUTH BOULDER CREEK

Location: About 10 miles southwest of Boulder
Length: 6.4 miles
Difficulty: Class IV (V) when water levels are less than

450 cfs; Class IV+ (V) at water levels greater than 450 cfs; final Eldo section Class V+ (VI–)

Put-in: Trailhead near Gross Reservoir Dam

Takeout: Eldorado State Park picnic area

Gauge: Call Watertalk, (303) 831-7135 1*6*; South Boulder Creek below Gross Reservoir; (Eldo only: (303) 831-7135 1*7*; South Boulder Creek near Eldorado Spring

Heads up: Brilliant boating, extreme finish.

Description: Close to Denver and Boulder, this fine, Class IV, remote creek run ends dramatically at Eldorado State Park. It's dramatic because the sheer cliffs of Eldorado rise on either side, and are probably flecked with brightly colored rock climbers who may be looking down at you and wondering why anybody would spend their leisure time in a freezing torrent. Also, there's drama at water level as the creek below the takeout at the picnic ground bridge turns

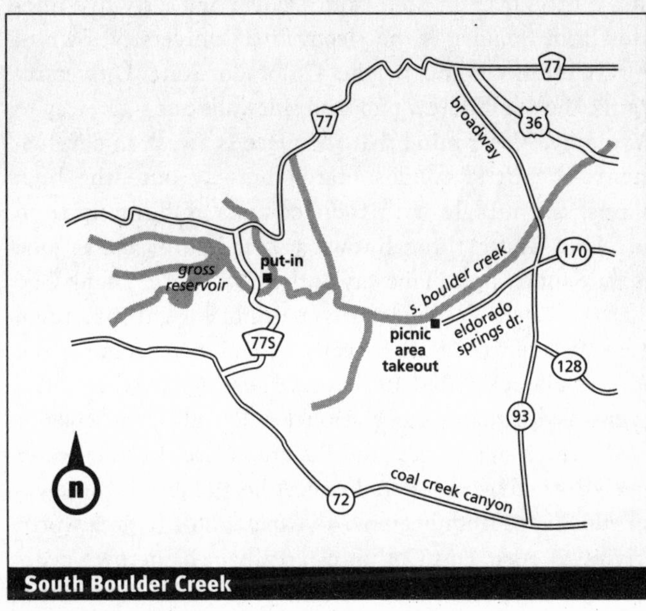

South Boulder Creek

decidedly ornery. The 3/4-mile, boulder-choked sluice is a Class V+–VI hair run that is fun to scout while pretending to think about paddling it. Until recently, South Boulder Creek required clandestine launch tactics. Now that it's legal, half the fun is gone, but so is the hassle. The run is mostly Class III and IV, but has two Class V drops. See *Colorado Rivers and Creeks* for all the details.

Directions: From Broadway (CO 93) in Boulder, take Baseline Road (77 RD) west up Flagstaff Mountain. At Gross Reservoir take Gross Reservoir Road (77S RD) to the trailhead and put-in.

Short Hops

Can't talk about Front Range boating without mentioning that a little over an hour from Denver and forty-five minutes from Boulder is the sleepy little university town of Fort Collins—home of the Colorado State University Rams, the quaint brew pub, and sidewalk café—gateway to Wyoming. Never mind that the place is awash in development—the little condos march bravely onto the high plains, and mingle with their cousins ambling up from Loveland. Traffic through town at rush hour is just as good as the Santa Monica Freeway or the FDR Drive. Thank God that the Cache la Poudre River tumbles right into town from its steep and reticent canyon, and offers some of the best, easily accessible and diverse boating anywhere. The river was designated as a National Wild and Scenic River in 1987, which means that the Poudre is free flowing; water levels depend on runoff and rain. A host of prime whitewater runs range from beginner to expert. This river is worth driving to. Also, Fort Collins can really be a fun town, reactionary antigrowth sentiments aside. For a fine perspective on the ranch country just above the canyon, read *The Meadow* by James Galvin. It's a terrific and poetic historical novel. Here are brief descriptions of several favorite runs on the Poudre, and a hair-boat mention on an archetypal, steep, wilderness tributary creek. There are many great runs between and above the ones included here. Again, refer to *Colorado Rivers and Creeks* for complete coverage and scary stories.

Note: The water levels in feet refer to the rock gauge in the river at Pineview Falls (CO 14 mile marker 112.7) 2′ equals roughly 330 cfs; 2.5′, 470 cfs; 3′, 650 cfs; 3.5′, 910 cfs; 4′, 1300 cfs; and 4.5′, 1800 cfs.

Location distance is measured from the intersection of CO 14 and US 287 in the middle of Fort Collins. Put-in and takeout directions refer to mile markers on CO 14 in Poudre Canyon.

CACHE LA POUDRE—FILTER PLANT

Location: About 16 miles west of Fort Collins

Length: 2.4 miles

Difficulty: Class II at water levels less than 2.5′; Class III at 2.5–4.0′; Class III+ at water levels greater than 4.0′

Put-in: Below the filter plant (mile marker 116.8)

Takeout: Picnic Rock Access (mile marker 119.0)

Gauge: Call Watertalk, (303) 831-7135 1*19*; Poudre at canyon mouth

Heads up: Great teaching run.

Description: This very popular, very riffly Class II–III beginner run is quite scenic and a good place to start a whitewater career.

Caution: Make sure you take out at the Picnic Rock River Access. You definitely do not want to float over the dangerous diversion dam just downstream.

Cache la Poudre — Filter Plant

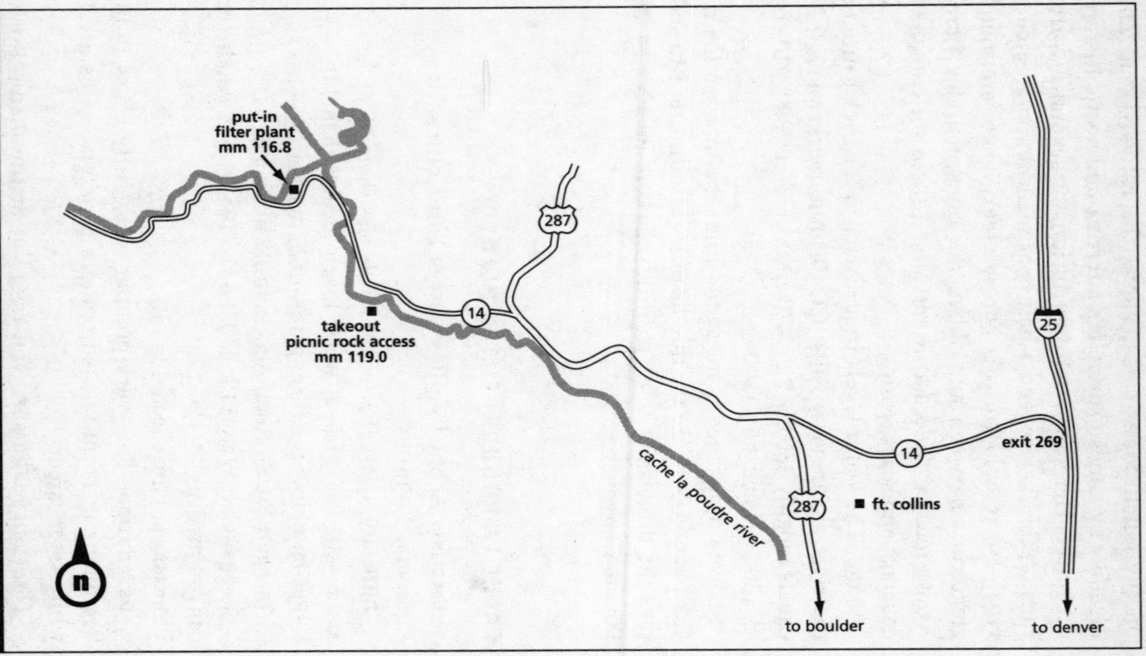

Directions: From Denver, take I-25 north to Fort Collins/CO 14 (exit 269). Take CO 14 west to its intersection with US 287 in the middle of town. Turn right onto US 287 north and drive about 10 miles to where CO 14 branches off again to the left (west). Turn left and follow CO 14 up the river. From Boulder, take 28th Street (US 36) north to the Diagonal (CO 119) on right. Turn right and follow CO 119 to Longmont and US 287. Take US 287 north into Fort Collins. About 10 miles out of town CO 14 takes off to the left (west). Turn left and follow CO 14 into the Poudre Canyon.

CACHE LA POUDRE—BRIDGES

Location: About 20 miles west of Fort Collins

Length: 2 miles

Difficulty: Class III at water levels less than 3.5′; Class IV– at water levels greater than 4.0′

Put-in: Just below Pineview Falls (mile marker 112.7)

Takeout: Bridges pullout (mile marker 114.7)

Gauge: Call Watertalk, (303) 831-7135 1*19*; Poudre at canyon mouth

Description: Dear to my heart, Bridges was the first run I did in Colorado my first season boating. I remember being a little nervous about the bridge abutment at Difficult Bridge, as it lies just below a rapid. The run is a great short intermediate paddle.

Directions: From Denver, take I-25 north to Fort Collins/CO 14 (exit 269). Take CO 14 west to its intersection with US 287 in the middle of town. Turn right onto US 287 north and drive about 10 miles to where CO 14 branches off again to the left (west). Turn left and follow CO 14 up the river. From Boulder, take 28th Street (US 36) north to the Diagonal (CO 119) on right. Turn right and fol-

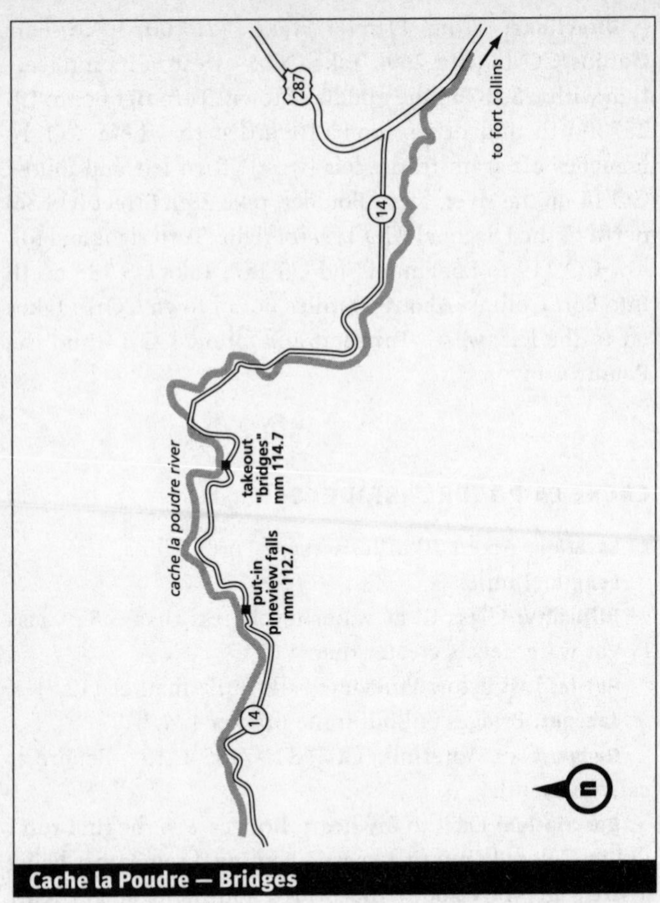

Cache la Poudre — Bridges

low CO 119 to Longmont and US 287. Take US 287 north into Fort Collins. About 10 miles out of town CO 14 takes off to the left (west). Turn left and follow CO 14 into the Poudre Canyon.

CACHE LA POUDRE—UPPER MISHAWAKA

Location: About 29 miles west of Fort Collins

Length: 3.3 miles

Difficulty: Class III+ at water levels less than 2.5′; Class IV at 25–4.0′; Class IV at water levels greater than 4.0′

Put-in: Steven's Gulch (mile marker 104.7)

Takeout: Mishawaka Inn (mile marker 108.1)

Gauge: Call Watertalk, (303) 831-7135 1*19*; Poudre at canyon mouth

Heads up: One of the funnest intermediate runs around. Harleys at the end.

Description: The best part of this run—aside from the whitewater—may be the takeout at the Mishawaka Inn. The deck looks over the river, and the leather-vested bikers look over the deck. A watering hole for Hogs, the inn offers with talents such as David Grisman and Bela Fleck on the weekends. The run has been tremendously popular for decades. It's known for primo playing at all water levels, and at good flows, it's a fast-paced Class IV. Silver Bullets and Born to Die tattoos right at the takeout.

Directions: From Denver, take I-25 north to Fort Collins/CO 14 (exit 269). Take CO 14 west to its intersection with US 287 in the middle of town. Turn right onto US 287 north and drive about 10 miles to where CO 14 branches off again to the left (west). Turn left and follow CO 14 up the river. From Boulder, take 28th Street (US 36) north to the Diagonal (CO 119) on right. Turn right and follow CO 119 to Longmont and US 287. Take US 287 north into Fort Collins. About 10 miles out of town CO 14 takes off to the left (west). Turn left and follow CO 14 into the Poudre Canyon.

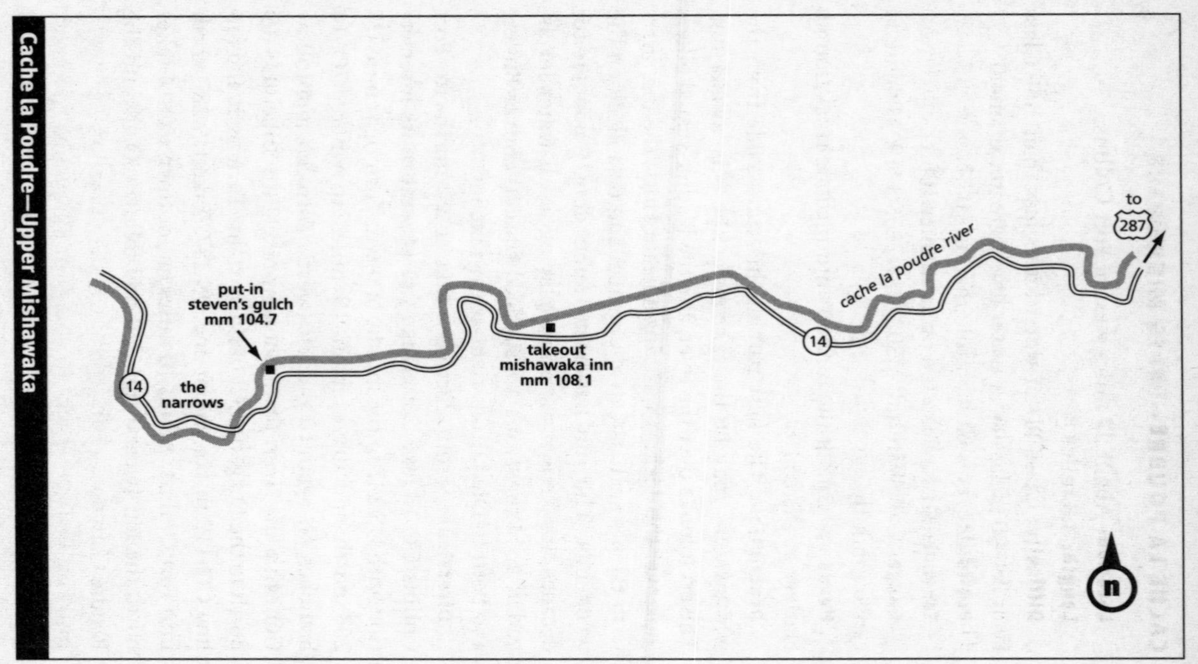

Cache la Poudre—Upper Mishawaka

CACHE LA POUDRE—THE NARROWS

Location: About 32 miles west of Fort Collins

Length: 3.4 miles if you run all sections

Difficulty: The Upper Narrows are Class V at water levels less than 2.5′; Class V+ at water levels greater than 2.5′. The Middle Narrows are Class IV at less than 2.5′; Class IV+ at 2.5–4.5′; and Class V– at greater than 4.5′. The Lower Narrows are Class V– at less than 2.5′; Class V at 2.5–4.5′; and Class V+ at greater than 4.5′.

Put-in: Narrows Picnic Ground (mile marker 101.9) or Sports Car Corner (mile marker 103)

Takeout: Steven's Gulch access (mile marker 104.7)

Gauge: Call Watertalk, (303) 831-7135 1*19*; Poudre at canyon mouth

Heads up: Easy to scout, close to the road Class V

Description: Just above Upper Mishawaka is a classic, feisty expert run. It's right along the road, so the three sections are easy to scout and can be run separately or all together. The Upper, Middle, and Lower Narrows have very different characters. The area is convenient for a group of mixed abilities, as experts wanting an adrenaline booster can paddle here and then meet others on the Mishawaka runs just below.

Directions: From Denver, take I-25 north to Fort Collins/CO 14 (exit 269). Take CO 14 west to its intersection with US 287 in the middle of town. Turn right onto US 287 north and drive about 10 miles to where CO 14 branches off again to the left (west). Turn left and follow CO 14 up the river. From Boulder, take 28th Street (US 36) north to the Diagonal (CO 119) on right. Turn right and follow CO 119 to Longmont and US 287. Take US 287 north into Fort Collins. About 10 miles out of town CO 14 takes off to the left (west). Turn left and follow CO 14 into the Poudre Canyon.

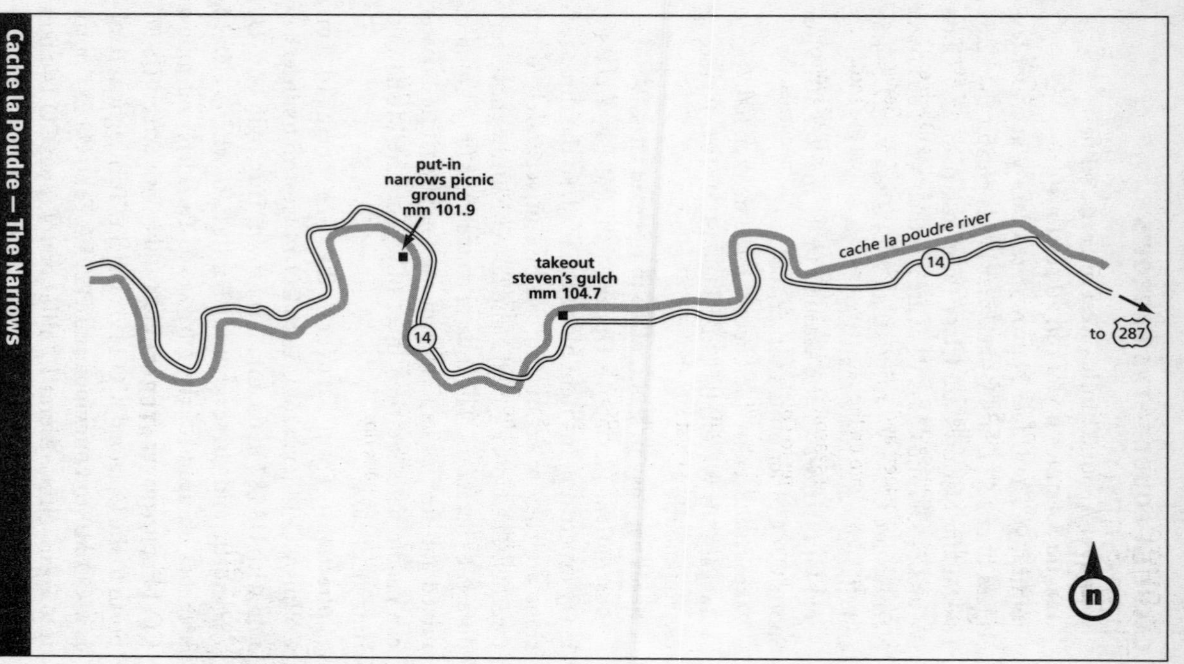
Cache la Poudre — The Narrows
put-in
narrows picnic
ground
mm 101.9
takeout
steven's gulch
mm 104.7
cache la poudre river
14
14
to 287
n

Longer-Than-Short Hops

FOUR HOURS OR so to the put-in, but this has to be mentioned: the Big South. It runs into the Poudre and it's a classic—a brilliant adventure for the expert paddler seeking remoteness and a steep creek with waterfalls (Double Trouble is forty feet) and Class V gorges. The U.S. Forest Service keeps the gate on the put-in road closed until all the snow is gone, so the season is short, usually from the end of June until mid-July. Refer to *Colorado Rivers and Creeks* for details.

And last of all, but beloved: Shoshone is located just over two and a half hours from the Denver–Boulder area, on the Colorado River just shy of Glenwood Springs, right off I-70. Although only about one and a half miles of Class III rapids (Class IV above 4,000 cfs), it has water all year, and there's great surfing and squirting and cartwheeling most of the way down. The put-in is at the Shoshone exit (exit 123), which can only be accessed from the eastbound lanes, so go on to the takeout at Grizzly Creek (exit 121) and double back. A smooth bike path parallels the length of the run, so it's easy to jog or bike back to the car, or throw your in-line skates in a dry bag and blade back up.

Golden

GOLDEN WHITEWATER PARK

Location: Downtown Golden

Gauge: Call Watertalk, (303) 831-7135 1*22*; Clear Creek near Golden

Heads up: Controlled chaos. Boaters come from all over.

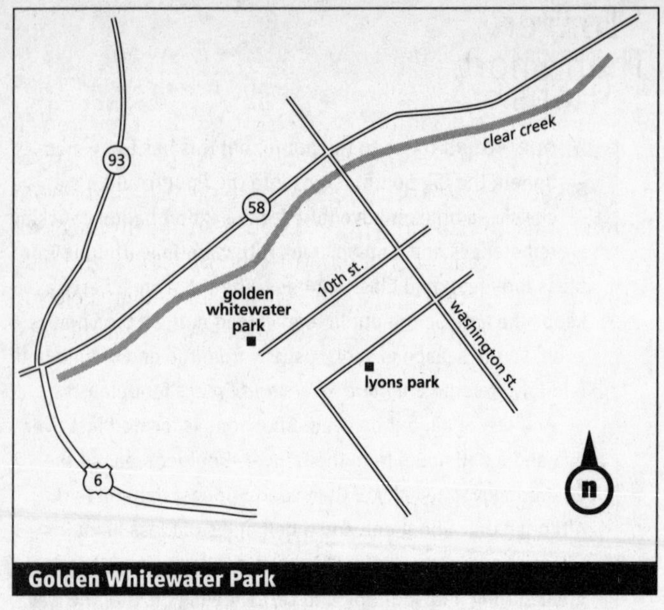

Golden Whitewater Park

Description: Circus Circus. Thank Gary Lacey again. I almost moved to Golden because of this play park, and still might. For a third of a mile or so, the designed Class II–III rapid offers boulder-to-boulder eddy hopping with deep eddy-lines for vertical moves, and several drops with good surf waves and holes. At the bottom is the Bottom Hole, a cartwheelers dream steed, where the rodeo riders line up like Saturday night at the Rock Island Club. This is world-class playing. The line for the hole can feel as bad as waiting for the bumper cars at Elitch's, so try to go at off-hours when the flow is good. Walk back up the bike path. Paddling is best when volume is over 600 cfs. On the weekends and after work, parking can be a challenge. A lot of camper vans and pickups and orange hair. You can see some top-notch freestyling here, and the dudes are friendly and encouraging, so it's a good place to pick up technique.

Directions: Just upstream of downtown Golden at the Rec Center park. From Denver, take 6th Avenue (US 6) west to CO 58 just outside of Golden. Turn right on CO 58 and get off at the Washington Street exit. Turn right and go a couple of blocks to 10th Street. Take 10th Street west past the pool and park in any space you can find. From Boulder, take Broadway (CO 93) south to its intersection with CO 58 outside of Golden. Turn left on CO 58 and take it to the Washington Street exit. Turn right and go a couple of blocks to 10th Street. Take 10th Street west past the pool and park in any space you can find.

Four Runs in Clear Creek

God gave Clear Creek to Denver and Boulder paddlers and the paddlers said "Thanks." God said, "Four good runs between Dumont and Golden." The paddlers said, "You're the Man." God said, "Class IV to Class V." "Right on." God said, "Not many eddies at high water, and the rocks are sharp thanks to the Highway Department which I created so that the serpent and his progeny unto the tenth generation might have government jobs—" Some paddlers put on face masks. Others simply didn't swim or even flip. God said, "Good. Clear Creek shall run with the runoff, and with the monsoonal rains. Stay in touch with Watertalk for flows." That was it. God had been so nice to the paddlers they decided not to get irritated at the casino buses that clogged their shuttles.

Stuck

I WAS PADDLING UPPER Clear Creek at high flood with my friend John Mattson and another paddler whose name I can't remember. It was a cool, rainy summer day. The water was brown with mud, the narrow canyon walls were stained dark with rain, and it seemed there was nothing left in the world but rock and water. Water in motion. At flood Clear Creek is a churning torrent. The eddies disappear. There are few places to pull over, to take a break; a swim would be horrendous. A paddler out of his boat could be swept along for miles. We leapfrogged each other, hitting the surging waves and breaking through, shaking our eyes clear. It was nonstop. The tongues around the big holes were jetstreams. At some point we caught a swirling eddy at a corner and John said, "Somewhere down here is a big hole." "OK," I thought. "I'll look out for a big hole."

I was ahead of the others and rode up a haystack wave. When I looked over the other side the river dropped away and I was looking straight down into a deep gnashing trough. "Oh, shit!" is all I thought as I plunged, was surfed sideways, and then cradled in a world of violent water gone suddenly silent. The upstream current fell from the wave crest at terrific speed, brown and smooth, almost touching my left shoulder. On my right, the wall breaking dirty white surged and churned well over my head. I braced hard against the wall to keep from being flipped upstream and rode it like a crazy horse. It was like leaning against the pressure wave of an explosion. At the end of the trough, in a small eddy, I could see the other two looking down at me. The scariest thing was their expressions. Their eyes were huge. I pried myself high up onto the pile but it wouldn't let me over. I worked the boat forward, trying to break out of the left side, then rocked it back. The hole was too deep. The kayak bucked violently. I was tiring fast. I wondered what I would do when I was too exhausted to brace anymore. I flipped upstream in an instant capsize and held my paddle straight over my head toward the bottom of the river, trying to catch the lower current pushing through. Nothing. I rolled back up. "This could be bad," I thought. Judging by their expressions, my pals were thinking it too. I pried again up onto the pile. Just then the hole surged, I dug, and was rocking over the top and downstream. We pulled out a mile below in a foamy pool and dragged our boats onto the rocks. John and I squatted in the rain and clasped hands. Adrenaline surged in my limbs and I looked at the broken rock walls and the river and my friend and I thought, "Nothing is better than this."

RUN ONE: DUMONT TO IDAHO SPRINGS

Location: 35 miles west of Denver; about 40 miles southwest of Boulder

Length: 5.5 miles

Difficulty: Class IV

Put-in: Lawson (6 Pipes Bridge) or Dumont

Takeout: Idaho Springs

Gauge: Call Watertalk, (303) 831-7135 1*23*; Clear Creek near Lawson

Heads up: Beautiful Class IV.

Description: This is the upper upper run. It differs in character from the runs below in that most of the drops are man-made reefs with a ledgy character. There's a lot of fun playing in a boat inclined to the vertical. Also, the run has a more remote feel because it isn't as exposed to the road. At the I-70 underpass on the west entrance to Idaho Springs, almost at the end of the run, is a surprisingly steep and gnarly rapid called Outer Limits. Give it a good scout. You can add a few miles and half a grade by putting in at the 6 Pipes Bridge above Lawson. The first time I did this run we pulled out at Idaho Springs and watched a kid on a

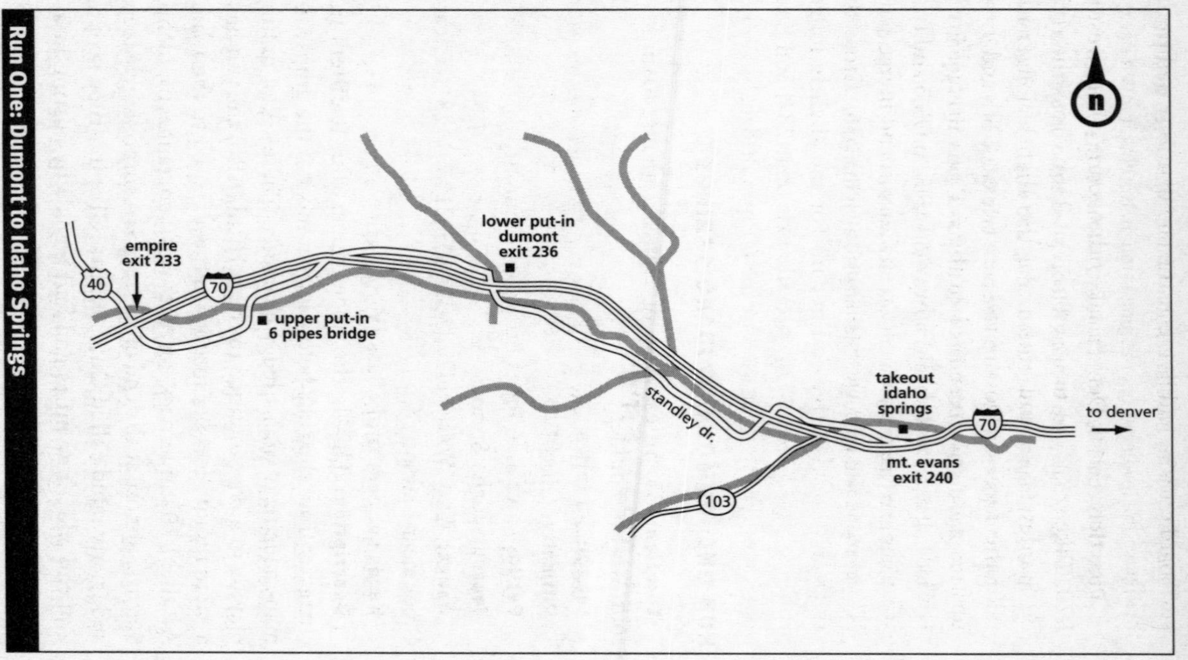
Run One: Dumont to Idaho Springs
n
40
empire
exit 233
70
upper put-in
6 pipes bridge
lower put-in
dumont
exit 236
standley dr.
103
takeout
idaho
springs
mt. evans
exit 240
70
to denver

surfboard cutting and jiving at the end of a rope tied to the bridge.

Directions: From Denver, take 6th Avenue (US 6) west to I-70. Take I-70 west to Dumont (exit 236). Cross the river on Stanley Drive and put in. For the slightly longer run take the Lawson/Downieville exit (exit 234) and head upstream on the river road to the 6 Pipes Bridge. From Boulder, drive south on Broadway (CO 93) to US 6 and turn west. Follow US 6 up Clear Creek Canyon and merge with I-70 west. Take I-70 west to Dumont (exit 236). Cross the river on Stanley Drive and put in. For the slightly longer run take the Lawson/Downieville exit (exit 234) and head upstream on the river road to the 6 Pipes Bridge.

RUN TWO: KERMIT'S

Location: 27 miles west of Denver; 32 miles southwest of Boulder

Length: 3.6 miles

Difficulty: Class IV at flows less than 600 cfs

Put-in: Junction of US 6 and US 40 (Kermit's)

Takeout: Junction of US 6 and CO 119

Gauge: Call Watertalk, (303) 831-7135 1*22*; Clear Creek near Golden

Heads up: After-work favorite.

Description: What is Kermit's Roadhouse? Does anyone go in there? The run below the little pub in the shadow of the elevated highway is all frolic and a favorite after-work run for Denverites. There are some open-ledge drops, good surf waves, and an exciting, solid IV drop called Double Knife just west of tunnel #6 (mile marker 258.9). Also look out for the riverwide hole called Terminator between tunnels #5 and #6 (mile marker 259.3). I got stuck in there in

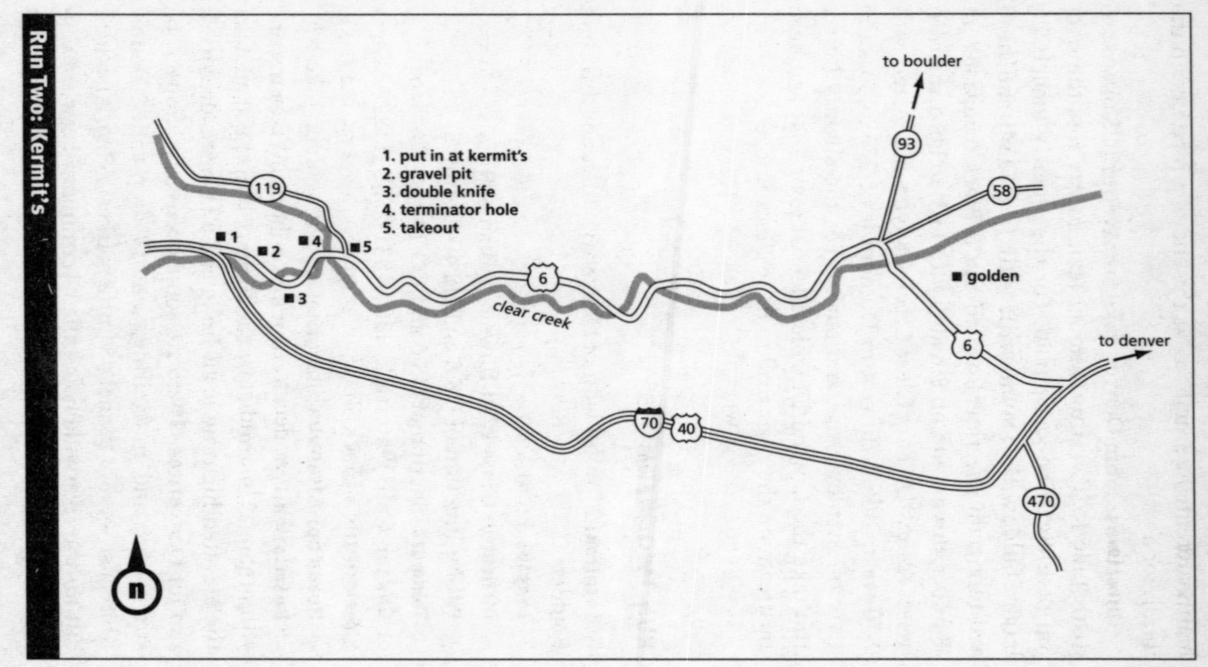
Run Two: Kermit's
1. put in at kermit's
2. gravel pit
3. double knife
4. terminator hole
5. takeout
1
2
3
4
5
119
6
clear creek
93
to boulder
58
golden
6
to denver
70
40
470
n

high water one June and thought I'd have to write my boss to ask for a year off.

Directions: From Denver, take 6th Avenue (US 6) west past Golden and up into Clear Creek Canyon. Continue to Kermit's Roadhouse just before the junction with I-70. From Boulder, drive south on Broadway (CO 93), to US 6 and turn right (west). Follow US 6 up Clear Creek Canyon and continue to Kermit's Roadhouse just before the junction with I-70.

RUN THREE: BLACK ROCK

Location: 22 miles west of Denver; 27 miles southwest of Boulder

Length: 5.5 miles

Difficulty: Class V–V+ at flows 400–900 cfs; Class V at flows greater than 900 cfs

Put-in: Green Bay Rock (mile marker 262.9)

Takeout: Rigor Mortis (Green Bridge, mile marker 267.2)

Gauge: Call Watertalk, (303) 831-7135 1*22*; Clear Creek near Golden

Heads up: Stay on your toes at high water: sharp rocks, a few big eddies.

Description: Black Rock is a serious, expert, roadside Class V run 45 minutes from Denver and Boulder. Like any Clear Creek run at decent flows, it is fast and constricted with a few sizable eddies, and a lousy place to swim. The first big drop, for which the run is named, is marked by a huge—guess what color—boulder visible from the road at mile marker 264. Watch the undercut rock wall on the left. Below, just past tunnel #2, is the Narrows. The river constricts and spills happily over a ramp into a wide, sticky hole flanked by a voracious, recirculating eddy against the left wall. Once I eddied out just above the drop at high

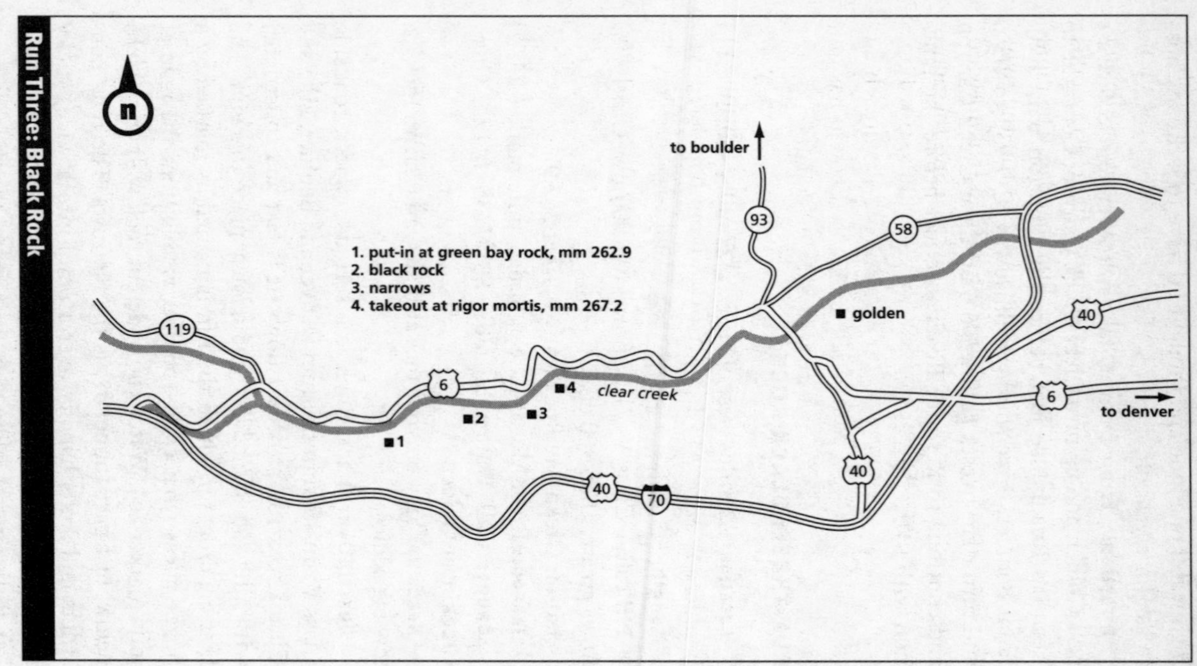
Run Three: Black Rock
n
to boulder
93
58
1. put-in at green bay rock, mm 262.9
2. black rock
3. narrows
4. takeout at rigor mortis, mm 267.2
119
6
■ golden
40
■4
clear creek
6
to denver
■2
■3
■1
40
40
70

water and watched an amazing hat trick: three of the best kayakers in the state charged one at a time over the drop, got stopped by the hole, pushed up against the wall, and swam. I'm not a rocket scientist, but I figured my odds weren't too good and I walked the drop that day. The rapid has changed since, and it's become easier to run the right side. Once you survive the Narrows, you can look forward to Rigor Mortis, just above the Green Bridge and the take-out. Picture this: An amusement park log flume, tilted up. Edge one side with an undercut wall and put a vicious hole at the bottom. Rigo, as it is affectionately known, has an insatiable appetite for boaters with karmic deficits.

Directions: From Denver, take 6th Avenue (US 6) west past Golden and up into Clear Creek Canyon. Continue to Green Bay Rock at mile marker 262.9. From Boulder, drive south on Broadway (CO 93) to US 6 and turn left (west). Follow US 6 up Clear Creek Canyon and continue to Green Bay Rock at mile marker 262.9.

RUN FOUR: LOWER CLEAR CREEK

Location: 18 miles west of Denver, 23 miles southwest of Boulder

Length: 5.7 miles

Difficulty: Class IV at flows of 400–900 cfs; Class IV+ at flows greater than 900 cfs

Put-in: Rigor Mortis (Green Bridge, mile marker 267.2); put in below the bridge!

Takeout: Tunnel #1 or Whitewater Park in Golden

Gauge: Call Watertalk, (303) 831-7135 1*22*; Clear Creek near Golden

Heads up: Another after-work Denver favorite.

Description: Somehow, though it is rated Class IV and it has all the sharp, broken rock and flumelike feel of the rest

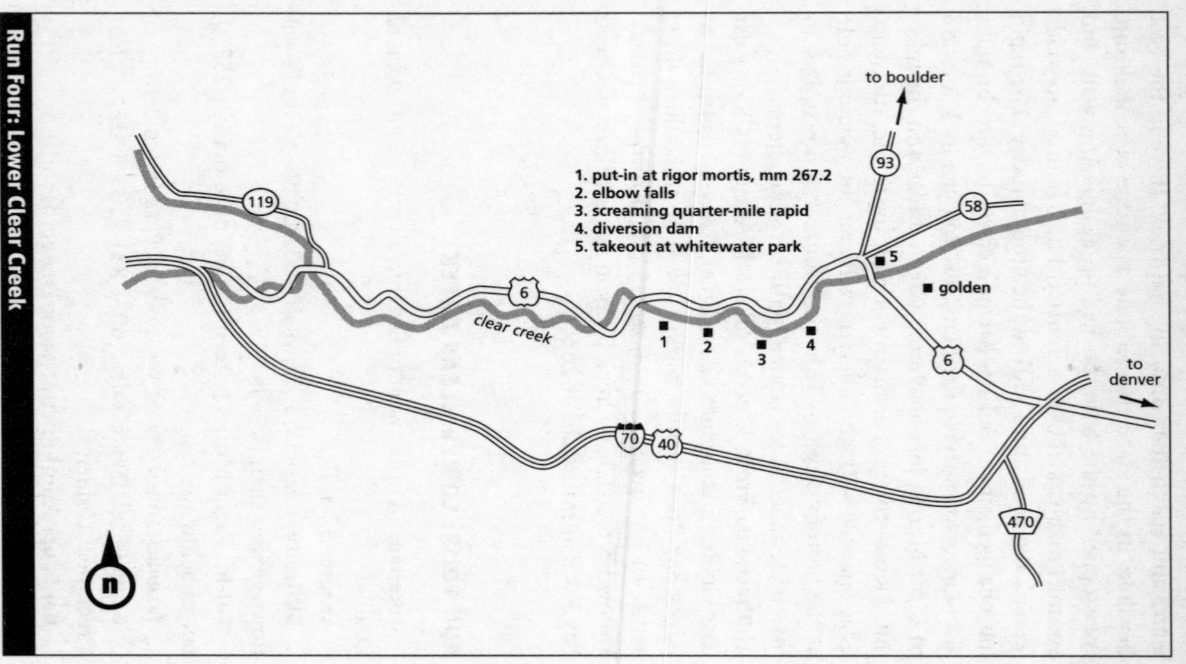
Run Four: Lower Clear Creek
to boulder
93
119
58
1. put-in at rigor mortis, mm 267.2
2. elbow falls
3. screaming quarter-mile rapid
4. diversion dam
5. takeout at whitewater park
5
golden
6
clear creek
1
2
3
4
6
to denver
70
40
470
n

of Clear Creek, this run feels more hospitable and forgiving. For an advanced boater it's plain fun, and ends at the Whitewater Park in Golden, so you can finish the river-run and enter Rodeo World, winding up the day with surfs and cartwheels, families cheering from the bank, and slalom racers in their knifelike boats cutting through everybody, just trying to get a workout on the permanent gates. The three drops to note are Elbow Falls, the Screaming Quarter-Mile Rapid, and a diversion dam that is best to walk, as pin potential is high.

Directions: From Denver, take 6th Avenue (US 6) west past Golden and up into Clear Creek Canyon. Continue to the Green Bridge at mile marker 267.2. From Boulder, drive south on Broadway (CO 93) to US 6 and turn left (west). Follow US 6 up Clear Creek Canyon and continue to the Green Bridge at mile marker 267.2.

Where to Connect

Book and Link

Colorado Rivers and Creeks, 2nd ed., by Gordon Banks and Dave Eckardt (Woody Creek Colo.: Published by the authors, 1999).

www.kayakingcolorado.com

Shops and Instruction

Denver

Confluence Kayaks and Telemark
1537 Platte Street
Denver, CO 80202
(303) 433-3676
www.confluencekayaks.com

Carries a full line of kayak gear; also offers demos, rentals, instruction for all levels, sea kayak instruction, guided river trips, and pool sessions.

Union Boat Yard
2045 West Union, Bldg. D
Englewood, CO 80110
(303) 783-3661

Confluence Kayaks' outpost at Union Chutes.

Boulder

Boulder Outdoor Center
2510 North 47th Street
Boulder, CO 80301
(303) 444-8420

Carries a full line of kayak gear; also offers boat rentals, instruction for beginners through experts, and pool sessions.

Wildwasser Sport
7161 Valtec Court
Boulder, CO 80301
(303) 444-2336

Carries a full line of Prijon kayaks, plus paddles, accessories, and paddling gear that complement the boats. The best selection of sea and touring kayaks on the Front Range.

Golden

Alpenglow Mountainsport
885 Lupine Boulevard, Suite B
Golden, CO 80401
(303) 277-0133

Carries a full line of kayak gear; also offers rentals, demos, boat outfitting and repair, instruction for all levels, and pool sessions.

Clubs and Organizations

Colorado Whitewater Association (CWWA)
P.O. Box 4315
Englewood, CO 80155-4315
(303) 430-4830
www.coloradowhitewater.org

Dinners, training camps, club weekends, and more.

American Whitewater Association
1430 Fenwick Lane
Silver Spring, MD 20910
(301) 589-9453
www.awa.org

American Canoe Association
7432 Alban Station Boulevard, Suite B-232
Springfield, VA 22150
(703) 451-0141
www.aca-paddler.org

Rocky Mountain Sea Kayak Club
www.dotzen.org/paddler/rmskc
E-mail: peck4500@aol.com

Regional trips and instruction.

Rocky Mountain Canoe Club
(303) 989-4833
www.ahssolar@quest.net

Events

Clear Creek Festival

This event, which occurs in early June, features awesome races, rodeos, demos, and a good time right in Golden. The best whitewater festival on the Front Range. Call Alpenglow in Golden at (303) 277-0133.

Amateur Rodeo Series

A wild amateur hot-dog series held weekly at locations all over the Front Range. Call Mike Paris at (303) 278-4902.

Paddlesports Expo

A fun day of free instruction and boat demos on Boulder Reservoir. Call Wildwasser Sport at (303) 444-2336 for more information.

Alpenglow's Boat Swap

Over three hundred boats and gear, plus rafts are for sale during the first weekend in April. Great opportunity to get into reasonably priced equipment. Call (303) 277-0133 for information.

Rocky Mountain Adventures Demo Day

Try out the hot new boats on City Park Lake in Fort Collins on the first Sunday in May. Also, the big Boat Swap occurs the first Saturday in June. Call (970) 493-4005 or (800) 858-6808 for more information.

Fly-Fishing

ONE FISH, TWO fish, 19,600 fish. That's how many catchable ten-inch rainbow trout the Colorado Division of Wildlife stocked in Wash Park's Smith Lake recently. Sixteen thousand in City Park, in the middle of Denver. A variety of other game fish can be found in local waters, including bluegills, largemouth bass, crappie, and channel cats. Dave Nessler, a fisheries biologist for the Division of Wildlife says you can do pretty well on a little mosquito pattern, or an Adams, or a Renegade—say size 16–20. If you want to fish pristine mountain creeks and rivers, there's more fishing an hour and a half from Denver and Boulder than you can shake a Sage 5-weight at. You could spend a lifetime and never get it done. When

I lived in Boulder, I used to fly-fish right from town and up into the canyon. I caught smallish rainbows; it was a fine respite later in the summer when the water was low. Within thirty-five minutes of Denver is a beautiful stretch of the South Platte in Waterton Canyon. No cars are allowed on the smooth dirt road that winds above the river, so you see whole families on bikes, cranking upstream with fishing rods sticking out of daypacks and off bike racks. An hour and a half from downtown, on the South Fork of the South Platte, below Cheesman Dam, is a stretch of trout water that is listed as one of the top ten producing trout streams in America and a favorite among Colorado anglers. I've described a very selective overview of some of the finest, most reasonably accessible waters in the area, from close-to-home creeks to farther-afield rivers worth driving to—and a few local urban fishing holes where the guy fishing next to you using bacon for bait may haul out a five-pound channel cat.

Thanks to Marty Bartholomew and his exhaustive and excellent *Flyfisher's Guide to Colorado,* and to Todd Hosman and his superb *Fly Fishing Colorado's Front Range: An Angler's Guide.* Much of the information below comes from these venerable sources. Thanks also to Dan Hatch, proprieter of the Hatch Fly Shop in Evergreen, for his generous advice and help.

Denver City Limits

CITY PARK LAKE

Location: Denver
Access: 200′ from car
Fish: Bluegill, bullhead, carp, channel catfish, crappie,

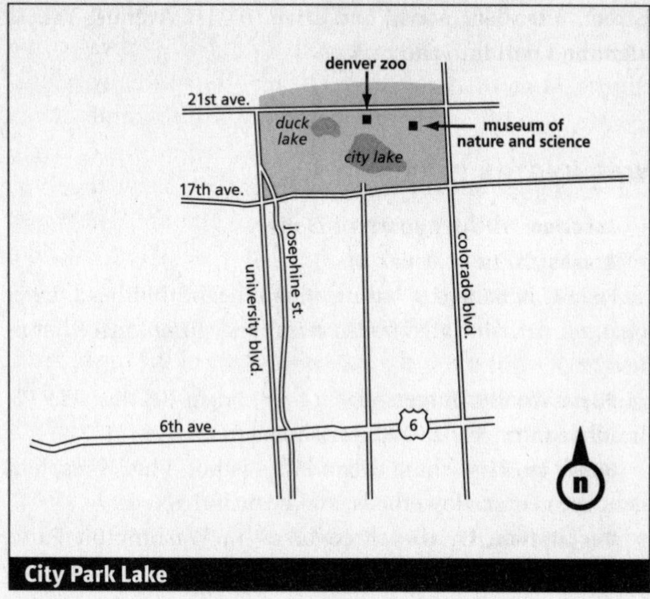

City Park Lake

gizzard shad, green sunfish, largemouth bass, yellow perch; catchable-sized rainbow trout are stocked in spring

Flies: Royal Wulff size 14, Elk Hair Caddis size 14–18, Black Woolly Buggers size 6, Beadhead Hare's Ear size 16

Heads up: Warm-water lake fly-fishing is the new frontier. Plus, the Museum of Nature and Science, Denver Zoo, and paddle boats.

Description: Yes, you can fly-fish here. No, you wouldn't be a fool. You can cast dry flies for stocked trout and poppers for bass. You can sight-cast for big tailing carp and imagine you're bonefishing in the Keys—with downtown Denver bristling below you and the mountains beyond, and the peacocks crying from over the lawns at the zoo. Really. Remember to buy a fishing license.

Directions: Drive east on 6th Avenue (US 6) to Josephine

Street. Turn left (north) and drive to 21st Avenue. Take a right and pull into the park.

WASHINGTON PARK

Location: Slightly south of Denver

Access: None to speak of

Fish: Catchable 10″ trout, plus bluegill, bullhead, carp, channel catfish, largemouth bass, and pumpkinseed sunfish

Flies: Woolly Burgers size 14–18, Foam Beatles size 12, Beadhead Prince size 12, Grasshopper size 4–6

Heads up: Fly-fishing urban lakes is hot. Plus, a resplendent rec center, flowerbeds, and beautiful people.

Description: Of the three lakes in Washington Park,

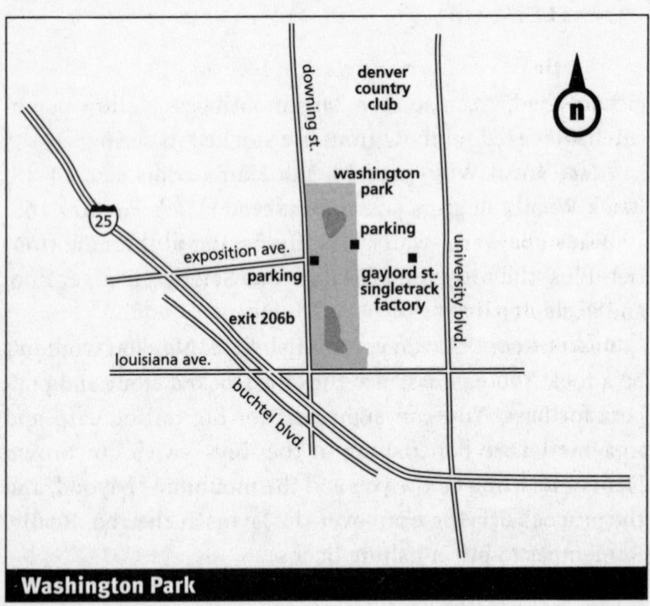

Washington Park

Smith Lake, the farthest north, is the only one stocked. The Colorado Division of Wildlife slips in up to 20,000 trout over the course of the spring, and apparently most of these end up in someone's frying pan. Throw on the vest, sunscreen, and polarized sunglasses and have at it. You can actually cast dry flies for rainbows and take dinner home. You might bag a few phone numbers too, if that's what you're after. For more description of the scene at this lovely, prosperous park, see "Mountain Biking."

Directions: Take I-25 south to Washington Street/Emerson Street (exit 206B). Merge onto Buchtel Boulevard going north to Louisiana Avenue. Turn left (east) onto Louisiana Avenue, then left (north) onto Downing Street. Parking is located on the street or in the parking lot, toward the north side of park.

BERKELEY LAKE

Location: 6 miles northwest of Denver

Access: Easy, within 200′ of parking

Fish: Rainbow trout (stocked in spring), largemouth bass, orange spotted sunfish, sucker, green sunfish, bluegill, bullhead, carp, channel catfish, and crappie

Flies: Bass Poppers size 14–18, Woolly Buggers size 14–18, Beadhead Prince Nymphs size 16–20

Heads up: If you've never fought a 10-pound carp you couldn't know that this is the new frontier in fly-fishing. Added attractions include a rec center, swimming pool, big trees, and a walking path.

Description: The Berkeley Lake Rec Center is where I workout. The weight room is crowded and hot, and loud rap pipes through the speakers. When I finish I wander dazedly out into the parking lot and look at the lake. Just seeing the water, the fringe of cattails, and the big old trees

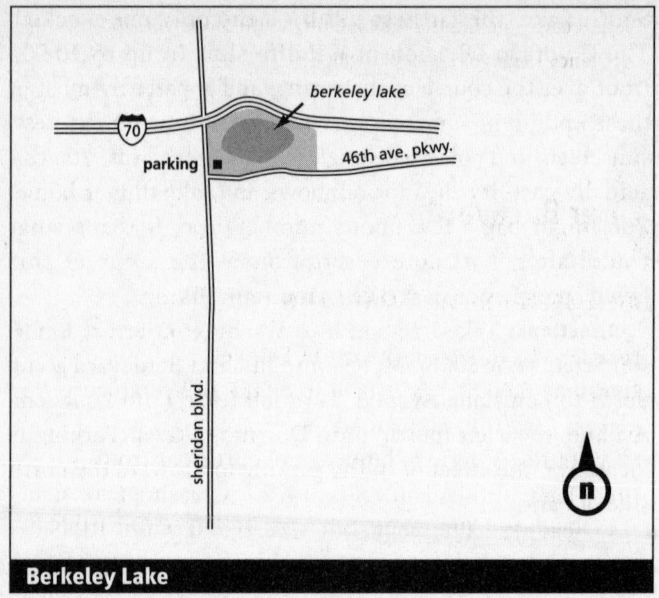

Berkeley Lake

scattered over the grass makes me feel better. I don't even notice the traffic on I-70 whizzing by on the other side of the lake. I've never tried it, but it's supposed to be an excellent warm-water fishery.

Directions: Drive west on 6th Avenue (US 6) to Sheridan Boulevard (CO 95). Turn right (north) and drive 4 miles to 46th Avenue Parkway. Turn right (east) onto 46th Avenue Parkway and take an immediate left into the parking lot.

Reservoir Fishing

OST OF THE big lakes and reservoirs around Denver are fishable, with the same opportunities and challenges mentioned in the other lake fisheries. A couple of good places to catch very big fish—catfish, bass,

and carp—are **Chatfield Reservoir,** south of Denver, and **Quincy Reservoir,** east of town.

Denver Backyard

BEAR CREEK ABOVE MORRISON

Location: 15 miles southwest of Denver

Elevation: 5,600′ in Morrison to 6,600′ in Evergreen

Access: Easy trail along road

Fish: Rainbow, brown, brooks, and cutthroat trout

Flies: Parachute Adam's size 14–20, Grasshoppers size 10–14, Beadhead Pheasant Tail size 16–20, Gold Ribbed Hare's Ear size 16–20

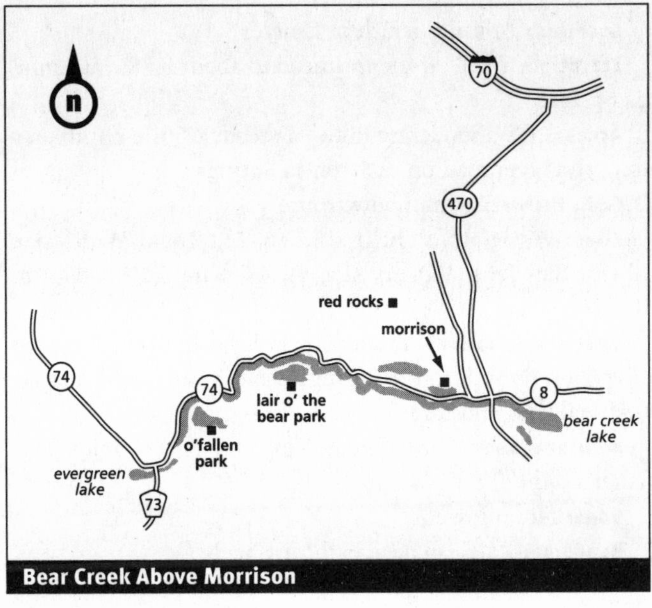

Bear Creek Above Morrison

Maps: *Colorado Atlas and Gazetteer*

Heads up: Close to town, small creek, beautiful canyon, stone houses.

Description: Just outside of Denver, above Morrison, Bear Creek offers a lot of good fishing in a pretty canyon. It's a small stream, crowded with trees and brush, and you can wade up the middle and hit the pockets. I've seen people fishing right behind Red Rocks Cyclery in Morrison. Great after-work respite.

Directions: Go west on 6th Avenue (US 6) to I-70 westbound and stay in the right lane so you can merge onto CO 470. Drive south on CO 470 to the Morrison (CO 8) exit and turn west. Drive through town and up CO 74 into the canyon.

WATERTON CANYON

Location: 14 miles south of Denver

Elevation: 5,520′ at the trailhead to about 5,786′ at Strontia Springs

Access: It's a moderate hike—a steady 6-mile climb on a smooth gravel road up to Strontia Springs

Fish: Brown and rainbow trout

Flies: Ak's Olive Quill size 16–22, Royal Wulff size 10–16, San Juan Worms size 12–14, Orange Scuds size 10–18

Special regulations: From 300 yards north of the Marston Diversion up to Strontia Springs Dam is catch-and-release, artificial flies and lures only.

Map and book: USFS Pike National Forest map, *Flyfisher's Guide to Colorado*

Dogs: Not allowed

Heads up: Rattlesnakes, bighorn sheep

Description: Waterton Canyon is one of the loveliest

places close to Denver to walk, run, ride a mountain bike, and fish. The rocky stream flows in runs, riffles, and long broad glides, and the trout higher up get well over 14 inches. The smooth dirt road that follows the river is closed to cars. As the best fishing is above the Marston Diversion, about 3 miles up the road, it's fast and fun to strap your rod to a daypack or bike rack and ride upcanyon to your favorite riffle. A herd of bighorn sheep reside in the

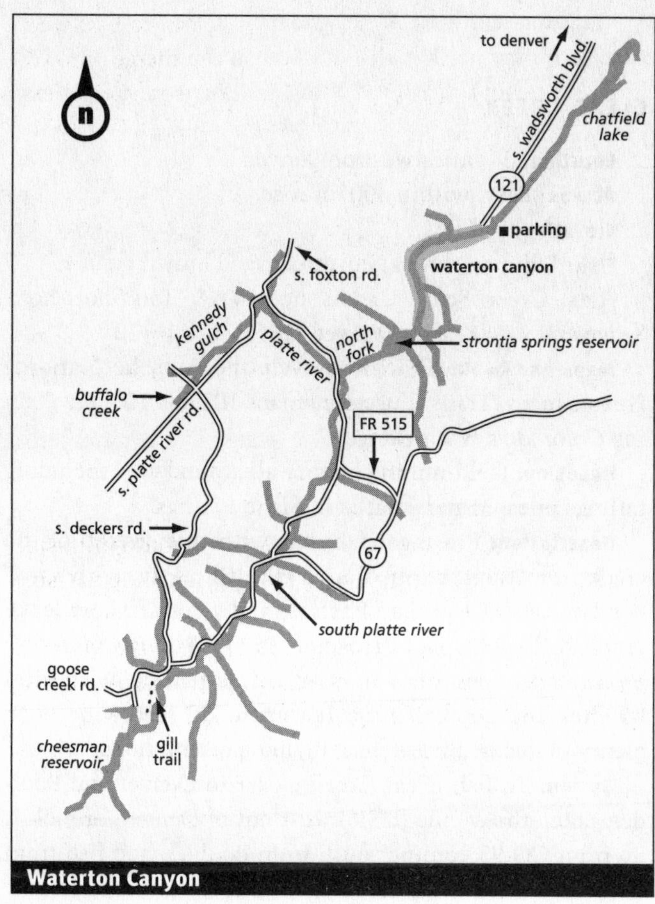

Waterton Canyon

Canyon; in the hot months they can often be found chilling in the cool mist exploding out of the Strontia Springs Dam. In the fall it's quieter, and the colors—the oak brush and willows, the grasses on the steep slopes—are inspiring.

Directions: Go west on 6th Avenue (US 6) to I-70 westbound. Stay in the right lane and merge onto CO 470. Take CO 470 to Wadsworth Blvd (CO 121), and go south 4 miles to the Waterton Canyon entrance. Turn left (east) into the parking lot.

CLEAR CREEK

Location: 24 miles west of Denver

Access: Easy, within 300′ of road

Elevation: 8,100′

Fish: Rainbow, brook, cutthroat, and brown trout

Flies: Green Sedge Caddis size 14–18, Tan Short-horn Sedge size 14–18, Blue-Winged Olives size 16–20

Maps and book: USFS Roosevelt and Arapaho National Forests maps; Trails Illustrated maps 103 and 104; *Fly Fishing Colorado's Front Range*

Heads up: Gold-mining history all around you, including tailings piles. Mineral baths in Idaho Springs.

Description: I'm most familiar with this stretch of the creek from the cockpit of a kayak. It's pretty, with some ponderosas, willows, and asters, and a lot of short ledge drops, riffles, and pools. Hosman, in *Fly Fishing Colorado's Front Range,* describes it as an active fishery, with vital hatches and good fishing. It's about 30 feet wide with plenty of opportunities for long line presentations.

Option: To fish Clear Creek closer to Denver and Boulder, take 6th Avenue (US 6) west out of Denver, or pick it up from CO 93 coming south from Boulder, and fish from the pullouts all along the road.

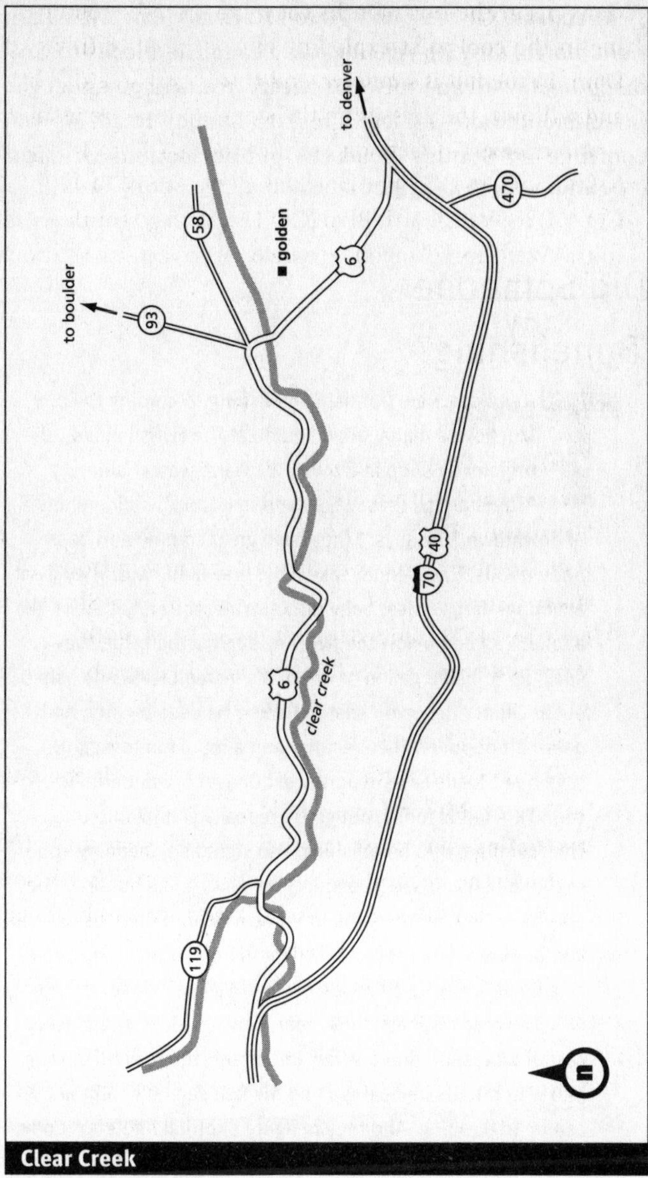

Clear Creek

Directions: Go west on I-70 to Mt. Evans (exit 240). Turn right (north) on 13th Avenue. Go a couple of blocks to Colorado Boulevard and turn left (west). You will go under the interstate and cross Clear Creek to Stanley Road. As you continue on Stanley Road the public sections of Clear Creek parallel the road.

Did Someone Say Bonefishing?

THERE'S A NEW frontier in fly-fishing, according to Cody Muchow, a manager and guide at The Flyfisher, Ltd., the premier fly shop in Denver. It's warm-water fishing.

"There are all these lakes and reservoirs within minutes of downtown," he says. "They have great crappie and bass populations. Bass readily take a fly; they fight hard. They'll eat anything—frogs, mice, baby ducks. When they hit, it looks like a toilet flushing below the fly. They don't actually hit, they suck, up to half a gallon of water. It's incredible." Cody fishes out at Quincy Reservoir east of Parker. He uses big-frog and deer-hair poppers. They're noisy and a lot of fun to cast. He says that Sloans Lake in northwest Denver is wonderful for carp. "It sounds funny, but guys are really getting into this. They compare it to bonefishing. You sight fish, meaning you cast to a fish you see. You stalk 'em, almost like hunting. They may be tailing, rooting around in the mud for little crustaceans and bugs and you drop the fly right in front of their nose and give it two quick tugs like it's fleeing. We use clouser minnows, little crawdad poppers, hare's ears. An accurate, well-placed cast and presentation are very important. You may be moving into water that's ankle deep and the fish can be enormous. It can be frightening. And they're fighters, brutal fighters." Cody pauses, as if the next concept may be hard to swallow. "They're considered more highly developed than trout," he says. "They're better adapted to their environment. More resourceful—they utilize more food sources, have a better sense of smell. And they're community fish. Carp are highly organized. They have a way of communicating with each other—like whales." Cody's getting into deep water, but he bravely goes on. "For some guys, this may be their only shot at a fifteen-, twenty-pound fish. The type of gear you'd use for bonefishing is ideal—heavier rods—but you can do fine with lighter gear. A lot of alternatives to stream fishing for trout are just being discovered. There's a whole other world for fly-fishermen that's being explored, that's affordable, and that's incredibly exciting." Say no more. Some of us are already pulling out the Sage 8-weight.

Boulder City Limits

BOULDER CREEK

Location: Downtown Boulder and up the creek into Boulder Canyon

Elevation: 5,300′ to 8,500′

Access: Easy to moderate, within 100′ of the road

Fish: Rainbow, brown, cutthroat, and brook trout

Flies: Parachute Adams size 14–18, Elk Hair Caddis size 16–24, Flashback Pheasant Tail size 14–18, Beadhead Prince size 16–20

Maps and book: USGS Boulder, Gold Hill, and Tungsten maps; USFS Roosevelt and Arapaho National Forests maps; *Fly Fishing Colorado's Front Range*

Heads up: From the local fishing Yoda: "Just a fun little, a good little creek to catch fish—use dry flies."

Description: Boulder proves itself again as an urban outdoorsperson's paradise with fun fly-fishing that starts in

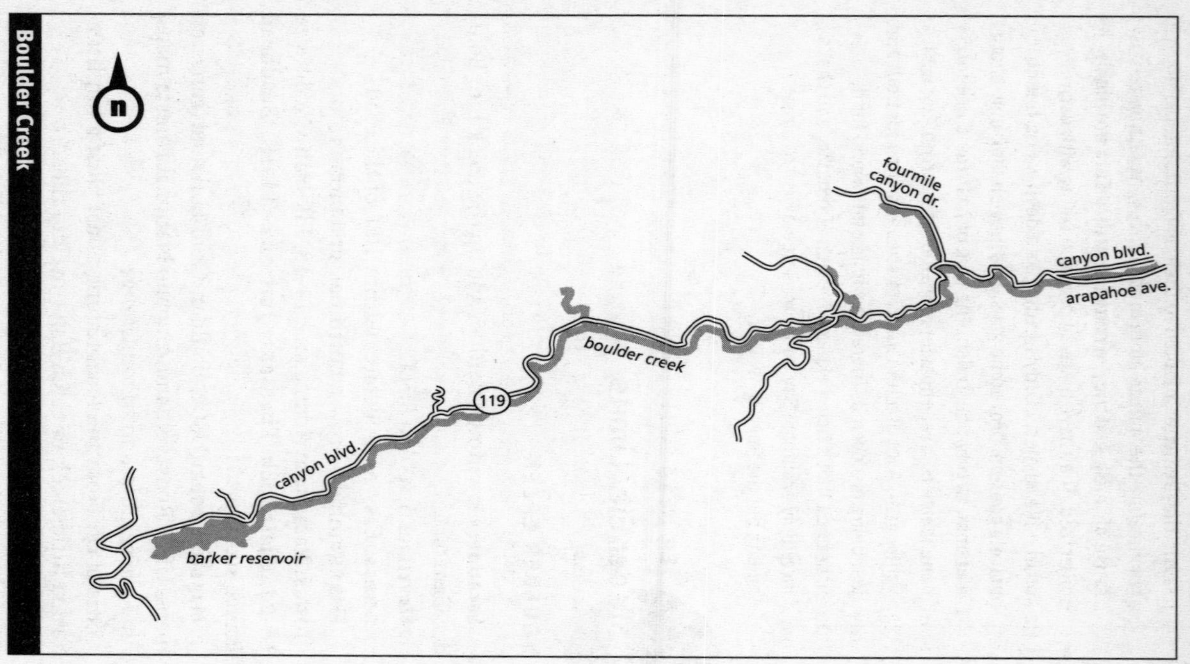

Boulder Creek

town. During low-water months I used to make an evening ritual of fishing the bends of Boulder Creek just above town behind the Elephant Rock climbing pullout. I caught a lot of small trout wading upstream and casting into the pockets. Todd Hosman recommends the 8-mile stretch above the national forest boundary about 6.5 miles above town.

Directions: To start in-town at Eben Fine Park, drive south on 28th to Arapahoe Avenue. Turn right (west) on Arapahoe and go to 3rd. Turn right down into the parking lot. Work your way upstream. Or drive west up Canyon Boulevard (CO 119) into the canyon and use the pullouts to park at likely spots.

BOULDER RESERVOIR

Location: 4 miles north of Boulder.

Access: Off North 51st Street

Fish: Walleye, channel catfish, black crappie, bluegill, largemouth bass, yellow perch, rainbow trout (catchable size are stocked), and carp

Flies: Muddler Minnows size 4, Umpqua Bait Fish size 2, Parachute Adams size 16–20, Beadhead Woolly Burgers size 6

Fee: $5.00

Heads up: Bring a kayak and fish the edges of the cattails from your boat.

Description: Boulder Reservoir is a beautiful place to do anything, especially on fall evenings, when squadrons of geese are coming in over the foothills and the grass and reeds are tawny. In spring, you are not hallucinating if you see pelicans. Warm-water lake fishing is a blast, with some of the scrappiest fighters pound for pound found anywhere.

Directions: From 28th Street (US 36) go north to the Longmont Diagonal (CO 119) and turn northeast (right). At

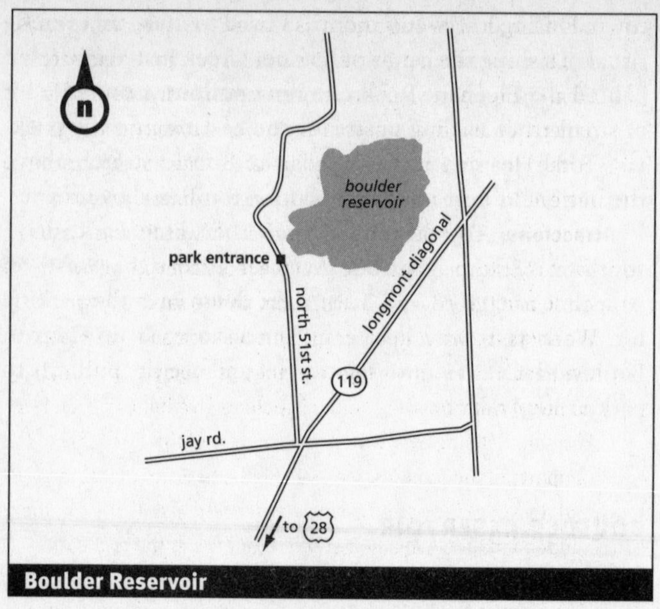

Jay Road turn left (west) and then almost immediately right (north) onto 51st Street. Access the park from 51st Street.

Dying to Fish

THIS IS A TRUE story. My friend Amy is a park ranger at Chatfield State Recreation Area south of Denver, and she told it to me. It happened in early June out at Catfish Flats. The flats are some shallows where the river flows into the reservoir and the lake is narrow. It was late afternoon. In the life of the old fisherman it was evening. He was in his eighties and sick. He had fought off his doctors, his family, the nursing home, and maintained his independence, making do in the house he had lived in most of his life. More than anything in the world now he loved to fish. He had fished since he was a boy, and he was a good fisherman. He loved the streams and the lakes around Denver like family, though he had seen them change a lot since he had first tossed a dry fly with his father. Now, his eyes weren't so good, and it was difficult to tie on the little simulated bugs, to thread the fine tippet through the eyes of the hooks, so he fished with spinners, shiny spoons he could snap on at the swivel. He was fishing. Casting carefully, standing at the edge of the red-stemmed willow brush and the grove of young aspen, on the sandy margin of the shore, he was careful to keep his balance and not to hook the trees. He reeled the lure in evenly, as evenly as he could, in no hurry, twitching the end of his pole to give it living action. The sun, hanging over Waterton Canyon and the first grassy ramparts of the foothills, was still high and warm on his face and neck. He had gotten a single strike and lost it. The hit, the sudden jerk, the sensation of that other life at the end of the line, had surged adrenalin into his arms and hands, and now he made his casts with that extra attention, the heightened awareness and excited expectation that all fishermen know. He made another cast, watched the spinner arc and catch the sun and flash and heard the splash, and he started to retrieve it, turning the handle of the reel and Wham! The fish hit hard, must be a bass, the rod doubled and Christ it was taking line, the drag was whining and he was leaning back against the pull on the rod and—his chest exploded, a blinding light, and then blackness. A fisherman on the opposite shore saw the old man fall. He turned and flagged Amy, who was driving by, and she spun the car on the gravel road and hit the lights and radioed for an ambulance. When she got to the man his rod lay across his neck. She knelt, moved it aside, and swiftly took his pulse. None, and no breathing—she started CPR, and within a minute got the pulse and breathing back. She cradled the head of the old man in her hands and stroked his forehead and told him everything would be fine, would be all right, and the ambulance skidded to a stop in a crunch of gravel and a whirl of dust. Two paramedics jogged through the trees with a stretcher and took the old man away. For the next six months, all through the summer and fall, the old man called Amy at work. He bitched her out. He couldn't believe it. How could she have done that to him. Through all his sick years he had dreamed of dying fishing, on a summer afternoon in the late sun, and she had snatched it from him. Who in hell did she think she was. How could she have played God with him. Denying the last dying wish of an old man. She had ruined everything. He hoped she thought about it. The next time she saw an old fisherman fall he hoped she would think twice. Amy stopped taking calls at work. State park policy required her to administer first aid. She prayed for the old fisherman. She hoped he got his wish and died fishing. She hoped it wasn't in her jurisdiction. "If you insist on coming back to the lake and trying to die," she thought, "please, please, please be on my day off."

Boulder Backyard

LEFT HAND CREEK

Location: 12–16 miles north of Boulder

Access: Easy, within 200′ of road

Elevation: 6,640′

Fish: Brown, rainbow, and brook trout

Flies: Parachute Adams size 14–18, Turcks Teranchula size 8–10, Quill Gordon size 12–14, Beadhead Olive Caddis Emerger size 14–18

Maps and book: USGS Boulder map; USFS Roosevelt and Arapaho National Forests maps; *Fly Fishing Colorado's Front Range*

Heads up: Fun, small-stream getaway close to Boulder.

Description: Ten miles from town you can lose yourself

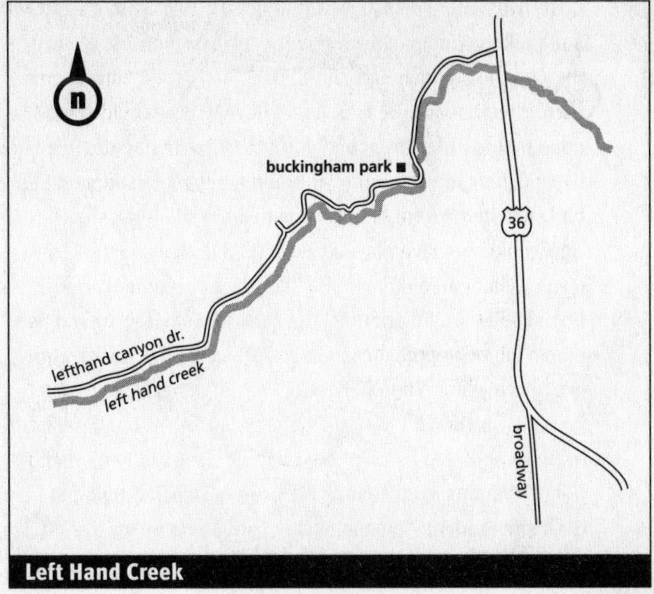

Left Hand Creek

on a challenging, small stream that cuts into steep banks of pines and willows. The water usually runs fast and clear over a rocky streambed—ideal for short-line, pocket-water fishing.

Directions: Drive north on 28th Street (US 36) to Left-hand Canyon Drive (94 RD) and turn left (west). Drive to Buckingham Park, about 2.4 miles. Anywhere along the road for the next 3 miles is great fishing.

SOUTH BOULDER CREEK—WALKER RANCH

Location: 9 miles southwest of Boulder
Elevation: 7,200′ at trailhead; 6,680′ at destination
Access: 1.1 miles (40 minutes), with 500′ of gradient

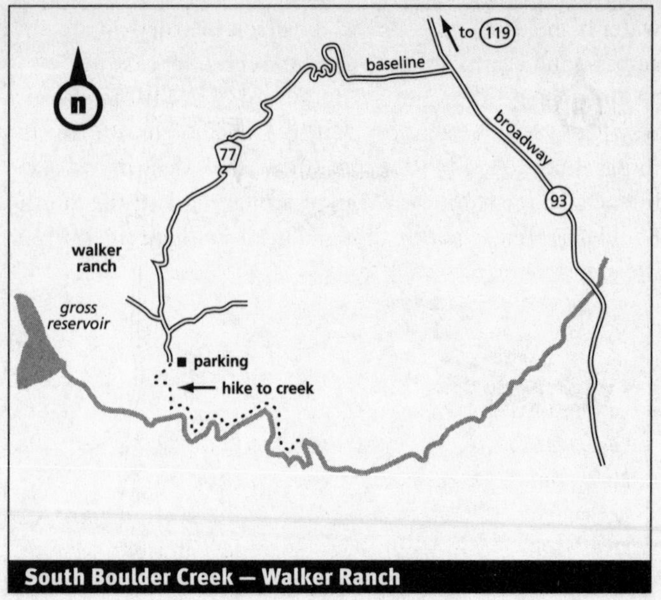

South Boulder Creek — Walker Ranch

Fish: Brown and rainbow trout over 11″ long; small brook and cutthroat trout

Flies: Pheasant Tail size 14–18, Olive Comparadun size 16–18, Rusty Spinner size 14–18, and Parachute Emerger size 16–18, Olive Diving Caddis size 16–18

Maps and book: USFS Roosevelt and Arapaho National Forests maps; USGS Eldorado Springs map; *Fly Fishing Colorado's Front Range*

Heads up: Bring a mountain bike for cross-training.

Description: A very active creek for the active angler, as the hike is demanding, especially on the way back up. It's close to Boulder, and very popular with mountain bikers, so don't become roadkill. But because the water isn't that easy to get to, you should find solitude and excellent fishing. When you hit the creek, follow a well-worn trail downstream for a while and fish back up. There's some fast water higher up. Lower down, the creek is wider—up to 40′ across—and easily wadable for some fun long casting.

Directions: Take Canyon Boulevard (CO 119) to Broadway (CO 93), and turn left (south). Continue on Broadway to Baseline Road (77 RD), and turn right (west) onto Baseline. Go about 8 miles to Walker Ranch. Park at the South Boulder Trailhead parking lot and head south on the trail to the creek.

ST. VRAIN CREEK

Location: 18–34 miles northwest of Boulder

Elevation: 6,000–12,000′

Access: Within 100′ of road, minimal elevation gain

Fish: Brown trout, rainbow, cutthroat, and brook trout higher up

Flies: AK's Olive Quill size 16–22, St. Vrain Caddis size 14–16, Beadhead Prince Nymph size 8–16, Beadhead Pheasant Tail Nymph size 16–22

Maps and books: USFS Roosevelt and Arapaho National Forests maps; *Flyfisher's Guide to Colorado; Fly Fishing Colorado's Front Range*

Heads up: Rattlesnakes and long steep hikes—bring a first-aid kit, food, and water.

Description: The St. Vrain is dreamlike mountain trout fishing—twisting, rock-strewn currents, deadfall and deep pocket water. Often hemmed in by trees and brush for challenges in presentation. You can fish pretty much anywhere on the three forks of the creek and have fun. I've listed three stretches, one with excellent roadside fishing, and the others involving tough hikes. If you're hiking, be prepared for bad weather and bring food and water.

Directions: To get to the South Fork, drive north on US 36 to CO 7 in Lyons. Turn left (west). The south fork of the

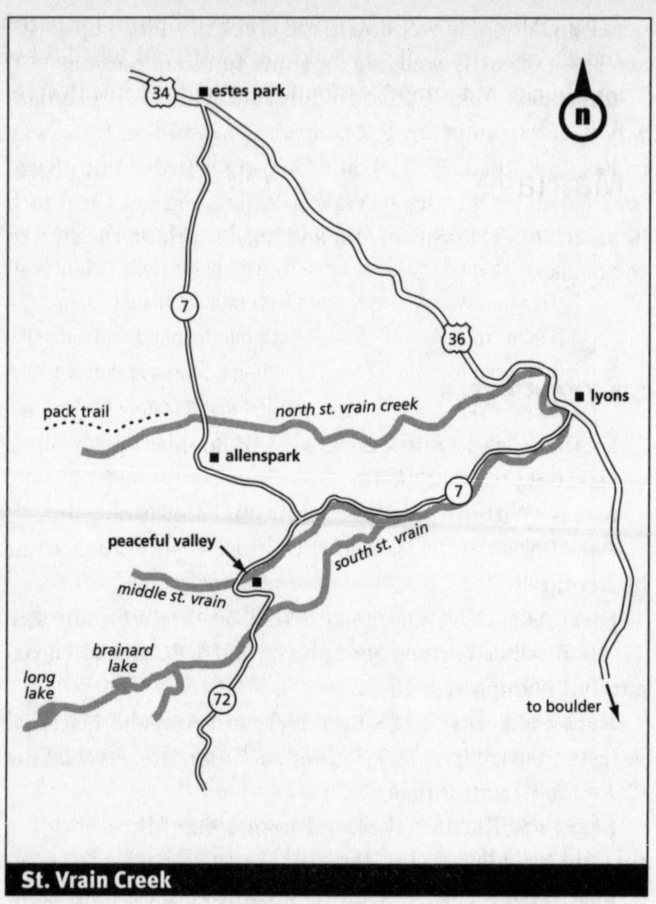

St. Vrain Creek

St. Vrain lies next to the highway for the next 10 miles to its confluence with the Middle Fork.

For the Middle Fork, continue west on CO 7 to the fork with the Peak to Peak Highway (CO 72). Turn left (south) to Peaceful Valley and the trailhead. A 5-mile hike takes you to the headwaters at St. Vrain glaciers (12,000′). This is a hard hike; bring food and water.

The North Fork is located farther north and west on CO

7, past Allenspark. Go left (west) at Wild Basin for parking and access. The Thunder Lake or Pack Trail will lead you into Rocky Mountain National Park and the headwaters.

Marriage

June Kistler has lived in Denver most of her life. She's in her seventies and has been fly-fishing for close to fifty years. Her son, Willy, a pretty good fisherman in his own right, claims that she can outfish both her husband and himself. "She can think like a fish," he brags. She says that she and her husband Bill had been married just a couple of years when they took a guided, three-day float trip on the Snake: "My very first cast I caught the guide in the ear." Since then, she caught the bug, and she and Bill have made a lifelong avocation of fly-fishing together up near Deckers on the South Fork of the South Platte. "The rainbows are the big fighters," she says. "They jump around toward the middle. I like to fish browns. You've heard of the wiley brown trout? They hang near the banks. They're natives and they're fun." One summer morning, twenty-five years into their marriage, she and Bill were fishing side by side up on the South Fork. "It was a big hatch. We don't seem to have hatches like we used to—some people blame it on insect sprays. Anyway, it started to warm up and the dry flies started to explode, a lot of blue quills and Adams. I've never seen a hatch like it. And they [the trout] were taking what we had. The fish were really boiling. And we made this game. One of us would cast at a time. You got three casts, and if you didn't catch a fish the other guy got to cast. We did that for over an hour. I'll never forget it." She says she fishes barbless, and one of the joys of fishing is to release a fish unharmed. When she releases them they hang around her feet, getting their energy back. There's a real connection between woman and fish. June says, "It's like they're saying 'Thanks. See you next time.'"

SOUTH PLATTE RIVER BELOW CHEESMAN DAM

Location: 53 miles southwest of Denver

Elevation: 6,560′

Access: About a 1-mile, easy-to-moderate, 20-minute walk up the Gill Trail to reach the river

Fish: Rainbow and brown trout

Flies: Black Beauty Pupa size 16–24, Miracle Nymph size 18–24, Flashback Pheasant Tail Nymph size 16–20, Trico Spinner size 18–26

Special regulations: Artificial flies and lures only. All fish must be released immediately

Maps and books: USFS Pike National Forest map; *Colorado Atlas and Gazetteer; Flyfisher's Guide to Colorado; Fly Fishing Colorado's Front Range*

Heads up: You saw it in a dream.

Description: About 1 hour and 20 minutes from downtown Denver is a stretch of archetypal trout water that is rated one of the ten most productive trout streams in America. A 20-minute walk on the Gill Trail brings you to the first view of red canyon walls and boulders rising out of deep pools. This is a popular spot, so as with most streams, the farther you're willing to walk, the quieter it gets. The trail follows the river upstream to Cheesman Reservoir, and the fishing tends to get better the higher you go. Another way into the upper canyon is a bit more strenuous and consequently less crowded (see Option). There are plenty of monster trout, though, and they tend to be less discerning than their jaded cousins below. The 1½-mile trail drops 300 feet in a third of a mile; remember that what goes down must come back up. Use a 10-foot, 6x leader for best results, and fish in lousy weather.

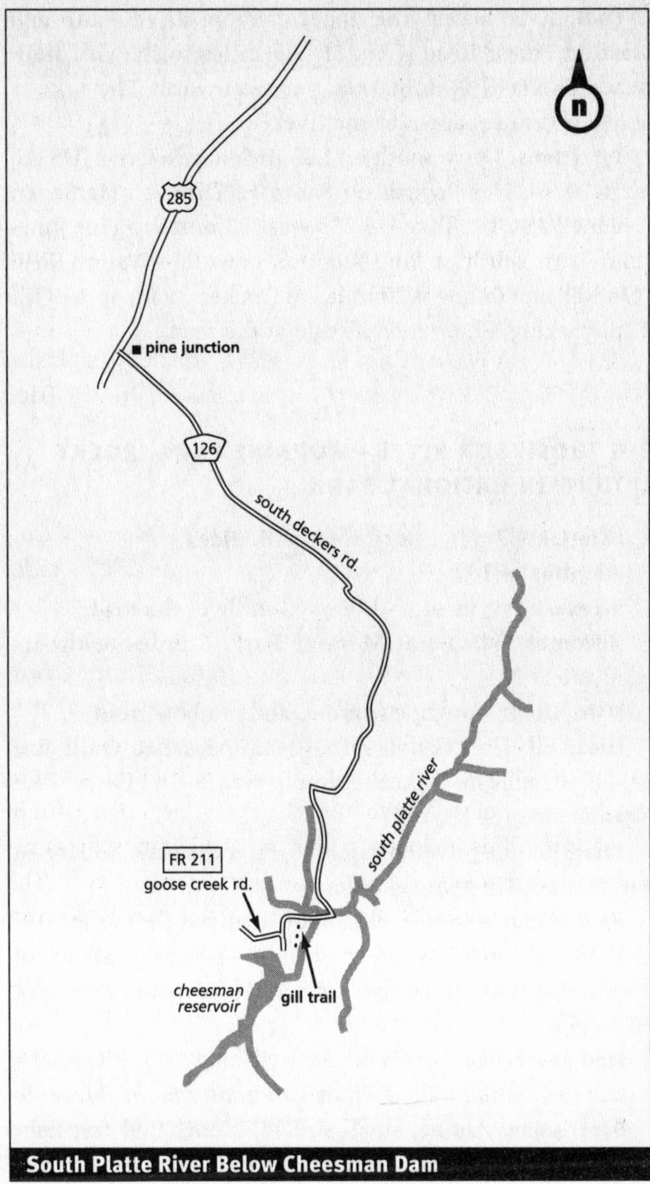

South Platte River Below Cheesman Dam

Option: To access the upper canyon, drive south and west on Forest Road (FR) 211, 2.5 miles to the Gill trailhead. The trail is unmarked yet well-worn. The hike is about 1 1/2 miles down to the river.

Directions: Drive south on I-25 to Santa Fe Drive (US 85) (exit 207B). Head south on Santa Fe Drive to Hampden Avenue (US 285). Take US 285 west 33 miles to Pine Junction. Turn south at Pine Junction onto Pine Valley Road (126 RD) and follow it 20 miles to Deckers. Park at the Gill Trail parking lot, on the left side of the road.

BIG THOMPSON RIVER—MORAINE PARK, ROCKY MOUNTAIN NATIONAL PARK

Location: 37 miles northwest of Boulder

Elevation: 8,100′

Access: Easy, most within a half mile of the road

Becomes fishable at Moraine Park, 6 miles below its headwaters

Fish: Brook, brown, cutthroat, and rainbow trout

Flies: Elk Hair Caddis size 10–22, AK's Red Quill size 14–18, Beadhead Prince Nymph size 8–16, Olive Biot Nymph size 18–22

Fee: $15 for a private vehicle to enter the park, $30 for an annual pass. Camping is extra

Special regulations: Single-hook artificial flies or lures

Heads up: Small-stream conditions—bring a small box of dry flies; a short, quick rod; a 7.5-foot leader; and a spool of 5X tippet.

Map and books: Trails Illustrated map 200; *Flyfisher's Guide to Colorado; Fly Fishing Colorado's Front Range*

Description: Alpine, small-stream, crouch-and-cast fishing at its best. The banks are grassy and undercut, without much cover, so walk back away from the bank and be

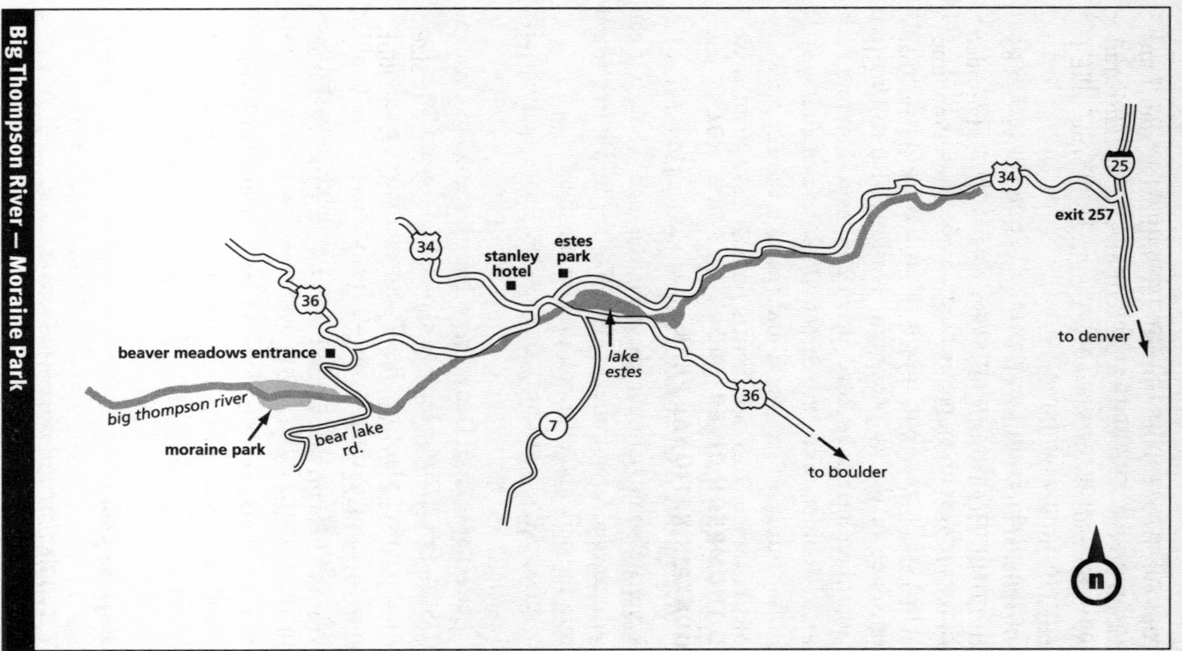

Big Thompson River — Moraine Park

wiley. The river splits 150′ upstream from parking area; follow the north fork (to the right) for the best fishing. This 2-mile section of the Big Thompson has brookies, browns, cutthroats, and rainbows.

Directions: From Denver, take I-25 north to Loveland (US 34, exit 257). Go left (west) on US 34 to Estes Park. Drive through town, past where US 36 merges with US 34. When US 36 forks left, take it to the Beaver Meadows Park entrance of Rocky Mountain National Park. Turn left (south) on Bear Lake Road; drive 2 miles to Moraine Park. From Boulder, take 28th Street (US 36) north and west 37 miles, through Estes Park, and through the Beaver Meadows entrance. Turn left (south) on Bear Lake Road; drive 2 miles to Moraine Park.

Option: Big Thompson Canyon below Lake Estes has some awesome fishing right along the road. Though it can get crowded in summer, most folks are in a hurry to get into the park and overlook this great fishery.

Flies: AK's Red Quill size 14–18, Rusty Spinner size 12–20

Directions: From Denver travel north on I-25 to Loveland (US 34, exit 257). Go left (west) on US 34 toward Estes Park. At the power plant the Big Thompson River parallels the road up through the canyon—fish anywhere. From Boulder, take 28th Street (US 36) north to the junction with US 34 in Estes Park. Turn right (northeast) and drive through town. Fish from the bottom of Lake Estes down through the canyon.

BLUE RIVER

Location: 57 miles west of Denver
Elevation: 8,100′

Access: Try to carry all your gear with a frozen cappuccino and hot dog from the 7-11

Fish: Rainbow, brown, and brook trout; Snake River cutthroat trout and Kokanee salmon

Flies: *Mysis* shrimp size 14–18, Black Beauty size 18–24, AK's Red Quill size 14–18, Green Drake size 10–12

Special regulations: Below Dillon Reservoir downstream to the northern city limits of Silverthorne, all fish must be

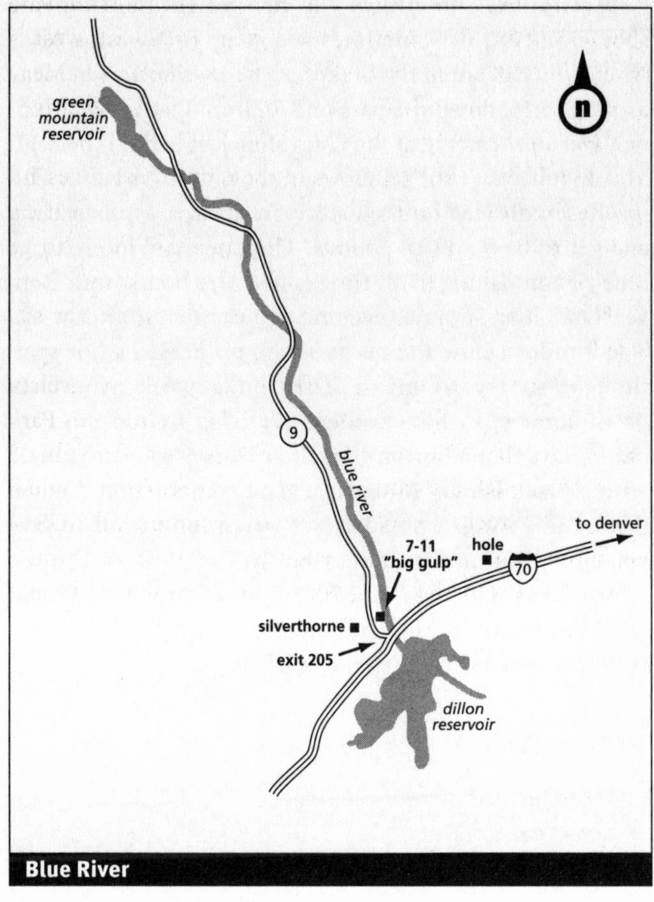

Blue River

returned immediately to the water. From the northern city limits of Silverthorne to Blue River's confluence with the Colorado, the possession limit is two trout, 16" or longer.

Maps and book: USFS Arapaho National Forest map; *Colorado Atlas and Gazetteer; Flyfisher's Guide to Colorado*

Heads up: Taut-line shrimping par excellence. If you want to catch a HOG don't get lazy—keep adjusting the strike indicator and weight so your shrimp bounces along the bottom.

Description: Sometimes you fish for the solitude and sheer beauty of it. Sometimes you go up to Asbestos Alley where you can smell the brakes of the 18-wheelers burning as they barrel down the pass on I-70 from Eisenhower Tunnel; you start casting at Big Gulp Hole just behind the 7-11. You do it because the rainbows in the tailwaters below Dillon Reservoir feed on prehistoric freshwater *Mysis* shrimp and get to be 5 and 10 pounds. The interstate-interchange blue-ribbon fishing of all time is just 1^1/2 hours from Denver. On a long summer evening you can fish it after work. The 2 miles below the reservoir are prime. It's a hot spot, though, so try to hit it early on a weekday. Marty Bartholomew, in his excellent *Flyfisher's Guide to Colorado,* says that a Burton's *Mysis* or Dorsey's *Mysis* teamed with a Black Beauty Midge is a great combination. "When fishing this setup," he advises, "watch for a trout to give you an indication that it ate your fly."

Directions: Go west on I-70 to Silverthorne (CO 9, exit 205). Turn right (north) and find the river behind the 7-11. Follow it down the valley along CO 9.

A Mecca Worth Driving To

THE FRYINGPAN—BASALT

Location: 160 miles west of Denver

Elevation: 7,800′

Access: Easy

Fish: Rainbow (below Ruedi Reservoir they reach double-digit weights), brown, cutthroat, and brook trout

Flies: *Mysis* shrimp size 14–18, Black Biot Midge size 16–24, Lawson's Parachute Green Drake size 10–12, Beadhead Bread Crust size 10–18, AK's Red Quill size 14–18

Special regulations: From Ruedi Reservoir downstream to the Roaring Fork River is Gold Medal Water—artificial flies and lures only; all trout except browns must be immediately returned to the water; bag and possession limit for browns is two fish less than 14″.

Maps: *Colorado Atlas and Gazetteer.* Call White River National Forest (970-945-1084) for additional information

Heads up: Best of the best. An 8-pound brookie was caught here in 1996.

Description: World-famous tailwater fishing below Ruedi Reservoir, with the trout fattening on the freshwater *Mysis* shrimp. The Fryingpan may be a circus—guys manically tying flies on tailgate vises, Germans with two thousand flies in fold-down chest tackle boxes—but most people who love to fish find the crowds worth an occasional visit. So much has been written about the Fryingpan . . . suffice it to say that it's worth the drive from Denver or Boulder.

Directions: Drive west on I-70 to Glenwood Springs (CO 82, exit 116). Go south on CO 82 to Basalt, where the Fryingpan converges with the Roaring Fork River. Take Fryingpan Road (FR 105) east to Ruedi Reservoir. Public and private sections are easily distinguished.

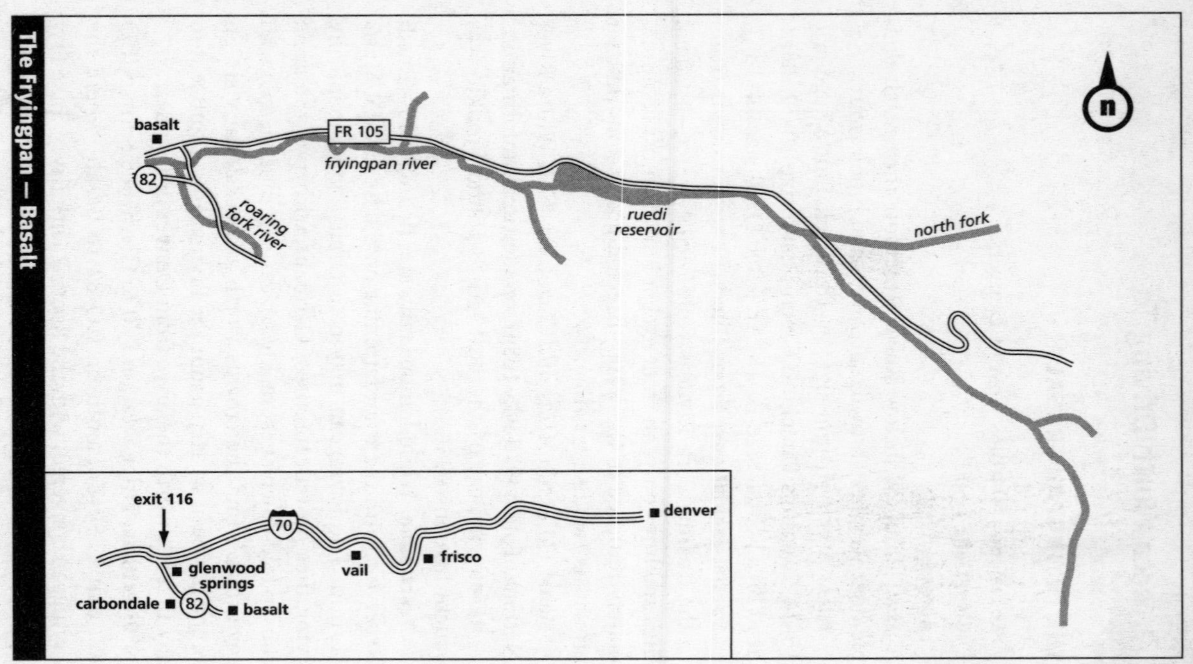
The Fryingpan — Basalt
n
basalt
FR 105
82
fryingpan river
roaring fork river
ruedi reservoir
north fork
exit 116
70
glenwood springs
vail
frisco
denver
carbondale
82
basalt

Where to Connect

Books

Flyfisher's Guide to Colorado, by Marty Bartholomew (Belgrade, Mont.: Wilderness Adventure Press, 1999).

Fly Fishing Colorado's Front Range: An Angler's Guide, by Todd Hosman (Boulder, Colo.: Pruett Publishing, 1999).

Fishing Close to Home: Fishing Spots and Information for All Age Groups, Metro Denver, Boulder and Nearby Lakes and Streams (Hudson, Colo.: Outdoor Books & Maps, 1999).

Shops

Denver

The Flyfisher, Ltd.
120 Madison Street
Denver, CO 80206
(303) 322-5014

Boulder

Front Range Anglers
629 South Broadway
Boulder, CO 80302
(303) 442-6204

Evergreen

The Hatch Fly Shop
28055 Highway 74, #202
Evergreen, CO 80439
(303) 674-0482

Rock Climbing

THE NUMBER OF serious rock climbers who live in Denver and Boulder and have real jobs is astounding. You can go to Yosemite in the summer and meet a lot of climbers who are just climbing, many living on a shoestring in order to pursue their passion. Go to Boulder, or to one of the Denver climbing gyms, and you meet people who are engineers and computer scientists and full-time moms who are very skilled climbers. For outdoor climbing, they hit Boulder Canyon after work, just minutes from downtown, with hundreds of routes. They run down to world-famous Eldorado Canyon for multipitch evening climbs, or work out the bouldering problems on Flagstaff Mountain and Mt. Sanitas. Denverites can be at

prime bouldering just outside of Morrison in half an hour, or on a tough single-pitch face climb at Table Mountain in Golden in twenty minutes.

Rock Gyms

It's becoming less and less of an oxymoron—a serious career and great climbing. Part of that is undoubtedly the booming growth of rock gyms and indoor sport climbing. Lead climbing in a rock gym is about as boiled down an urban adventure experience as you can get. In the middle of the city, on a black and sleety night, you can be in a tank top and shorts, thirty feet up on an overhanging wall, reaching for a 5.12 move and a clip-in you could be proud of on any cliff. Climbing gyms are a new phenomenon, only about fifteen years old, and their popularity is a testament to the hunger for adventure in the cities.

Climb on lunch break, climb before bed. Run down and do pull-ups on the sloped holds of the fingerboard. Finesse the boulder problem you've been working on so hard for so long you see it in your dreams. Even the most die-hard crag climber will admit the usefulness of a climbing gym for technique and strength training. As one Boulder mom put it as she belayed her three-year-old, "You can get so much stronger in a gym. It's so much less time consuming than a climb outside. Here, you can do twenty routes in a couple of hours. And you can bring your kids." And quite a few climbers, while they may be slow to admit it, only like indoor sport climbing. They like the athleticism and tactics of climbing, but in the controlled, relatively safe setting of a gym. Also, on a cliff, you're committed to climbing the same route as your partner. In a gym, you can belay your partner up a 5.13, then switch routes and have her belay you up a 5.9. A place for siblings, friends, lovers, and spouses of different ability levels to climb together and have a great time.

If you've never been to a rock gym, it's worth going just for the spectacle. It's like walking into a crypt commissioned by Jackson Pollack: putty colored walls arch into overhangs, all spackled and specked and flagged with strips of electric tape in every color, and chips and blobs and ovals and tiny skulls (the eye holes are finger holds) set in faux granite and sandstone. Quick draws—carabiners on short slings clipped to protection bolts—zag up the bedazzled faces and swing from the overhanging roofs. Giant spiders live in this crazy lair. The ropes dangle like webs from the tops of the walls, from the harnesses of the lead climbers who stretch and cling and pull up a length of rope to clip into the next fixed piece. There's usually some bad rock 'n' roll playing out of the high speakers, but you can hear breathing, and the short commands of the climbers, and the grunt or sigh as someone loses it and peels. Through all of this the spiders move, upward, outward, at impossible angles, with surprising grace and smoothness and distilled strength. It's a study in coiled and collected power to watch the good ones, and there are so many good ones at the gyms. The measured, tactical gymnastic flow up a face is almost magical. I loved these gyms from the first one I walked into. And I was surprised at how many families were climbing together—little sons belaying big dads, mothers and daughters.

Included in this chapter are the climbing gyms of the metro area, three in Denver and one in Boulder, and a climber/gymnast training center in Boulder. All of the gyms have weight-training rooms and pro shops with full lines of rental gear. Chalk up and go.

The Climbing Areas

When I was eighteen I was almost shot off the rough stone facade of a bank in Brooklyn. I don't think the security guys understood what the chalk bag dangling from the orange-and-white harness was, or why I was heading for the second-story window ledge and a good rest. In Blois, France, I was yelled off the crumbling wall of a medieval chateau by indignant locals in berets carrying baguettes. When I apologized in my strange accent they took me for a Quebecois, which apparently explained everything.

Boulderites and Denverites are spared these indignities by the proliferation of climbing gyms and by the proximity of some of the world's best rock climbing—Eldorado Canyon is twenty minutes from Boulder, forty-five from Denver. Hundreds and hundreds of superb routes are nearer still, from 5.4 classic slab climbing on the Flatirons to delicate crack-and-face climbing in Boulder Canyon and up on North Table Mountain in Golden. The weather is usually temperate enough, and there are enough south-facing cliffs, that a dedicated climber can have fun all year. Included in this chapter are five climbing areas very close to Boulder or Denver or both. This book isn't the place for route descriptions, which are highly technical, so these entries include only brief descriptions of the kinds of climbing you'll find at each spot and directions to the parking areas. Also listed are the best guidebooks for each spot, in which you'll find detailed route descriptions, safety precautions, gear recommendations, climbing history, regulations, and anything else you'll need to know.

Thanks to Stewart M. Green, Phillip Benningfield, Richard Rossiter, Mark Rolofson, Peter Hubbel, and Deaun Schovajsa for the great information in their excellent guidebooks. You'll definitely need their books to climb well at the different crags.

Denver City Limits

PARADISE ROCK GYM

6260 North Washington Street, Unit 5
Denver, CO 80216
(303) 286-8168
www.ParadiseRock.com

Location: 9 miles north of Denver

Description: The oldest climbing-only gym in the country. A lot of greats have come out of this gym. With 27-foot walls, it's not the highest, but it makes up for it with an extensive bouldering loft upstairs featuring a lot of severely angled overhang problems and pea gravel landing surface for the roped routes.

This gym is about the friendliest to a newcomer—the staff was warm and helpful, as were most of the climbers, which can mean a lot for a novice stepping into this intimidating sport. Charles Fryberger, one of the trainers, says, "Nowadays, most of the cutting-edge climbers are boulderers, so a lot depends on your bouldering terrain. We have some of the best angles going." Paradise offers the excellent and inexpensive Monday Night Special, a 1½-hour introductory lesson that includes rental gear for about $20. Definitely the best deal in the area for beginners. The gym also has many kids' programs, including the Denver Climbing League. Each year, from October through March, this competition series, the biggest of its kind in the country, invites kids in grades 7 through 12 to participate in this fun, seven-event series held on Saturday nights.

Directions: Drive north on I-25 to 58th Avenue (exit 215) and turn right (east). Drive to Washington Street and turn left (north). Go four blocks and turn right into industrial warehouses. It's clearly marked.

ROCK'N & JAM'N (GYM)

9499 North Washington Street, Unit C
Thornton, CO 80229
(303) 254-6299
E-mail: belayme@worldnet.att.net

Location: 11 miles north of Denver

Description: A little bit up the road from the venerable Paradise is the flashy upstart ROCK'n & JAM'n climbing gym. The walls have been pushed up to an impressive 37 feet, with a section crowned by overhanging terrain; these are good, long lead climbs for an urban gym. The bouldering grotto is upstairs. With air conditioning, an air-filtration system, and about eight new routes set every week—oh, and as this is the only climbing gym in Denver to have a spacious locker room with showers—the owners are confident in describing their gym as being "a little more upscale." This seems to be the case, with a concurrent rise in prices, and a significant increase in attitude among the climbers. ROCK'n & JAM'n offers excellent introductory classes (about $30 with gear) and ongoing instruction, an afternoon Belay Time For Kids age 6 and above, and a Kids' Climbing School for climbers age 12–18.

Directions: Drive north on I-25 to Thornton Parkway (exit 220) and turn right (east). Drive to Washington Street and turn right (south). Go to the backside of the shopping center and turn right into the parking lot.

THRILLSEEKERS (GYM)

1912 South Broadway
Denver, CO 80210-4005
(303) 733-8810
www.thrillseekers.cc

Location: Just south of downtown

Description: Welcome to downtown funk, in-the-heart-of-the-city, South Broadway serious indoor climbing. Thrillseekers resides in the old Jewel movie theater, which also was Kitty's Triple-X. On the marquee, the silhouette of a nude has been replaced with a climber stretching for an overhang move. Inside, the ambience is cryptlike, with a climbing pillar dividing the grottoes and 26-foot walls arching to a 40-foot roof traverse, the only one of its kind in the area. A weight-training area with the feel of Muscle Beach sits on a platform in the middle of the gym, along with a difficult balance traverse, finger boards, and campus boards. The atmosphere is friendly and dedicated. A couple of the country's best sport climbers have come out of this gym, which prides itself on setting climbs "true to grade," which means that a 5.12 at Thrillseekers is really a 5.12. Kevin, one of the managing staff, explained, "A lot of gyms grade their climbs soft so that their climbers come out all pumped up saying, 'Hey, I climbed a 5.11,' when they really climbed a 5.10. Here, we set true to grade so that when you get out on the cliff you know what you're getting into." Kevin went on to say that one of the gym's philosophies relies on Checking Your Ego at the Door. "A lot of climbers get a real attitude. If you're not housing the homeless or feeding the poor you don't impress me. It's just rock climbing." *Note:* Children under 8 are not allowed to climb.

Directions: Drive south on I-25 to Broadway (exit 207A) and turn right (south). Go just over a mile on Broadway. Thrillseekers sits between West Jewel Avenue and West Asbury Avenue on the east side of Broadway.

Denver Backyard

MORRISON WALL—MORRISON

Location: 15 miles southwest of Denver

Book: *Colorado Bouldering*

Heads up: Killer bouldering.

Description: Twenty-five minutes from Denver is some of the best, most accessible bouldering anywhere. Phillip Benningfield, in his comprehensive and excellent book, *Colorado Bouldering,* calls the Morrison Wall "pure, undistilled urban bouldering," and says that the "severely overhanging walls of the Lobby Area and the Black Hole offer the most concentrated sections of desperate bouldering in Colorado and possibly in the States." He also mentions that the Wall's proximity to Denver and its almost instant access from the road make it grossly popular. Great for winter days, because the Wall faces south. If it's too crowded, try the north-facing hillside across the highway and the creek from the main wall.

Directions: Go west on 6th Avenue (US 6) to I-70 westbound. Take I-70 to the Morrison (CO 26) exit. Drive south on CO 26 to Morrison. At the stoplight turn left and park at the end of town on the right. The wall is across the road. You can't miss it.

Boulder City Limits

BOULDER ROCK CLUB (GYM)

2829 Mapleton Avenue
Boulder, CO 80301

(303) 447-2804
www.boulderrock.com

Location: North of Boulder

Description: It may be just rock climbing, but you'd never guess it here. The attitude at this gym is so thick it gives the climbers extra resistance training. This said, the Boulder Rock Club is a premier gym that prides itself on the best route setting in the land, on everchanging routes, and on the high skill level of its trainees. The club also offers amazing programs for kids, starting at age 5, and two coed junior teams who train as seriously as any soccer or football squad. An extensive bouldering cave is upstairs. Introductory and advanced lessons, personal training, and an outdoor guide service are available. There is no age cut-off as long as the little climber fits into the gear: "Typically, younger than 2 is too small." (!)

Directions: Go north on 28th Street to Mapleton Avenue and turn right (east). Turn left (north) into the parking lot.

COLORADO ATHLETIC TRAINING SCHOOL (GYM)

2400 30th Street
Boulder, CO 80301
(303) 939-9699

Location: North of Boulder

Description: It's odd to walk into a huge gymnasium full of little tykes in leotards, and balance beams, and hanging rings, and learn that CATS is also an enclave for serious climbers. If you walk around to the right, and are careful not to get run over by a 4-year-old doing handsprings, you get to an intensely angled, hold-encrusted, bouldering nook. Past that is a wild looking wing of climbing walls, all angles and suspended ropes. Some of the very best climbers have trained here. If you want to be a serious acolyte, and don't care much about a social scene or an exhibition fest, then this may be the place for you. CATS owner and director, Rob Candelaria, is as unconventional as his gym. He is warm and unassuming, and you'd have to ask to find out that he was a geologist–cum–All American gymnast, a world-class rock climber, and the coach of some internationally ranked gymnasts and climbers, including five-time World Champion rock climber Robyn Erbesfield and U.S. champion Katy Brown. The drop-in fee to use the bouldering and climbing facility is a ridiculously cheap $5.

Directions: Go north on 28th Street to Pearl Street and turn right (east). Go to 30th Street and turn left (north). The school sits 100 yards east of Pearl on the east side of 30th.

Boulder Backyard

ELDORADO CANYON STATE PARK

Location: 10 miles southwest of Boulder, 31 miles northwest of Denver

Fee: This is a state park, so there's an entrance fee of $4 per day, $40 for an annual pass, and a host of regulations to be aware of.

Books: *Rock Climbing Eldorado; Rock Climbing Colorado*

Heads up: Climbing area.

Description: Southwest of Boulder lies one of the top three climbing areas in the United States. The canyon is cut by South Boulder Creek and edged with soaring sandstone crags that have become famous around the world: the Bastille, Red Garden Wall, Rincon Wall, Wind Tower, the West Ridge. The names of classic climbs like the Naked Edge, Psycho, and Rosy Crucifixion ring with almost

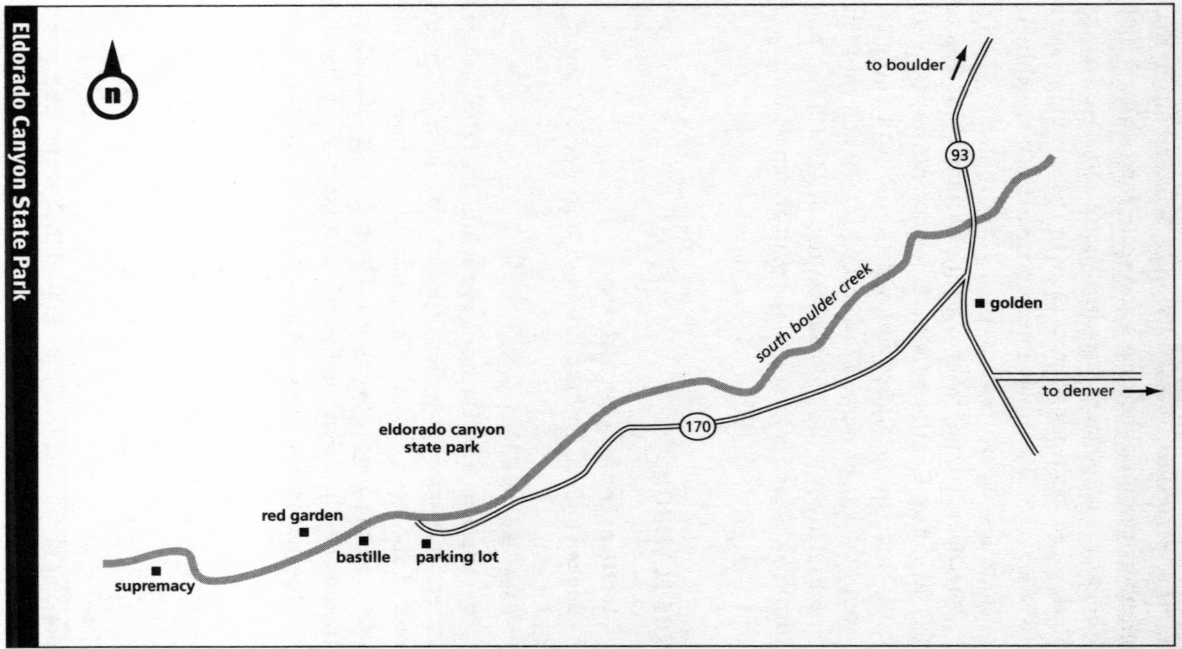

Eldorado Canyon State Park

mythic resonance. Generally mild winters mean that climbers can pick their days and scale routes year-round. The area is so popular that the classics can have waiting lines, so go midweek or very early in the morning. Use a 165-foot rope. Watch out for thunderstorms and lightning on summer afternoons.

Directions: From Denver, take 6th Avenue (US 6) west to CO 93 north. Continue to the Eldorado Springs (CO 170) exit. Turn left (west) and follow it to the park entrance. From Boulder, go west to Broadway (CO 93) and turn left (south). Drive to the Eldorado Springs (CO 170) exit and turn right (west). Follow it to the park entrance.

THE FLATIRONS

Location: South of Boulder

Books: *Rock Climbing the Flatirons; Rock Climbing Colorado*

Heads up: Climbing area.

Description: The Flatirons are Boulder's Eiffel Tower. Except that one never tires of looking at them. They are one of the most distinctive geographic features in Colorado, in the West, in America. There is something about their angle, their rhythm, the raw rock faces that bring the eye upward in a kind of visual song. Somehow they have survived being on a million logos, kept their freshness. While the slabs are cocked at 50 degrees and route ratings may not be difficult, the First and Third Flatirons are exposed, committing climbs, over 1000′, and not to be trifled with. Backing off is difficult. The East Face of the Third Flatiron is hugely popular, maybe the state's most popular climb, and has been dubbed by Yvonne Chouinard as the "finest beginner's climb in the country." But it has had its share of fatalities. So go prepared. Watch for afternoon lightning and be ready to do a three-pitch rappel off the backside.

Route: From the parking area hike up the closed road, called Kinnikinik, to the Bluebell Shelter and the road's end at 0.75 mile. To get to the First Flatiron follow the Bluebell Baird Trail northwest to the well-marked First Flatiron Trail. Take it west up a ridge. Soon the trail turns north to the base of the First Flatiron's east face. For the Third Flat-

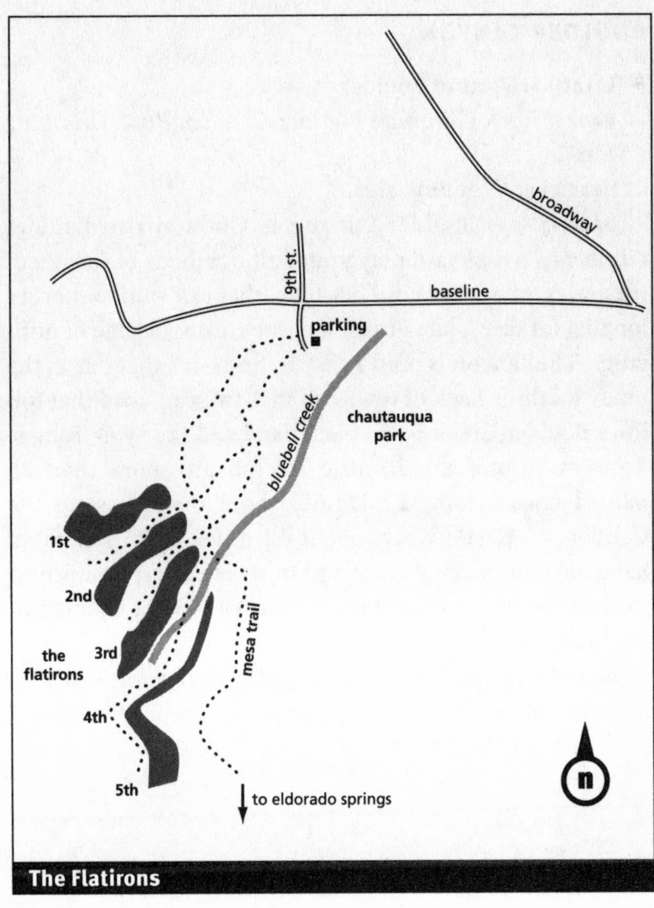

The Flatirons

iron, allow about an hour's walk. Find the Third Flatiron Trail southwest of the Bluebell Shelter and follow it to the Third Flatiron. Head for the East Bench on the northeast flank of the Flatiron for the East Face route.

Directions: From Boulder drive south on 28th Street (US 36) to Baseline and turn right (west). The entrance to Chautauqua Park is just west of Baseline and 9th Street.

BOULDER CANYON

Location: West of Boulder

Books: *Rock Climbing Boulder Canyon; Rock Climbing Colorado*

Heads up: Climbing area.

Description: Boulder Canyon is God's gift to Boulder climbers—a backyard playground of hundreds of fine granite routes, one to four pitches long, that can work out every longing for face, slab, or crack climbs, every degree of difficulty. The canyon is pretty easy to find—it's that cut in the piney foothills back of town, up that twisting road that follows Boulder Creek up to Nederland and the Wolf Tongue Brewery. Along the 16-mile stretch are more than 25 named crags, from the Dome, about 0.5 miles up the Canyon, to Castle Rock, about 12 miles up. All of them have obvious parking areas and most offer very fast access to the climbs. *Note:* Don't try to cross Boulder Creek during high water!

Directions: Head west up Canyon Boulevard (CO 119) into the canyon.

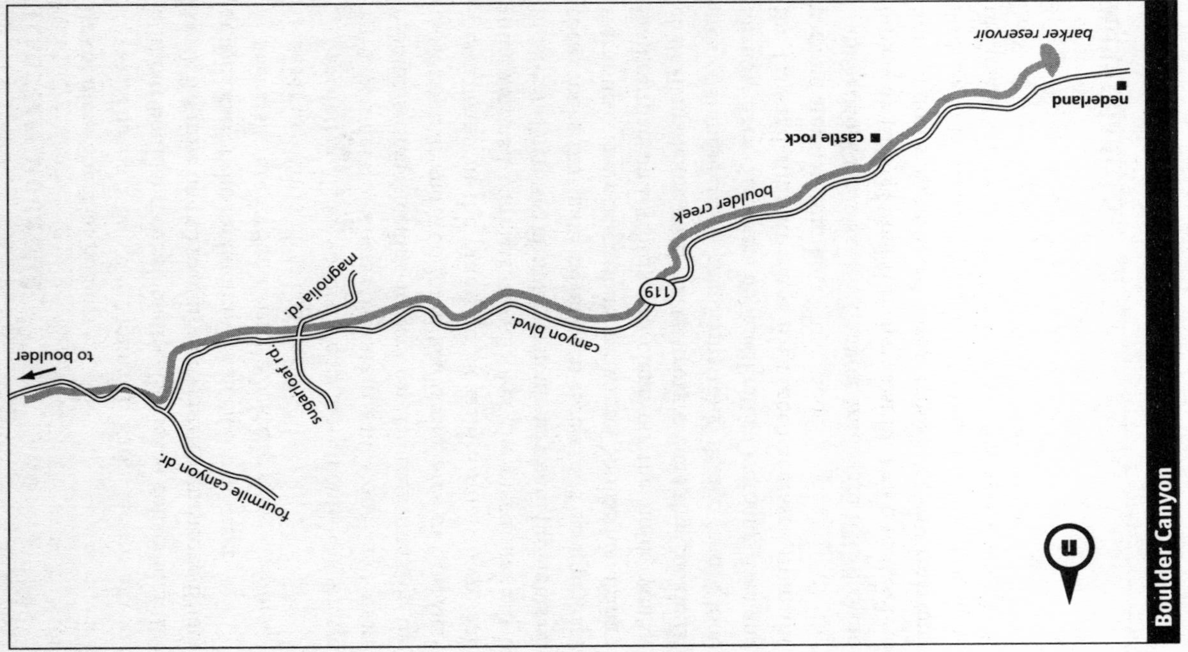
Boulder Canyon
to boulder
fourmile canyon dr.
sugarloaf rd.
magnolia rd.
canyon blvd.
119
boulder creek
castle rock
nederland
barker reservoir
n

FLAGSTAFF MOUNTAIN

Location: South of Boulder

Fee: There's a Boulder Mountain Parks fee for anyone without Boulder County plates. The fee is collected at the kiosk 0.5 mile up the road from the little Armstrong Bridge at the base of the mountain.

Books: *Colorado Bouldering; Rock Climbing Colorado*

Heads up: World-class bouldering.

Description: This wooded slope above Boulder is strewn with boulders of coarse Fountain sandstone, and more problems than bleeding fingers can count. It may be the most popular and well-loved bouldering area in Colorado. Views, wind in the pines, quick respite from town, and totally honed compatriots all over the place make it a must-try. There are brutally, ridiculously hard problems on these rocks that have never been repeated. There are easy warm-ups. There is sunshine for winter bouldering. Bring a landing pad and a brush to clean off the holds you've chalked up. Some good places to explore are the Cookie Jar area, 0.8 mile from the Armstrong Bridge; the Cloud Shadow Area, 1.5 miles up; and Pratt's Overhang Area and the Flagstaff Amphitheatre Area, both accessed from the parking area at 1.6 miles.

Directions: Go west on Canyon Boulevard (CO 119) to Broadway (CO 93) and turn left (south). Drive to Baseline Road and turn right (west). Head up Baseline to Armstrong Bridge and the start of Flagstaff Mountain Road. Park along the road.

MOUNT SANITAS

Location: 2 miles west of Boulder

Books: *Colorado Bouldering*

Heads up: Bouldering.

Description: Another fine bouldering spot on the outskirts of Boulder. Mt. Sanitas raises its steep ridge right at the western end of Mapleton Avenue. There's great hiking and running here, and the slopes are scattered with sandstone boulders offering scores of problems. Good bouldering all winter. From the parking area take the left-hand trail headed north and continue west around Mt. Sanitas on a well-engineered trail. Boulders are on the right after the steep landscaped portion of the trail.

Directions: Drive north on 28th to Mapleton Avenue and turn left (west). Go past the hospital and park in the Mt. Sanitas parking area.

Golden

NORTH TABLE MOUNTAIN

Location: 15 miles west of Denver, 19 miles south of Boulder

Books: *Classic Rock Climbs: Golden Cliffs, Colorado; Rock Climbing Colorado*

Heads up: Climbing area.

Description: A band of hard basalt cliffs yielding hundreds of sunny, 20–80′ routes looks over the suburban subdivisions of Golden, with the Coors Brewery glimmering across the valley. Mostly delicate, technical face climbing, and a lot of bolted routes for the sport climber. Great sunny exposure in the winter for year-round climbing. All of this minutes from Denver. Watch out for rattlesnakes, loose blocks, and nesting raptors. A bonus: the Golden Rec Center off of 9th Street has a sauna, whirlpool, and swimming pool available for a reasonable fee.

Directions: From Denver, take 6th Avenue (US 6) west to its intersection with CO 58 at the stoplight outside of Golden. Turn right (north) onto CO 58 and take the Washington Street exit. Turn left (north) up Washington to 1st Street. Turn right (east) and continue to Ptarmigan. Turn right (south) again and follow it to the obvious parking area. From Boulder, take Broadway (CO 93) south to Ford or Washington Streets, in Golden. Drive southeast, turn left on 1st Street and continue to Ptarmigan.

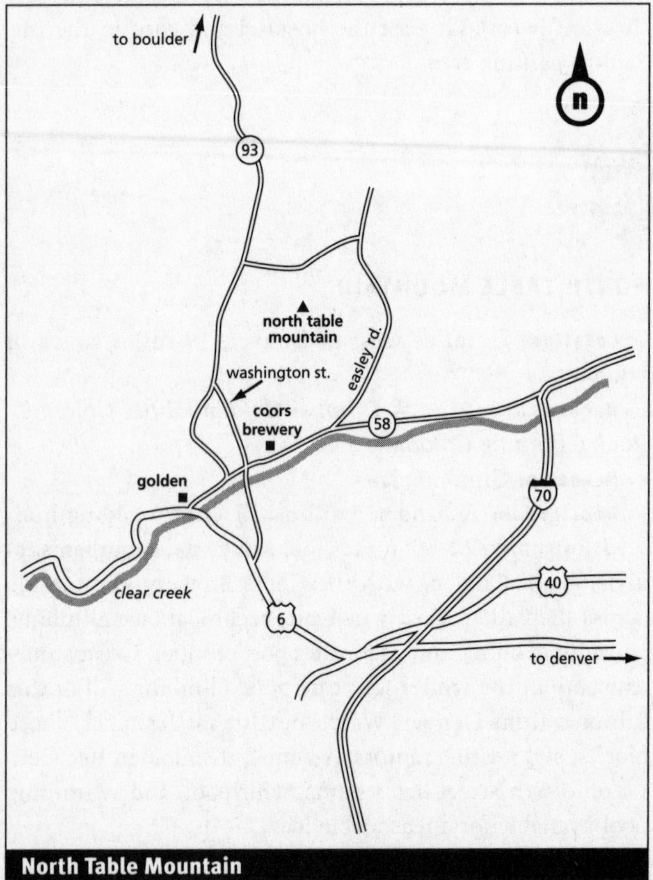

North Table Mountain

CLEAR CREEK CANYON

Location: 13 miles west of Denver, 18 miles south of Boulder

Books: *Clear Creek Canyon Sport Climbers Guide; Rock Climbing Colorado*

Heads up: Climbing area.

Description: Until 1989, Clear Creek Canyon was only of interest to kayakers, fishermen, gold panners, and those passing through on the treacherously winding US 6. That's when Boulder Mountain Parks said "No more bolts," and climbers who liked to drill abandoned Boulder Canyon and descended on Clear Creek. Now nearly 200 routes on dozens of crags thread the ancient, 1.7-billion-year-old gneiss and schist. There are a lot of steep faces and overhangs. The Sport Wall is 1.1 miles up the canyon from the intersection of US 6 and CO 58; Red Slab is at 4.1; and Anarchy Wall is at 6.4 miles, to name a few. Most of the routes are bolt-protected sport routes, though some require gear. On a clear winter day a crag can always be found soaking up the sun, and shady routes can be climbed in the heat of summer. The canyon's proximity to Denver—about half an hour from downtown to the nearest climbs—makes it a fantastic place to go after work. Watch for rattlers; park in the obvious pullouts, as far off the road as you can; and don't even try to cross Clear Creek when it's running high.

Directions: From Denver, go west on 6th Avenue (US 6) to the stoplighted intersection of US 6 and CO 58 just outside of Golden. Turn left (west) up US 6 into Clear Creek Canyon. From Boulder, take Broadway (CO 93) south to the intersection of US 6 and CO 58. Turn right (west) up US 6 into Clear Creek Canyon.

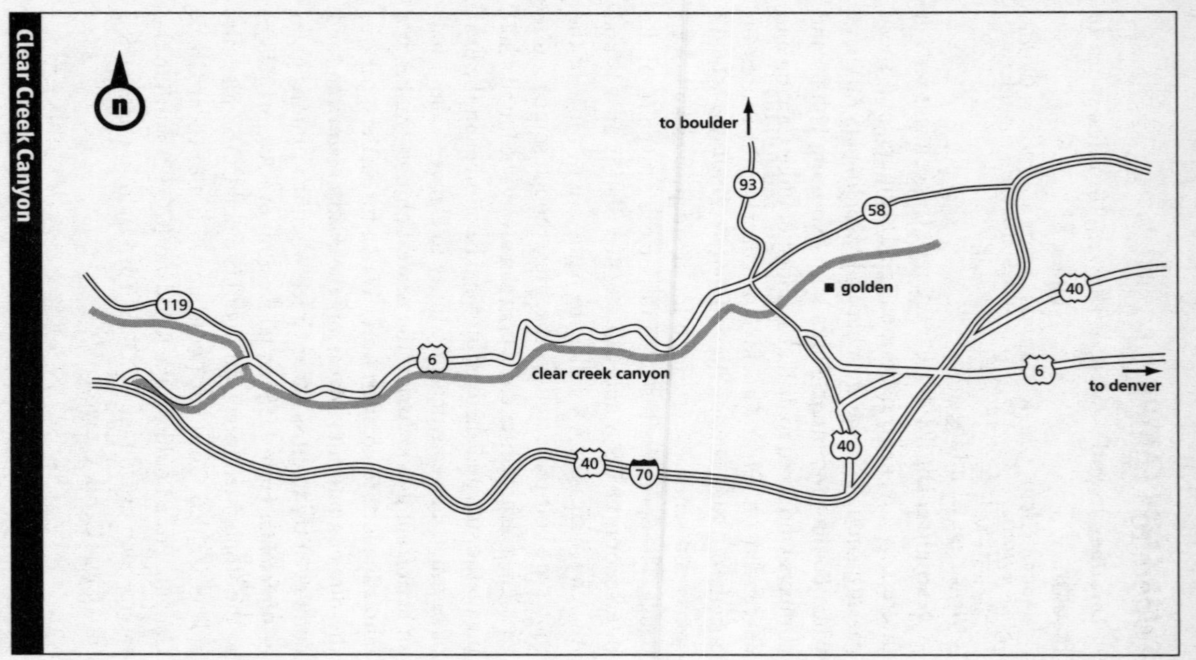

Clear Creek Canyon

Where to Connect

Books

Rock Climbing Colorado, by Stewart M. Green (Helena, Mont.: Falcon Publishing, 1995).

Colorado Bouldering, by Phillip Benningfield (Boulder, Colo.: Sharp End Publishing, 1999).

Rock Climbing Boulder Canyon, by Richard Rossiter (Helena, Mont.: Falcon Publishing, 1999).

Rock Climbing Eldorado, by Richard Rossiter (Helena, Mont.: Falcon Publishing, 2000).

Rock Climbing, the Flatirons, by Richard Rossiter (Helena, Mont.: Falcon Publishing, 1999).

Clear Creek Canyon Sport Climbers Guide, by Mark Rolofson (Boulder, Colo.: Free West Rock Guides, 1999.)

Classic Rock Climbs: Golden Cliffs, Colorado, by Peter Hubbel and Deaun Schovajsa (Helena, Mont.: Falcon Publishing, 1998).

Links

www.frontrangebouldering.com
www.rocklist.com
www.bouldering.com
www.webclimbing.com
www.freeclimbing.com

Schools and Guides

Colorado Mountain School
351 Moraine Avenue
Estes Park, CO 80517
(970) 586-5758
www.cmschool.com

Boulder Rock Club
2829 Mapleton Avenue
Boulder, CO 80301
(303) 447-2804
www.boulderrock.com

Front Range Mountain Guides
P.O. Box 17294
Boulder, CO 80308
(303) 666-5523
www.mtnguides.com

Also, climbing classes available at all of the rock gyms described.

Shops

Denver

REI
1416 Platte Street
Denver, CO 80202
(303) 756-3100

Mountain Miser
209 West Hampden Avenue
Englewood, CO 80110
(303) 761-7070

Boulder

Neptune Mountaineering
633 South Broadway
Boulder, CO 80303
(303) 499-8866

Mountain Sports
2835 Pearl Street
Boulder, CO 80301
(303) 442-8355

Golden

Bent Gate Mountaineering
1300 Washington Avenue
Golden, CO 80401
(303) 271-9382

Running

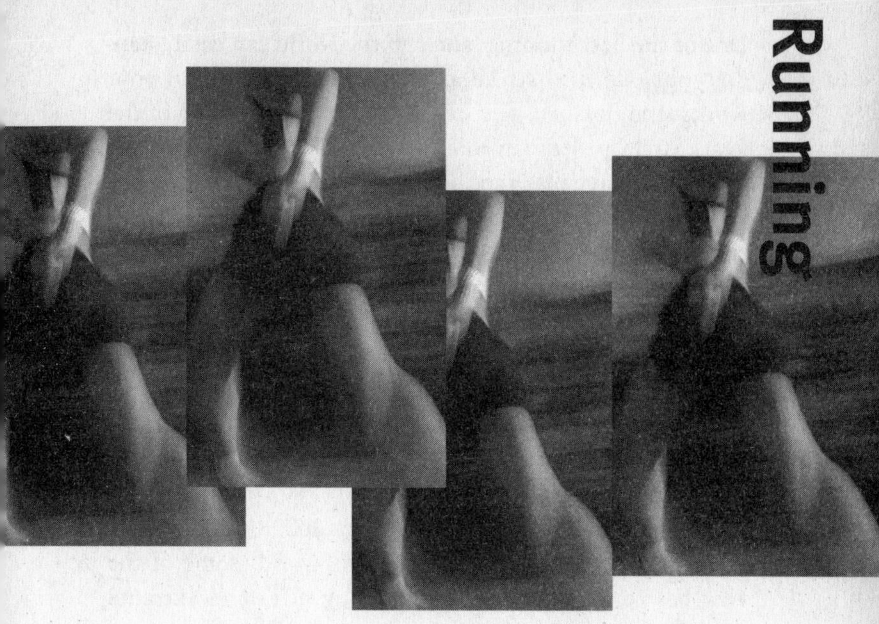

A SERIOUS RUNNER LIVING in Boulder is like a fly fisherman with a house on the banks of the Madison. There's not a lot more you could ask for. The altitude, over 5,300 feet, insures that your hemoglobin will thrive like geraniums in a hothouse. Spectacular dirt trails begin right out of the city, climb and roll through pine woods with soaring sandstone ramparts on one side and the high plains on the other. Foothill runs string along the skirts of meadowed ridges. Every combination of gradient and distance is right at the tips of your toes. A very serious running community that includes the elite of the elite in marathon and extreme endurance running is there to inspire and support and compete against you.

One of the best running stores in the world can easily handle your odd heel-strike and pronation. And when your workout is finished, you can stroll the swept bricks of the Pearl Street pedestrian mall on thighs of steel. While the slopes you have just run loom above the end of the street, you can watch the tourists gathering around the contortionist and the man who throws playing cards onto roofs, and grab a cup of French roast at Pour La France, a copy of *Cold Mountain* at the Boulder Bookstore. I'm not a serious runner, but I used to live in downtown Boulder and ran almost every day up through Chautauqua Park and into the forest beneath the Flatirons. I loved it—how quickly I could run out of the busy town and be on a lilting, narrow trail in deep woods.

Runner's World magazine (January 2000) rated Boulder the number one runners' town in the world. Some of the very best distance runners, including ultra and extreme marathoners, reside here, and almost every big name at one time or another passes through to take advantage of the tremendous terrain and camaraderie—and altitude—to train in Boulder. High plains and woods and alpine trail runs abound, most runnable from the middle of the city. There's a ton of support, from the renowned Boulder Running Company, where you can get the biomechanically perfect running shoe, to a battalion of bodyworkers, acupuncturists, Bhuddist centers, and personal coaches to ease the pain and steady the mind. A number of restaurants and health-food stores are concerned about the purity of your nutrition. Also, there's something to be said for the energy that comes from doing something you love in a beautiful place. The dramatic country—oceanic high plains washing up against the foothills of the Rockies, cresting in waves of jutting sandstone slabs and wooded ridges—it makes for an inspiring setting in which to cut loose and run. Through the woods and across the meadow and over the creek, up into the cooler evening, break out on a high bench and see half of America rolling out east below you.

Denver is no slouch either. Dirt trails edge most of the concrete bike paths, so one can hop out of work downtown and get in a good lick in the trees along Cherry Creek or the South Platte, or drive a short distance up to the High Line Canal. These are flat runs along streams. Twenty minutes from town are a host of foothill runs, from steep to rolling, with the meadowed climbs and groves of woods and big views characteristic of the Front Range. A little further out is the beautiful, wild-feeling Roxborough State Park with its red rock formations and thickets of scrub oak. Included in this chapter is a small selection of what's out there. I've varied gradients and length as much as possible. There are runs on trails that are dedicated to foot travel, and some that allow mountain bikers. Art Ives, a long-distance endurance runner and trainer in Boulder, pointed out that dedicated pedestrian trails aren't always a great advantage. He said, "The biggest danger is older folks walking little dogs. They take to the hiking-only trails because there are no bikers. And the little dogs run back and forth, and the leashes are so low. Man, you can really get tripped up."

Denver City Limits

WASHINGTON PARK

Location: Slightly southeast of Denver
Length: 3 miles around the outer loop
Terrain: Paved road edged with dirt trail
Elevation gain: None
Map: Bicycling Metro Denver Route Map
Dogs: Yes

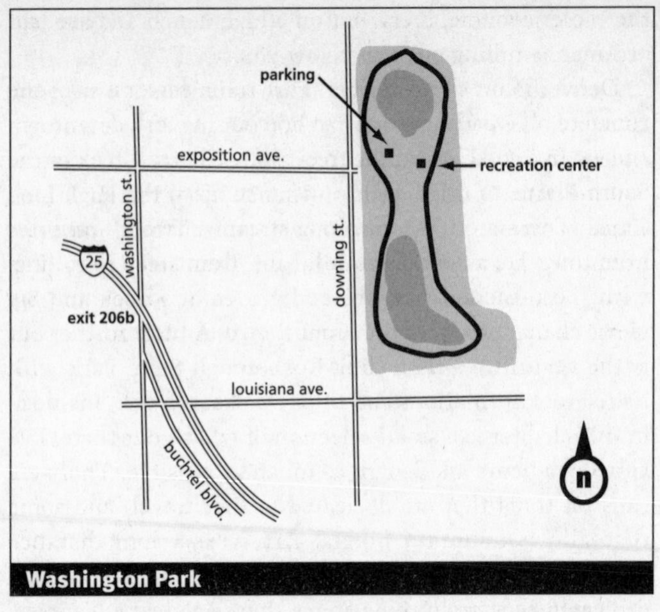

Heads up: Run to see and be seen! Flowerbeds and little lakes.

Description: This is great city running. It's the busiest park in Denver and truly lovely, with great swards of lush grass, big flower gardens, two lakes, and a stream. There's an ultra-modern rec center with a huge weight room and pool, along with tennis and basketball courts, soccer fields, lawn-bowling greens, and a lot of pick-up volleyball games. Big old oak trees and peace and prosperity. Enough said. Except that this is where the fittest of Denver, the young and the restless, the degreed and endowed, come to run. And to be seen. You can tell a lot by the fashionably frayed T-shirts that say PRINCETON CREW. Bikers whirl past around this relatively short loop—and the only reason I can figure is that they too have come to soak up the ambiance and check out the runners. It's fun and worth a visit, if not a regimen. Don't miss the statue of Wynken, Blynken, and Nod, a memorial to Denver poet Eugene Field who wrote "Dutch Lullaby," in which the three children "one night sailed off in a wooden shoe of crystal light." Hmm.

Route: Get on the dirt path and go!

Directions: Drive south on I-25 to Washington Street/ Emerson Street (exit 206B). Merge onto Buchtel Boulevard going north to Louisiana Avenue. Turn left (east) onto Louisiana. Turn left (north) onto Downing Street. Parking is located on the street or in the parking lot, toward the north side of the park.

HIGH LINE CANAL—THREE POND PARK TO ORCHARD ROAD

Location: Just south of Denver

Length: 12 miles out and back

Terrain: Flat crushed granite

Elevation gain: Minimal

Map and book: Bicycling Metro Denver Route Map; *Guide to the High Line Canal*

Dogs: Yes

Heads up: Flat gravel cruiser, flowing water in summer, big shade trees, close to downtown.

Description: This run comprises the prettiest section of the canal. The broad gravel path loops around Blackmer Commons, a meadow and wetland wildlife preserve, and through the affluent gentleman-farm horse country of Cherry Hills. Bird-watchers come from all over to scope out the sloping fields. The trail is shaded by giant cottonwoods and oaks, and in summer the cool breath of running water comes off the ditch. The trees open to occasional views of the mountains and the city to the north. Great for running with dogs or a stroller as the track is wide enough

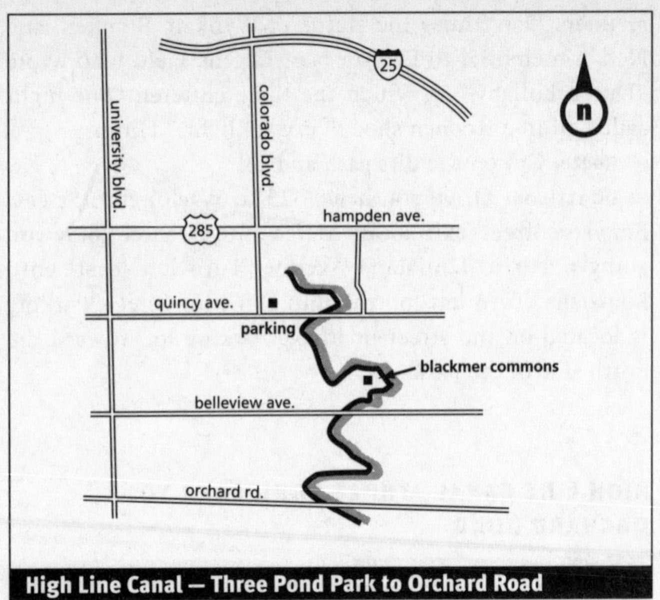

High Line Canal — Three Pond Park to Orchard Road

to accommodate enthusiasts of all sizes and degrees of furbearingness.

Route: Run south out of the parking lot along the canal. Turn around at Little Dry Creek Trail.

Option: Turn around at Belleview for a 6-mile run.

Directions: Drive south on I-25 to Colorado Boulevard (CO 2). Take Colorado Boulevard south to its end, about 1 mile, just past Hampden Avenue (US 285). The parking lot is located just north of Quincy Avenue.

BEAR CREEK LAKE TRAIL LOOP

Location: 15 miles southwest of Denver
Length: 8-mile loop
Terrain: Mostly paved trail edged by a dirt path

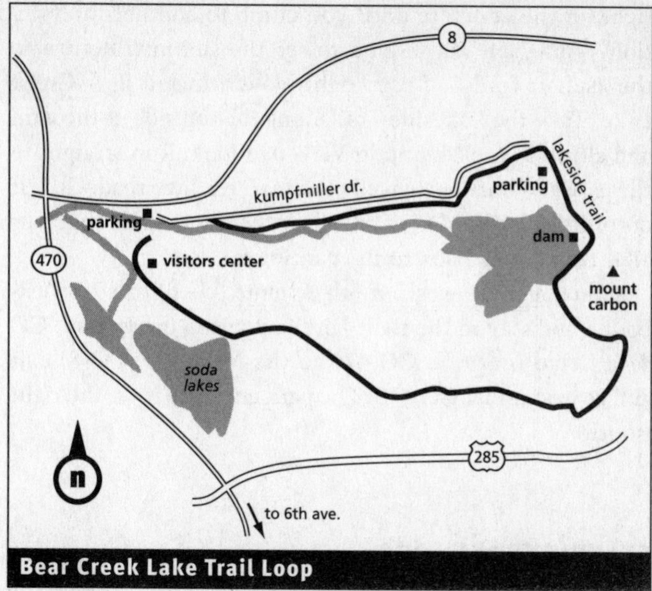

Bear Creek Lake Trail Loop

Elevation gain: 210′

Fee: This is a city park, so the cost is $5 per vehicle for a day pass. Ouch.

Map: Bear Creek Lake Park brochure

Dogs: Yes

Heads up: A little country in the city.

Description: Bear Creek is a lovely city park within the western edge of the city limits, near Morrison. The trail runs along the creek in a riparian wood of oaks and willows, skirts Bear Creek Lake, and climbs up on Mt. Carbon, which is a hill by any other name.

Route: Head south (left) out of the parking lot to the red concrete path. Cross the park road and pass the visitors center, the dirt road, the picnic sites, and continue straight on. Cross Turkey Creek and ascend toward the summit of Mt. Carbon. At the intersection with an asphalt trail, stay right on the concrete until you climb to another intersection—going left allows you to see the summit. Return to the asphalt trail and turn right, down toward Bear Creek Lake. Take the Lakeside Trail along the top side of the dam and climb to the Mountain View overlook. Run straight to the gate and onto the paved park maintenance road. Go left onto Kumpfmiller Drive or follow the horse trails that parallel Bear Creek back to the parking lot.

Directions: Go west on 6th Avenue (US 6) to I-70 westbound and stay in the right lane so you can merge onto CO 470. Drive south on CO 470 to the Morrison (CO 8) exit and go east under CO 470. The park entrance is on the right (south).

STANDLEY LAKE LOOP

Location: 14 miles northwest of Denver

Length: 2-mile loop

Terrain: Mostly paved trail edged by dirt path

Elevation gain: Minimal

Dogs: Yes

Heads up: Views of foothills and city lights.

Map: Bicycling Metro Denver Route Map

Description: Wide open grassland around a big lake. A good run for people on the northwest side of town. It is possible to see coyotes, foxes, and hawks. There are options for much longer runs. The only drawback is lack of shade and the subdivisions along the right side on the first leg.

Route: Run out of the parking lot toward the lake and bear right over the wooden bridge. Continue hard right (east) on the dirt trail that climbs a hill. You'll see a picnic shelter at the top. Continue on the trail to an intersection at 1 mile. Turn left down the hill, loop around the wood bench, and run back along the lake to your car.

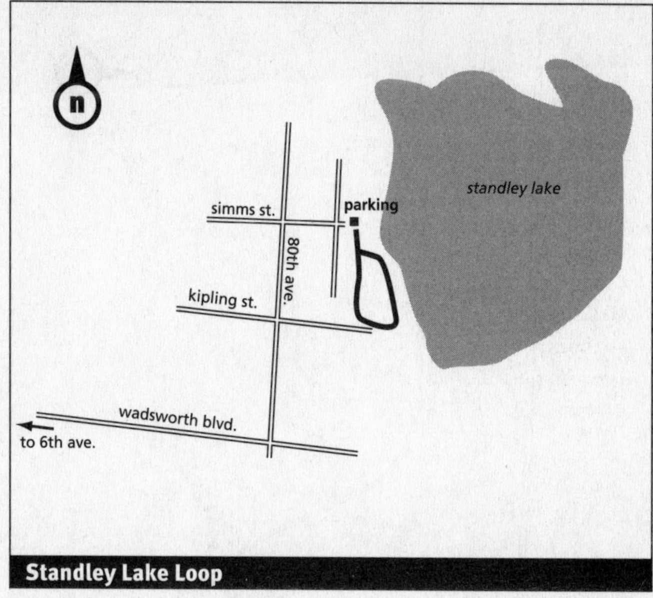

Standley Lake Loop

Directions: Drive west on 6th Avenue (US 6) to Wadsworth Boulevard. Go north on Wadsworth to 80th Avenue. Turn left (west) on 80th and drive past Kipling Street to Simms Street. Turn right on Simms and take it to its end at the lake parking lot.

Denver Backyard

GREEN MOUNTAIN—LONESOME LOOP

Location: 9 miles west of Denver
Length: 8-mile loop
Terrain: Singletrack and jeep road
Elevation gain: 800′

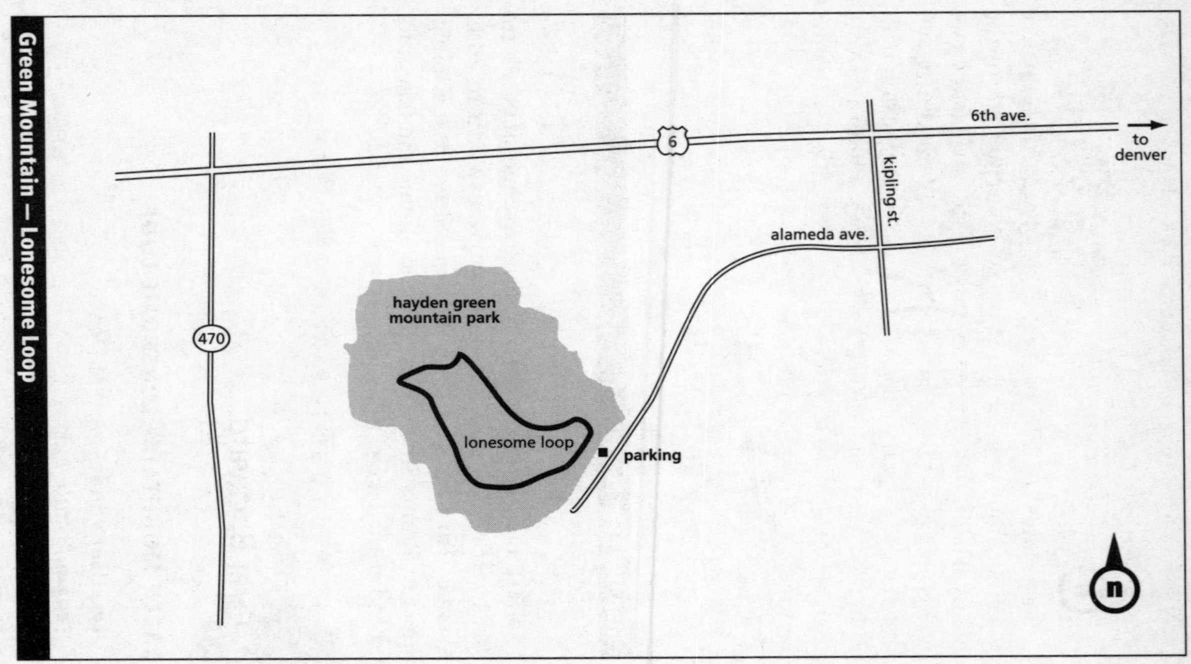
Green Mountain — Lonesome Loop
6th ave.
to denver
6
kipling st.
alameda ave.
470
hayden green mountain park
lonesome loop
parking
n

Map and book: Green Mountain Park Map; *Denver Hiking Guide*

Dogs: Yes

Heads up: Close to town, no shade!

Description: Fifteen minutes from Denver, this is one of the first mountains encountered as you chug out of the plains. The run has a good climb on a jeep road and views of Red Rocks and the city. Because of its proximity and excellent terrain, the Lonesome Loop is anything but, with mountain bikers and little dogs, so choose your time. Also, there's no shade, so don't do it on a sweltering day in midsummer; in the spring the meadows are flush with wildflowers.

Route: From the parking lot run counterclockwise to get the climb done first. Climb on the jeep road to a trail along the top of the mountain. Pass the radio towers and descend on rocky singletrack. *Note:* There are two other parking lots, but the loop is the same from each.

Directions: Take 6th Avenue (US 6) west to Kipling Street. Go south on Kipling to Alameda Avenue. Go right (west) on Alameda 3 miles to a parking area on right. The trail is part of Hayden Green MountainPark.

ROXBOROUGH STATE PARK—CARPENTER PEAK TRAIL

Location: 22 miles southwest of Denver

Length: 6.4 miles out and back

Terrain: Singletrack

Elevation gain: 1,000′

Fee: $4 state park fee

Contact: Call (303) 973-3959 for more information.

Maps and book: Trails Illustrated map 135—Deckers/Rampart Range; Roxborough State Park brochure; *Denver Hiking Guide*

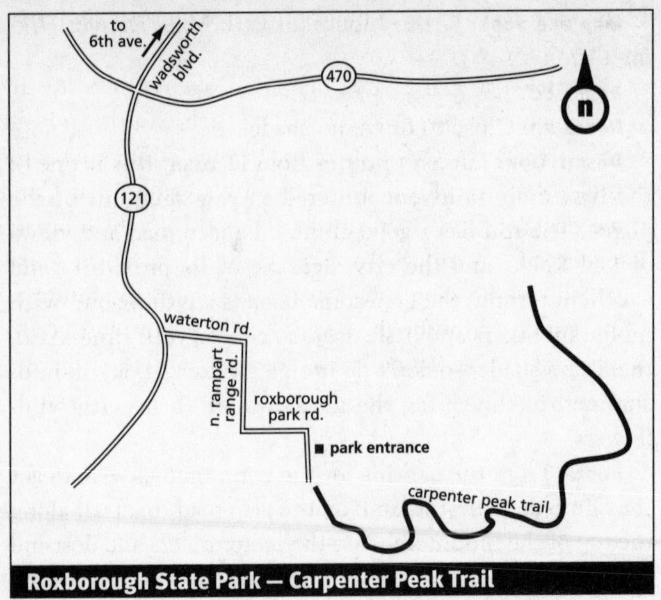

Roxborough State Park — Carpenter Peak Trail

Dogs: No

Heads up: Pedestrians only. A 360-degree view of red-rock formations, Denver, and the foothills at top.

Description: No bikes, no dogs, no ferrets. Just a beautiful, wild-feeling trail through red-rock sandstone formations and scrub oak. This is a great summit run on mostly smooth trails, with a tough climb that gains most of its 1,000 feet in 2 miles. It's pretty exposed, so don't run it in the midday heat. Excellent for sunsets! During the summertime there are concerts and full moon hikes. Be sure to look up and watch for golden eagles hunting small mammals. There are foxes, coyotes, and mountain lions—oh my!

Route: Head south on the South Rim Trail and stay right until you come to the turnoff right for Carpenter Peak Trail. Moderate to steep climb into foothills, a short break, then climb again to incredible 360-degree views at summit. Return the way you came.

Directions: Drive west on 6th Avenue (US 6) to Wadsworth Boulevard (CO 121). Turn south, follow Wadsworth under CO 470, and continue 5 miles to Roxborough/Waterton Road. Turn left on Waterton Road. Continue on Waterton Road until it ends at North Rampart Range Road (1.6 miles). Turn right (south) on North Rampart Range Road. Continue south 2.3 miles to the intersection with Roxborough Park Road. Turn left onto Roxborough Park Road. Take the next right to enter the park.

DEER CREEK CANYON PARK—MEADOWLARK TRAIL

Location: 19 miles southwest of Denver

Length: 2.7-mile loop with an option to go 5.2 miles

Terrain: Mostly smooth, hardpack trail; the beginning is a bit sandy

Elevation gain: 550′; optional route has 1,100′ gain

Map: Deer Creek Canyon Park brochure

Dogs: Yes

Heads up: High desert to low forest with a 5.4-mile option. The Meadowlark section is pedestrian only and great for kids.

Description: Beautiful red-dirt loop from high plains into foothill forest. Views of the Hogback and city lights. A sustained climb and fast descent down a foot-traffic-only trail section make it an ideal run. Mule deer, elk, turkey, grouse, mountain lion, and bear are all regulars.

Route: Start on Plymouth Creek Trail. After 1.1 miles, turn right onto hikers-only Meadowlark Trail. Switchback up into the trees and descend to the parking lot.

Option: For a 5.2-mile, 1,100′ elevation gain run, con-

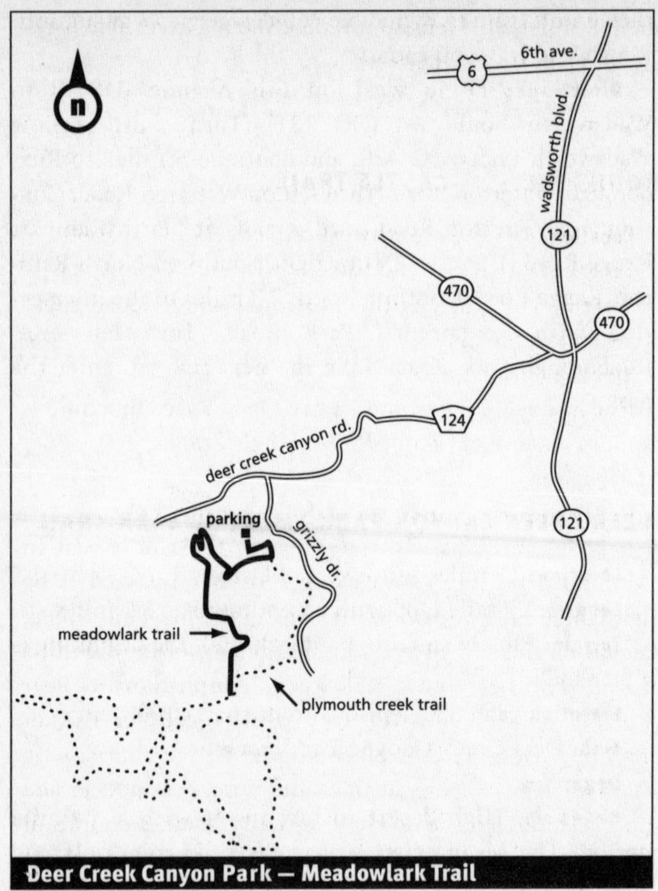

Deer Creek Canyon Park — Meadowlark Trail

tinue up Plymouth Creek Trail past the Meadowlark Trail junction to the Plymouth Mountain Trail on the left. Run the loop and return to the parking lot on the Plymouth Creek Trail.

Directions: Go west on 6th Avenue (US 6) 3.5 miles to Wadsworth Boulevard (CO 121). Turn left (south) and continue about 12 miles to Deer Creek Canyon Road (124 RD) Turn right (west) onto Deer Creek Canyon Road. After about 3 miles turn left (south) on Grizzly Drive. The parking lot is on the right (west).

MOUNT FALCON—CASTLE TRAIL

Location: 15 miles southwest of Denver

Length: 7 miles out and back

Terrain: Hardpack with occasional small loose rock. Steps and waterbars

Elevation gain: 1,620′

Map and book: Jefferson County Open Space brochure—Mount Falcon Park; *Front Range Single Tracks*

Dogs: Yes

Heads up: Long climb, watch for mountain lions.

Description: This route duplicates the ride listed in "Mountain Biking." One Denver runner insisted it be highlighted as a run because it's one of the most sustained, steep runs close to Denver. An up-the-face-of-the-foothills classic with big views (Red Rocks Amphitheater, Bear Creek Reservoir, and the city itself). Another runner described it as the best place around to see charismatic megafauna and the city at the same time. Lots of deer and the occasional big cat. He'd actually seen a couple of mountain lions. (See cautions, p. 28.) The nice thing about this run is that history awaits you at the top in the form of a rolling wooded plateau with a ruined castle. The castle is actually the remnants of John Brisben Walker's rock house, which burned in 1918. Walker planned to build a summer White House for presidents just to the east, but World War I and a "waning of Walker's good fortunes" nixed it. Another nice thing is that if you're feeling wimpy you can take 285 to Parmalee Gulch Road and drive around the back side (check the road map) straight to the top, run the short trails through the woods, and get the

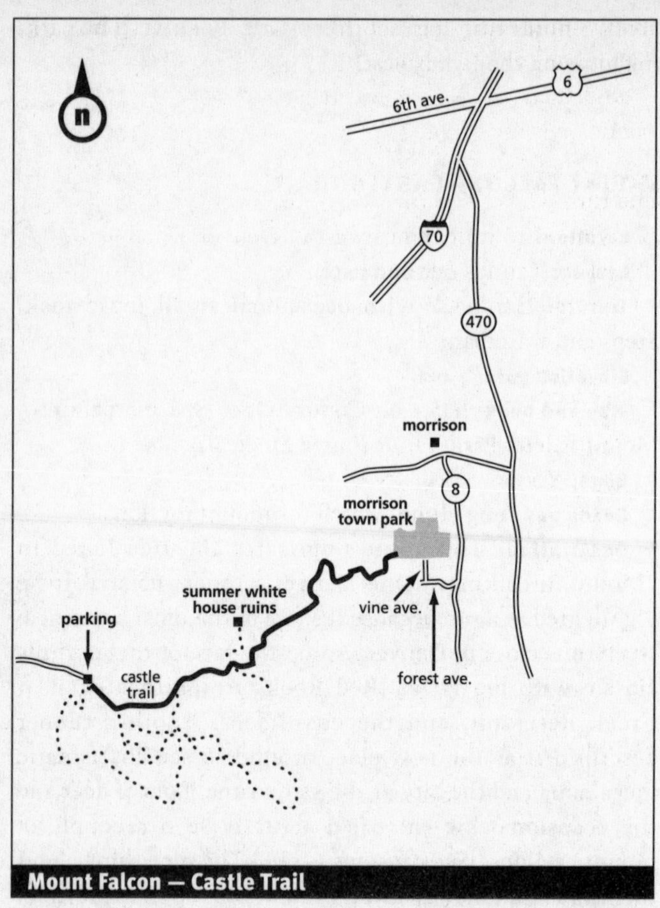

views without breaking a sweat. A third bonus is that you access this run near the little gateway hamlet of Morrison, which has the charm of a small mountain town, though it's next door to Denver. Check out Red Rocks Cyclery and the T'n'T Café.

Route: The Castle Trail is pretty much straight up for almost 3 miles. The trail then mellows and widens for another half mile to Walker's Dream ruins. Check out the many short loop options through the woods at the top. Then point yourself back downhill.

Directions: Go west on 6th Avenue (US 6) to I-70 westbound and stay in the right lane so you can merge onto CO 470. Drive south on CO 470 to the Morrison (CO 8) exit and turn west. CO 8 turns sharply south before Bear Creek Canyon; stay on it to Forest Avenue. Turn right (west). Take Forest to Vine Avenue and turn right (north); continue to the trailhead.

Perfect Fit

WHEN I NEEDED a new pair of running shoes I always went to the sporting goods store, looked over the racks on the wall, found some shoes in my price range, decided that the expensive ones must be better, forced a recalcitrant salesman who was almost on lunch hour to carry the boxes out of the back, tried them on for comfort, and then picked the ones that would look cool and competitive and go well with blue jeans. Some serious runners told me that this time it would be worth the trip to drive thirty-five minutes to Boulder and see the guys at the Boulder Running Company.

It's in the little Kinko's Mall on 28th and Pearl. When you walk in, there are no basketballs or baseball mitts or swimming goggles. There's a couple of anatomical charts of muscle and bone, some plastic joints on a ledge, an electronic treadmill, a video camera, and nothing but running stuff—shoes and shorts and energy bars. Co-owner Mark Plaatjes, a small, slight man with black curly hair and kind, humor-filled eyes, greeted me and took my quest for a shoe very seriously. He asked me how much I run, and on what kind of surfaces. He listened carefully. He had a clipped accent which I learned was South African. He asked me to stand barefoot and flex my knees. He asked me to twist my torso. He was checking the rigidity, pronation, and supernation of my foot. He put me in a pair of shoes, led me to the treadmill, and then filmed me as I walked and ran. He analyzed my gait and foot strike.

Plaatjes, it turns out, knows a bit about running: he won a World Championship in the marathon in Stutgardt in 1993. He won the Los Angeles Marathon in 1991. His personal best was twenty-six 4:55 miles in a row over rolling terrain. He had been the very best in the world. He is a certified physical therapist who gave lectures on body mechanics around the country. He knows about patience and compassion and stamina—he grew up black in apartheid South Africa, and overcame all the obstacles to pursue his dream. His hero, one of the best runners in South Africa, a champion at the five thousand- and ten thousand-meter races, was a man named John Halberstadt. Johnny is white. He took Mark under his wing, told him to run less for ultra-length, train at cross-country, and pick up his marathon times. He was instrumental in getting Mark a scholarship to the University of Georgia.

Today Johnny was right in the shop, on the other side of the video monitor, analyzing my stride and shoe. The two are best friends and had seen a need for knowledgeable service to Boulder's burgeoning running community when they started the store in 1996. The Boulder Running Company had fast gotten a reputation as one of the best running stores in the country, if not the world. I noticed that some of the signs over the shoe racks were in kanji—Japanese characters. "A lot of Japanese runners and teams train here," said Johnny. "It's our way of showing respect." He continued, "Our favorite slogan is 'We don't sell shoes, we sell tools to solve problems.' "

What I noticed right away was the warmth of these men. The miles and miles of pushing their own limits on the trail had distilled their spirits to an absolute presence and compassion. A patience, a focus, an energy. Humor. No hurry. Nothing else, at this moment, was more important than the task at hand—

which was learning about my biomechanics and finding me a good shoe. Every runner, every body is different. I discovered that I pronate, that one leg is slightly longer than the other, that my foot is flexible. Johnny has done a lot of work in shoe design and owns patents on shoe technology. I watched my stride in different shoes, and settled on a shoe that had a dual-density heel and kept my foot aligned straight up on the foot strike. They are the most comfortable running shoes I've ever owned. And well below a hundred dollars. "Most of the shoes we recommend are in the $79 to $89 range. We sell the shoe that best fits the person, not the most expensive shoe."

ELK MEADOWS

Location: 23 miles southwest of Denver
Length: 6-mile loop
Terrain: Smooth hardpack, occasional rocks, waterbars
Elevation gain: 700′
Dogs: Yes
Heads up: Hundreds of elk possible in the fall.
Map and book: Jefferson County Open Space brochure—Elk Meadow Park; *Front Range Single Tracks*

Description: This is a rolling, smooth hardpack run through woods and meadow. It's a great run to revisit throughout the year, as wildflower meadows yield to tawny grass and the aspens yellow, and later, the tall pines catch the first snows. It's terribly popular with mountain bikers, so stay aware. You always have the right-of-way, but having the law on your side may not be much consolation if you get run over by an ignorant peddler. You can add 5.9 miles, with 2.7 miles of killer climbing, by taking the Bergen Peak Trail. It's a marked spur trail on the left. Take it to the top and return the same way, then continue the standard loop.

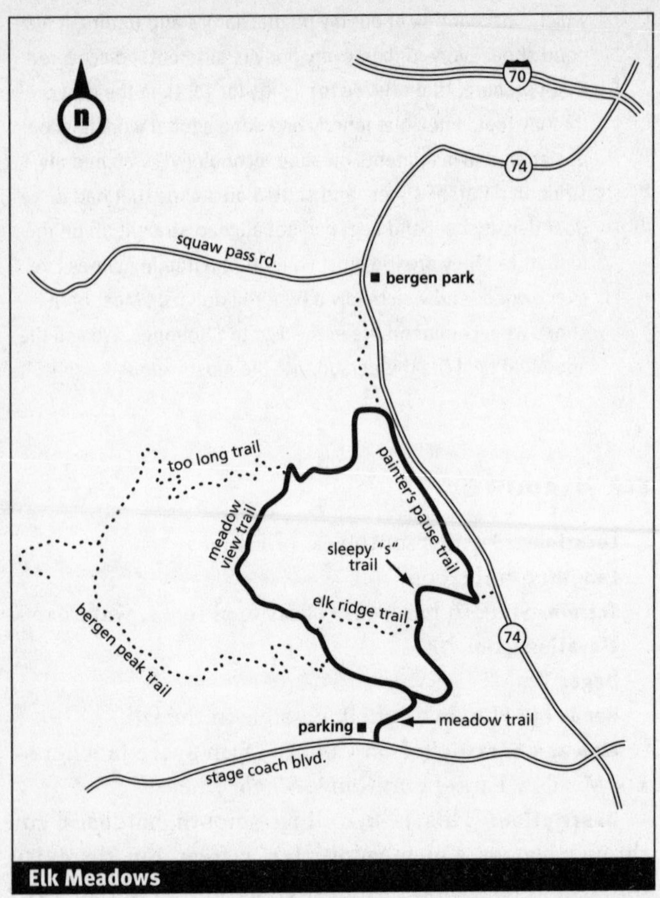

Elk Meadows

Route: Leaving the parking lot, head up the Meadow Trail to Meadow View Trail and turn left onto Meadow View. Pass the Bergen Peak Trail (don't take it unless you want an unmerciful climb) and veer left at the junction with Elk Ridge Trail. Staying on Meadow View, continue past Too Long Trail to Painter's Pause Trail. Turn right onto it and continue to the junction with Sleepy S Trail and turn right. Go past Elk Ridge Trail to Meadow Trail, and turn left. Head back to the car.

Directions: Drive west on 6th Avenue (US 6) to westbound I-70. Drive about 17 miles to Evergreen Parkway (CO 74, exit 252). Drive 5 miles south on Evergreen to Stage Coach Boulevard (476 RD) and turn right (west). Go about 1 mile to the south parking lot.

Boulder City Limits

CHAUTAUQUA PARK—MESA TRAIL

Location: Slightly southwest of Boulder

Length: 14 miles out and back

Terrain: Smooth hardpack fire road and singletrack, rocky singletrack, some steps

Elevation gain: 410′

Map: Sky Terrain Boulder/El Dorado map

Heads up: A classic. Foot-traffic only. Pines, Flatirons, foothills, and Eldorado Springs.

Description: Archetypal Boulder. The standard, the classic. And pretty demanding, as it climbs for a mile at the start—up to Enchanted Mesa—and then drops in and out of several canyons along the way, taking in some sections with steep log steps. A real beauty—mostly in the pine woods, up under the Flatirons, with views of the plains, and finishing with a fast, mile-long descent through a big meadow. Four tributary trails drop from the Mesa Trail down into West Boulder, so there are good opportunities for neighborhood access and route variation.

Route: From Chautauqua Park, take the Mesa Trail, heading southwest along Bluebell Creek, to a fork. Bear right. You'll cross three trails—Enchanted Mesa, Kohler

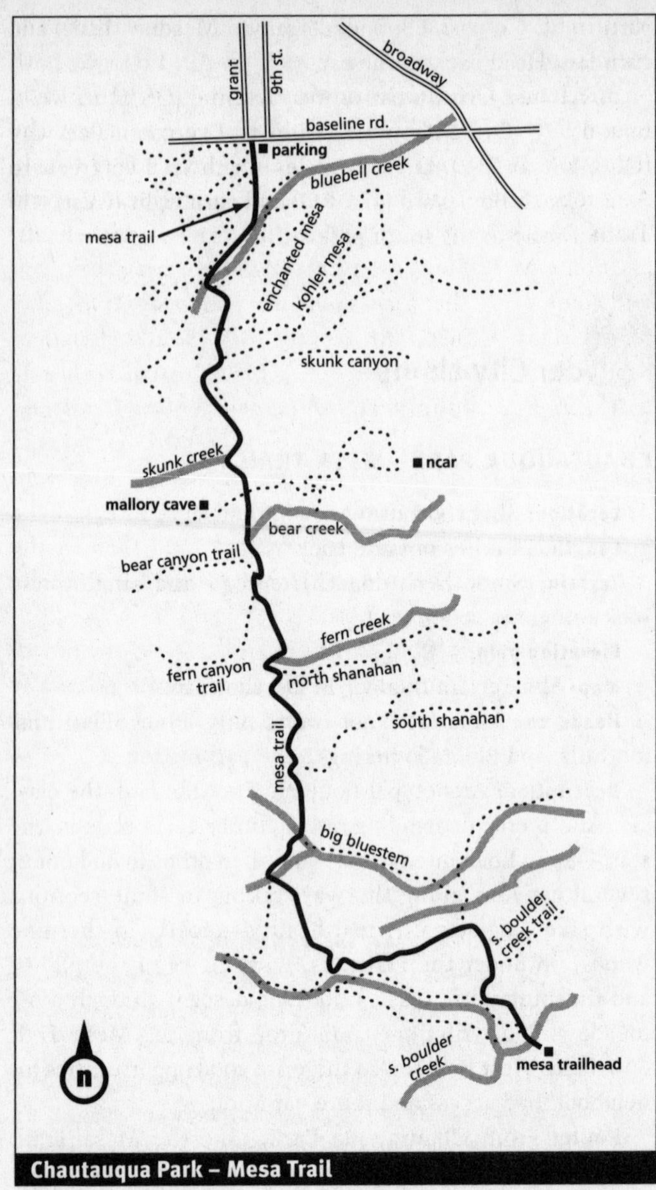

Chautauqua Park – Mesa Trail

Mesa, and Skunk Canyon. Cross Skunk Creek, still on the Mesa Trail. Then cross three more trails (the first two, both on the left, go to the National Center for Atmospheric Research [NCAR], the last, to Mallory Cave, is on the right). Join Bear Creek Canyon Trail and cross Bear Creek. At a fork in the road join Fern Canyon and Bear Canyon Trails. You'll want to go left and then take another left, back onto Mesa Trail. After crossing over Fern Creek, you will come to another fork (the North Shanahan Trail); stay to the right. Quickly to another fork (South Shanahan Trail); again stay to the right. Cross Big Bluestem Trail, stay to the right. At the next intersection (Mesa Trail and Shadow Canyon Trail) go left—a quick descent. At the next fork go right. Keep descending to join the Big Bluestem Trail. Stay to the right. Here you will be running through a grassy field, over South Boulder Creek, and then to the Mesa trailhead on the road to Eldorado Springs. Return the way you came.

Directions: Take Canyon Boulevard (CO 119) to Broadway (CO 93), and turn left (south). Continue on Broadway to Baseline Road, turn right (west), and drive to just past 9th Street. Turn left (south) into the parking lot.

Chautauqua Park

CHAUTAUQUA PARK, LOCATED on the south side of Baseline Road just west of 9th Street, is the gateway to the city of Boulder's Mountain Parks. Big meadows climb to pine woods and the jutting Flatirons. A tremendous place to run, just stroll, or walk your dog, if it's on a leash. Chautauqua Park is easily accessible by car, although it's a snap to get to on a bike. The Park Ranger Cottage, located at the south end of the parking lot just inside the park's entrance, is a good place to get oriented. It's generally staffed Monday through Friday, 8:30–5:00, weekends 9:00–5:00. They have park maps, brochures, information, and an emergency phone for after-hours use. Numerous trails originate from this area.

The Chautauqua is also a living history district that provides education and cultural enrichment for the community. The light-filled octagonal dining hall serves delicious meals year-round (check out the brunch—I mean it), and the acoustically perfect Chautauqua Auditorium is a venue for concerts, films, and lectures. Interestingly, for all its glorious cultural cachet, Chautauqua is reputed to have been the headquarters for the region's KKK in the 1920s.

CHAUTAUQUA PARK—THE "ULTIMATE" LOOP

Location: Slightly southwest of Boulder

Length: 9-mile loop with 2/3-mile out-and-back option to Green Mountain summit

Terrain: Rocky creek crossings, steep hardpack jeep road, semi-rocky singletrack, pine needles

Elevation gain: 1,600′

Map: Sky Terrain Boulder/El Dorado map

Dogs: Yes

Heads up: Great variety of terrain: canyon, mountain, woods, and meadow.

Description: From Chautauqua, this loop links together half a dozen trails for a long, demanding run of great variety. There are smooth, wide sections for speed and stride work and technical, rocky sections that require agility and concentration. "Either way," says one elite Boulder runner, "it's a little rough on the quads." And it's beautiful. One section crosses and recrosses Bear Creek, so you'll probably get your feet wet. Then it climbs up onto the West Ridge of Green Mountain, with huge views to the Divide. If you

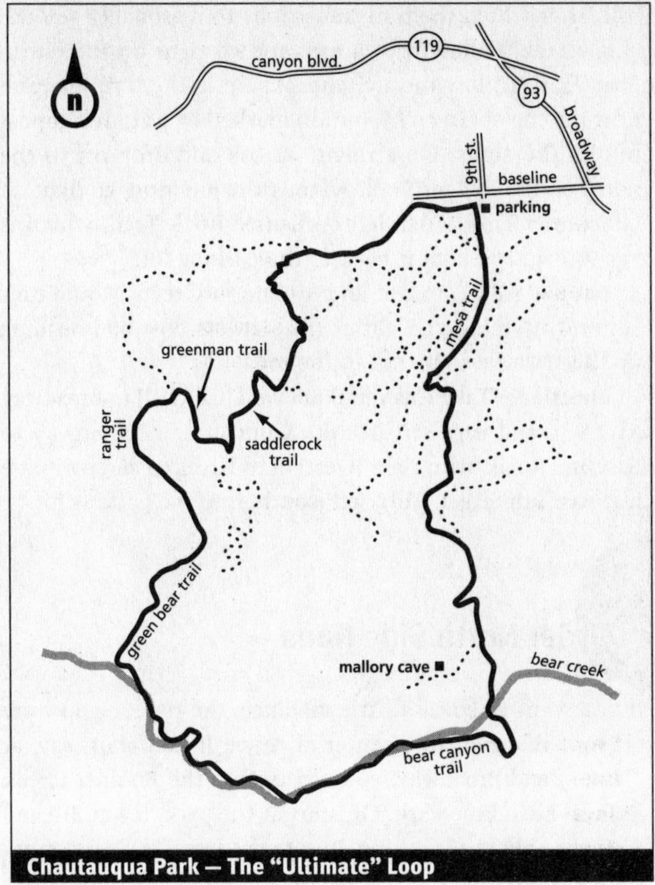

Chautauqua Park — The "Ultimate" Loop

have time, take the 1/3-mile spur trail up to the summit (8,144′) and take in the limitless views from above the Flatirons. Thanks to Art Ives for detailing the route.

Route: The best thing to do is to get ahold of the Sky Terrain Boulder/El Dorado map and connect the dots. Head out from the park on the Mesa Trail. After about 3 miles, take a right up the Bear Canyon Trail, which turns off to the west and follows Bear Creek. You'll come to a short, steep hill, after which the trail transitions to reasonably smooth singletrack. Follow it to a fork and go right on the Green Bear Trail. Follow the switchbacks up to the trail junction near the top of Green Mountain marked by a stout signpost minus the signs. Go straight across and drop off to the north on the Ranger Trail. At the next junction, go right on Greenman Trail. Then left on Saddle Rock Trail, which is very steep, and hoof it back to the parking lot.

Option: Add 2/3 mile and a visit to Green Mountain's summit by taking a right at the signless post and heading up the 1/3-mile spur trail to the top.

Directions: Take Canyon Boulevard (CO 119) to Broadway (CO 93), and turn left (south). Continue on Broadway to Baseline Road. Turn right (west) onto Baseline and continue just past 9th Street. Turn left (south) into the parking lot.

Boulder North Side Runs

If you want to cover a little distance, the routes below are all runnable from the center of town. If you start, say, at Canyon and Broadway, you can run up the Boulder Creek Path to Eben Fine Park. Or, start at the park; it's at 3rd and Arapahoe, and has parking. Run to the top of the park, cross the footbridge over the creek, and go through the underpass to Settler's Park. From here you can take the Red Rocks Trail, which is a gorgeous, steep, short jaunt through ponderosas and fins of rose sandstone—particularly lovely in the evening as the sun hits the mountains and sidelights the rock. The trail tops out in a little open saddle, and you can jog down to the start of the Sanitas Mountain Trail. From Eben Fine Park this is less than a mile. To continue on to the Foothills Trail, and the trail network by Boulder Reservoir, continue on the Sanitas Valley Trail, run up the valley, and, just where it merges with the Dakota Ridge Trail, take a hard right onto a nameless singletrack to Hawthorne Street. Take Hawthorne east one block to 4th Street. Go left (north) and run to Wonderland Lake and the Foothills Trail.

MOUNT SANITAS—SUMMIT LOOP

Location: 2 miles west of Boulder

Length: 3-mile loop

Terrain: Steep, often rocky trail

Elevation gain: 1,200′

Map and book: Mount Sanitas brochure; *Best Easy Day Hikes: Boulder*

Dogs: Yes

Heads up: A Boulder favorite. Steep, zagging ridge climb. Great views of the Indian Peaks and the plains. Rock climbing and a rock grotto en route.

Description: Divide the elevation gain by the distance and you get the idea. The run begins almost immediately with a bunch of stair steps. Then up the ridge and back and forth across the ridgeline. Lovely views of the gentle Sanitas Valley and the plains beyond, and back west of the snowy peaks of the Continental Divide. It all ends with a switchbacking dive off the top. This is literally Boulder's backyard, and the sense of seclusion right out of town is lovely.

Route: Run past the picnic shelter at the trailhead and across a footbridge, and bear left onto the stair steps. Stay straight on the main trail and climb the ridge to rocks at the summit. Descend on steep East Ridge Trail into Sanitas Valley. At about mile 2, pick up the wide Sanitas Valley Trail and run south. Stay on the main, broad path back to the trailhead.

Directions: Drive north on CO 93 to Mapleton Avenue

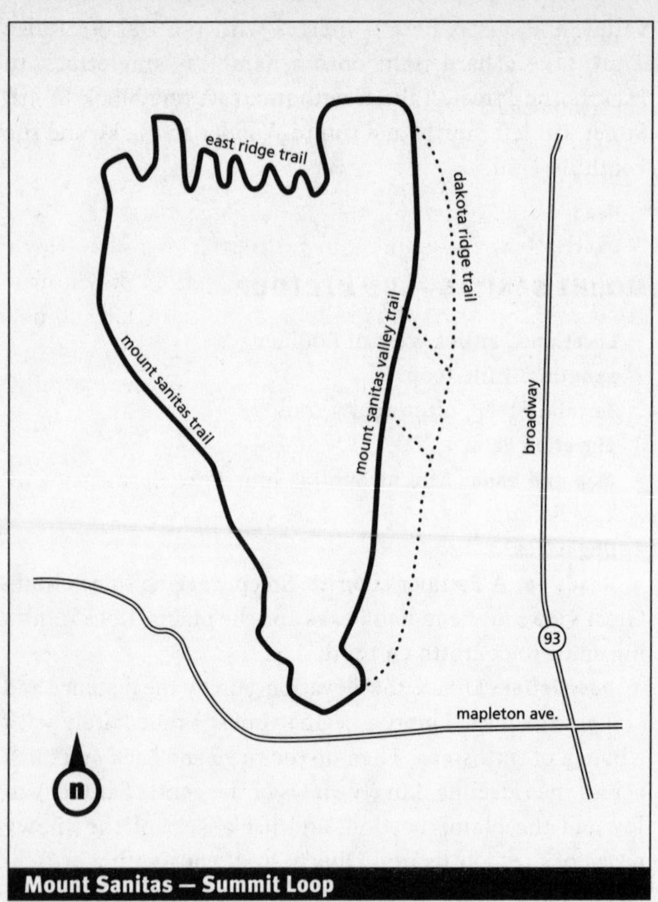

Mount Sanitas — Summit Loop

and turn left (west). Go about 2 miles to the trailhead on the right side (north).

FOOTHILLS TRAIL—US 36 TO WONDERLAND LAKE

Location: 4 miles northwest of Boulder
Length: 5 miles out and back

Terrain: Trail—crushed gravel, some loose rock, waterbars

Elevation gain: Minimal

Map: Zia Designs' Boulder County Mountain Bike Map

Dogs: Yes

Heads up: Flat and rolling—phew! Paragliders.

Description: A popular run because it's close to town (you can get on the Foothills Trail right from downtown) and because it's pretty and rolling, without the long climbs and descents typical of Front Range runs. It's fun to run through the meadows right along the base of the foothills, but it's completely open, so be ready for no shade in summer. Also, watch out for mountain bikers.

Route: Run through the underpass beneath US 36 and follow the trail up the meadow toward the mountains. Climb over steep waterbars as the trail swings south and

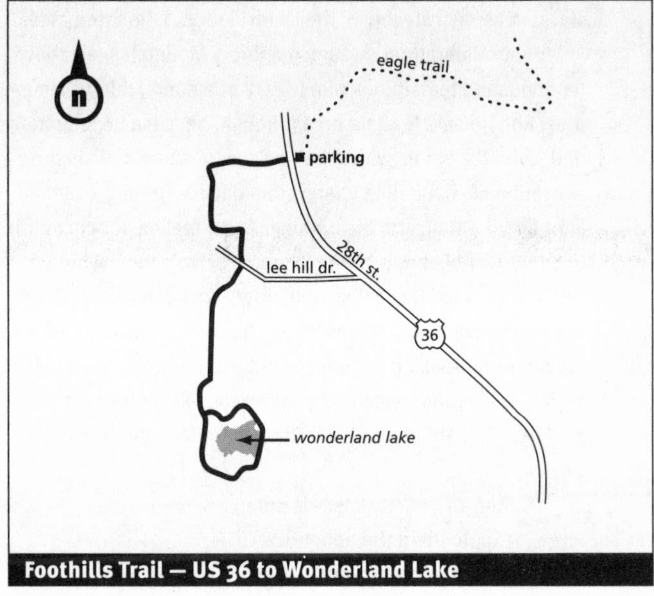

Foothills Trail — US 36 to Wonderland Lake

parallels the foothills. Cross Lee Hill Drive and continue on to Wonderland Lake. Run back the way you came.

Option 1: You can run east out of the other side of the parking lot onto a dirt road. Go left and continue onto Eagle Trail, which drops off a beautiful bench to the fields and trails just west of the Boulder Reservoir. Chew up as much of this route as you can handle, then run back.

Option 2: Run to the Foothills Trail from downtown (see "Boulder North Side Runs," pp. 242–43).

Directions: Go north on 28th Street (US 36) 4 miles north to the trailhead. It is on the right (east) side of the road.

Divine Madness

ART IVES ISN'T your run-of-the-mill personal trainer and running coach. In August, 2000, at age 45, he won the Masters category of the Leadville 100, a hundred-mile, ultra-marathon through the Rocky Mountains, all above ten thousand feet. It took him twenty-one hours, thirty-six minutes, and he said it was a breakthrough, because he felt strong and joyful the whole way. When he's in the Zone, he has the sensation of channeling energy from outside, from the air and light and the trail, into his running. And a feeling of being both in and out of his body. "The technique I give people who run with me is called the 'Horse and Rider.' Your consciousness is above your body: calling the shots, registering sensations, pushing and relaxing the body simultaneously. Your body is strong, willing, and able underneath you, like a horse would be." Ives thought about it, and then he quoted Whitman from *Leaves of Grass*:

> Sure as the most certain sure . . .
> . . . plumb in the uprights
> stout as a horse, affectionate

Haughty, electrical,
I and this mystery, here we stand!

"That's the feeling," he finished.

You get the impression, talking to Ives, that running and winning over long distances is about more, a lot more, than being strong and putting one foot in front of the other. Ives is lean, with thinning hair, a deeply lined face, and gentle eyes. He has a relaxed warmth, a kind of patience about him that doesn't hide a thrum of internal energy. "All these other levels go into it," he says. "Diet, nutrition, your discipline and scheduling, how you organize your week so your running can fit into and enhance the rest of your life. Your personal energy. Your meditation practice. We do a consistent amount of Sitting Practice when preparing for 100-mile racing, because you're gonna have to keep your wits about you under adverse circumstances." Like a bruised foot and a mountain in your way at mile 70.

Ives came to serious running over twenty years, along a path that included fighting back from injury and aversion. This, he says, makes him compassionate when other people are struggling with their training. In 1995, he joined about thirty Boulderites who started to take legendary weekly training runs of thirty and fifty miles. The group became known as Divine Madness, and its members placed extremely well in ultramarathons. One of its runners and Ives' longtime training partner, Steve Peterson, went on to win the Leadville 100 four times. "We knew we were onto something," says Ives. Divine Madness broke up after a marital scandal that engulfed its leader, and, according to Ives, was sensationalized and exploited by the national press. "The training was beautifully conceived and very challenging, as you can imagine," he says. "There were many that perceived it as zealous and extreme. Some media portrayed it as a cult. That hurt me a lot. We're just ordinary runners who run extraordinary runs." A lot of the members still train together and win races. Ives started offering personal training and coaching to augment his own training.

"You want to build your life on a continuum where you get energy from what you do. If I can give people just a piece of what I've learned, maybe they'll become fascinated with their own true capabilities, as I did." He is particularly excited about work he's done with kids and Running Wild, the camp he directs in southwestern New Mexico.

For information on personal training with Ives, on weekly marathon training groups in Denver and Boulder, and on the New Mexico camp, call (720) 890-1744 or (303) 263-1523.

Boulder Backyard

EAST BOULDER TRAIL—TELLER FARM AND WHITE ROCKS

Location: 5.5 miles east of Boulder

Length: 4 miles or a 12-mile out and back

Terrain: Smooth farm road and smooth rolling single-track

Elevation gain: Minimal

Map: Zia Designs' Boulder County Mountain Bike Map

Dogs: Yes

Heads up: A great long flat run.

Description: This is a wide open, rolling run through swales of pasture, across a meandering Boulder Creek, and past a band of startling white cliffs that look like something from the middle of the Australian Outback. A favorite among elite runners, because you can hit your stride on the smooth trail and it's very fast on the descending return. Also, this is one of the few trails around that isn't up up up then down down down. Eagles and bluebirds, wildflowers, cottonwoods along the creek—the high plains the way it used to be—except for the pricey homes skylin-

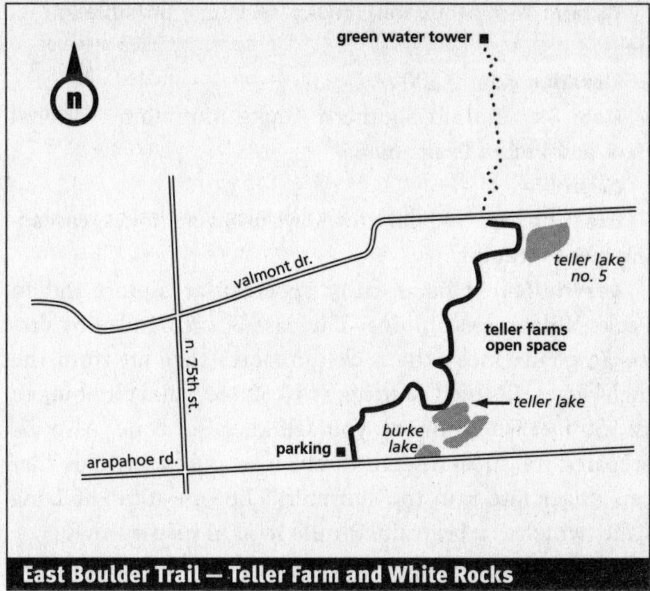

East Boulder Trail — Teller Farm and White Rocks

ing the ridge. Stunning views of the Divide. Native Americans used to run buffalo off the cliffs. A short and a long run are described.

Route: For 4 miles, run north to Valmont and return.

Option: For 12 miles, continue past Valmont to the green water tower and return.

Directions: Drive east on Arapahoe Road, past 75th Street. The trailhead is about 1 mile east of 75th on the left (north).

PAWNEE PASS VIA LONG LAKE AND LAKE ISABELLE

Location: 29 miles west of Boulder

Length: 9 miles out and back; there are options for a 3-mile loop and a 4-mile out and back

Terrain: Mountain trail, rocky sections, possible snowfields

Elevation gain: 2,500′

Map: Sky Terrain Southern Rocky Mountain National Park and Indian Peaks map

Dogs: No

Heads up: Spectacular views, wildflowers, lakes, cascading creeks, tundra.

Description: This is truly spectacular alpine, Indian Peaks Wilderness running. The pass is surrounded by dramatic gendarmes—the rock pinnacles that jut from the high ridges. It's high, starting at 10,520 feet and climbing to 12,550 feet, so acclimate yourself ahead of time. Also, be prepared for sudden weather changes and snowfields that can linger late into the summer. The run starts at Long Lake, which is a beautiful 3-mile loop in its own right.

Historic note: Niwot Ridge, the swale of tundra across the Lake Isabelle drainage from Pawnee Pass, was established as one of only 17 long-term ecological research stations in the country in 1980 by the National Science Foundation. The site is internationally famous for alpine research conducted by the University of Colorado Mountain Research Station.

Route: From the Long Lake Trailhead, run into the Indian Peaks Wilderness at Long Lake. The Jean Lunning Scenic Trail heads left at the lower end of Long Lake; the Pawnee Pass Trail is to the right. Take Pawnee Pass and climb through the woods to Lake Isabelle (2.1 miles). This is stunning country, some of the best of the Indian Peaks. Just before the lake, rock hop across South St. Vrain Creek and ascend a small ridge, coming out above the lake. Here the trail splits, with the Isabelle Glacier Trail straight ahead. Turn right, staying on Pawnee Pass Trail, which crosses the creek several times before climbing through the last trees into the tundra and talus. Pass bogs, tarns, mead-

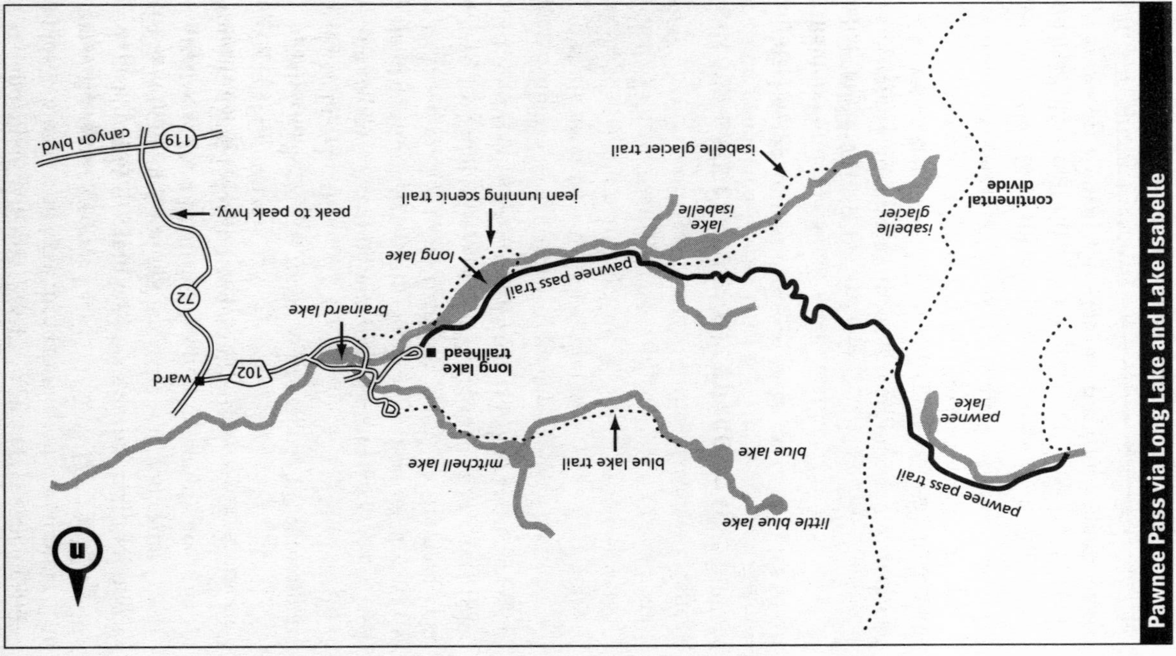

Pawnee Pass via Long Lake and Lake Isabelle

ows, and miles of alpine flowers. And be prepared for snowfields, which can survive through most of the summer. The top of the run at Pawnee Pass is obvious. Descend the other side a short way to catch big views of the crags to the west. Then turn around and run back the way you came.

Option 1: For a beautiful 3-mile run, simply hoof the 1/4 mile to Long Lake and run around it on the 2.5-mile Jean Lunning Scenic Trail.

Option 2: Begin the route as described, but turn around at Lake Isabelle.

Directions: Drive up Canyon Boulevard (CO 119) to Nederland and turn right onto the Peak to Peak Highway (CO 72). Drive to Ward and turn left (west) on Brainard Lake Drive (102 RD), just north of Ward, toward Brainard Lake. Park in the Long Lake and Mitchell Lake parking areas.

Golden

GOLDEN GATE CANYON—THE BURRO TRAIL

Location: 29 miles northwest of Denver, 32 miles south of Boulder

Length: 4-mile loop

Terrain: Trail with some loose rock and sand, gravel road

Elevation gain: 520′

Fee: $4 state park day fee, $40 for an annual pass

Map and book: Golden Gate Canyon State Park map; *Denver Hiking Guide*

Dogs: Yes

Heads up: Above 7,500 feet in the cool shadow of the pines. A summer respite.

Description: Best medicine for summer in the city. Golden Gate is a gem, with a web of trails winding from the cool creek and beaver ponds of the canyon up into steep hills of lodgepole and ponderosa. Lovely meadows, too. Campsites and shelters are available. This is a demanding run considering its length, with a lot of gradient (a fancy word for steep) and some rocky sections.

Route: From the pullout, run 100 feet up to a junction and turn left. Climb steeply for 1.1 miles and bank a right onto the Burro and Mt. Lion Trails. Shortly after, turn right onto Burro Trail. Descend to a stream, cross a bridge, and bear right. At the next fork (0.2 mile from the bridge) bear left and put the maintenance shed behind you. Turn left onto a dirt road at the next junction. After about 0.5 mile turn right onto Mt. Lion Trail. Turn left at the next junction and drop into a parking lot. Cross it, pick up the trail on the other side, and kick back to your car.

Directions: From Denver, drive west on 6th Avenue (US

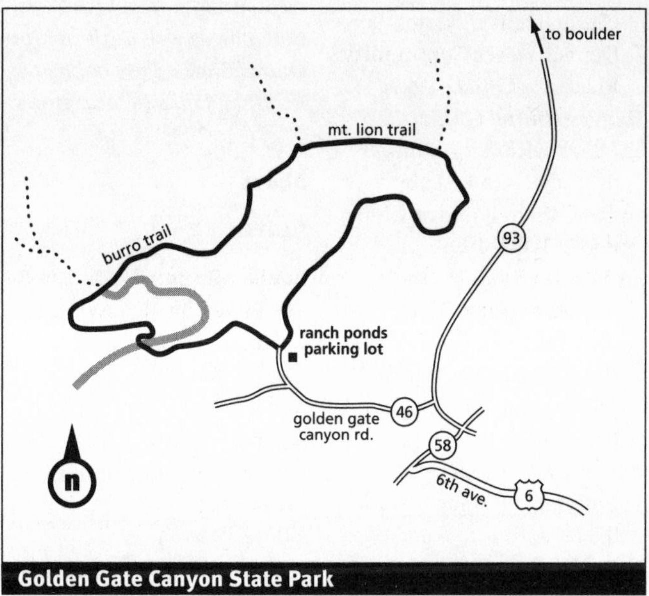

Golden Gate Canyon State Park

6) through Golden to CO 93. Turn north onto CO 93 and drive to Golden Gate Canyon Road (CO 46) and turn left (west). Continue 14 miles to the park entrance. Turn right toward the visitors center and continue 3 miles to the Ranch Ponds parking lot. From Boulder, drive west on Canyon Boulevard (CO 119) to Broadway (CO 93) and turn left (south). Drive 19 miles to Golden Gate Canyon Road (CO 46) and turn right (west). Continue 14 miles to the park entrance. Turn right toward the visitors center and continue 3 miles to the Ranch Ponds parking lot.

Where to Connect

Books and Link

Guide to the High Line Canal (Denver, Colo.: Denver Water Community Relations Office, 1999).

Denver Hiking Guide: 45 Hikes within 45 Minutes of Denver, 2nd ed., by Dave Rich (Boulder, Colo.: Books West, 1999).

Front Range Single Tracks: The Best Single Track Trails near Denver and Boulder, by Tom Barnhart (Littleton, Colo.: Fat Tire Press, 1999).

Best Easy Day Hikes: Boulder, by Tracy Salcedo (Helena, Mont.: Falcon Publishing, 2000).

www.active.com

Great site! Lists tons of races, usually weekly, in Colorado as well as the entire United States. Easy online registration. Links to local stores.

Shops

Denver

Boulder Running Company
8116 West Bowles Avenue
Littleton, CO 80123
(303) 932-6000

Runner's Roost
1685 S. Colorado Boulevard
Littleton, CO 80222
(303) 759-8455

The Sporting Woman
2902 East 3rd Avenue
Denver, CO 80206
(303) 316-8392

Boulder

Boulder Running Company
2775 Pearl Street
Boulder, CO 80302
(303) 786-9255

Runner's Choice
2460 Canyon Boulevard
Boulder, CO 80302
(303) 449-8551

Fleet Feet Sports
1035 Pearl Street
Boulder, CO 80302
(303) 939-8000

Clubs

Denver

Rocky Mountain Road Runners
(303) 871-8366
www.rmrr.org

Check out the Web site for weekly run times and locations. The club has a $25 annual enrollment fee, but includes all 12 of the monthly trophy series races, weekly runs, training with a partner program, Thursday night trail runs (all around CO 470) April to October, and snowshoeing runs in the off-season.

Phidippides Track Club
(303) 721-1520

The Phidippides Track Club is an organization for runners and fitness enthusiasts of all ages and abilities. The purpose of the club is to enhance personal life quality, promote social interaction, and develop physical fitness and wellness through running for fun and competition. The club provides interval track workouts (weekly, March through October) and social activities to improve the knowledge and enjoyment of running and training.

Boulder

Boulder Road Runners
(303) 492-8776
www.boulderroadrunners.org

Sunday runs at 9:00 A.M. bring out 100–150 people (honestly) every week. Cinnamon rolls and coffee after the run. Great way to meet and partner up with other runners, learn about training and other groups, and talk about the running community. You can bring your dog. Great Web site as well.

Events

Denver

Race for the Cure
(303) 744-2088
www.raceforthecure.com

The largest series of 5K run/fitness walks in the world, with races in 107 U.S. cities and over a million participants. Proceeds benefit the Susan G. Komen Breast Cancer Foundation. A festive fall run through downtown Denver.

Boulder

Bolder Boulder
4571 North Broadway
Boulder, CO 80304-0585
(303) 444-RACE
E-mail: race@bolderboulder.com

One of the largest road races in the world. More than 42,000 runners, walkers, and wheelchair racers, and as many as 32 international professional teams participate. The race starts in northeast Boulder, winds through many neighborhoods, and features live music and entertainment at every corner.

Always on Memorial Day weekend.

Boulder Backroads Marathon
P.O. Box 1889
Boulder, CO 80306
(303) 939-9661
www.boulderbackroads.com

Boulder Backroads Marathon is a 26-mile, 385-yard, professionally timed road race. Both marathon and half-marathon runners begin at the Boulder Reservoir and travel out through Boulder County's beautiful rural neighborhoods on mostly soft-packed dirt roads and quiet country lanes. You'll pass farms, cattle, horses, cottonwood groves, and tranquil ponds, returning to the reservoir for the finish and post-race festivities. An annual fall run that's entry deadline is usually around September 1.

In-Line Skating

SARAH KNOPP, THE researcher for this book, grew up in Denver on in-line skates. There was no place she and her pals didn't go. They tore up the 16th Street Mall, which is illegal and a public nuisance. She said that getting away from a cop car was a snap, and a cop on foot wasn't even worth troubling about. They made a slalom course out of the shoppers. They rolled down the steps at the Denver Center for the Performing Arts—backward, because it's easier that way. They took to Speer Boulevard at 3 A.M. and played hockey. Downtown, they made the stop-and-go rush hour streets a fluid battlefield and, using the cars as cover, killed each other with slingshot paintballs. Now, as adults, her friends have neither ceased nor desisted. They still skate the mall, but its touchier because the cops now have bikes. For Rockies baseball games, rather than deal with the crowds and parking downtown, they park at the free lot at the Cherry Creek Mall and skate down Cherry Creek and South Platte bike paths to Coors Field. It takes them about half an hour. One crazoid in their group heads west in the spring and actually skates the Slickrock Trail in Moab.

Denver and Boulder are good towns for skating. You can usually blade all winter, barring snow days. From downtown Denver, smooth concrete paths slide along Cherry Creek and the South Platte for scores of miles. You can hop on the Cherry Creek path after work and blade all the way to Chatfield Lake—over 20 miles. Or head up-creek to Cherry Creek Lake, about 12 miles, and take a swim. It's cooler and often shady in the riparian zone along the path, and there's the sound of running water, and the little rapids, and paddling ducks. On a summer night you'll never feel lonely and better be dexterous, because it seems like half the city is on the trail, running and biking and walking—and sleeping. (Homeless people sometimes sleep right on the path.)

In Boulder, the best skating is also along the creek, on a beautifully designed, smooth trail that follows the stream past fishing pools and paddling holes, through the middle of town and east out onto the high plains, linking up to a network of paths that comprise miles of perfect blading. A helmet and good people skills are a must—dodge people, finesse them, and know when to give way.

SOUTH PLATTE TRAIL—BOWLES AVENUE TO CHATFIELD

Location: 9 miles south of Denver

Length: 10 miles out and back

Elevation gain: Minimal

Map: Bicycling Metro Denver Route Map

Dogs: Yes

Heads up: Meadows!

Description: Smooth concrete follows the South Platte River upstream (south). It's amazing how much wildlife has the same idea as you—willows, cottonwoods, and Russian olive trees, shelter snakes, ducks and geese, herons, dip-

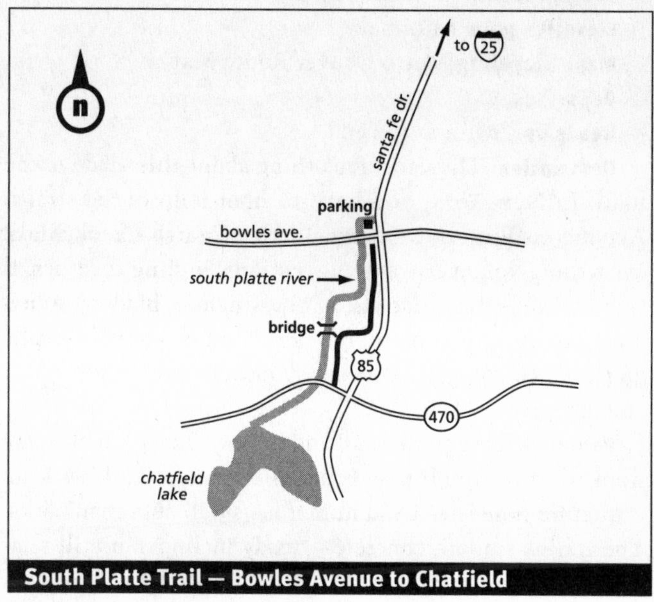

South Platte Trail — Bowles Avenue to Chatfield

pers, raccoons, and beaver. There are numerous ponds along the trail, beautiful views of the foothills and open meadows. Bridge crossings. You may encounter horses. Fall through spring is beautiful blading—less crowded with people and bugs. Good sun exposure throughout the day, warmer in the afternoon.

Route: Get on the trail and go.

Directions: Go south on I-25 to Santa Fe Drive (US 85) exit 207B. Go south on Santa Fe to Bowles Avenue and turn right (west). Drive about 100 yards and park in the dirt lot on the south side. Walk to the trail on the east side of the river.

CHERRY CREEK TRAIL—CHERRY CREEK MALL TO CHERRY CREEK LAKE

Location: Slightly southeast of downtown

Length: About 16 miles out and back

Elevation gain: Minimal

Map: Bicycling Metro Denver Route Map

Dogs: Yes

Heads up: Swim at the end.

Description: The dangerous thing about this blade is the mall. In New York, you have to hoof it from Saks Fifth Avenue to Victoria's Secret. In the Cherry Creek Mall, everything you ever wanted is perilously close together. If this becomes a regular route, you might consider leaving your credit cards on the bureau. This is a lovely bit of creek. Once you get to the lake you can blade to the beach and dive in.

Route: Go east on the trail and follow Cherry Creek away from the city. You'll pass Four Mile Historic Park with its miniature homestead and numerous small suburban parks. The trail is smooth concrete—steady incline, but still relatively flat, except for one big hill before the lake.

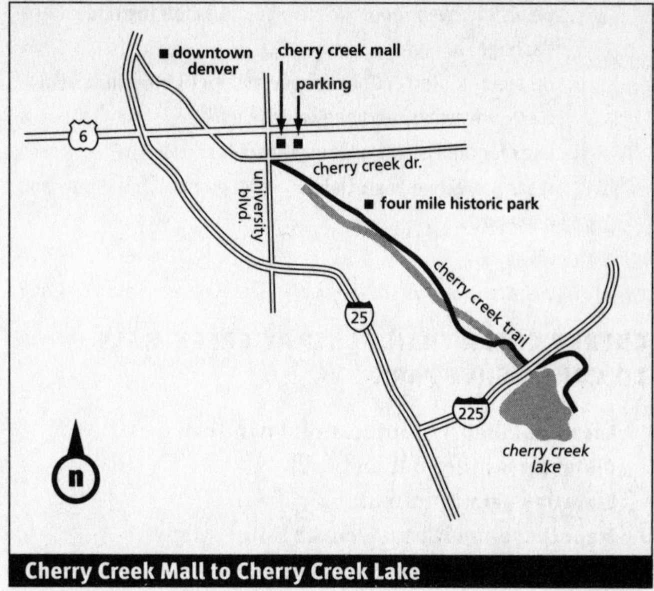

Cherry Creek Mall to Cherry Creek Lake

Directions: Take 6th Avenue (US 6) east to University Boulevard.. Take a right (south) to Cherry Creek Drive and turn left (east). Park in the Cherry Creek Mall parking lot.

In-Line Skating Safety

1. Stay to the right unless passing slower trail users. When passing, give an audible signal such as, "on your left" to let others know where you are.
2. Obey skating restrictions. It is illegal to skate on commercial property, including malls and where posted.
3. Always yield to pedestrians. They have the right of way—especially in Boulder.
4. Skate tricks should be done in skate parks.

5. Be visible: Wear appropriately colored clothing and carry a flashlight at night.
6. Be alert at intersections (especially for right-turning vehicles), driveways, and alley crossings.
7. Look for debris and uneven sidewalks.
8. Wear protective gear: Helmet, wrist guards, and elbow and knee pads.

CHERRY CREEK TRAIL—CHERRY CREEK MALL TO CONFLUENCE PARK

Location: Slightly southest of downtown
Distance: 8 miles out and back
Elevation gain: Minimal
Map: Bicycling Metro Denver Route Map
Heads up: Summer night social.

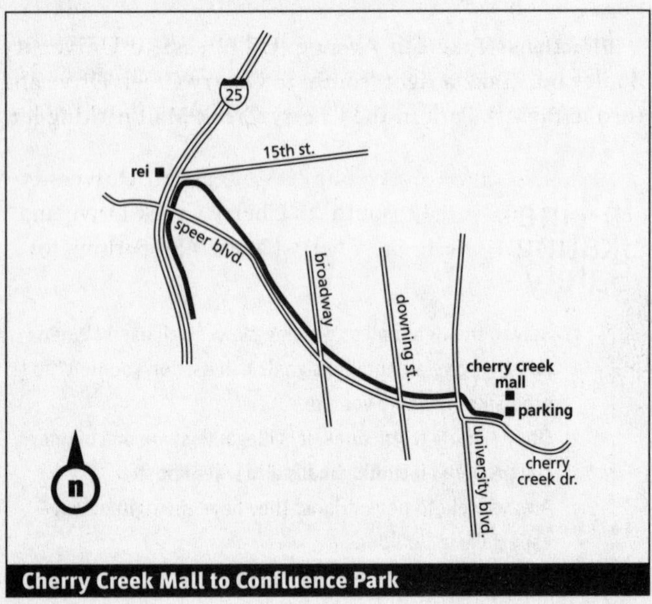

Cherry Creek Mall to Confluence Park

Description: Down along the creek it's hard to believe you're in the middle of Denver. It's deeply shaded, grape vines festoon the retaining walls, the creek burbles and foams. Near the beginning of the route, the path runs unnervingly close to the traffic of Speer Boulevard. One false move and you're roadkill, so take it easy and watch the kids. The route ends at the confluence of Cherry Creek with the South Platte. Here rodeo paddlers are honing their skills in the Whitewater play park. Just over the footbridge is the mammoth REI flagship store and Starbucks, which serves excellent tuna melt sandwiches with Caesar's salad. Some people I know simply take off their skates in summer and jump in at the top of the boisterous rapid. Not recommended.

Route: Get on the path and skate west.

Option: From Confluence Park, you can make a longer skate by going north or south along the South Platte, though north gets industrial and a little creepy pretty quickly. Heading south seems okay, but still not recommended for a woman by herself, as recreational traffic is light to moderate, and the trail passes through some rough parts of town.

Directions: Take 6th Avenue (US 6) east to University Boulevard. Take a right (south) to Cherry Creek Drive and turn left (east). Park in the Cherry Creek Mall parking lot.

Denver Backyard

JOHNSON RESERVOIR AT CLEMENT PARK

Location: 12 miles south of Denver

Length: 1.4 mile-loop

Elevation gain: Minimal

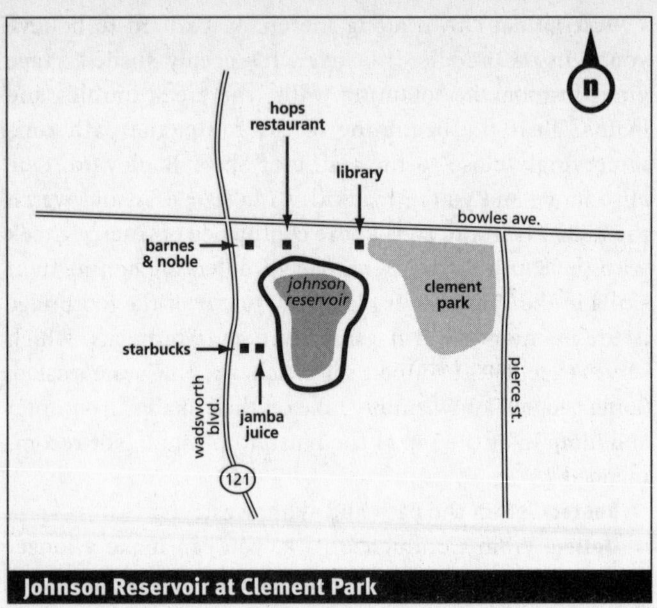

Johnson Reservoir at Clement Park

Map: Bicycling Metro Denver Route Map

Dogs: Yes

Heads up: Family frolic.

Description: This is a nice concrete path around a reservoir in southwest Denver. Skate, drink latte, and shop. The shores of Johnson Reservoir are lined with mall stores—Barnes and Noble, which is open until 11 pm, Starbucks, Jamba Juice, and a Hops restaurant that has an outdoor patio and live music on summer weekend nights. You can link up with other Clement Park paths to lengthen your loop. Free music concerts here in the summer, and the path is lit for nighttime use. Great for the family; Clement Park has a toddler area, playground, soccer field, and batting cages.

Route: Find the path around the lake and go. Loop off into Clement Park for longer skates.

Directions: Go west on 6th Avenue (US 6) to Wadsworth

Boulevard (CO 121) and turn south. Drive past Bowles Avenue and turn left (east) on Ark Hill Road and into Bowles Crossing shopping center. Park close to the reservoir. Path circles the reservoir.

CROWN HILL PARK

Location: 7 miles northwest of Denver

Length: 1.2-mile loop

Elevation gain: Minimal

Maps: Bicycling Metro Denver Route Map; Crown Hill Park brochure

Dogs: Yes

Heads up: Great to roll around the lake a few times and watch the sunset.

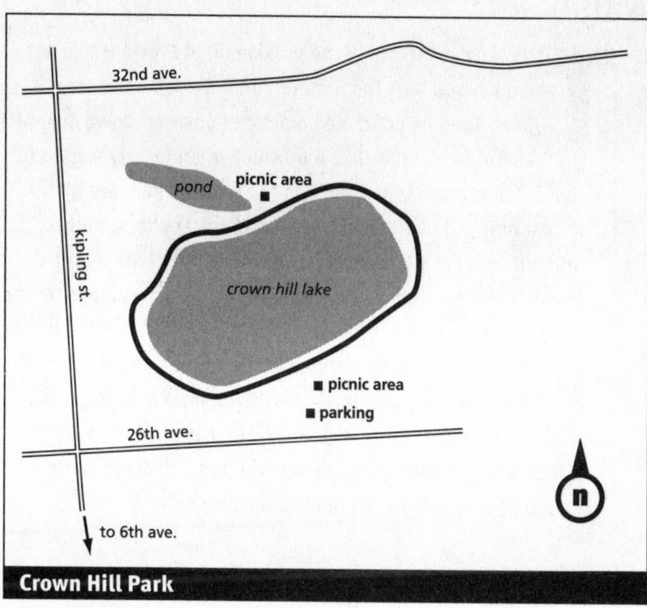

Crown Hill Park

Description: This is a lovely little park with a wildlife sanctuary, a smooth concrete path around a pretty lake, picnic tables and benches, and dirt trails that branch off for short running and biking loops. It's popular with horseback riders, and a great place to watch the sunset over the mountains on warm summer evenings. The cattails are alive with redwing blackbirds and loud peepers, and the lake is full of waterfowl. Take a picnic. The park is popular with old people who like to stroll and play chess, so it's a nice place to feel connected with other generations.

Route: Get on the path and go.

Directions: Drive west on 6th Avenue (US 6) to Kipling Street (CO 391) and turn right (north). Go to 26th Avenue and turn right (east). The signed parking lot is on the left (north) side of the street.

Mush

THE GUY CAME out of the parking lot at Crown Hill in a crouch and took the first turn onto the lake path at 15 plus. Then he got more compact, hunkered down over his skates in a stance like a downhiller, and really started to move. Counterclockwise, lake on the left. The sun had hit the mountains and bled the sky like a bad blade wreck. Joggers and old couples stepped aside, aghast, though the man seemed in total control. He was hanging on to two leads. At the end of them, four feet out, were two huge huskies, running flat-out. Redwing blackbirds keened in the cattails and a hatch of mayflies came off the smooth water. The man and the dogs took the hard turn west. A group of old men played chess on a bench. One looked up, distracted. He had a VFW cap on. He squinted across the water and said, "Mush."

Boulder City Limits

Boulder is skate-friendly. The streets are "smooth-enough," drivers are usually considerate, and there are a ton of smooth paths, which go all over town, but often don't link in easy-to-follow loops. Described here is the classic Boulder skate on the beautiful smooth path that follows Boulder Creek. There are miles of concrete paths that branch off from this main artery, offering myriad opportunities to link and loop, get lost, and explore variations through the streets. One of Boulder's fanatic skaters, Sarah Mannelin, likes to skate the rollercoaster hills on 4th Street, over a mile of fun from Spruce to Kalmia. She likes speed and distance, and will head down Boulder Creek, loop on a nice path south to Arapahoe Road, then link streets and bike paths along the south side of Flatirons Country Club and back. Lamar Simms, the Denver Deputy D.A., was one of the first people to skate in Boulder. He likes to skate south on Boulder Creek to Foothills Parkway, then head north on a smooth path for a couple of miles before coming back. Some people like to skate the mile or so from Eben Fine Park up Boulder Canyon, but it gets sandy. The best thing to do is get ahold of the GO City of Boulder Bicycle and Pedestrian Map—they're free and all over town—and make up your own routes.

BOULDER CREEK—EBEN FINE PARK TO 55TH STREET

Location: Slightly west of Boulder
Length: 7 miles out and back
Elevation gain: Minimal
Map: GO City of Boulder Bicycle and Pedestrian Map

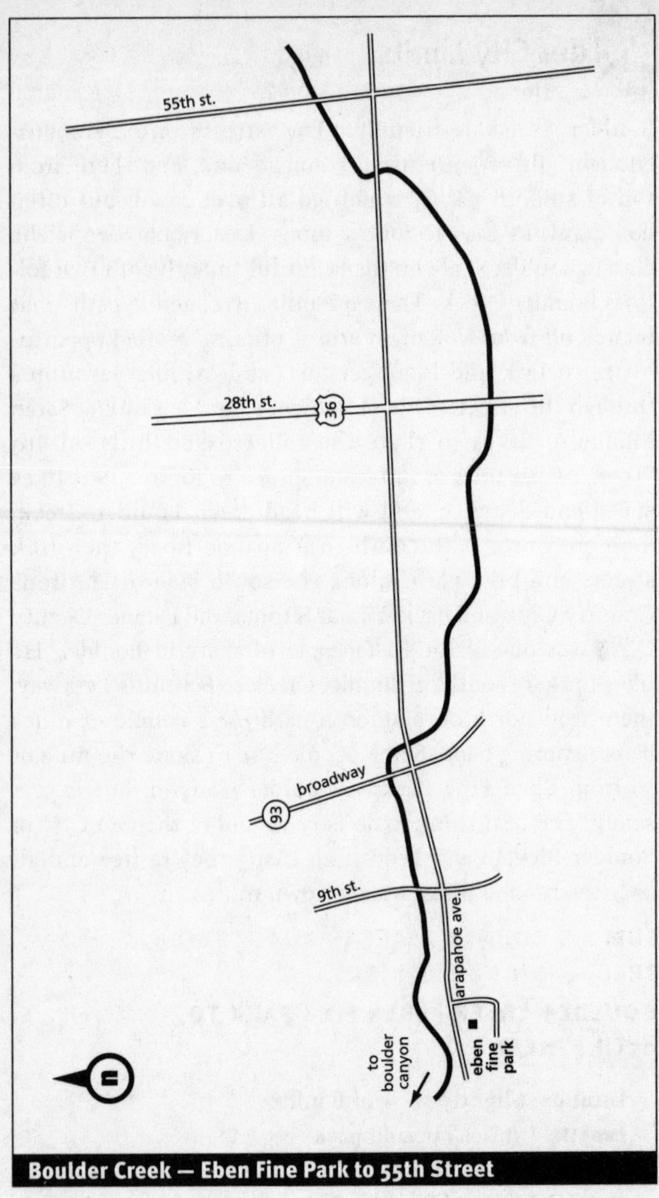

Boulder Creek — Eben Fine Park to 55th Street

Dogs: Yes

Heads up: Exercise-fanatic slalom.

Description: This was my first-ever skate. Not many people were skating in Boulder at the time. I followed my expert friends down the creek and didn't notice much of the spilling water, the rustling willows, the beautifully designed curves and underpasses. Sascha and Lamar sailed along, gracefully swerved around runners, tucked on the hills. I was terrified. I was a menace, and can't believe that the walkers on the path survived my trip unscathed. This is a pretty long skate for the average person. Remember that water flows downhill: coming back is a very gradual climb back up the creek. You can make it shorter any time by simply turning around.

Route: Follow the creek downstream. At 55th take a deep breath and come back. You can also skate upstream into Boulder Canyon for a mile or so, but it gets dirty pretty quickly with sand and gravel from the road.

Directions: Drive south on 28 Street (US 36) to Arapahoe Avenue and turn right (west). Drive 2 miles; the road to Eben Fine Park drops steeply on the left.

Short Hops

SUMMIT COUNTY RECREATIONAL TRAIL—BRECKENRIDGE TO FRISCO

Location: 57 miles west of Denver

Length: 10 miles one-way

Elevation gain: Drops about 500 feet

Dogs: Yes

Heads up: Thrilling and beautiful mountain skate.

Description: Alpine skating at its best. If you had a mind to, and the quads, you could skate on this pretty, smooth, blacktop trail all the way from Breckenridge to Vail. This less ambitious and popular route, which links two hopping mountain towns, is a 10-mile, breathtaking blade from 9,600 feet down to 9,100 feet, with big views of Peaks 7, 8, 9, and 10, and a rolling fast forest trail that smells of fir and pine and is blessedly cool in the summer. Cool-er. Start at the Breck Rec Center and skate north to Frisco. Stop at Main Street, eat, shop, stroll, and then catch the Summit Stage, a free shuttle bus back up to the rec center. There are several bus stops on Main Street in Frisco, and they are well marked. In the off-ski-season, the buses run every hour at about the hour from Frisco. Make sure you take it on the side of the street heading back toward Breck or you'll get a nice ride to Copper Mountain.

Route: Start at the Breckenridge Rec Center, hop on the path, and skate north to Frisco.

Directions: Drive west on I-70 to Breckenridge (CO 9, exit 203) and take CO 9 south. As you get into Breckenridge the rec center is one of the first buildings on the right. Turn right (west) on Valley Brook Road, and left (south) on Airport Road and you'll see the center. Park in the lot.

Skate Parks

Skate parks are increasingly popular. They are thronged with young skateboarders, but more and more in-line skaters are taking to them for the kind of thrills and spills that would be suicidal on the street. Below are a couple of the best skate parks in Denver and Boulder.

THE BLADIUM—DENVER

Next to the old Stapleton Airport, and next to a giant hangar that houses skate hockey and volleyball courts, is an outdoor *wooden* skate park with half-pipes, rails, and drops. Skateboarders tell me it's one of the best around. Nonmember fee is $10. The address is 8797 North Montview Blvd., Bldg. 65; telephone (303) 320-3033.

Directions: Drive north on I-25 to Colfax Avenue (US 40, exit 210A) keep right at the fork in the ramp. Merge onto Colfax heading east. Go 6 miles to Quebec Street and turn left (north). Go to Montview Boulevard and turn right.

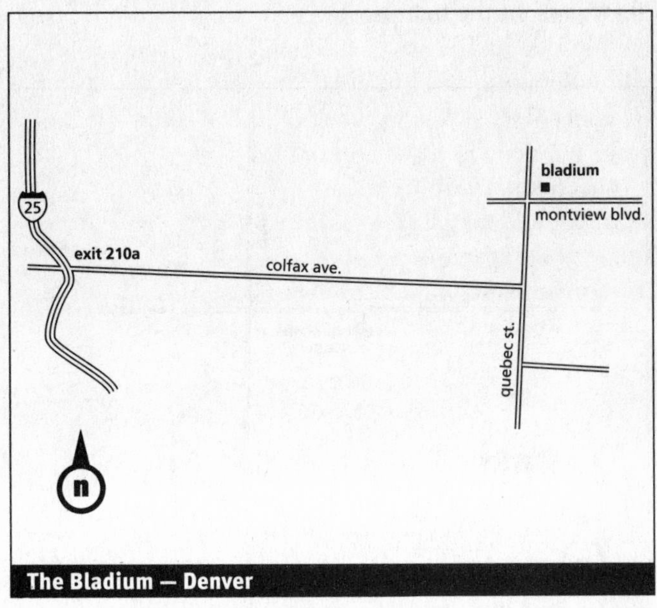

The Bladium — Denver

SCOTT CARPENTER PARK—BOULDER

This is a beauty. Leave it to Boulder to design a skate park that has everything a skater or skateboarder could dream of—rails, steps, ramps, half-pipes—and have it look like a modern sculpture. This place is worth visiting just to spectate. The skateboarders are serious and mostly silent, so all you hear is the granite slide of the wheels, the clap of a flipped board hitting concrete, the metallic grind of a rail. It's a trip. The park is located at 30th Street and Arapahoe.

Directions: Drive south to Arapahoe Road, turn east and head to 30th. Turn right (south) on 30th and then take an immediate right into Scott Carpenter Park. You'll see the skate park on the right.

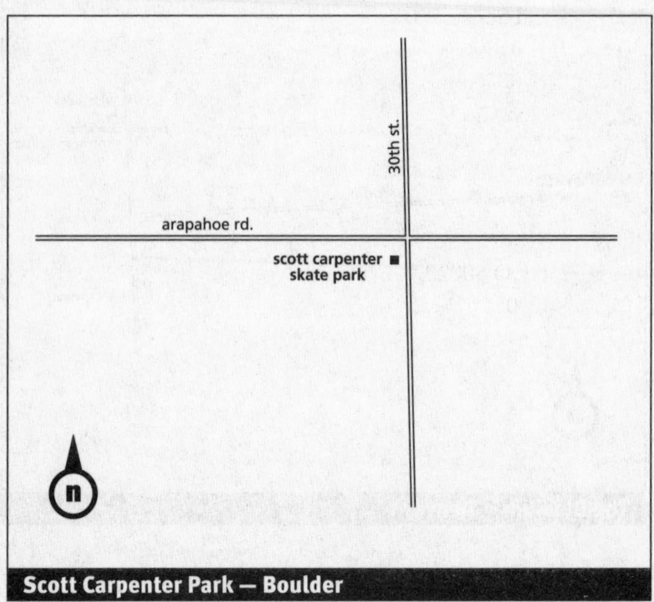

Scott Carpenter Park — Boulder

Where to Connect

Link

www.active.com

Shops

Denver

Grand West Outfitters
801 Broadway
Denver, CO 80203
(303) 825-0300

Boulder

Doc's Ski and Sport
627 South Broadway
Boulder, CO 80303
(303) 499-0963

Galyan's
Flatirons Mall
31 West Flatiron Circle
Broomfield, CO 80020
(720) 887-0900

Farther Afield

Christy Sports
849 Summit Blvd. (near Walmart)
Frisco, CO 80443
(970) 668-5417

Group Skate

K2 Days. Sometime between April and November, around 5 or 6 P.M. a group gets together at Grand West Outfitters with the K2 rep and skates various fun routes around town. Call Grand West Outfitters for current info.

Hiking & Backpacking

THERE'S A FINE line between walking and hiking. The *Oxford English Dictionary* defines hiking as walking "vigorously or laboriously." I don't think that's quite it. To me, hiking always meant going up, which also meant at some point going down. You walk on the flats and hike in the hills. You don't hike in the city. A hike has a sense of deliberateness about it, something you choose to do, which implies pleasure and distinguishes it from a Commute or a Forced March. All this to say that the *hikes* listed are all outside of town, some just barely; and they will bring you into contact with some wildness and beauty.

This chapter is relatively brief, because all the trails described in this book are good hikes. You can multiply the good hiking routes by referring to the chapters on running, mountain biking, snowshoeing, cross-country skiing, telemarking, and horseback riding. Almost all of the trails mentioned there are excellent for hiking, though some of the longer routes may require that a hiker turn back early. Keep in mind the trailheads at Brainard Lake, Eldora, Mathews Winters Park, Waterton Canyon, and White Ranch. For walks in town, refer to the City Limits sections in the chapters on mountain biking, in-line skating, and running. All of these sections contain good routes for urban walking, whether it's along the South Platte or Cherry Creek, the High Line Canal, or in Bear Creek Lake Park.

Backpacking is another story. There's so much wonderful, classic backpacking all over Colorado, it's a little hard to figure out what to corral for an urban adventure guide. The best thing to do may be to explore an area or mountain range, rather than think in terms of taking a specific trail, so I've briefly described a half dozen stunning wilderness areas within an easy drive of Denver and Boulder. These are large roadless areas that allow a backpacker to experience true Colorado wildness. You'll find a description of each area and directions to the nearest major trailhead. The wilderness areas are laced with trails, giving a backpacker opportunities for easy or difficult trips; for trips from one night out to several weeks. A brilliant guide, with detailed trail and trip descriptions, is *The Complete Guide to Colorado's Wilderness Areas* by John Fielder and Mark Pearson.

Another distinction between walking and hiking seems to be that hiking requires the practitioner to think about safety. Be prepared for bad weather, and have enough water and food. It's a good idea to purchase a Colorado Hiking Certificate. This is an extraordinary insurance policy that costs $5, lasts for five years, and can be obtained at REI and most serious outdoor stores. Should you ever need to be searched for and rescued, it covers these costs. Note that all Colorado hunting and fishing licenses automatically include the certificate.

Several authors and their fine guidebooks were crucial to compiling this chapter. Thanks to Tracy Salcedo, Caryn and Peter Boddie, John Fielder and Mark Pearson, and Dave Rich.

The Colorado Mountain Club

IT WOULD BE remiss to not highlight this resource for Colorado outdoorspeople. The club's activities run broad and deep. Started in 1912, the volunteer organization of over ten thousand members runs seminars and trips year-round, beginner to advanced—mountain hikes and climbs, cross-country and telemark skiing, camping and backpacking, technical rock and ice climbing. Their seasonal catalog is almost unbelievable—there will likely be over a hundred snowshoe trips, from half-day to multiday, in areas from the Front Range to the San Juans. Thousands of hikes. Classes in avalanche safety and mountaineering. All run by volunteers and all for very reasonable prices. There are groups that tend to be younger and groups that are older, and a lot of mixed trips where vast amounts of accumulated knowledge is generously shared. An ideal place to improve skills, see the country, and get to know others who share the same loves. The CMC has joined with the esteemed American Alpine Club to build the remarkable American Mountaineering Center in Golden. The center houses the largest mountaineering library in the Western Hemisphere, an auditorium, and a climbing and exploration museum. Contact the CMC at 710 10th Street, #200, Golden CO 80401; (303) 279-9690 or (800) 633-4417; fax: (303) 279-9690; www.cmc.org/cmc/index.html. The American Mountaineering Center is at the same address, Suite 110; (303) 384-9145.

DEER CREEK PARK

Location: 19 miles southwest of Denver

Length: 5-mile loop

Difficulty: Moderate

Elevation gain: 1,260′

Highest elevation: 7,440′

Map: Jefferson County Open Space brochure—Deer Creek Park

Dogs: On leash

Heads up: Popular, multiuse trails; a great weekday hike.

Description: Deer Creek Canyon has one of the best views of the swelling hogback, with its banded sandstone cuts and grass slopes. The trail wends into the canyon through scrub oak and juniper. Good place for birds and wildflowers and seclusion. Dawn and dusk are the best times to see deer, elk, and wild turkeys. If you're there at midday, bring a lunch and eat it at one of the picnic shelters.

Route: Start on the Plymouth Creek Trail, turning to the right at the intersection with Plymouth Mountain Trail. Take the second left for the Red Mesa Loop. It eventually rejoins the Plymouth Creek Trail, which takes you back to your car.

Directions: Drive west on 6th Avenue (US 6) for 3.5 miles to Wadsworth Boulevard (CO 121) and turn left (south). Continue about 12 miles to Deer Creek Canyon Road (124 RD). Turn right and in about 3 miles turn left (south) on Cougar Road. The parking lot is on the right (west).

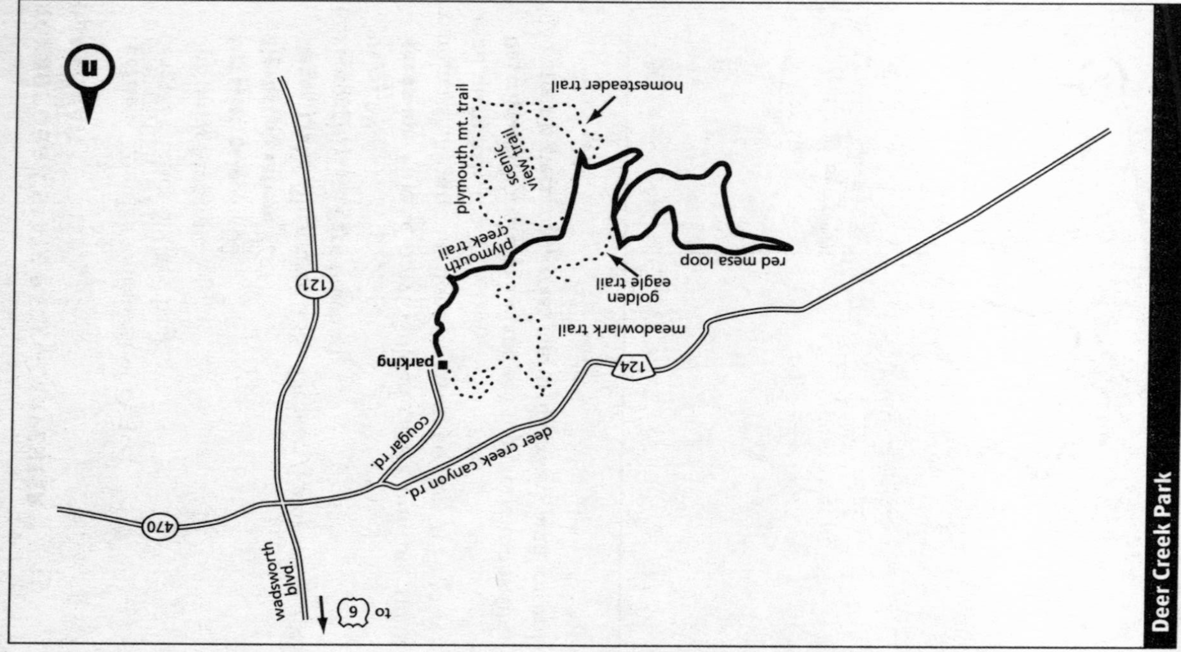

Deer Creek Park

ROXBOROUGH STATE PARK—CARPENTER PEAK TRAIL

Location: 22 miles southwest of Denver

Length: 6 miles out and back

Difficulty: Moderate

Elevation gain: 1,100′

Highest elevation: 7,200′

Maps: Trails Illustrated 135—Deckers/Rampart Range; Roxborough State Park brochure

Dogs: No

Heads up: Hiking only! Golden eagles hunting small mammals. Mountain lions—pray that they're hunting small mammals too.

Description: For seclusion and red-rock formations tumbled among green oak, grass and wildflowers, and for bril-

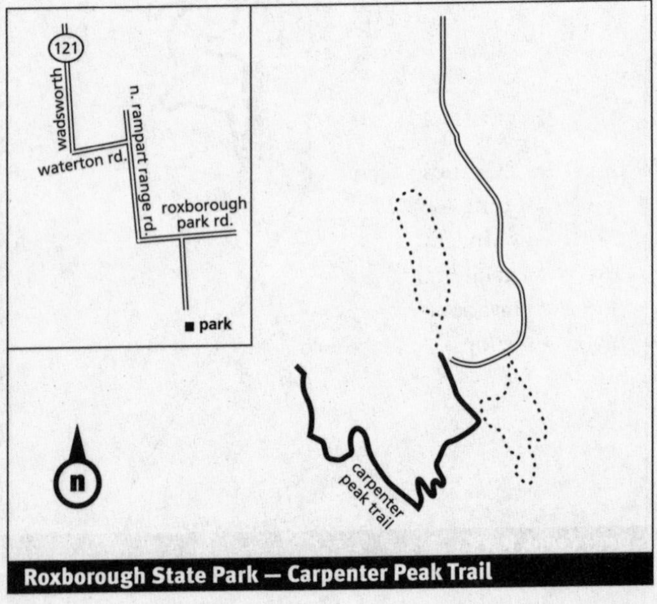

Roxborough State Park – Carpenter Peak Trail

liant contrasting colors of rock and brush in the fall, Roxborough is queen of the parks. Plains, foothills, and montane zones make for great birding. Not much cover, so it's best to avoid the heat of the day. There's a visitors center with restrooms, bird checklists, and wildlife information.

Route: Hike the South Rim Trail to the turnoff for Carpenter Peak Trail. A moderate to steep climb to a small plateau, then a steep pitch to the summit with 360-degree views. Return the way you came.

Directions: Drive west on 6th Avenue (US 6) to Wadsworth Boulevard (CO 121). Turn south and follow Wadsworth under CO 470 and continue 5 miles to Roxborough/Waterton Road. Turn left on Waterton Road and follow it until it ends at North Rampart Range Road (1.6 miles). Turn right (south) on North Rampart Range Road. Continue south 2.3 miles to the intersection with Roxborough Park Road. Turn left onto Roxborough Park Road. Take the next right to enter the park.

MOUNT FALCON

Location: 20 miles southwest of Denver

Length: 3-mile loop

Difficulty: Moderate

Elevation gain: 560′

Highest elevation: 7,760′

Map: Jefferson County Open Space brochure—Mt. Falcon Park

Dogs: Yes

Heads up: Many trail options—grab a brochure. Great for families.

Description: A great hike if you want to start with some altitude, enjoy big views out to Denver and over the plains, and meander on the piney ridge tops. There's one rocky

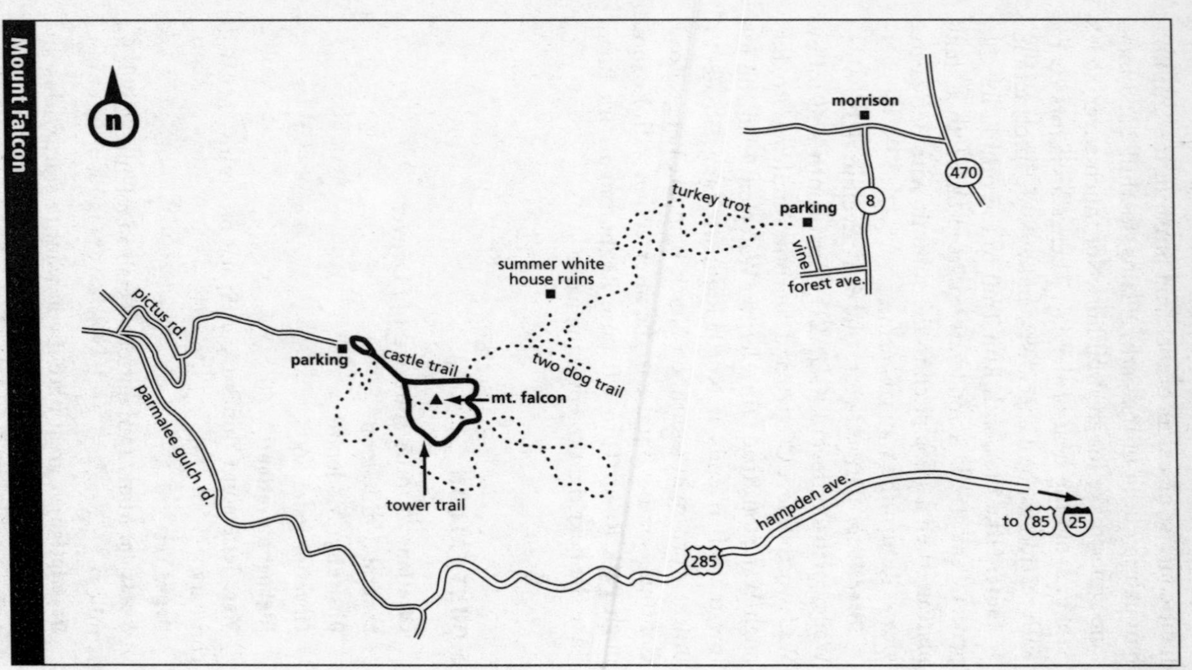
Mount Falcon
n
morrison
470
8
parking
turkey trot
vine
forest ave.
summer white
house ruins
pictus rd.
parking
castle trail
two dog trail
mt. falcon
parmalee gulch rd.
tower trail
hampden ave.
285
to 85 25

descent on this loop, and many other trails and features to explore, including remnants of an old stone mansion. A good spot for hikers of all abilities.

Route: Take Castle Trail east to the Parmalee Trail. It winds around to a junction with five other trails. Take the Tower Trail heading southwest around the south side of Mt. Falcon. It meets back up with the Castle Trail, which you can take back to the parking lot.

Directions: Drive south on I-25 to Santa Fe Drive (US 85, exit 207B) Head south on Santa Fe to the Hampden Avenue (US 285) exit. Take US 285 south (which actually heads west, go figure) about 13 miles to Parmalee Gulch Road (120 RD). Go right (north) on Parmalee Gulch Road about 5 miles to Pictus Road and turn right (east). Follow signs to the west parking area.

BEAVER BROOK

Location: 31 miles west of Denver

Length: Up to 17 miles, or about 8-plus miles one way

Difficulty: Moderate to difficult

Elevation gain: 1,160′

Highest elevation: 7,760′

Map and books: USGS Morrison and Evergreen (7.5 minute); *Foothills to Mount Evans; Best Easy Day Hikes: Denver*

Dogs: Yes

Heads up: Watch for gold markers. If you are not good with topo maps, or get lost easily, start at Windy Saddle at the Lookout Mountain Nature Center (for directions to the center, see *Shorter Option*). Not recommended for small children.

Description: A very popular Denver hike through ponderosa pine and aspen forests, with a good chance of hawks

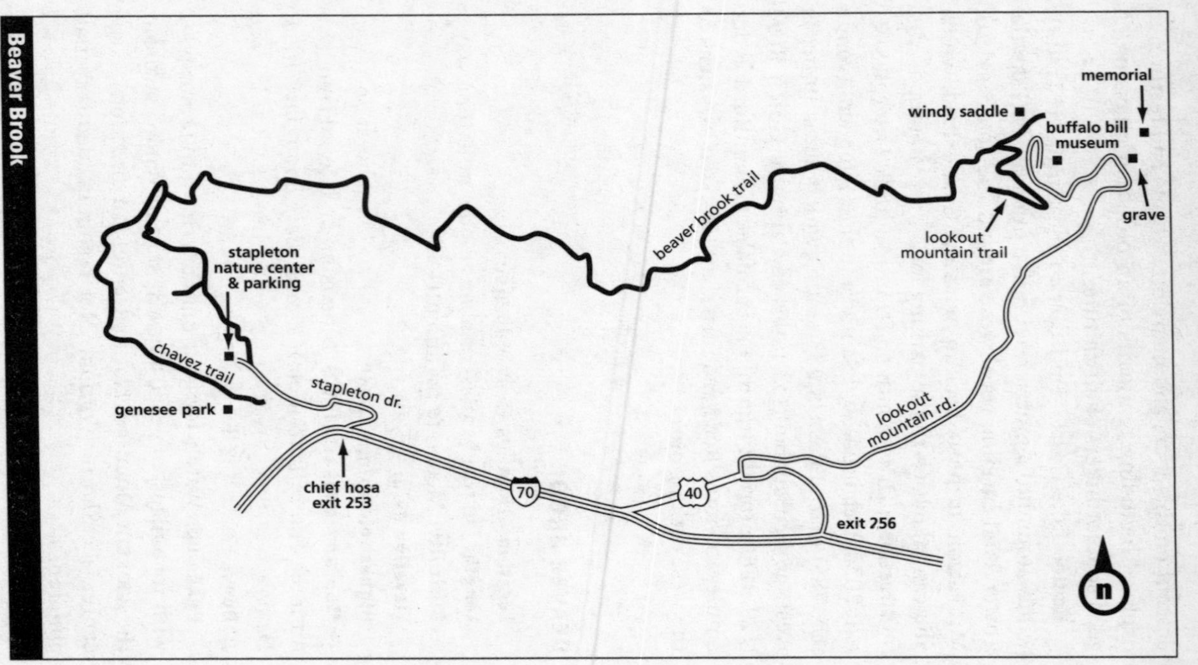
Beaver Brook
memorial
windy saddle
buffalo bill museum
grave
lookout mountain trail
beaver brook trail
stapleton nature center & parking
chavez trail
genesee park
stapleton dr.
chief hosa exit 253
70
40
exit 256
lookout mountain rd.
n

and eagles flying overhead. Great views of Denver, the high plains, Clear Creek Canyon, South Table Mountain, and the Continental Divide. Abrupt drops, steep climbs, and rock fields.

Route: From Genesee Park walk from the trailhead to the picnic area. The Stapleton Nature Trail, to the north, connects you with the Beaver Brook Trail. Once on the Beaver Brook Trail watch for the yellow diamonds that mark the trail. Note that the trail is not always well worn and it could use a few more markers—it's easy to be diverted onto an unsigned trail. Soon after the start, the trail drops to the left (northwest) at an unmarked Y intersection. Rejoin the old trail at 0.6 mile and continue generally north. Go right at the next obvious trail junction. (A left will loop you back to the parking lot via the Chavez Trail for a 2.8-mile hike.) As you climb out of Bear Gulch, watch for access trails and a jeep road joining the Beaver Brook Trail. Don't take them. You'll then scramble through rock fields, and across a couple of talus slopes, and descend to the Lookout Mountain Nature Center.

Shorter option: You can leave a car at the Nature Center on Lookout Mountain for a shuttle and an 8-mile one-way hike.

Directions: To get to Genesee Park, head west on I-70 to the Chief Hosa exit (exit 253), and go north on Stapleton Drive to the Stapleton Nature trailhead. (From October to April the road is closed after about 1 mile. Park at the gate and walk half a mile to the trailhead.) To get to Lookout Mountain Nature Center, take I-70 west to the Buffalo Bill Memorial Museum and Grave exit (exit 256). Turn right (north) on Grapevine Road to US 40. Turn left (west) onto US 40. Turn right (north) on Lookout Mountain Road (68 RD). Turn left (west) on Colorow Road and follow it to the nature center.

BERGEN PEAK

Location: 23 miles southwest of Denver

Length: 10-mile loop

Difficulty: Moderate

Elevation gain: 1,730′

Highest elevation: 9,680′

Map: Jefferson County Open Space brochure—Elk Meadow Park

Dogs: Yes

Heads up: Steep climbs, switchbacks.

Description: This is a strenuous, steep climb close to town, with rewarding views of Pikes Peak, Mt. Evans, and the Continental Divide at the top. Lovely pine forest. Mountain bikers actually climb the mountain too, so watch for dazed-looking cyclists.

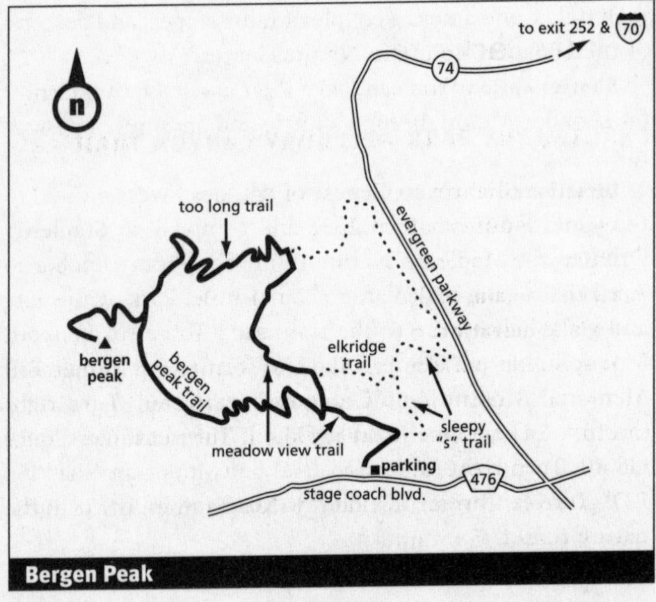

Bergen Peak

Route: Head south out of the parking lot on the Meadow Trail. It quickly joins the Meadow View Trail and Sleepy S Trail. Stay to the left and continue on the Meadow View Trail. At the Bergen Peak trailhead go to the left (west) and climb to the left turnoff for Bergen Peak (steep ascent to the top). You can cut off about a mile and come back the way you came, or for the full loop, take a left onto the Too Long Trail when you come down from the mile-long spur trail to the summit. This descends steeply back to the Meadow View Trail. Take a right onto Meadow View and another right onto the Meadow Trail to get back to the lot.

Directions: Head west on 6th Avenue (US 6) to westbound I-70. Take I-70 about 17 miles to the Evergreen Parkway (CO 74, exit 252.) Drive 5 miles south to Stage Coach Boulevard (476 RD) and turn right (west). Go about 1 mile to the south parking lot.

Boulder Backyard

CHAUTAUQUA PARK—GREGORY CANYON TRAIL

Location: Slightly southwest of Boulder
Length: 5 miles out and back
Difficulty: Moderate
Elevation gain: 950′
Highest elevation: 6,650′
Fee: If you park at the Gregory Canyon parking area there's a $3 daily fee for cars not registered in Boulder County. Season pass is available at the seasonal Chautauqua Park Ranger Cottage.
Maps: Sky Terrain Boulder/El Dorado map; USGS Eldorado Springs (7.5 minute)
Dogs: Yes

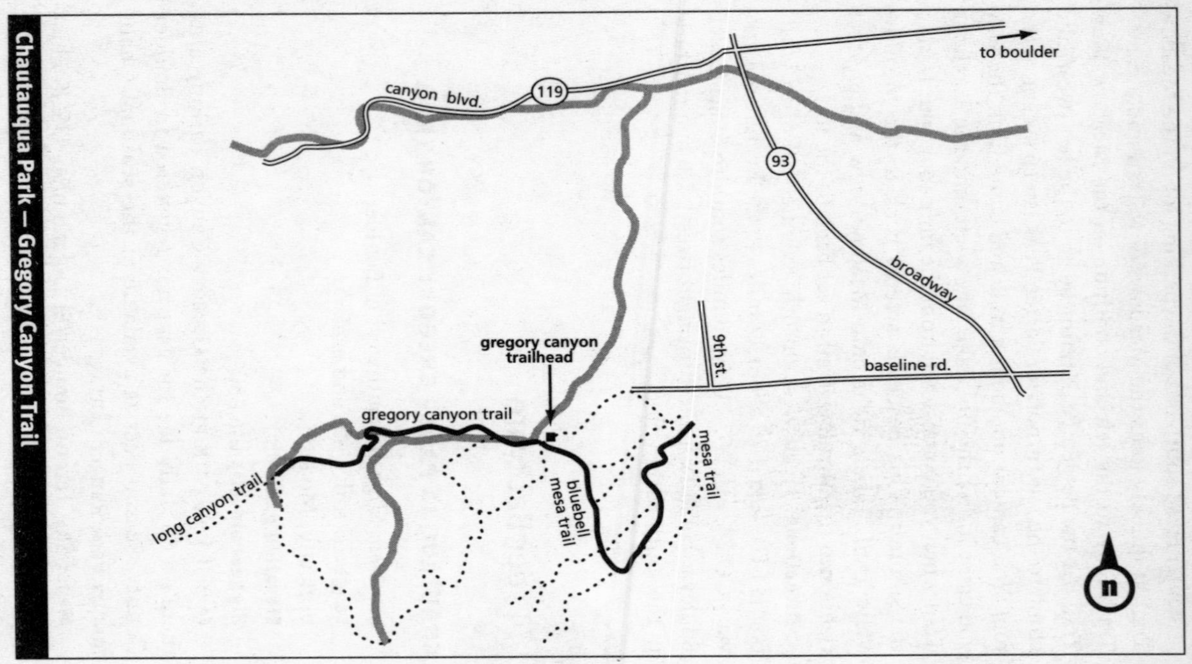
Chautauqua Park — Gregory Canyon Trail
to boulder
canyon blvd.
119
93
broadway
9th st.
baseline rd.
gregory canyon trailhead
gregory canyon trail
bluebell mesa trail
mesa trail
long canyon trail
n

Description: At Chautauqua, right at the edge of town, you climb out of the lovely open grasslands beneath the Flatirons, skirt the north slope of Green Mountain, and enter one of the prettiest canyons that cut the foothills. The slopes are covered in Douglas fir and ponderosa pine, and scented like a sachet. You hike along Gregory Creek.

Route: Hike southwest out of the parking lot, up the closed road, to the Bluebell Mesa Trail. Turn right, north, onto the Bluebell-Baird Trail. At the Gregory Canyon trailhead continue north up the Gregory Canyon Trail to the Long Canyon Trail. Turn around at this junction.

Longer options: There are many options for longer hikes and loops. It's a little over a mile further to the top of Green Mountain. See the Sky Terrain Boulder/El Dorado map.

Directions: Take Canyon Boulevard (CO 119) west to Broadway (CO 93), and turn left (south). Continue on Broadway to Baseline Road and turn right (west). Take Baseline to just past 9th Street. Turn left (south) into the well-marked Chautauqua parking lot.

BALD MOUNTAIN LOOP—PINES TO PEAK TRAIL

Location: 7 miles northwest of Boulder

Length: 1.25 miles

Difficulty: Easy

Elevation gain: 240′

Highest elevation: 7,100′

Map and book: USGS Boulder (7.5 minute); *12 Short Hikes in the Boulder Foothills*

Dogs: Yes

Heads up: Great views and a shaded bench at the summit.

Description: A short, lovely hill climb through ponderosa woods to a big open meadow at the top and a little bench in the shade of the trees. From here the views are magnifi-

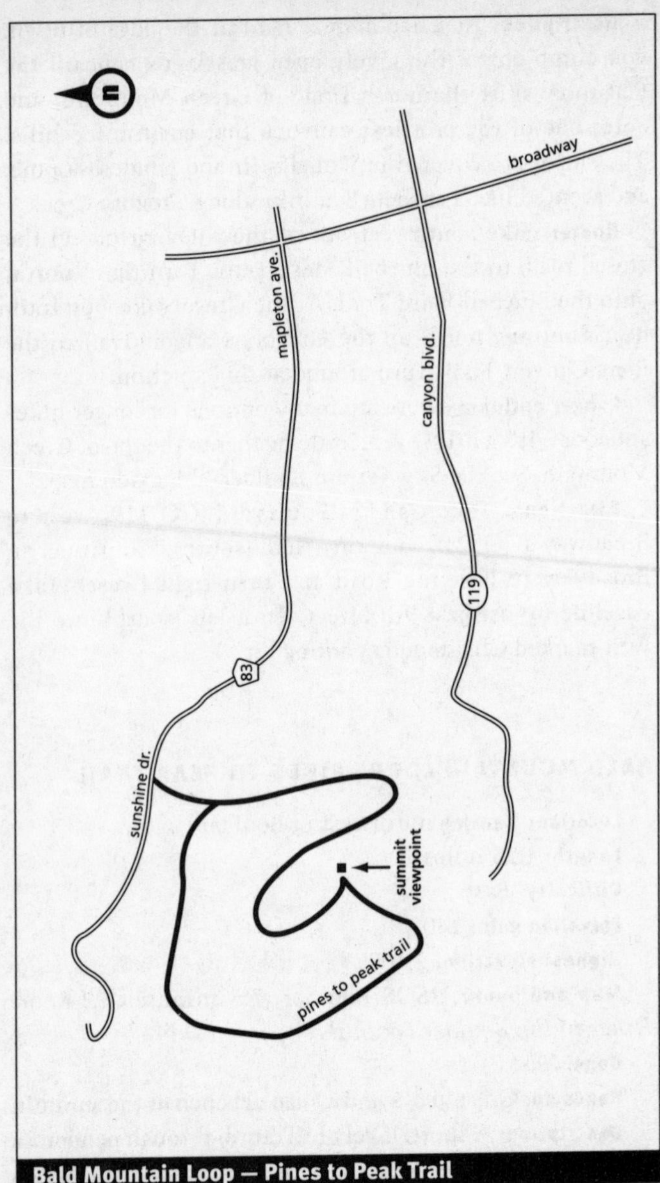

Bald Mountain Loop — Pines to Peak Trail

cent—Indian Peaks, the back of Flagstaff Mountain and the Flatirons, and Denver shimmering on the sea of the plains. Good gentle stroll for families.

Route: Head south out of the parking lot on the Pines to Peak Trail. Stay to the left at the junction—the trail climbs to the meadowed summit and loops back around.

Directions: Drive west on Canyon Boulevard (CO 119) to Broadway and turn right (north). Take it 1.8 miles north to Mapleton Avenue and turn left (west). Take Mapleton Avenue about 1 mile; it becomes Sunshine Drive (83 RD). Continue 4.2 miles up the canyon to the parking lot on the left side of the road.

ELDORADO STATE PARK—ELDORADO CANYON TRAIL

Location: 10 miles southwest of Boulder, 31 miles northwest of Denver

Length: 9 miles out and back

Difficulty: Difficult

Elevation gain: 1,040′

Highest elevation: 7,250′

Fee: $4 day pass, $40 annual pass per vehicle

Maps and book: Eldorado State Park brochure; Sky Terrain Boulder/El Dorado map; *12 Short Hikes in the Boulder Foothills*

Dogs: Yes

Heads up: Rock climbers on the cliffs. If you are using the Sky Terrain Boulder/El Dorado map, the Eldorado Canyon Trail is unlabeled—it's the hiking trail below North Draw.

Description: Wild kingdom. Beautiful forests of ponderosa pine, Douglas fir, and juniper. Small wetlands and riparian communities offer glimpses of raptors, songbirds, and waterfowl. Golden eagles, red-tailed hawks, and prairie fal-

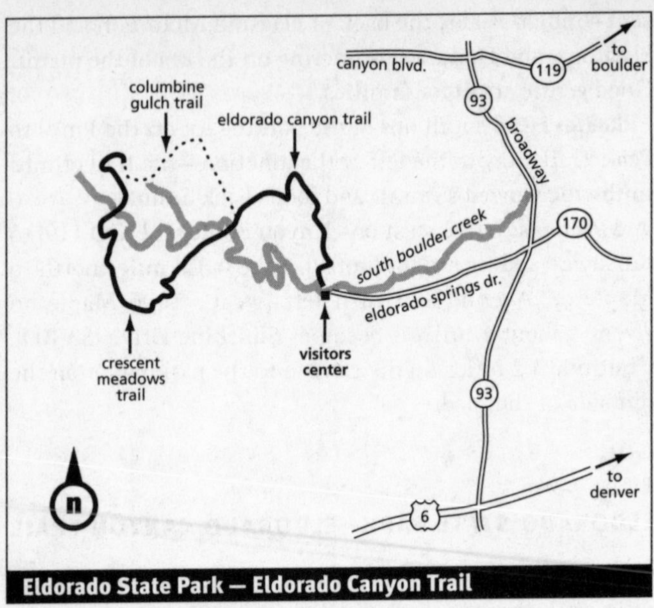

Eldorado State Park — Eldorado Canyon Trail

cons nest within and adjacent to the park. Commonly seen are mule deer, coyote, raccoon, striped skunk, cottontail rabbit, porcupine, ground squirrel, and red fox. Also around, but more rarely seen, are black bear, mountain lion, and elk.

Route: Park at the new visitors center at the west end of the road. The trailhead is located to the north. Follow the well-marked Eldorado Canyon Trail through a series of switchbacks. It traverses the ridge with views of the Continental Divide. At the junction with the Crescent Meadows Trail stay right and continue on the Eldorado Canyon Trail. As you leave the side of South Boulder Creek you enter Walker Ranch Park; this was the site of a forest fire in the summer of 2000. Please stay on the trail to avoid hampering regrowth. Turn around at the junction of the Eldorado Canyon Trail and the Columbine Gulch Trail.

Directions: From Boulder, drive west on Canyon Boulevard (CO 119) to Broadway (CO 93) and turn left (south). Go 5 miles to Eldorado Springs Drive (CO 170) and turn right (west). Continue to the park entrance west of the town of Eldorado Springs. From Denver, take US 6 west 12 miles, through Golden to CO 93 and turn right (north). Drive 13 miles to Eldorado Springs Drive (CO 170); turn left (west) and follow CO 170 to the park entrance.

Golden

GOLDEN GATE CANYON STATE PARK—MOUNTAIN LION TRAIL

Location: 29 miles west of Denver, 32 miles south of Boulder

Length: 6.7-mile loop

Difficulty: Moderate

Elevation gain: 1,200′

Highest elevation: 9,000′ at Windy Peak

Map: Golden Gate State Park brochure

Dogs: Yes

Heads up: Winter backcountry camping.

Description: The whole of this glorious park is great for hiking, and its network of trails offers many options in steepness and length. Mountain biking is permitted in most of the park, but there are a few hiking-only trails, which the park map shows clearly. The Mountain Lion Trail isn't one of them, but it's a great hike anyway. The park contains several designated backcountry camping areas and lean-to shelters. For camping, call (303) 582-3707 to obtain a permit. The steep hills of Golden Gate are blanketed with Douglas fir and logdepole pine, patched with aspen groves, threaded with little creeks, pocketed with

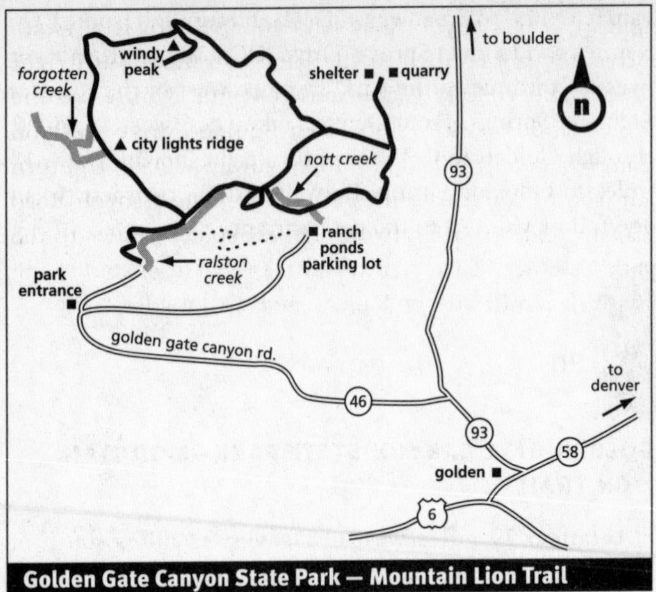

Golden Gate Canyon State Park — Mountain Lion Trail

meadows and grassy valleys. Deer are common, and you may see turkey vultures, red-tailed hawks, and golden eagles. A short excursion to Forgotten Creek will land you at a barn and pond—great for an afternoon of lolling and reading.

Route: Park your car at Nott Creek and head northwest. The Mountain Lion Trail loops around City Lights Ridge and Forgotten Creek. A quick ascent up Windy Peak and you'll be at the halfway point and a great spot to eat lunch. Continue to the quarry for backcountry campsites and a three-sided shelter. If you're camping: there are no fires allowed in the backcountry, and you must sign in at the visitors center. Go northeast out of the parking lot and do the loop in reverse so you won't have to carry your gear as far.

Directions: From Denver, drive 12 miles west on US 6 through Golden to CO 93. Continue north on CO 93 to

Golden Gate Canyon Road (CO 46) and turn left (west). Drive about 14 miles to the park entrance. Turn right toward the visitors center and continue 3 miles to the Ranch Ponds parking lot. From Boulder, drive west on Canyon Boulevard (CO 119) to Broadway (CO 93) and turn left (south). Drive 19 miles to Golden Gate Canyon Road (CO 46) and turn right (west). Drive about 14 miles to the park entrance. Turn right toward the visitors center and continue 3 miles to the Ranch Ponds parking lot.

Short Hops

CHIEF MOUNTAIN

Location: 31 miles west of Denver

Length: 3 miles out and back

Difficulty: Easy

Elevation gain: 1,060′

Highest elevation: 11,709′

Map and books: USGS Idaho Springs (7.5 minute); *Best Easy Day Hikes: Denver*

Dogs: Yes

Heads up: As good a view is hard to find. Rivals any Fourteener. Limited parking, windy on summit.

Description: Start high, hike through spruce-fir forest, and top out with exquisite views of the Continental Divide to the west, Mt. Evans to the southwest, Pikes Peak to the south, Longs Peak to the north, and the high plains to the east. A solid, short climb; watch for thinning air and take your time.

Route: The trail is marked by a metal stake on the south side of the road, and switchbacks up the embankment to a small white post marked 290. Cross Old Squaw Pass Road

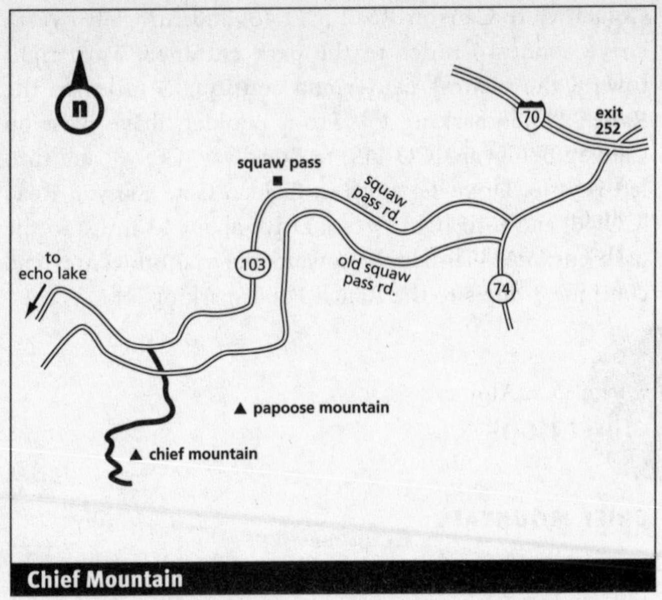

Chief Mountain

through spruce-fir to the saddle of Chief Mountain to the west and Papoose Mountain to the east. Hike up the switchbacks to another saddle. The right-hand outcrop, to the north, is the summit. Return the way you came.

Directions: Take I-70 west to Evergreen Parkway (CO 74, exit 252). Head south on CO 74 to Squaw Pass Road and turn right (west); it becomes CO 103. In about 12 miles look for a pullout on the north side of CO 103. Neither trailhead nor parking area is marked. Look for mile marker 19. The more well-defined parking area for Old Squaw Pass road is 0.4 mile east on CO 103.

SCOTT GOMER

Location: 57 miles southwest of Denver

Length: 8 miles

Difficulty: Moderate to difficult

Elevation gain: 3,030′

Highest elevation: 12,650′

Map and book: USGS Mount Evans (7.5 minute); *Skiing Colorado's Backcountry: Northern Mountains—Trails and Tours*

Dogs: Yes

Heads up: Alpine lake, bighorns. Good for snowshoeing.

Description: This trail was highly recommended by my neighbor and senior consultant Ardis Rohwer. It's a high-altitude alpine jaunt, with great views of Mt. Bierstadt and Mt. Evans. The rocky slopes surrounding Abyss Lake are home to bighorn sheep and mountain goats.

Route: The first 4 miles of the trail heads in a northeast direction up the Scott Gomer Creek drainage. Approximately 2 miles from the trailhead the trail makes the first of three crossings of Scott Gomer Creek. Shortly after this first crossing, Mt. Bierstadt will come into view ahead and on your left. After the third crossing of Scott Gomer Creek you will reach a trail junction sign with the Rosalie Trail. Continue to your left at the sign to Abyss Lake. For the next 7 or 8 minutes of hiking you will be on both the Abyss Lake and Rosalie Trails. At the next sign the Rosalie Trail bears left up to Guanella Pass and the Abyss Lake Trail continues straight ahead in a northeast direction across several small streams. Stay on the Abyss Lake Trail. Note that this portion of the trail was rerouted several years ago and the trail is not located as it appears on the "photorevised 1974" copy of the Mt. Evans quad map. After the two small stream crossings the trail begins a series of fairly steep switchbacks, still bearing northeast. The trail leaves the trees and enters thick willows just

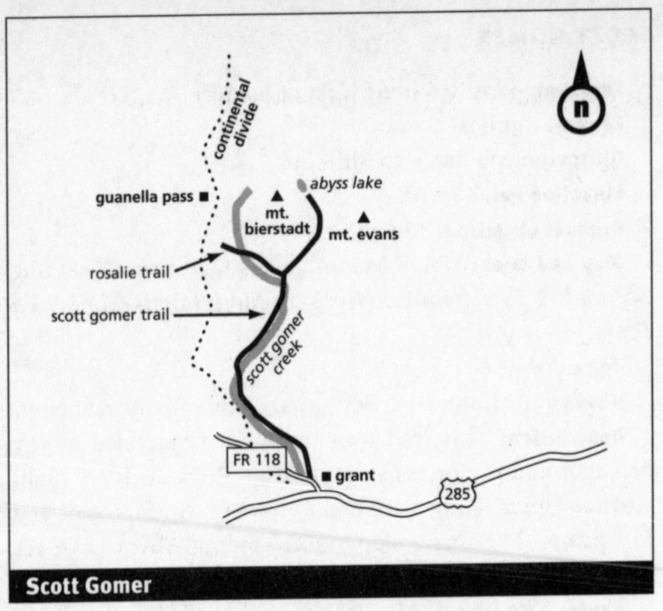

Scott Gomer

to the southwest of the small lake labeled "elevation 11,730" on the quad map. After crossing the drainage outlet of this lake watch for rock cairns to identify the trail through the willows. After about 30 minutes of hiking from Lake 11,730 you will cross the Lake Fork stream draining out of Abyss Lake. From this point the trail begins to head in a more westerly direction on tundra. Several remnants of an airplane crash will be visible along this portion of the trail. Trail terminates at Abyss Lake.

Directions: Drive south on I-25 to Santa Fe Drive (US 85, exit 207B). Head south on Santa Fe to Hampden Avenue (US 285). Drive west on US 285 for 51 miles to Grant. Turn right (north) onto FR 118 (toward Guanella Pass) and drive 5.5 miles. The trailhead is on the east (right) side of the road and is located just south of Burning Bear Campground. There is a parking area at the trailhead.

MISSOURI LAKES LOOP

Location: Minturn—95 miles west of Denver

Length: 9-mile loop

Difficulty: Moderate

Elevation gain: 10,500′

Highest elevation: 12,000′

Maps and book: USGS Minturn (7.5 minute); Trails Illustrated 108—Vail/Frisco/Dillon; *The Complete Guide to Colorado's Wilderness Areas*

Dogs: Yes

Heads up: Holy Cross Wilderness. Waterfalls!

Description: Hike along Fancy Creek past Fancy Lake and over Fancy Pass. Short alpine hike gives you views of the peaks of the Sawatch Range and high-altitude lakes. As you descend along Missouri Creek from Missouri Lakes watch for waterfalls and cascades.

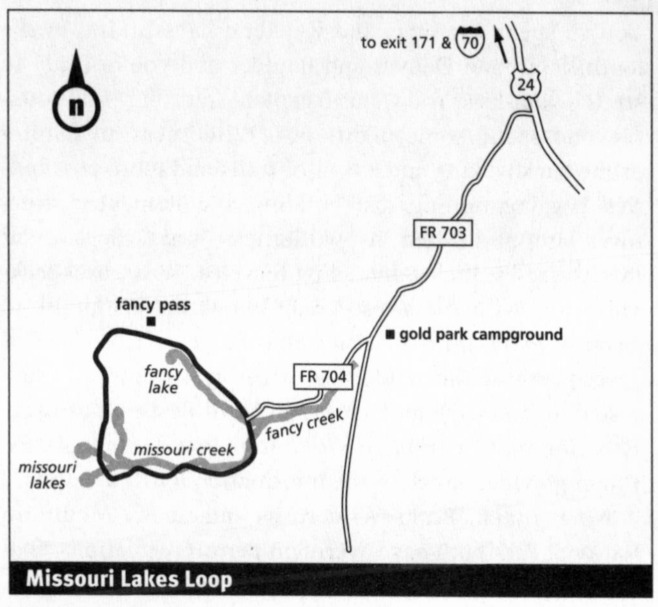

Missouri Lakes Loop

Route: A counterclockwise loop from the Missouri Lakes trailhead. Hike uphill along Homestake Pipeline to the parking area on FR 727. The Fancy Pass Trail (TR 2006) takes off from this lot. Hike the trail along Fancy Creek to Fancy Lake. The trail joins an old wagon road and continues to Fancy Pass. It then loops and contours past Treasure Vault Lake to Missouri Pass, and descends to the Missouri Lakes. The trail turns to the east as you descend along Missouri Creek back to the trailhead.

Directions: Drive west on I-70 to Minturn (US 24, exit 171). Drive south on US 24 to FR 703 and turn right (southwest). Follow FR 703 just past Gold Park Campground to FR 704, and turn right (west) to the Missouri Lakes trailhead.

Wilderness Areas

You've spent evenings and weekend days hiking in the foothills around Denver and Boulder and you're ready to stretch your legs. You want to explore some big, wild country, and spend some nights out. Wilderness areas offer prime backpacking and a host of trails and route possibilities. Logging, mining, road building, and permanent structures are prohibited in wilderness areas. So are all mechanized vehicles, including bicycles. When backpacking in the wilderness, use Leave No Trace techniques to minimize your impact (see p. 28). For an excellent, detailed description of the wilderness areas and numerous suggested routes, see John Fielder and Mark Pearson's brilliant *The Complete Guide to Colorado's Wilderness Areas,* which provided much of the information for this section.

Note: Indian Peaks Wilderness and Rocky Mountain National Park both have overnight permit regulations. Call the numbers given for each to obtain permits and other information.

INDIAN PEAKS WILDERNESS

General location: 25 miles west of Boulder and a few miles northwest of Nederland, which is 14 miles from Boulder

Permits: Backcountry permits are required for overnight camping between June 1 and September 15. Quotas are in place during peak season for areas within the wilderness area. A $5 per reservation fee applies. Reservations can be obtained by phone, at the Boulder Ranger District Office (Monday–Friday, 8 A.M.–4:30 P.M.), or at selected area vendors. For more information call the Boulder Ranger District: (303) 444-6600.

Contact: Dillon Ranger District, White River National Forest, (970) 468-5400, or Holy Cross Ranger District, White River National Forest, (970) 827-5715

Maps: USFS Arapaho and Roosevelt National Forest maps

Description: The wilderness area sprawls across the Arapaho and Roosevelt National Forests. Its 74,000 acres are filled with notched peaks, glaciers, brilliant lakes, creeks, and breathtaking views. Ecosystems range from lodgepole pine to spruce-fir to bristlecone pine to timberline-alpine tundra. Wildlife common to the area are elk, moose, mule deer, black bear, mountain lion, and beaver. Birds include red-tailed hawk, ptarmigan, and golden eagle. Fishing, hiking and backpacking, climbing, and canoeing are all popular in the Indian Peaks. There are numerous campgrounds, backcountry sites, and trailheads. Be aware that Indian Peaks has more restrictions than other wilderness areas in Colorado, so call for information.

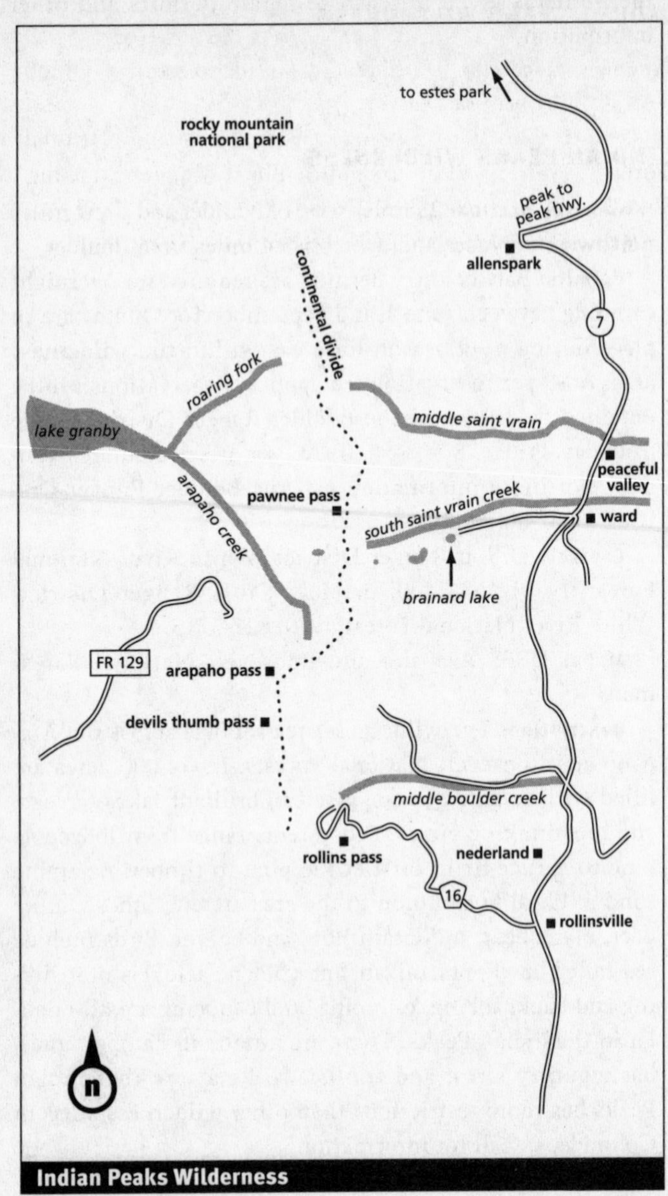
to estes park
rocky mountain national park
peak to peak hwy.
allenspark
continental divide
7
roaring fork
lake granby
middle saint vrain
peaceful valley
arapaho creek
pawnee pass
south saint vrain creek
ward
brainard lake
FR 129
arapaho pass
devils thumb pass
middle boulder creek
rollins pass
nederland
16
rollinsville
n
Indian Peaks Wilderness

MOUNT EVANS WILDERNESS

General location: 10 miles south of Idaho Springs, which is 30 miles north of Denver

Contact: Clear Creek Ranger District, Arapaho National Forest, (303) 567-2901, or South Platte Ranger District, Pike National Forest, (303) 275-5610

Maps: USFS Arapaho and Pike National Forest maps

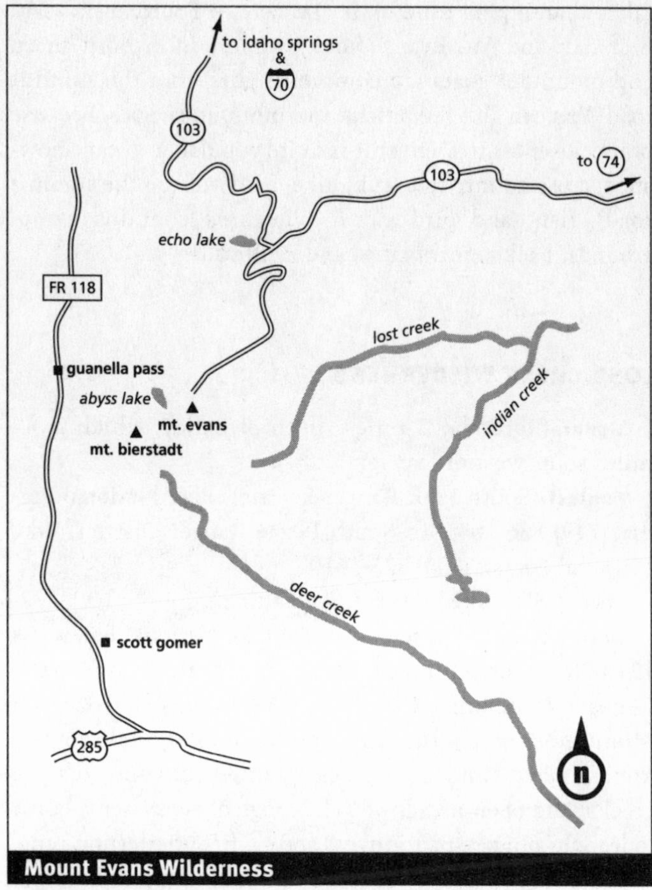

Mount Evans Wilderness

Description: This wilderness lies in the Arapaho and Pike National Forests. Roughly 73,000 acres, it contains lodgepole pine, spruce-fir, bristlecone pine, and timberline-alpine tundra ecosystems. A great portion of the wilderness lies above timberline, and is graced with ancient glaciers and a prime stand of bristlecone pine. Some of these trees are 1,500 to 2,000 years old. Plan a visit to the Mt. Goliath Natural Area. This is one of a few places outside of the Arctic Circle to contain arctic tundra (arctic tundra has more lakes than alpine tundra). It claims two Fourteeners—Mt. Bierstadt and Mt. Evans. Rocky Mountain bighorn sheep and mountain goats are common sights from the summit road. You can also see hawks, marmots, and eagles. Because of its closeness to Denver it is quite popular. You can snowshoe, cross-country ski, run, hike, road ride (up the summit road), fish, and bird-watch. The area contains campgrounds, backcountry sites, and trailheads.

LOST CREEK WILDERNESS

General location: 3 miles south of Bailey, which is 42 miles southwest of Denver

Contact: South Park Ranger District, Pike National Forest, (719) 836-2031, or South Platte Ranger District, Pike National Forest, (303) 275-5610

Map: USFS Pike National Forest map

Description: Lost Creek is in the Pike National Forest. Its 121,000 acres embrace three mountain ranges—the Kenosha Mountains, Platte River Mountains, and Tarryall Mountains—and stunning granite domes, half-domes, knobs, spires and buttresses, granite canyons, roaring creeks, and open meadows. The range of ecosystems cover lodgepole pine, aspen groves, spruce-fir, bristlecone pine, and timberline-alpine tundra. Lost Creek repeatedly loses

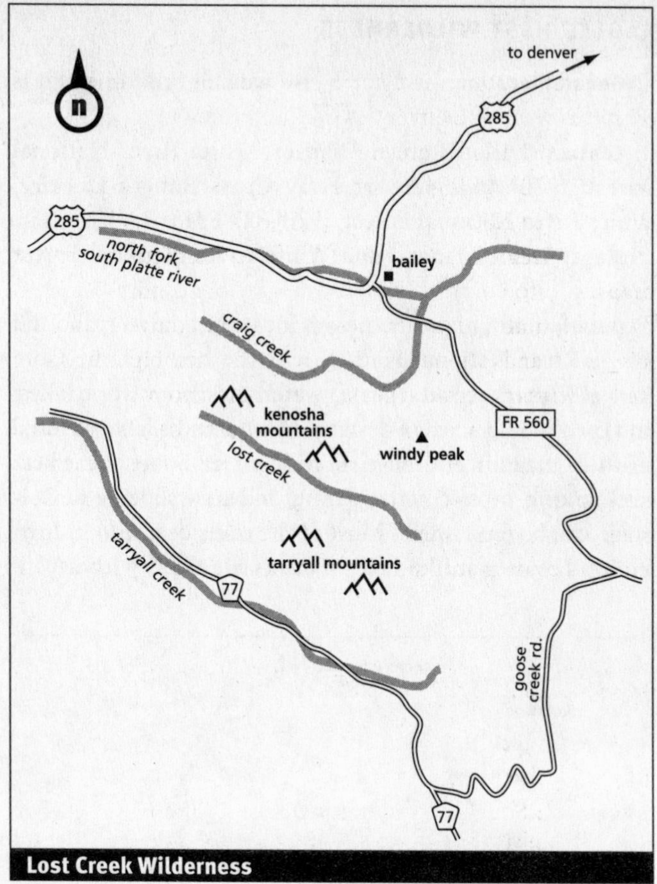

Lost Creek Wilderness

itself into the rock, hence its name. Elk, bobcats, black bears, and mule deer are residents, in addition to Rocky Mountain bighorn sheep. There are numerous campsites and over 100 miles of trails.

EAGLES NEST WILDERNESS

General location: Just north and west of Frisco, which is 59 miles west of Denver

Contact: Dillon Ranger District, White River National Forest, (970) 468-5400, or Holy Cross Ranger District, White River National Forest, (970) 827-5715

Maps: USFS Arapaho and White River National Forest maps

Description: This wilderness is located in the Arapaho and White River National Forests. It is the home of the Gore Range, with its serrated peaks, waterfalls, and pristine lakes, and the 134,000 acres of designated wilderness have ensured that this magnificent range survives intact. Some of the best telemarking, cross-country skiing, and snowshoeing in Colorado can be found here. Most of the trails dead-end in high valleys beside gemlike lakes. Forests are filled with aspen,

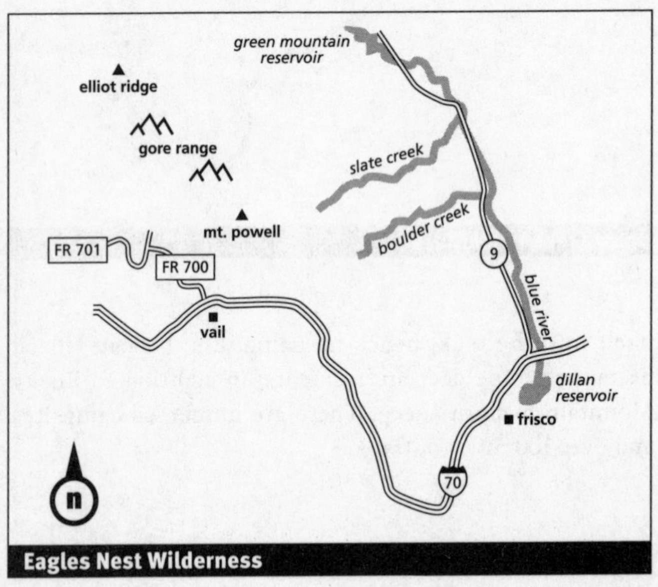

Eagles Nest Wilderness

lodgepole pine, spruce, and fir. There are numerous campsites and trailheads, and over 180 miles of trails.

HOLY CROSS WILDERNESS

General location: Just southwest of Minturn, which is 91 miles west of Denver

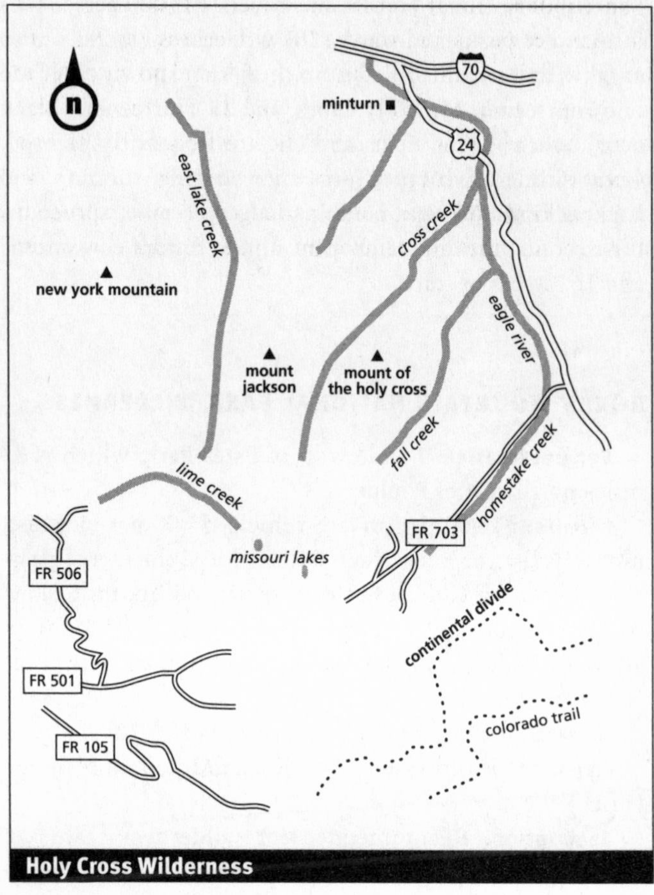

Holy Cross Wilderness

Contact: Holy Cross Ranger District, White River National Forest, (970) 827-5715, Eagle Ranger District, White River National Forest, (970) 328-6388, Sopris Ranger District, White River National Forest, (970) 963-2266, Leadville Ranger District, San Isabel National Forest, (719) 486-0749

Maps: USFS White River and San Isabel National Forest maps

Description: Holy Cross is located in the White River and San Isabel National Forests and covers 122,000 acres. This is a land of peaks and water. The wilderness cradles scores of lakes and streams filled from the spring snowmelt of the one Fourteener, Mt. Holy Cross, and 25 Thirteeners. Black bear, bobcat, lynx, deer, and elk are frequently sighted. Great skiing of all types, plus snowshoeing, running, and backpacking. The area contains lodgepole pine, spruce-fir, bristlecone pine, and timberline-alpine tundra ecosystems and 164 miles of trails.

ROCKY MOUNTAIN NATIONAL PARK WILDERNESS

General location: 1 mile west of Estes Park, which is 37 miles northwest of Boulder

Permits: $15.00 per private vehicle; $5.00 per bicyclist, motorcyclist, or pedestrian; $10.00 for Golden Age passport; $50.00 for Golden Eagle passport; and free for Golden Access passport. An annual pass for Rocky Mountain National Park is available for $30. Backcountry permit fee is $15.00.

Contact: Rocky Mountain National Park, (970) 586-1206

Maps: Trails Illustrated 200—Rocky Mountain National Park

Description: Recommended for wilderness status in 1974, Rocky Mountain National Park is still sitting on the

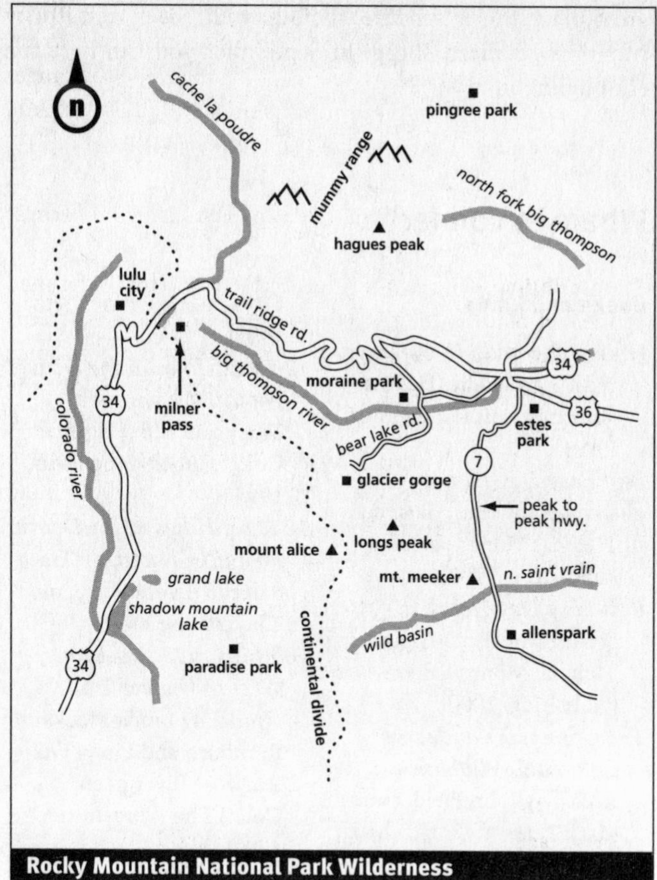

Rocky Mountain National Park Wilderness

congressional back burner. In the meantime, it is managed as wilderness, so all the same rules apply. The park encompasses 265,000 acres—415 square miles. Go any distance from the main roads and you're in pristine and remote country. Backpacking, bird-watching, camping, rock climbing, mountaineering, cross-country skiing, fishing, hiking, horseback riding, nature walks, skiing, snowshoeing, stargazing, and wildlife viewing are all hugely popular. A great place to see wildlife, including elk, deer, and Rocky Mountain bighorn sheep. In September you can hear the elk bugling.

Where to Connect

Books and Links

Hiking Colorado II, by Caryn and Peter Boddie (Helena, Mont.: Falcon Publishing, 1999).

Best Easy Day Hikes: Denver, by Tracy Salcedo (Helena, Mont.: Falcon Publishing, 2000).

Best Easy Day Hikes: Boulder, by Tracy Salcedo (Helena, Mont.: Falcon Publishing, 2000).

The Complete Guide to Colorado's Wilderness Areas, by John Fielder and Mark Pearson (Englewood, Colo.: Westcliffe Publishers, 1994).

Denver Hiking Guide: 45 Hikes within 45 Minutes of Denver, 2nd ed., by Dave Rich (Boulder, Colo.: Books West, 1999).

12 Short Hikes in the Boulder Foothills, by Tracy Salcedo (Evergreen, Colo.: Chockstone Press, 1995).

12 Short Hikes in the Denver Foothills: Central, by Tracy Salcedo (Evergreen, Colo.: Chockstone Press, 1995).

12 Short Hikes in the Denver Foothills: North, by Tracy Salcedo (Evergreen, Colo.: Chockstone Press, 1995).

Foothills to Mount Evans, West-of-Denver Trail Guide, by Linda McComb Rathburn and Linda Wells Rihgrose (Evergreen, Colo.: The Wordsmiths, 1980).

Skiing Colorado's Backcountry: Northern Mountains—Trails and Tours, by Brian Litz and Kurt Lankford (Golden, Colo.: Fulcrum Publishing, 1989).

www.gorp.com
www.cmc.org

Shops

REI
1416 Platte Street
Denver, CO 80202
(303) 756-3100
Equipment rentals available; reserve one week in advance.

Grand West Outfitters
801 Broadway
Denver, CO 80203
(303) 825-0300
Equipment rentals.

Neptune Mountaineering
633 South Broadway
Boulder, CO 80303
(303) 499-8866

Mountain Sports
821 Pearl Street
Boulder CO 80301
(303) 442-8355
www.mountainsportsboulder.com
Equipment rentals available; reserve one week in advance.

Clubs and Organizations

You only need one in Colorado!

The Colorado Mountain Club
The American Mountaineering Center
710 10th Street, #200
Golden, CO 80401
(303) 279-3080, (800) 633-4417; fax: (303) 279-9690
www.cmc.org
One of the oldest, finest mountain clubs in the country, with chapters all over the state. Invaluable information on trails, fine maps, hundreds of weekly trips all year.

Bird-Watching

COLORADO'S OFFICIAL BIRD list stands at 466 species, ranking it sixth in the country for bird diversity. The area around Denver and Boulder is literally an ornithological crossroads. The grasslands of the high plains attract eastern birds. The mountains and canyons, plateaus and mesas host western birds. In addition, "birds such as snowy owls and rough-legged hawks, migrate from the north to overwinter here, but because of our position we also have [more southern] birds whose range extends no further north, such as scaled quail and greater roadrunners," adds Front Range ornithologist Kevin Cook. Cook says that there are anthropogenic reasons as well: people have diversified the landscape, constructing reservoirs that bring water into places where it was historically unavailable, attracting water- and shorebirds that normally would have flown over without stopping. There are loons and pelicans, sandpipers and plovers, and a lot of ducks. Legendary local birder Norm Lewis points out that the Denver–Boulder area is at the extreme western edge of the Mississippi Flyway, and that birds also wander in from the Pacific "for God only knows what reason." Lewis says wryly that ornithologists at the Colorado Bird Observatory banding station at Barr Lake are "constantly catching birds that have no business here."

The rise in elevation along the Front Range contributes to a remarkable juxtaposition of habitats, from high plains riparian to alpine tundra in just a few miles, making birding in the area terrifically exciting. Several of these spots have been designated Important Bird Areas—that is, they provide critical habitat for many species—by the National Audubon Society. There are some remarkable and unique opportunities for Denver–Boulder birders, such as the reservoirs that host a huge variety of waterfowl. In the spring the Dakota Hogback Hawkwatch, located just out of town on Dinosaur Ridge by Red Rocks, has been described as the best place in Colorado to observe migrating hawks, eagles, falcons, and other diurnal birds of prey. Two trails in the Boulder Mountain Parks are also very popular with birders.

Birding in the region, and in the entire United States, has become increasingly popular, and is now one of the fastest growing pastimes. One reliable source claims that there are now more birders than golfers. The reasons are that it requires only a pair of binoculars and a bird book. One local birder, Ann Bonnell, says that when you're traveling you can easily throw the two items in your carry-on. "Airports are great places to bird," she says.

Listed here is a selection of some of the area's best accessible birding spots, the best guidebooks and Web sites, and clubs and organizations that conduct regular field trips and lectures. It's worth noting here that aside from a good field guide, Harold R. Holt's seminal *A Birder's Guide to Colorado* will prove invaluable in making your birding in the area more productive.

Denver City Limits

DENVER CITY PARK LAKES

Location: Downtown Denver

Description: Believe it or not, this central downtown locale just behind the Museum of Nature and Science and next to the zoo has been listed as an Important Bird Area by the National Audubon Society, meaning it provides crucial habitat. Birders can regularly see cormorants, a variety of ducks, gulls, geese, and grebes on the lake and sparrows and finches in the park. Restrooms are available.

Directions: Go east on US 6 to Josephine Street. Turn left (north) up Josephine to 21st Avenue and take a right (east) into the park.

Denver Backyard

ROCKY MOUNTAIN ARSENAL NATIONAL WILDLIFE REFUGE (RMA)

Location: 10 miles northeast of Denver

Contact: U.S. Fish and Wildlife Service, (303) 289-0232

Description: It may be the oddest wildlife refuge on the planet: Ten miles northeast of Denver are 27 square miles of deciduous woods, shortgrass prairie, lakes, and wetlands on the site of a former arsenal where chemical weapons such as napalm and mustard gas were manufactured from World War II to the 1960s; pesticides were produced until 1982. In 1992 the land was designated a National Wildlife Refuge and slated for cleanup. It's home to coyotes, prairie dogs, hawks, eagles, burrowing owls, and lark buntings. During migration, you may see, among others, osprey, sandhill crane, Say's phoebe, mountain bluebird, sage thrasher, and grasshopper and Cassin's sparrows. The RMA will become one of the largest urban wildlife refuges in the country once remediation is complete.

The refuge is fenced, with access controlled by the U.S. Fish and Wildlife Service through the west gate at 72nd Avenue and Quebec Street. It may be closed over the next year or two to assess new hazards. There's a visitors center, restrooms, and bird checklist available.

Directions: Drive north on I-25 to I-70 east, exit 214A. Drive east on I-70 to Quebec Street, exit 278. Go north on Quebec 3.4 miles to the west gate entrance.

CHATFIELD STATE PARK

Location: 17 miles southwest of Denver

Fee: A state parks pass costs $4 per vehicle per day, $40 per vehicle per year.

Contact: (303) 791-7275

Description: One of the most popular spots for area birders and an Audubon Important Bird Area. A huge draw for waterfowl, including a remarkable congregation of winter gulls. Also parasitic jaegers, pomarine jaegers, western grebes, Clark's grebes, red-tailed hawks, rough-legged hawks, cormorants, and herons. There are plenty of restrooms. A bird checklist is available at the park office; fol-

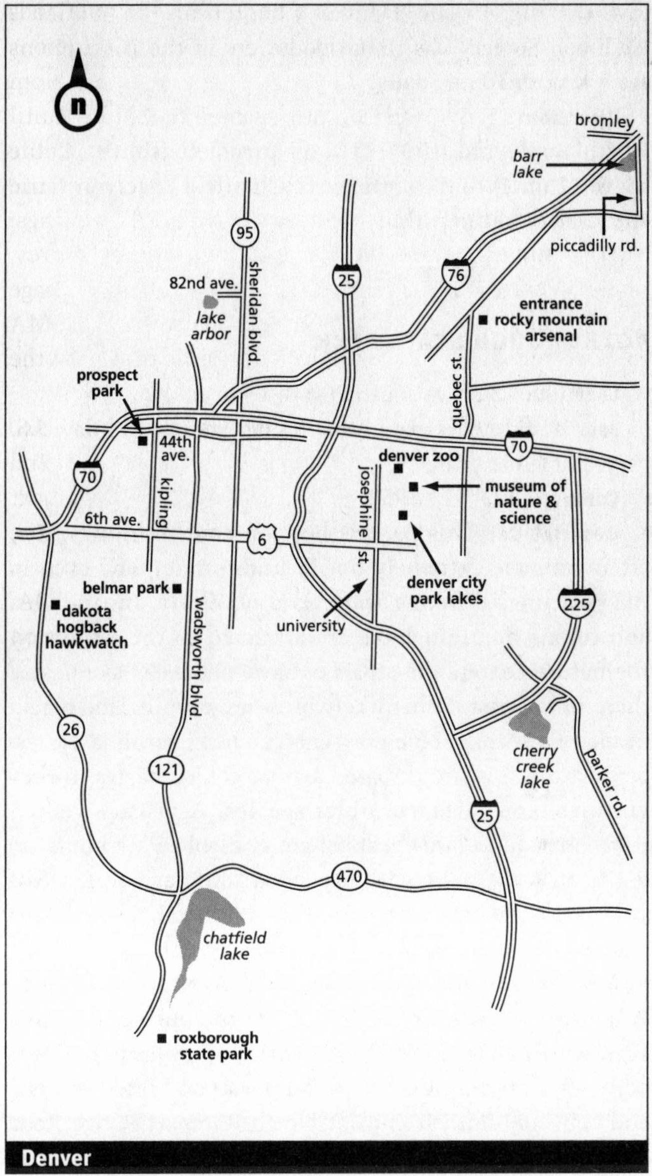
n
bromley
barr lake
piccadilly rd.
95
sheridan blvd.
25
76
82nd ave.
lake arbor
entrance rocky mountain arsenal
quebec st.
prospect park
44th ave.
70
denver zoo
museum of nature & science
70
kipling
6th ave.
6
josephine st.
denver city park lakes
belmar park
dakota hogback hawkwatch
wadsworth blvd.
university
225
26
121
cherry creek lake
parker rd.
25
470
chatfield lake
roxborough state park

Denver

low the signs. The Denver Chapter of the National Audubon Society has its headquarters in the park. Hours are 5 A.M. to 10 P.M. daily.

Directions: Drive west on 6th Avenue (US 6) to Wadsworth Boulevard (CO 121) and turn left (south). Drive south 12 miles to the entrance to Chatfield Reservoir. Turn left (east) into the park.

ROXBOROUGH STATE PARK

Location: 22 miles southwest of Denver

Fee: A state park pass costs $4 per vehicle per day, $40 per vehicle per year.

Contact: (303) 973-3959

Description: This park is best on cool mornings. The afternoons are extremely hot in midsummer, and even in the mornings drinking water is a necessity. Broad-tailed and rufous hummingbirds are attracted to the feeders by the nature center, and a pair of Say's phoebes have nested there in the past. Other likely birds are evening and black-headed grosbeaks, blue-gray gnatcatchers, scrub jays, vesper sparrows, white-throated swifts, golden eagles, turkey vultures, and several warbler species. A visitors center, restrooms, and a bird checklist are available. Park hours are 9 A.M. to 4 P.M. daily with expanded summer hours. Leave your pets at home: Roxborough is a National Natural Area and pets aren't allowed on leashes or in your car.

Directions: Drive west on 6th Avenue (US 6) to Wadsworth Boulevard (CO 121). Turn south and follow Wadsworth under CO 470 and continue 5 miles to the Roxborough/Waterton Road. Turn left (east) on Waterton Road and continue until it ends at North Rampart Range Road (1.6 miles). Turn right (south) on North Rampart Range Road. Continue south 2.3 miles to the intersection of

North Rampart Range Road and Roxborough Park Road. Turn left onto Roxborough Park Road. Take the next right to enter the park.

CHERRY CREEK STATE PARK

Location: About 12 miles southeast of Denver

Fee: $5 per vehicle per day, $43 per vehicle per year

Contact: (303) 699-3860

Description: Similar birding to that found at Chatfield. For the past few years a great black-backed gull has stopped here on his way to the Pueblo Reservoir, where he arrives in late December. The park has a visitors center with a bird feeder, restrooms, and bird checklists. There are nesting sites throughout the park.

Directions: Drive south on I-25 to I-225. Take I-225 east to Parker Road (CO 83). Go south 1 mile to the park entrance, on the right.

BEL MAR PARK, KOUNTZE LAKE

Location: About 5 miles southwest of Denver

Contact: (303) 231-1307

Description: There is always something good here, and this is an excellent spot for ducks in the winter: bufflehead, hooded merganser, common and Barrow's goldeneye, wood and Ruddy ducks, wigeon, Canada geese, and mallards are common, along with the ubiquitous circle of northern shovelers. In spring and summer American coots and pied-billed grebes nest in the marshy areas, and black-crowned night-herons, great blue herons, and the occasional green heron stalk their prey. Several species of swallows spend the warm months here, as well as many warbler species and lots of red-winged blackbirds and common grackles. The park also contains an historical village and museum, and restrooms.

Directions: Drive west on 6th Avenue (US 6) to Wadsworth Boulevard (CO 121) and turn left (south). Go about 1.25 miles to West Ohio Avenue and turn right (west). You're there.

PROSPECT PARK

Location: About 8 miles northwest of Denver

Description: Prospect Park accesses the Wheat Ridge Greenbelt and its four lakes. The area is notable not only for birds but for the resident foxes. Warblers are common throughout the spring and summer, especially during migration. Waterfowl include greater and lesser scaup, goldeneye, canvasback, bufflehead, and ruddy ducks. There are restrooms, and a bird checklist is available at one of the Wild Bird Center stores. The trail around Prospect Lake is handicapped accessible.

Directions: Drive west on 6th Avenue (US 6) to Kipling Street (CO 391) and turn right (north). Go 3 miles to 44th Avenue and turn left (west). Continue about 1 mile to Robb Street. The park is on the left.

LAKE ARBOR

Location: About 8 miles northwest of Denver

Contact: (303) 420-0984

Description: Despite the number of people, this has proven to be a good area to bird. Species seen include pied-billed and western grebes, American white pelican, double-crested cormorant, great blue heron, snow and Canada geese, wood duck, green-winged and blue-winged teals, mallard, cinnamon teal, northern shoveler, American wigeon, ring-necked duck, lesser scaup, common golden-eye, bufflehead, ruddy duck, red-tailed hawk, American kestrel, American coot, killdeer, spotted sandpiper, Wilson's phalarope, ring-billed gull, forster's tern, rock and mourning dove, belted kingfisher, northern flicker, tree swallow, violet-green swallow, barn swallow, blue jay, black-billed magpie, American crow, black-capped chickadee, American robin, European starling, yellow-rumped warbler, western meadowlark, red-winged blackbird, yellow-headed blackbird, common grackle, house finch, American goldfinch, and house sparrow. There are restrooms and a path around the lake.

Directions: Drive west on 6th Avenue (US 6) to Sheridan Boulevard (CO 95) and turn right (north). Go to west 82nd Avenue, turn left (west), and continue to Ames Street. Turn left (south) on Ames and follow it as it curves around and becomes 80th Place and then Gray Street (go figure). Turn left (west) on Pomona Drive and look for the parking lot.

BARR LAKE STATE PARK

Location: 21 miles northeast of Denver

Fee: A state parks pass costs $4 per day per vehicle, $40 per vehicle per year.

Contact: (303) 659-6005

Description: Notable for the resident bald eagles, and great blue heron and double-crested cormorant rookeries. To the left of the nature center bridge is good birding for shorebirds and waterfowl, and a path leads to the gazebo where eagles and rookeries can be observed, and where a permanent spotting scope is set up. To the right of the bridge is good songbird territory. This is an excellent spot any time of year. The Colorado Bird Observatory and banding station is located here. The park has a nature center (closed Mondays and Tuesdays), restrooms, bird feeders, and bird checklist, available at the nature center.

Note: Pets are not allowed on the trails west of the visitors center in the Critical Wildlife Habitat Area.

Directions: Drive north on I-25 to I-76, exit 216A. Keep right at the fork in the ramp and merge onto I-76 east. Go to Bromley Lane, exit 23, and take Bromley east to Piccadilly Road. Turn south on Piccadilly and continue to the park entrance.

DAKOTA HOGBACK HAWKWATCH

Location: 12 miles west of Denver

Description: Located minutes from downtown Denver, across the road from Red Rocks Park, the Hawkwatch is located along one of the few spring raptor migration corridors in the western United States, and is the best place in Colorado to see migrating hawks, falcons, eagles, and other birds of prey. Osprey, bald eagles, golden eagles, ferruginous hawks, northern harriers, American kestrels, turkey vultures, and sharp-shinned and cooper's hawks are all regularly sighted. Go between mid-April and early May. No facilities are available, but they're close by, just across the road at Mathews Winters Park.

Directions: Drive west on I-70 to Morrison/Golden, exit 259. Go south on CO 26 and turn right (west) almost immediately into the Mathews Winters parking lot. Dakota Ridge is across the street to the east. From the lot walk south to an old road and follow it northeast almost to the top of the ridge. A signed trail heads south just below treeline. Follow it for 0.5 mile. The Hawkwatch is on the high point, 50 yards south of the three power poles.

Boulder City Limits

GREGORY CANYON TRAIL

Location: Just south of Boulder

Fee: A fee is charged to visitors from outside Boulder County.

Description: Harold Holt, in his indispensable *Birder's Guide to Colorado,* says that many local birders consider this canyon the best foothill birding near Boulder. He suggests birding from the trailhead parking lot back along the road toward Baseline. Yellow, Wilson's and MacGillivray's warblers, lazuli bunting, spotted towhee, and gray catbirds may all be seen. Return and climb the trail for brown creeper, house wren, brown thrasher, solitary vireo, and yellow warbler. In recent years hooded warblers have been breeding here. Restrooms are available.

Directions: Drive north on Canyon Boulevard (CO 119) to Broadway (CO 93) and turn left (south). Take Broadway to Baseline Road and turn right (north). Follow Baseline 0.8 mile to its end. Just past the bridge at the base of Flagstaff Road turn left into the canyon drive and follow it to the parking lot.

THE McCLINTOCK NATURE TRAIL—CHAUTAUQUA PARK

Location: Just south of Boulder

Fee: A fee is charged to visitors from outside Boulder County.

Directions: The trail starts opposite the covered picnic area in Chautauqua. It follows the streambed up Bluebell Canyon for about 0.5 mile to the ponderosas on the top of the hill. Recommended by Holt as excellent birding during spring migration. There are many other trails in Chautauqua Park that are wonderful hikes with good birding.

Directions: Drive north on Canyon Boulevard (CO 119) to Broadway (CO 93) and turn left (south). Take Broadway to Baseline Road. Turn right (west) and follow Baseline to 12th Street. Turn left and go two blocks to the trailhead.

Boulder Backyard

SAWHILL AND WALDEN PONDS

Location: 7 miles east of Boulder

Description: An excellent, close-to-town spot comprising a mosaic of small ponds and wetlands. These reclaimed gravel ponds recently played host to a tufted duck. This area usually produces good waterfowl including canvasback, hooded merganser, bufflehead, lesser (and sometimes greater) scaup, and ring-necked ducks. Also, Sawhill and Walden can see a breeding attempt by the least bittern plus a spring visit of the little blue heron (immature or adult). Others that may be seen include Virginia rail, sora, olive-sided flycatcher, western wood-pewee, western and eastern kingbirds, Swainson's and hermit thrushes and solitary and warbling vireos.

Restrooms, bird checklist, and map are located at the information sign. Handicapped-accessible paths lead around all the small ponds. The two areas, while administered under separate jurisdictions, are adjacent, and the birds don't know the difference. You can park at either one and walk through to the other. Most birders prefer to start at the Walden Ponds Wildlife Habitat Area.

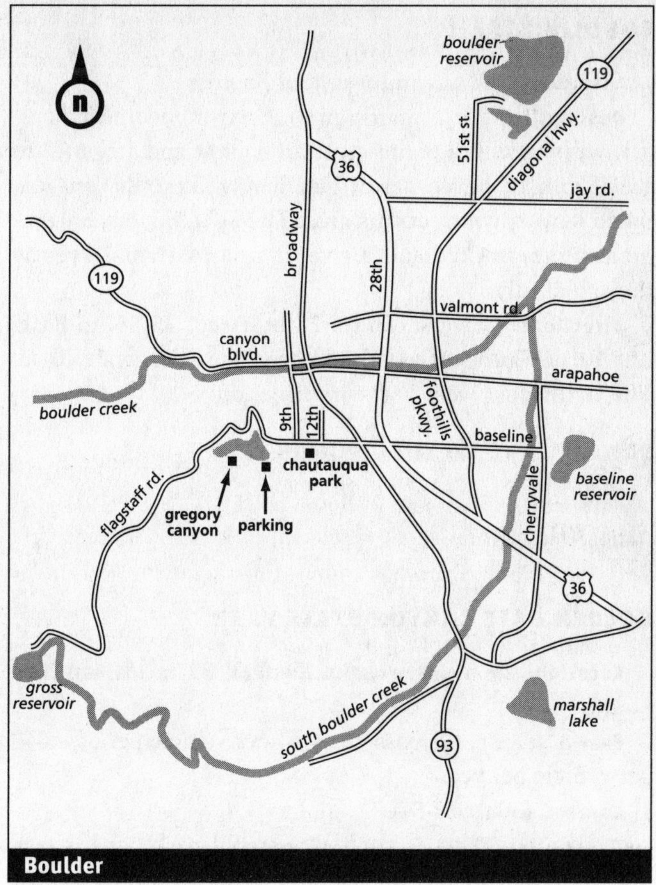

Boulder

Directions: Drive north on 28th Street (US 36) to Valmont Road. Turn right (east) and drive to 75th Street. Turn left (north), pass the Sawhill Ponds access, and turn west into Walden Ponds. Continue west and south to the Cottonwood Marsh parking lot.

BOBOLINK TRAIL

Location: 3 driving miles east of Boulder

Description: For a prairie birding experience near Boulder, with excellent plains riparian habitat and a chance to see bobolinks, orioles, great blue herons, kestrels, and red-tailed hawks, consider this area. The bobolink, an uncommon species in Colorado, arrives in mid-May and leaves by the end of July.

Directions: Drive south on 28th Street (US 36) to Baseline Road. Turn left (east) and drive to Cherryvale Road. The trail is just west of the intersection.

Golden

GOLDEN GATE CANYON STATE PARK

Location: 29 miles west of Denver, 32 miles south of Boulder

Fee: A state parks pass costs $4 per vehicle per day, $40 per vehicle per year.

Contact: (303) 582-3707

Description: This is such a beautiful park, with steep, pine-covered hills, meadows, and aspen groves, it almost doesn't matter how many birds you see. The park has almost 35 miles of trails and excellent birding. Blue grouse, three-toed woodpecker, Clark's nutcracker, red crossbill, and rosy-finches are among the scores that can be seen here. Black swifts in summer. There's a visitors center, restrooms, and bird checklist. Also, camping is available.

Directions: From Denver, drive west on 6th Avenue (US 6) through Golden to CO 93. Continue north on CO 93 to Golden Gate Canyon Road (CO 46) and turn left (west).

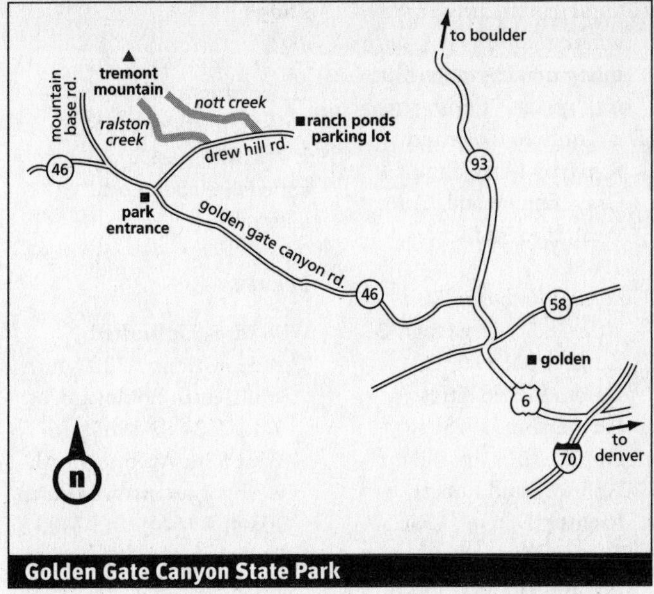

Golden Gate Canyon State Park

Continue 14 miles to the park entrance. Turn right toward the visitors center and continue 3 miles to the Ranch Ponds parking lot. From Boulder, drive west on Canyon Boulevard (CO 119) to Broadway (CO 93) and turn left (south). Drive 19 miles to Golden Gate Canyon Road (CO 46) and turn right (west). Continue 14 miles to the park entrance. Turn right toward the visitors center and continue 3 miles to the Ranch Ponds parking lot.

Where to Connect

Books

A Birder's Guide to Colorado, by Harold R. Holt (Colorado Springs, Colo.: American Birding, 1997).

Complete, amazing guide to where the birds are, with many driving loops that link specific birding areas.

The Guide to Colorado Birds, by Mary Taylor Gray (Englewood, Colo.: Westcliffe Publishers, 1988).

Colorado Breeding Bird Atlas, edited by Hugh E. Kingery (Denver, Colo.: Colorado Bird Atlas Partnership, 1998).

Colorado Birds, by Robert Andrews and Robert Righter (Denver, Colo.: Denver Museum of Natural History, 1992).

Field Guide to the Birds of North America, 2nd ed., by the National Geographic Society (Washington, D.C.: National Geographic Society, 1987).

Birds of Denver and the Front Range, by Chris C. Fisher and Greg Butcher (Edmonton, Canada: Lone Pine Publishing, 1997).

Shops

The stores below are designed specifically for the birder. Binoculars, bird guides, bird feeding gear, and a lot of knowledge about local hotspots.

Denver

Wild Birds Unlimited

Three locations: 2720 South Wadsworth Boulevard (at Yale; 303-987-1965); 7677 West 88th Avenue (northwest corner at Wadsworth; 303-467-2644); and 7400 East Hampden Avenue (303-694-1088).

Wild Bird Center

Three locations: 1685 South Colorado Boulevard (just north of I-25; 303-758-7575); at I-70 and Youngfield (between Chili's and Applejack's; 303-231-9252); and 5270 East Arapahoe Road (303-694-4616).

Boulder

Wild Bird Center of Boulder

1641 28th Street (south of Canyon)

(303) 442-1322

Clubs, Organizations, Field Trips, Links

DENVER

Audubon Society of Greater Denver
9308 South Platte Canyon Road
Littleton, CO 80128
(303) 973-9530

They're building a Nature Center at Chatfield State Park; call them for information on field trips. Their Walk the Wetlands trips are very popular.

Denver Field Ornithologists
Rare Bird Alert Hotline: (303) 424-2144
www.geocities/dfobirders

An extremely active, respected group with regular field trips, lectures, and a wealth of birding information. Regular monthly meetings. Contact their Web site for membership and all other information.

The Denver Museum of Nature and Science
(303) 370-6303

Regular area field trips with local expert birders, as well as occasional trips farther afield to southern Colorado and Nebraska.

Colorado Bird Observatory
13401 Piccadilly Road
Brighton, CO 80601
(303) 659-4348

Located at Barr Lake, this nonprofit group is active in conservation and protection and conducts bird research throughout the state. Educational programs. Banding station at the lake.

BOULDER

National Audubon Colorado
3107 28th Street, Suite B
Boulder, CO 80301
(303) 415-0130

Boulder Bird Club
(303) 666-9827

Open to all, regular field trips.

GENERAL

Colorado Field Ornithologists
www.cfo-link.org

These are the folks that update the official state bird list. Visit their Web site for a wealth of information on field trips, Rare Bird Alerts, annual bird counts, books, and other links.

CoBirds List Serve
listproc@lists.co.edu

To subscribe, send an e-mail. Leave the subject field blank; in message type: subscribe cobirds.

A very active bulletin board of birders around the state. Up-to-the-minute sightings and a constant flow of bird info.

Events

Bird Walks

Guided bird walks are also available throughout the year at all state parks. You will want to keep in mind that December through March is the best time to see both bald and golden eagles. Call the numbers provided at each park description for more information.

International Migratory Bird Day Celebrations

Early May at many locations around Colorado. Test your birding basics, explore the sounds of birds, or discover the art of woodcarving. In particular, Lookout Mountain Nature Center has numerous events for you to celebrate International Migratory Bird Day. Contact: Lookout Mountain Nature Center, 910 Colorow Road, Golden, CO 80401; (303) 526-0594, www.co.jefferson.co.us/dpt/openspac/natstart.htm.

Dawn Chorus

First Sunday in May at many Front Range locations. Greet the sunrise and listen for bird songs. See local papers for information.

Fall Flight

Explore the wonders of Barr Lake State Park in late September. As warbler migration begins to wane and sparrow migration picks up, the lake and wetlands come alive with many species, including waterfowl. Other nearby wildlife areas that are especially interesting during fall migration includes Pawnee National Grasslands and Rocky Mountain National Park. Contact the Colorado Bird Observatory.

Horseback Riding

I GREW UP READING Louis L'Amour Westerns and always dreamed of drifting the High Country on horseback. The fact is, few people today own their own horses. So, while there is a quite a lot of equestrian activity going on around Denver and Boulder, from dressage to pony club to polo, this chapter is limited to a handful of good area stables where you can take lessons and hire out a horse for an hour or a day. Beyond that, should you own a horse, parks, open spaces, and trails that are open to riding are listed. The only place where riding is allowed within the city limits of Denver is along the High Line Canal. (See "Running" and "Mountain Biking" for access.) The Denver Water Board puts out a comprehensive and inexpensive

little guidebook, *The Guide to the High Line Canal Trail,* available at the Tattered Cover, the landmark bookstore in Denver.

The city of Boulder is extraordinarily horse friendly, with a host of trails within Boulder open spaces. So many, in fact, that only the locations of trailheads are given here; the trails themselves are left to you to explore. If you are a horseman, don't forget the Colorado Trail. It's 500 miles long, from Denver to Durango, traverses some of the finest high country in the world, and is well loved by those who have ridden it. A few years ago I decided it was time to fulfill that long-held dream. I hadn't ridden since I was twelve, so I trained for two months, then took a horse and a pack horse from southwestern Colorado to Wyoming. It took just under a month and was one of the finest trips I've ever taken.

Denver Backyard

BARR LAKE STATE PARK

Location: 21 miles northeast of Denver

Fee: $4 day pass, $40 annual

Contact: Call (303) 659-6005 for more information

Description: Although horses are not permitted on the boardwalks, visitors may ride their horses on park trails, which provide a fine opportunity for wildlife watching. A 9-mile trail follows the perimeter of the lake. Bring your binoculars. Several observation stations have been constructed at particularly good viewing locations, so you can dismount, stretch your legs, and look for ospreys and herons. These are small shelters that provide screening for the viewer and shelter from the weather.

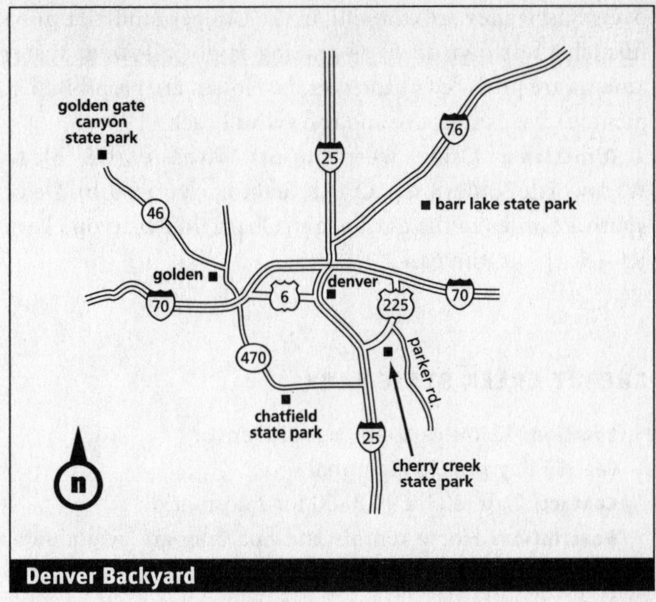

Denver Backyard

Directions: Drive north on I-25 to the I-76/Grand Junction/Ft. Morgan exit (exit 216A). Keep right at the fork in the ramp and merge onto I-76 east. Go to Bromely Lane (exit 23), turn right (east) to Piccadilly Road, then turn south on Piccadilly Road to the park entrance.

CHATFIELD STATE PARK

Location: 17 miles southwest of Denver

Fee: $4 day pass, $40 annual

Contact: Call (303) 791-7275 for information

Description: Horse trailer parking, corrals, unloading ramps, and the trailhead are on the park's west side, which is most easily reached from the Deer Creek entrance. Horses may be leased at the B&B Livery, west of the swim beach. Visitors may leave their horses in the corrals overnight if they are camping in the campground, but must furnish their own feed, as grazing is not allowed. Water faucets are provided at the corrals. Horses are prohibited at picnic sites, campsites, and the swim beach.

Directions: Drive west on 6th Avenue (US 6) to Wadsworth Boulevard (CO 121) and turn left (south). Drive south 12 miles to the entrance to Chatfield Reservoir. Turn left (east) into the park.

CHERRY CREEK STATE PARK

Location: 12 miles southeast of Denver

Fee: $5 day pass, $43 annual

Contact: Call (303) 699-3860 for information

Description: Horse rentals and boarding are available at *Paint Horse Stables*, near the east gate entrance. Twelve miles of trails offer equestrians a close-to-town, pretty place to ride. Horse owners find it a good place to condition their horses, too. Call the stable at (303) 690-8235.

Directions: Drive south on I-25 to I-225. Take I-225 east to Parker Road (CO 83). Go south 1 mile to the park entrance (on the right).

GOLDEN GATE CANYON STATE PARK

Location: 32 miles west of Denver, 35 miles south of Boulder

Fee: $4 day pass, $40 annual

Contact: Call (303) 582-3707 for information

Description: Horseback riding in the park is permitted on all trails rated "easy." Ample parking space is provided at the Nott Creek trailhead. Twelve trails at Golden Gate Canyon are each named after an animal and marked with the animal's footprint. The difficulty of the trail is indicated by the background shape of the trail marker. Circles denote easy trails, squares are moderate, and diamonds are difficult. Trailheads with parking areas are easily accessible from the main roads in the park.

Directions: From Denver, drive west on 6th Avenue (US 6) through Golden to CO 93. Continue north on CO 93 to Golden Gate Canyon Road (CO 46) and turn left (west). Continue 14 miles to the park entrance. Turn right toward the visitors center and continue 3 miles to the Ranch Ponds parking lot. From Boulder, drive west on Canyon Boulevard (CO 119) to Broadway (CO 93) and turn left (south). Drive 19 miles to Golden Gate Canyon Road (CO 46) and turn right (west). Continue 14 miles to the park entrance. Turn right toward the visitors center and continue 3 miles to the Ranch Ponds parking lot.

Boulder Backyard

BOULDER OPEN SPACE AND MOUNTAIN PARK TRAILHEADS

Contact: (303) 441-3440 or www.ci.boulder.co.us/open space/ (Use the link if possible—it's the easiest way to extract information.)

Note: Regulation horseback riding is allowed on all trails mentioned below, but off-trail riding is discouraged to protect rare plants and wildlife habitat.

Trailhead: Bobolink

Location: Just west of the intersection of Baseline and Cherryvale Roads

Parking: Parking lot on southwest corner of intersection

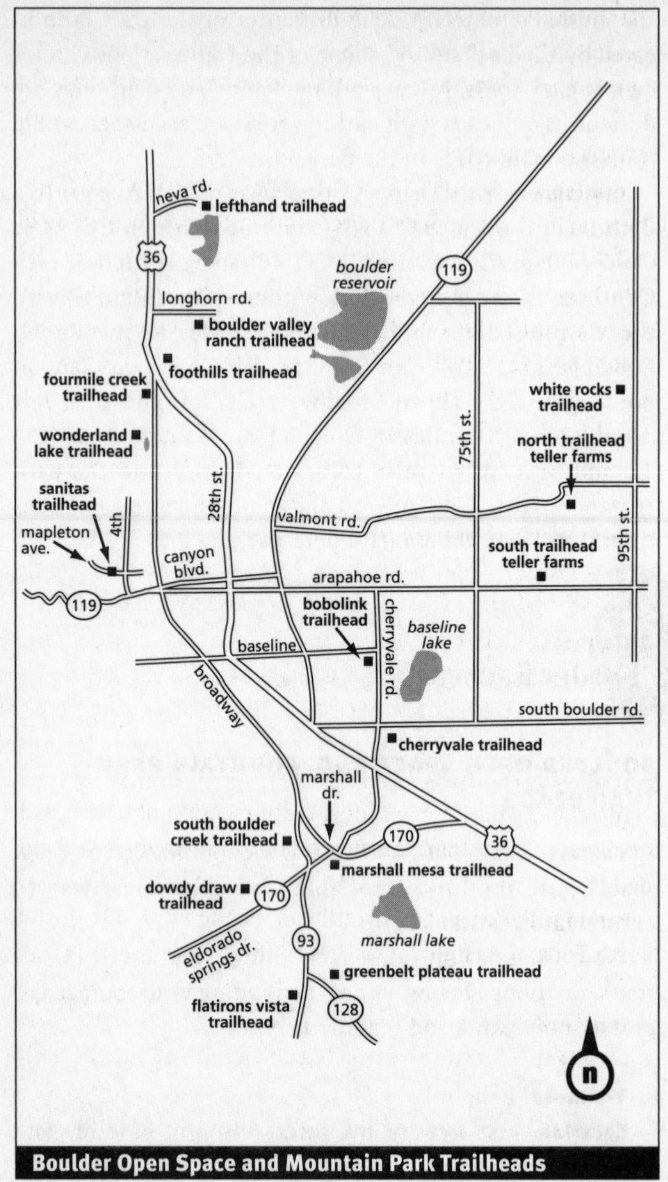

Boulder Open Space and Mountain Park Trailheads

Trailhead: Boulder Valley Ranch

Location: 1 mile east of US 36 on Longhorn Road

Parking: Parking lot on south side of Longhorn Road

Trailhead: Cherryvale

Location: 66 South Cherryvale Road (west side of south Cherryvale Road approximately 0.1 mile south of South Boulder Road)

Parking: Parking lot at the trailhead and north of the driveway into the open space operations center. Horse trailer parking is available

Trailhead: Doudy Draw

Location: 1.8 miles west of CO 93 on Eldorado Springs Drive (CO 170)

Parking: Parking lot on the south side of Eldorado Springs Drive

Trailhead: Flatirons Vista

Location: 0.3 mile south of CO 128 on CO 93

Parking: Parking lot on west side of CO 93

Trailhead: Foothills

Location: 0.4 mile north of the intersection of US 36 and Broadway (CO 93) on the North Foothills Highway access road

Parking: Parking at the trailhead on the west side of the North Foothills Highway access road

Trailhead: Fourmile Creek

Location: 0.3 mile west of North Broadway on Lee Hill Road

Parking: Paved parking lot is available at the trailhead

Trailhead: Greenbelt Plateau

Location: North side of CO 128, 0.1 mile east of the intersection of CO 128 and CO 93

Parking: Parking lot on north side of CO 128

Trailhead: Lefthand

Location: 1 mile east of CO 36 on Neva Road

Parking: Parking lot at the trailhead is large enough to accommodate horse trailers

Trailhead: Marshall Mesa

Location: 0.3 mile east of South Cherryvale Road on Marshall Drive (CO 170)

Parking: Limited parking on south side of Marshall Drive (CO 170)

Trailhead: Mesa Trail, south trailhead

Location: 1.7 miles west of CO 93 on Eldorado Springs Drive (CO 170)

Parking: Parking lot on the north side of Eldorado Springs Drive

Trailhead: Sanitas

Location: 0.5 mile west of 4th Street on Mapleton Avenue

Parking: Limited parking off Mapleton Avenue

Trailhead: South Boulder Creek, west trailhead

Location: 1401 South Foothills Highway. West of CO 93 at Thomas Lane, approximately 0.5 mile north of the intersection of CO 93 and Eldorado Springs Drive (CO 170)

Parking: Parking lot just south of Thomas Lane at the trailhead

Trailhead: Teller Farms, north trailhead

Location: South of Valmont Road between 75th and 95th Streets

Parking: Parking lot at the trailhead

Trailhead: Teller Farms, south trailhead

Location: On the north side of Arapahoe between 75th and 95th Streets

Parking: Parking lot at the end of a 0.5-mile dirt road north of Arapahoe

Trailhead: White Rocks

Location: West of 95th Street on West Phillips Road, approximately 1.5 miles north of Valmont Road

Parking: A small parking lot just north of West Phillips Road at the trailhead

Trailhead: Wonderland Lake

Location: 4201 North Broadway at Wonderland Lake

Parking: Parking lot at 4201 North Broadway

Where to Connect

Stables

B&B Livery
Chatfield State Park
11500 North Roxborough Park Road
Littleton, CO 80125
(303) 933-3636

Hourly rentals, hay rides (only in winter), BBQ, lessons, and pony rides. A $4.00 park entrance fee is charged.

Bear Creek Lake Stables
14600 West Hampden Avenue
Morrison, CO 80465
(303) 697-9666 for the stables; (303) 697-1522 for Soda Lakes Marina, the winter number.

Rentals, year-round by reservation

Bradley Stables
1375 North 111 Street
Lafayette, CO 80026
(303) 665-4637
www.bbcyber.com/bbstables

Rentals, lessons, training, trail riding, and boarding. Also, birthday parties with horses, "your place or mine."

Pine Cliff Stables
21517 West 56th Avenue
Golden, CO 80403
(303) 279-1221
www.pinecliff.netfirms.com

Mountain trails, hunting, rentals year-round, boarding, and pony rides.

Sombrero Ranches, Inc.
3300 Airport Road
Boulder, CO 80301
(970) 586-4577 or (303) 442-0258
www.sombrero.com

Wild West Ranch
8001 Alkire Street
Arvada, CO 80005
(303) 425-8902
"Web site? Nope, we ride horses. We're cowboys out here."

Rentals, ponies, pig roasts, boarding, lessons, training, and trail rides.

Clubs and Equestrian Centers

Denver

Colorado Horse Council, Inc.
220 Livestock Exchange Building
4701 Marion Street
Denver, CO 80216
(303) 292-4981
www.cohoco.com

Rocky Mountain Region Pony Club
Check the Web site:
www.rockymountainupsc.org
www.ponyclub.org/FindAClub/uspcmap.htm

Rocky Mountain Back Country Horsemen
P.O. Box 41
Penrose, CO 81240
(719) 372-0317

Columbine Polo Club & Equestrian Center
6900 South Platte Canyon Road
Littleton, CO 80128
(303) 933-7881
www.columbineequestrian.com

High Prairie Farms Equestrian Center
7522 South Pinery Parkway

Parker, CO 80134
(303) 841-5550
www.highprairiefarms.com

Boulder

Peak to Peak Pony Club: Boulder
15 Copperdale Lane
Golden, CO 80403
Instruction Coordinator: Julia Clavette
(303) 642-0401
www.ponyclub.org/FindAClub/uspcmap.htm

Joder Arabian Ranch LLC
7497 North Foothills Highway 36
Boulder, CO 80302
(303) 449-6040

Paragliding & Hang Gliding

THERE ARE SUPERB flying sites practically in downtown Boulder, and a world-class spot at Lookout Mountain, 20 minutes from Denver. Hang gliding's been around a while and its practitioners established many of these areas. But the sport has changed: Modern gliders weigh between 48 and 90 pounds, can get glides of 20 to 1, and achieve speeds of over 70 mph. In the hands of a good pilot they are capable of 300-mile flights and can be landed on a small spot with a couple of quick steps. Paragliding, in spite of the risks of flying around with a soft chute, is growing increasingly popular. The appeal is obvious: the modified parachutes weigh only 10 pounds and easily fit into a backpack. You hike or drive up to a suitable

ridge or hillside, open the canopy, and take off—simplest aircraft in the world. Simplicity aside, flying safely around Denver and Boulder demands considerable experience and skill. A "rotor of the Rockies" effect makes flight hazardous when the winds aloft are strong. Before launching, it's imperative that you call a local expert and find out about wind conditions and other considerations. The guys at Fly Away Paragliding (303-642-0849), Mark and Paul Ferguson of the Rocky Mountain Paragliding School of Colorado (303-579-9971) and Mark Windsheimer of Airtime Above Hang Gliding (303-674-2451) are good folks to call; they'll be very glad to fill you in.

Since contacting the locals is the first, best move, I've reversed the usual order for this chapter and listed the area's schools and shops first, followed by places to fly.

Where to Connect

Paragliding Shops

Fly Away Paragliding
30590 Highway 72
Golden, CO 80403
(303) 642-0849
E-mail: flyaway@diac.com
Certified instruction, sales, and service.

Rocky Mountain Paragliding School of Colorado
29170 Golfway
Eveergreen, CO 80439
(303) 579-9971
www.rmparagliding.com

E-mail: lessons@rmparagliding.com

Certified instruction, sales, and service.

Hang Gliding Shops

Airtime Above Hang Gliding
1372 Sinton Road
Evergreen, CO 80439
(303) 674-2451
E-mail: airtimehg@aol.com

Certified instruction program, glider repairs and inspections, chute repacks, and new and used gliders and harnesses for sale. By all accounts, the best place around to learn to fly. They teach foot launching, and utilize a scooter tow for those days that the training hill doesn't work. They also teach truck towing. All instructors are certified, and they only use certified equipment. Great safety record.

Bolder Flight
(303) 444-5455
E-mail: thermals1@aol.com

All equipment and accessories, as well as service. Gliders, harnesses, helmets, radios, ball varios, equipment, and accessories.

CloudStreet AirSports
4623 East County Road 54
Ft. Collins, CO 80524
(970) 493-5339

Ultralight and hang glider introduction flights, instruction, sales, service, and aerotowing.

Clubs

Rocky Mountain Hang Gliding Association (RMHGA)
P.O. Box 28181
Lakewood, CO 80228

Inquiries about flying sites, or where people are flying can be made through the local discussion board, or visit the site guide at: www.rmhga.org

Link

www.intellicast.com

This is a great site! A weather Web site for active people —use it for all sailing activities, gliding, and trip planning.

Flying Sites

DAKOTA RIDGE FLYING SITE

Description: A very popular walk-up site on the north side of Boulder for pilots of all levels. The ridge is about 800′ above the landing site, and is steep enough to offer excellent ridge soaring lift. There's also a 50-foot training hill near the landing area. P2 site.

Directions: From Canyon Boulevard and 28th Street, go north on 28th (US 36) 4 miles to the trailhead. It's on the right (east) side of the road. Walk through the tunnel under the highway to get to the landing area. Then climb the obvious trails to the ridge crest. The main takeoff faces east and works well with south to southeast winds. For northeast winds, walk around the corner to the north and launch.

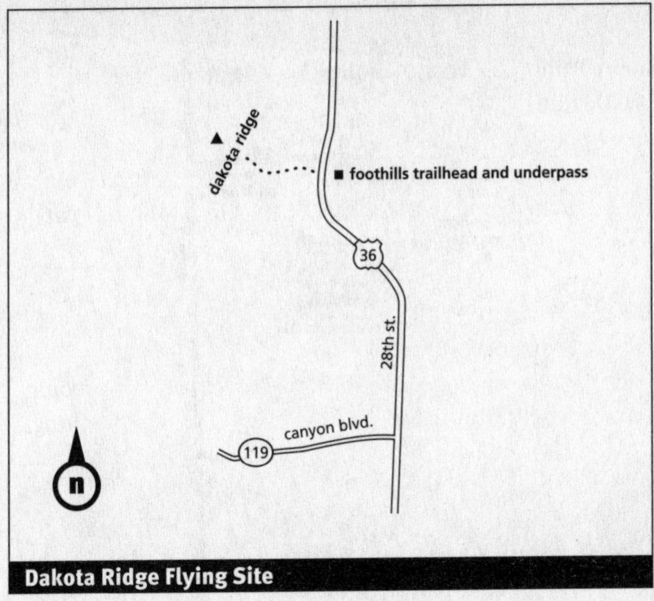

Dakota Ridge Flying Site

NORTH BOULDER FLYING SITE

Description: This is urban flying—primarily a training hill, with a large landing area and two launch sites at 200 and 600 feet. Don't underestimate it: flights of up to 7 miles have been recorded on paragliders, over 50 miles on hang gliders, including glides to Pueblo, Colorado. Good in northeast to southeast winds. P2 or H2 site.

Directions: The walk-up site lies on the north side of Boulder at the corner of Broadway and Locust Street. You'll see the parking area as you turn into Locust.

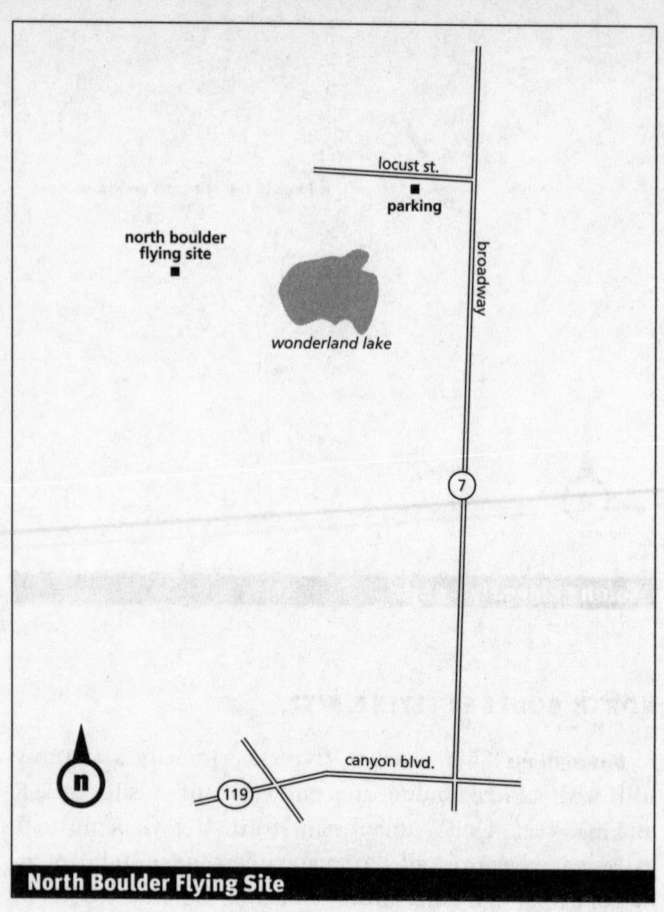

North Boulder Flying Site

SOUTH BOULDER TRAINING HILL

Contact: For more information, call Mark Windsheimer of Airtime Above Hang Gliding at (303) 674-2451

Description: A good, 200-foot-high training hill for paragliders in South Boulder near Eldorado Springs, with another training hill that's better for hang gliders just 1.5

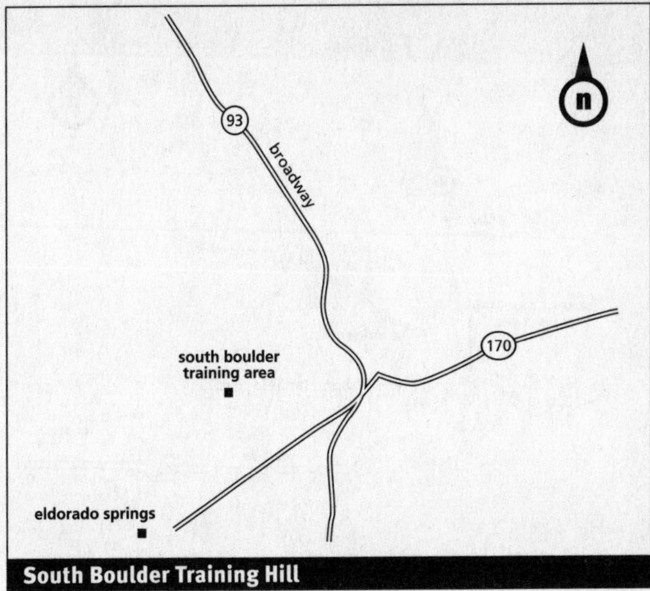

South Boulder Training Hill

miles away. With decent north winds it's possible to soar. P2 site.

Directions: Take Broadway (CO 93) south toward Eldorado Springs. At the crest of the long hill you'll see the parking area on the right. About 1.5 miles east is the hill more suitable for hang gliders, that is, the landing area is free of cactus and rock.

LOOKOUT MOUNTAIN

Location: Just west of Golden on 6th Avenue

Description: This is a very popular drive-up site for intermediate and advanced pilots. Lookout has over 1,000 vertical feet and steep faces. Excellent soaring and cross-country potential. The distance record for a paraglider is 82 miles;

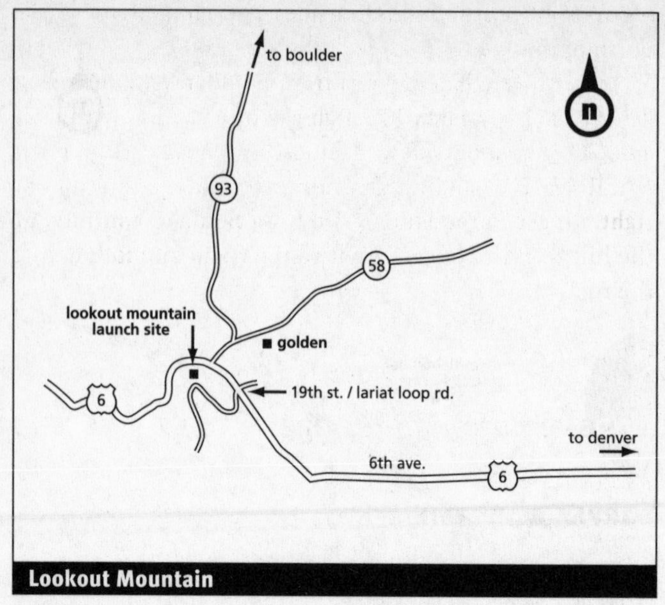

Lookout Mountain

20-mile cross-country flights are not uncommon. Hang glider pilots have flown to the Colorado–New Mexico state line! The mountain can be flown in north to southeast winds. P3 site or P2 site with local sponsorship. Helmet, radio, and reserve chute are required. Definitely call an experienced local before flying here. Signs at the landing area list phone numbers of local experts to call.

Directions: To get to the landing area from Denver, take US 6 west to Golden. Just before you hit CO 58 you come down a long hill. As it curves to the right at the bottom there are some big trees and a parking area on the left. You'll see the meadow. To get to the launch site from Denver, drive west on US 6. Go left onto 19th Street (19th is at the last stoplight before the junction of US 6 and CO 58, so if you hit CO 58 you've gone a little too far). Take 19th Street up the hill, stay on the main drag, and arrive at the big rock M on the mountainside. The launch site is just north of the M.

To get to the landing area from Boulder, take Broadway (CO 93) south, straight through the intersection with US 6 and CO 58 just outside Golden. As you head east on US 6, you'll see the landing area almost immediately on the right. To get to the launch site from Boulder, continue up the hill to 19th Street, take it to the right, and follow it to the rock M.

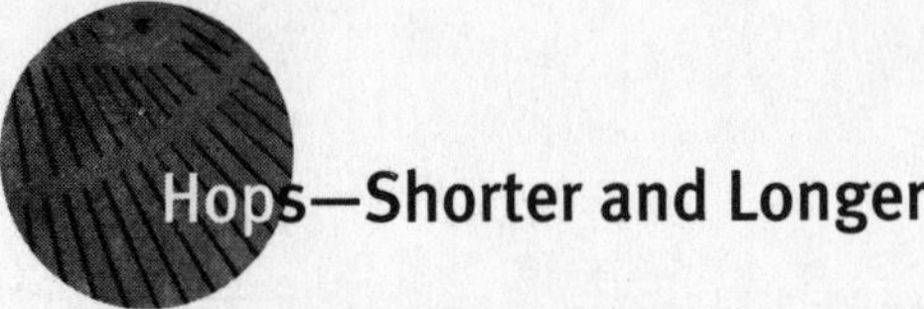

Hops—Shorter and Longer

COPPER MOUNTAIN

Contact: For more information, call Granger Banks at (303) 494-2820

Description: Copper Mountain (elev. 12,200′) has a 2,500-foot vertical, a good landing area at the Superbee lift, and, yes, chairlift access to the top. Launches west, north, and east. P4 site or P3 with sponsorship.

WILLIAMS PEAK

Location: Near Heeney

Contact: For more information, contact Mark Windsheimer of Airtime Above Hang Gliding at (303) 674-2451

Heads up: Not usually flown by paragliders in the middle of the day. Storms and sudden gust fronts are not uncommon.

Description: This is a very popular site for Denver area hang glider pilots. Launches are at approximately 10,200,

9,400, and 9,000 feet. The lakeside landing area is a large grass field next to Green Mountain Reservoir. The north landing zone is the size of a football field and cut out of sagebrush. Both lie at approximately 8,000 feet. Launches are possible to the southwest, west, and northwest. Primarily a thermal site without much ridge soaring opportunity. The usual season is April to October. Excellent cross-country potential. P2 and H2 during morning and late evening. Hang 3 other times.

Windsurfing

THERE ARE MORE windsurfers in the high desert and mountains of Colorado than on all of America's Gulf Coast. Thousands. Because the mountains and climate make the winds unpredictable and wild, Front Range windsurfers have developed interesting adaptive strategies. Some in Boulder keep their cars loaded with gear, and when the wind kicks up clean and hard out of the north or northwest, they hit Boulder Reservoir—whether it's the middle of a workday or the middle of winter—as long as there's open water. Denverite Karen Marriott, who won the U.S. Open course race in Corpus Christi in 1998, says "There's no such thing here as 'The wind blows every day at 2 P.M. in June.' The place in town

that's kind of unique is Soda Lakes. It's the only place around that has an almost predictable thermal." So in summer, if it's a clear morning looking to get hot, passionate board sailors get up early and catch the thermal that blows from sunrise until 9 A.M. They also hop over to popular Aurora Reservoir, which just filled up in the mid-1990s. Because it's a little farther east, the wind is cleaner and stronger than the old local favorites, Chatfield and Cherry Creek Lakes. Devoted windsurfers also drive 1 1/2 hours northeast to Jackson Lake for the clean, high plains wind. The lake hosts a big race, the Cold Water Classic, every May. There are other annual windsurfing events in the area, and lots of good instruction. Also, some wild ice sailing when the water's just too hard to surf. It's getting more and more popular. Ice sailors use the same sail and rig as a windsurfer, and fashion their own innovative boards.

For general Colorado boating regulations that apply to windsurfers, call (888) 593-2628 or visit the Web site at www.coloradoparks.org.

Denver City Limits—Sort Of

SODA LAKES

Location: 16 miles southwest of Denver

Size: Small lake — 1/4 mile long by 1/8 mile wide

Elevation: 6,000′

Fee: $4 per day, $40 per year for a Denver City Parks Pass

Season: Year-round

Map: Bear Creek Lake Park brochure

Heads up: Winds, winds, winds . . . and a reliable, early morning summer thermal.

Description: This is really a tiny lake, but beloved by

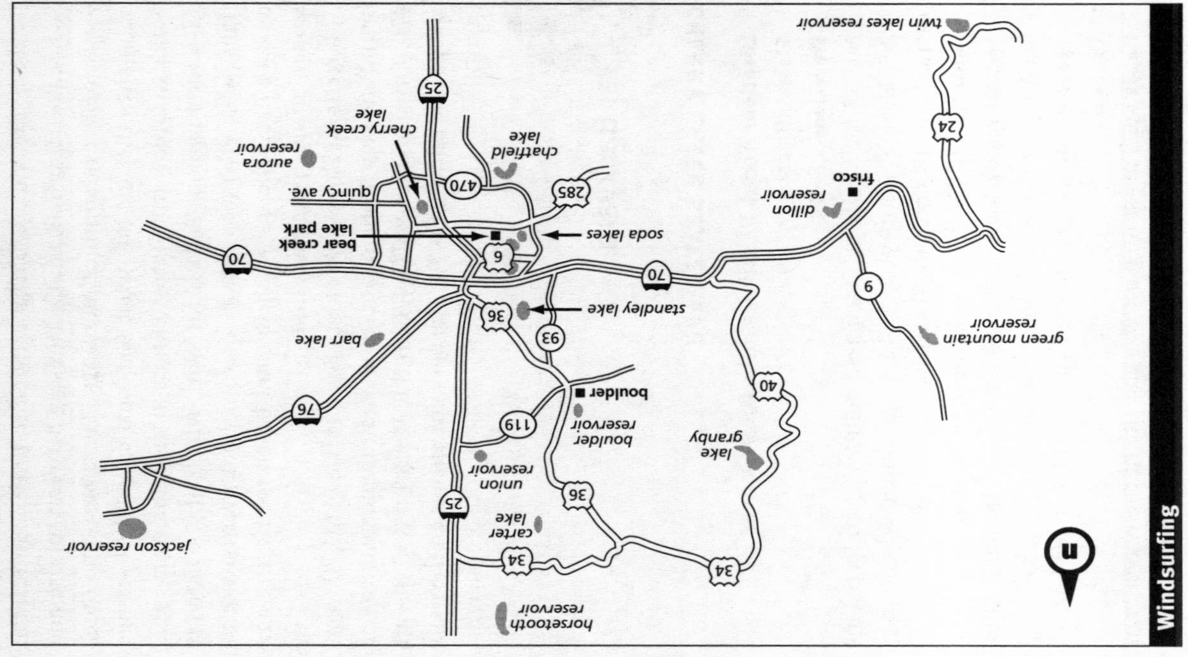
Windsurfing
n
jackson reservoir
barr lake
76
25
70
bear creek
lake park
quincy ave.
aurora
reservoir
cherry creek
lake
25
470
chatfield
lake
6
soda lakes
285
standley lake
36
93
union
reservoir
119
boulder
boulder
reservoir
carter
lake
34
36
horsetooth
reservoir
34
lake
granby
40
70
dillon
reservoir
frisco
9
green mountain
reservoir
24
twin lakes reservoir

locals for the one reliable bit of wind in three counties: the Soda Lakes Thermal, which kicks up between sunrise and 9 A.M. on warm summer mornings. There are some other anomalies that include what one local calls "Real strange winds that blow from 0 to 30 knots in the blink of an eye." Also the infamous Soda Lake Swirl, which, if you catch it right, will let you sail in a circle without ever having to tack or jibe. There's a coarse sand beach for rigging and launching along the east shore.

Directions: Drive west on 6th Avenue (US 6) to I-70 westbound and stay in the right lane so you can merge onto CO 470. Drive south on CO 470 to the Morrison (CO 8) exit and go east under CO 470. The park entrance is on the right (south).

Denver Backyard

CHERRY CREEK STATE PARK

Location: About 12 miles southeast of Denver

Size: 880 acres

Elevation: 5,550′

Fee: $5 for a daily vehicle pass (includes $1 collected for Water Basin Authority) or $43 for an annual vehicle pass (includes $3 collected for Water Basin Authority)

Contact: Call (303) 699-3860 for information

Special regulations: If there's any ice on the lake, they won't allow any boats (iceboats excepted).

Season: The gate is manned year-round, but see *Special regulations.*

Heads up: This state park was the site of the prayer vigil and papal mass with Pope John Paul II during World Youth Day 1993. Pray for wind.

Map: Cherry Creek Lake brochure available at park entrance

Description: Old local favorite. Moderate- to light-wind sailing with south to west winds. A good-size lake, but too much powerboat traffic to relax. On the plus side, it's set in a natural prairie environment of gentle, rolling hills and is very pretty.

Directions: Drive south on I-25 to I-225. Go northwest on I-225 to Parker Road (CO 83, exit 4) and turn right (south). Go 1 mile south on Parker to the park entrance.

CHATFIELD STATE PARK

Location: 21 miles southwest of Denver

Size: 1,550 acres

Elevation: 5,430′

Fee: A state parks pass costs $4 per vehicle per day or $40 per year.

Contact: Call (303) 791-7275 (general information); (303) 791-5555 (Chatfield Marina)

Special regulations: If there's any ice on the lake, they won't allow any boats (iceboats excepted).

Season: The gate is manned year-round, but see *Special regulations*.

Map: Chatfield State Park brochure

Heads up: Powerboats and jet skis; ice sailing in the winter.

Description: Chatfield used to be a favorite until Aurora Reservoir filled up and offered cleaner, stronger winds. It's a large reservoir, with very erratic light to big winds hailing from the south to west. One drawback is all the powerboat traffic. There's an excellent rigging and launching area on the north shore. When the ice gets thick enough, Chatfield is a hot (cold) spot for ice sailing.

Directions: Drive west on 6th Avenue (US 6) to Wadsworth Boulevard (CO 121). Turn left (south) on Wadsworth. Drive past CO 470 to the Deer Creek entrance on the left—it's well marked.

AURORA RESERVOIR

Location: 21 miles southeast of Denver

Size: 820 acres

Elevation: 5,000′

Fee: $4.00 daily or $35 annually for an Aurora City Parks pass

Contact: Call (303) 690-1286 (general information); (303) 766-0020 (Windline)

Special regulations: No motorboats, except fishing boats with electric motors.

Season: Year-round

Map: Aurora Reservoir Park brochure

Heads up: No powerboats, no jet skis, no wakes!

Description: This is the most popular lake for windsurfing in the Denver area. Karen Marriott, who's been windsurfing in town for 15 years, says that because it's a little farther east where the plains start to flatten out, the lake has cleaner, stronger winds. She says of Denver, "The city, where it sits down in the Platte River Valley, means that the winds are up 50 to 80 feet." She says that when Aurora filled up in the mid-90s it became an instant hit with windsurfers. There's an excellent grass and sand rigging and launching area at the marina. Light- to big-wind sailing with south to west to northerly winds. Northerlies are nasty because the marina buildings can block a lot of wind and can make launching and returning a real pain. No obstructions other than an occasional fisherman!

Directions: Drive south on I-25 to I-225. Go northwest on I-225 to Parker Road (CO 83), exit 4, and turn right (south).

Drive to Quincy Ave and turn left (east). Go 2 miles past Gun Club Mile Road to the park entrance.

BARR LAKE STATE PARK

Location: 21 miles northeast of Denver

Size: When the lake is full there are nearly 1,000 acres for boating

Elevation: 5,100′

Fee: A state parks pass costs $4 per day per vehicle or $40 per year.

Contact: Call (303) 659-6005 for information

Special regulations: Only sailboats, hand-propelled craft, and boats with electric trolling motors or gasoline motors of 10 horsepower or less are allowed. A boat ramp is located adjacent to the north parking lot. Boating on the northern half of the lake only.

Season: High-water levels April through June. The levels drop quickly in July and August, and the lake could be closed in September and October. Refill occurs in late October or November.

Map: Barr Lake State Park brochure

Heads up: Great nationally and internationally known bird-watching.

Description: Barr Lake is a midsize lake with light to medium westerly and northerly winds. In the 1880s it was an elite outing area for sportsmen from Denver—"The finest fishing in the west." Pollution almost ruined it, but strong laws and controls instituted in the 1960s helped stop the flow of toxins into the lake. What makes it special now is that it's edged by huge old cottonwoods and marshes, and the south half of the lake is a wildlife refuge. Three hundred and thirty species of birds have been spotted here, giving it an international reputation. Regular visitors include herons, pelicans, grebes, and other waterfowl. It also hosts one of the few successful bald eagle nests on the Front Range. You can ride the wind with some proud compatriots.

Directions: Drive north on I-25 to I-76, exit 216A. Keep right at the fork in the ramp and merge onto I-76 east. Go to Bromely Lane (exit 23) and turn right (east) on Bromely Lane/152 Avenue to Piccadilly Road. Turn right (south) on Piccadilly Road and drive to the park entrance. It's well marked.

Nature vs. Nurture

KAREN MARRIOTT LOVES to windsurf. She grew up in Denver, learned to sail here, trains here. She says despite the lack of big waves, Coloradans have gotten pretty good. They're fast, and they do flatwater tricks like Spocks and Vulcans. (If you didn't know, a Spock is a 360-degree spin—in the air.) In 1998 Marriott won the U.S. Open at Corpus Christi, Texas.

There are a couple of things she loves about the sport: "One, there's no such thing as being done. There's always something left to learn. And two, how good you are is directly related to how much you do it. You might say, 'I wanna be a pro basketball player,' and you could practice every day for years and never be any good. If you say, 'I'm gonna be a pro windsurfer,' that's different. Sail five hours a day for the next five years and you're gonna get *really* good. There's no such thing as being too short or too stocky. There's no such thing as being genetically gifted." Or, it seems, too far from a coast.

Or too old. The sport is wildly popular among retirees of all ages. One youngish veteran says he often sees a seventy-three-year-old man sailing. "There are a ton of people in their sixties windsurfing," he said, with a hint of envy. "And they're usually better than us pups in our forties because they have so much time to practice."

Boulder City Limits—Sort Of

BOULDER RESERVOIR

Location: 7 miles north of Boulder

Size: 540 acres

Elevation: 5,173′

Fee: Daily: $4 adults; $1.75 under 18; 4 and under free. Seasonal: Resident—$80 family; $35 adult; nonresident—$110 family, $50 adult

Contact: For information, call Boulder Parks and Recreation, (303) 413-7201; gate (303) 441-3468; boathouse (303) 441-3456; guard shack (303) 441-3469

Special regulations: Motorboats allowed only with city permit, nonmotorized boats need no permit.

Season: Labor Day to Memorial Day the gate's open, but no one's home, so have at it!

Map: Boulder Reservoir brochure, available at park entrance.

Description: One fall I paddled around the lake almost every evening. Sometimes I hammered into very stiff winds, and was a little awed by the athletic windsurfers tearing around on their short boards, especially when the weather got really cold. It's a beautiful, fair-size reservoir, with the mountains cresting to the west and a lot of bird life. There are osprey, northern harriers, American pelicans, white-faced ibis, least bitterns, and flocks of geese and duck V-ing down, squadron after squadron, for a night's rest in spring and fall. There's a decent rigging and launching area that can get pretty crowded on a nice evening when the wind is kicking. Light- to big-wind sailing with north to west winds. The reservoir is right next to the foothills, so the wind is pretty "dirty"—fickle and inconsistent.

Directions: Drive north on 28th Street (US 36) to Jay Road and turn right (east). Go to 51st Street and turn left (north). The entrance to Boulder Reservoir is well marked.

Sailing on Ice

YOU ARE A fanatic windsurfer. Thanksgiving arrives with a twenty-pound turkey and an arctic wind out of the northwest that raises a white-flecked chop on your favorite lake and kills the last durable little marigolds in your flowerbed. You go sailing anyway. Overnight the bitter cold turns the surface of the lake into a dense precursor of ice—a floating, unsympathetic layer of slush just this side of a slurpee. You go sailing anyway. The sound as you rip and jibe sets your teeth on edge. Two days later some dumb kids are playing broom hockey on the cove where you performed your first Vulcan in August. Shut down. You begin to drink. Your performance at the office slips. You forget to shave and to walk the dog, and the new glint of mistrust and hurt flashing in the eye of your spouse deepens your despair. One night, slumped against the basement bar you've set up, you notice your first windsurfer propped in the corner, the sail and rig, all grimed with dust and cobwebbed. A swell of nostalgia and real grief rises in your gullet. You turn away, nauseous with longing, and in some kind reprieve from destiny, notice your old college hockey skates hanging from a hook, tangled and entwined with the white figure skates of your betrothed, a depleted memorial to the days you skated together on Occum Pond and your love was fresh and crisp as a fall apple. Suddenly you sit up. A current of light surges through your aching head. You bolt off the stool. The skates are too high to reach on tiptoes and you almost break your neck falling off an upended milk crate. You dislodge the old board . . . ice sailing is born.

That's not exactly Mike Charboneau's story, but he did come to ice sailing from windsurfing, and he says that he made his first board with hockey skates. "It's like a giant skateboard with four skates," he says. Same sail and rig as a windsurfer. He says that sailing on the ice is actually easier than windsurfing because you take out the third dimension, the water that rocks and unsteadies your floating board. "It's actually a great way to learn windsurfing. And tricks are a lot easier." He says even with a light breeze you can have a blast, because on ice you can sail three to five times faster than the wind. "We probably max out at about 40 mph. The sheer speed is incredible. There's no sound but the wind going by your helmet." He explains that wiping out isn't as bad as it might seem. "When you're ice fishing, walking across the lake, and you fall, you fall straight down and it really hurts. When you spill at 20 mph you just slide."

Mike says an average person can be up and ice sailing in about ten minutes. The reservoir up at Georgetown is one of the first to freeze and a popular spot. When Chatfield freezes they go there. Every year, in January, Mike and his cohorts put on a "Windsurfing on Ice Day" at either Chatfield or another nearby frozen lake, with instruction, equipment, and safety clinics, and a chance to hop on and try it. I did it. It was fun. If you're interested call him at (303) 973-9660. Or contact the Rocky Mountain Windsurfing Association.

Short Hops

JACKSON LAKE STATE PARK

Location: 45 miles northeast of Denver
Size: 2,600 acres
Elevation: 4,440′

Fee: A state parks pass costs $4 per vehicle per day or $40 per year.

Contact: Call the park office, (970) 645-2551, for information

Special regulations: None

Season: The lake is closed to boats November 1. Boating at Jackson Lake State Park does not resume until *all* ice is off the reservoir in spring.

Heads up: First warm place to go in early summer.

Description: Sailors from Denver and Boulder make the popular trek for the cleaner, steadier high plains winds. Also for the warmth. The lake is shallow and heats up quickly in the early summer. It has attractive sandy beaches. Launch from any of the campsites along the west side. Light- to big-wind sailing with north to west winds.

Directions: Drive north on I-25 to I-76, exit 216A. Keep right at the fork in the ramp and merge onto I-76 east. Drive northeast 60 miles to the US 34/I-76 interchange (exit 66). Turn left (north) on CO 39 and go 7.25 miles through Goodrich. Turn left (west) on Y.5 Road and follow the paved road for 2.5 miles to the park entrance.

GREEN MOUNTAIN RESERVOIR

Location: 79 miles northwest of Denver

Size: 2,125 acres

Elevation: 8,000′

Fee: None

Contact: Call the U.S. Forest Service, (970) 468-5400, for more information

Special regulations: None

Heads up: Big. Mountain views.

Description: Launch from anywhere along the east side of the reservoir, though most people launch from about the northern third of the lake. Light- to big-wind sailing with north to west winds. The water gets *real* cold! The land around the reservoir consists mostly of gently sloping, sagebrush plains.

Directions: From Denver, take I-70 west to Silverthorne (CO 9, exit 205) and turn right (north). Drive about 24 miles on CO 9 to the north end of the reservoir.

Where to Connect

Shops

Larson's Ski & Sport
4715 Kipling Street
Wheatridge, CO 80034
(303) 423-0654

The *place in the Denver metro area to get gear and wisdom.*

Chip Graham Windsurfing Academy
(303) 426-6503

Clubs

Rocky Mountain Windsurfing Association
P.O. Box 27961
Denver, CO 80227-0961
E-mail: RMWA@windsurfing-co.com

The extremely active windsurfing club in Colorado. They put on big weekend events, races, and lovingly embrace their ice sailing wing.

Events

Cold Water Classic

Held at Jackson Lake State Park on the second Saturday in May. A race around buoys and freestyle events. Entrance fee: $15. Contact Karen at Larson's Ski and Sport.

Toucan Open

Held at Lake McConaughy in northeast Nebraska outside of Ogalala, 210 miles from Denver, the weekend after Labor Day. The event is as big as the winds screeching down the lake—four days of demo gear, professional windsurfers (mainly Coloradans) and lessons. One of the biggest events in the country. Contact Karen at Larson's Ski and Sport.

Willams Fork Weekend

Outside of Winter Park, the second weekend of August. It is hosted by Rocky Mountain Windsurfing Association and boasts fun races, camping, and a potluck dinner. Contact the RMWA.

Sailing

THERE'S QUITE A bit of sailing going on around the Front Range. We weren't sure if this was an adventure activity or not. We're certain it is out on the high seas, having suffered our share of seasickness and terror. This said, we know it's a hoot when the Rocky Mountain trade winds are tearing out of the canyons. There are a host of regattas on the lakes and reservoirs around Denver and Boulder, and many clubs offer racing and instruction in a range of boat classes. For descriptions of each lake and reservoir, please see "Windsurfing."

Lake	Phone Number	Marina	Storage	Lessons	Rentals	Races & Regattas	Open Sailing
Aurora Reservoir	(303) 690-1286	yes	yes	yes	yes	no	yes
Barr Lake	(303) 659-6005	no	no	no	no	no	yes
Carter Lake	(970) 667-1062	yes	yes	yes	yes	yes	yes
Chatfield State Park	(303) 791-7275	yes	yes	yes	yes	yes	yes
Cherry Creek Lake	(303) 690-1166	yes	yes	yes	yes	yes	yes
Dillon Reservoir	(970) 468-6562	yes	yes	yes	yes	yes	yes
Union Reservoir	(303) 772-1265	yes	yes	yes	yes	yes	yes
Jackson Reservoir	(970) 645-2551	yes	yes	no	no	yes	yes
Boulder Reservoir	(303) 441-1807	yes	yes	yes	yes	yes	yes

Clubs	Web site
Colorado Sail and Yacht Club	www.csyc.org
Denver Sailing Association	www.denversailing.org
Carter Lake Sailing Club	www.sailcarter.org
Dillon Yacht Club	www.summitnet.com/dyc/dyc.html

Schools	Web site	Phone number
Victoria Sailing School	www.victoriasailingschool.com	(303) 697-6601
Community Sailing of Colorado	www.members.tripod.com/~CommunitySailing/index.html	(303) 757-7718
The Anchorage	www.theanchorage.com	(303) 833-6601

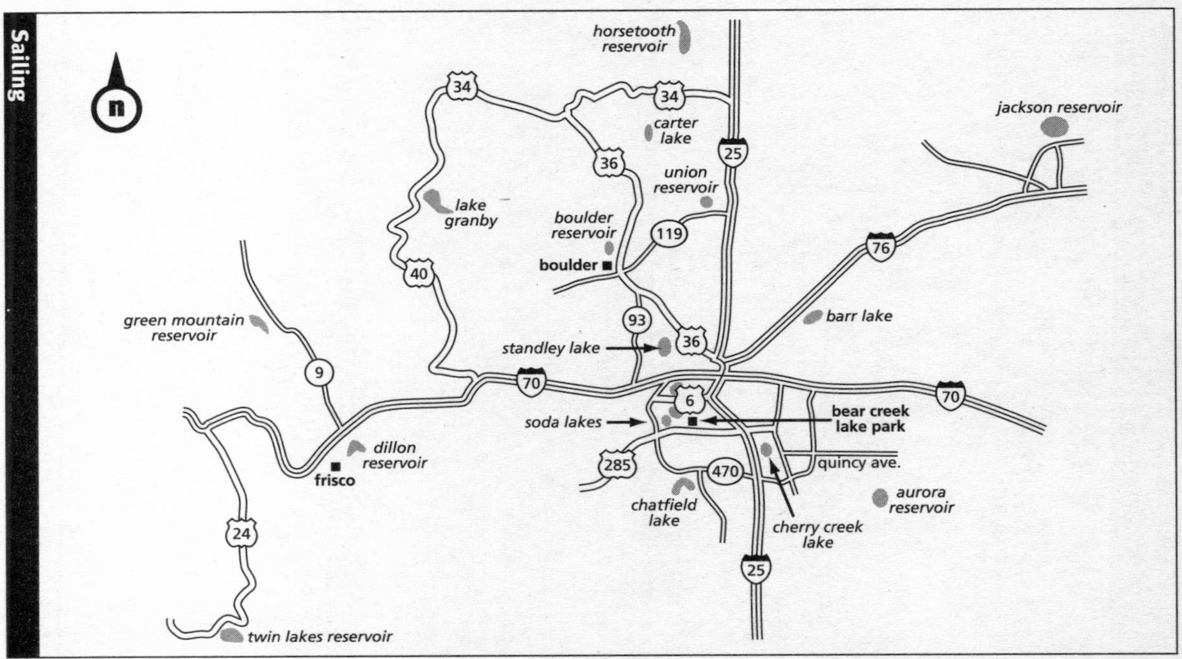
Sailing
n
horsetooth reservoir
34
34
carter lake
25
jackson reservoir
36
union reservoir
lake granby
boulder reservoir
119
76
boulder
40
green mountain reservoir
93
barr lake
standley lake
36
9
70
6
70
soda lakes
bear creek lake park
dillon reservoir
285
470
quincy ave.
frisco
aurora reservoir
chatfield lake
cherry creek lake
24
25
twin lakes reservoir

Scuba Diving

QUESTION: Which state has the most certified scuba divers per capita?

A) Colorado
C) California
B) Florida

Congratulations. It's true. Colorado has more certified scuba divers per capita than California, than Florida, than anybody. And since the coral reefs here haven't been doing too well since something like the Miocene, I can't figure out why except maybe that we have the mountains and the snow, and so when a Coloradan goes on vacation she or he goes someplace balmy with umbrellas in the drinks. This, actually, is the theory of Ray Brienza at Rocky Mountain Diving Center, which is about the oldest dive shop in Colorado. Ray also says that the Denver metro area is a great place to "train." Meaning there are a lot of reservoirs close by without a whole lot to look at, and a couple of fun dive holes within shot of a weekend trip. These include the Blue Hole in Santa Rosa, New Mexico, and the Homestead Crater outside of Park City, Utah, which maintains a constant water temperature of 94°F for fun midwinter dives. Some other interesting spots include high-altitude diving at nine thousand feet in Jefferson Lake near Leadville, which requires special dive tables and specialized training; winter ice diving with Underwater Phantaseas of Lakewood up at Twin Lakes north of Buena Vista; and the Aurora Reservoir where, in the mid-1990s, the Colorado Scuba Association sank a Cessna 172 airplane in thirty feet of water. If this seems a bit contrived, Horsetooth Reservoir, by Fort Collins, is not. There's a turn-of-the-century town under there. Ray had heard about it, but was still awed when he swam up to a barn in eighty feet of water. "It was eerie, yeah," he says. "It had algae all over it. I saw a couple of houses too." There's an intact town under Lake Dillon as well, but the Denver Water Board, which controls the reservoir, has strict rules against people-to-water contact: they don't allow swimmers, windsurfers, or divers, for fear they might contaminate the water. It's a goofy rule, and very frustrating to Front Range scuba folks. One says dryly, and with a bit of bitterness seasoned by periodic nitrogen overdoses, "A lot of gas and oil goes into the water from powerboats. A lot. And sailboats dump sewage into it as well. The Water Board knows all about it. But a few divers are going to pollute the lake. Oh, man. I mean . . . I gotta go."

So here is a simple list of the favorite lakes and some of the best dive shops that offer gear and certification instruction. Note the listing for Scott Taylor at A-1 diving—another shop that may have a legitimate title to oldest in Colorado. Scott is the only Master Diver in Colorado certified to teach disabled divers, and he runs an excellent program, including dives for the blind.

Denver Backyard

AURORA RESERVOIR

Location: 21 miles southeast of Denver

Contact: Aurora City Parks, (303) 690-1286

Heads up: Submerged Cessna airplane. Dive certification open-water area.

CHATFIELD STATE PARK—KING FISHER LAKE

Location: 21 miles southwest of Denver

Contact: Chatfield State Park, (303) 791-7275

Heads up: Murky and cold. Dive certification open-water area.

Diver under Glass

ON ANY GIVEN day, Denver Dive Master and instructor Shawna Morgan will go diving in the Sea of Cortez, in the cold Pacific somewhere off of Monterey, and in the South China Sea. More precisely, she'll dive in little bits of these seas, in simulated bits, among hosts of representative fish, and most likely will be gawked at by hordes of children who dream one day of shouldering a scuba tank and taking the plunge. Morgan is the director of divers at the Ocean Journey Aquarium, where one hundred volunteer and fifteen staff divers work in three 3-hour shifts every day, keeping the tanks clean and feeding the fish. Shawna says that eighty to ninety percent of the time the divers are "doing windows, scrubbing rocks, cleaning gravel, and also feeding the fish, which is the fun part." They mostly use a hookah system—long hoses of surface-supplied air, but in the Open Blue exhibit in the South China Sea area they use tanks so as not to disrupt the swim patterns of several species of shark. Good idea. All the divers are extremely well qualified, having at least one hundred dives and one hundred hours in open water. "It's a fixed environment," she says. "There's nowhere for the animals to go if you flail. And all of the coral is man-made, so if you knock off a piece there's no way it'll grow back." Shawna says that some of the divers get attached to certain specific fish; a few even love the homely moray eels, who look, to the layman, like all teeth and deadly intention. She says they're pretty friendly, and have gotten used to being hand-fed. "They're nearsighted, so you don't want to make sudden wriggly movements with your fingers right in front of their face. They might think it's food." The most aggressive fish? "The little tiny damsel fish. They peck at you once you get into their territory—bump your mask and pull at your hair." Divers interested in volunteering should call Ocean Journey's Volunteer Hotline, (303) 561-4429.

Boulder Backyard

HORSETOOTH RESERVOIR

Location: 45 miles north of Boulder

Contact: Larimer County Parks and Open Lands, (970) 679-4570

Heads up: You can dive to submerged barns and houses. Currently undergoing dam repairs; low-water levels. Carter Lake is an alternative, (970) 667-1062.

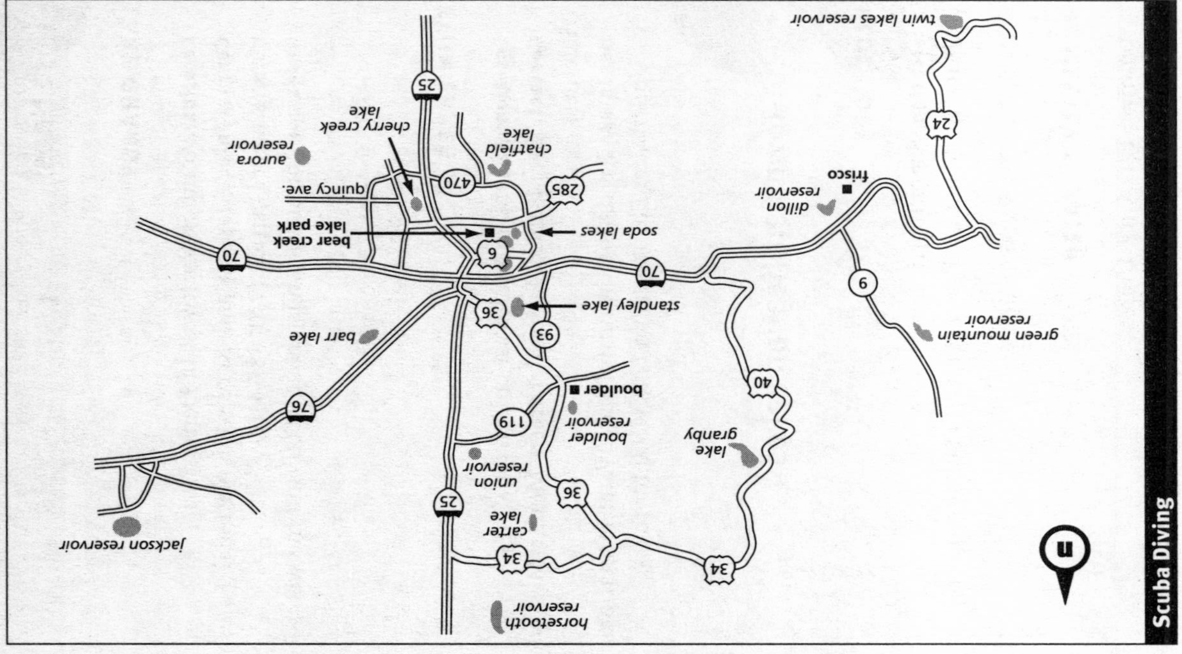
Scuba Diving
jackson reservoir
horsetooth reservoir
carter lake
union reservoir
barr lake
boulder reservoir
boulder
standley lake
soda lakes
bear creek lake park
quincy ave.
aurora reservoir
cherry creek lake
chatfield lake
lake granby
dillon reservoir
frisco
green mountain reservoir
twin lakes reservoir
n
25
34
36
119
93
76
70
6
470
285
40
9
24

Short Hops

LAKE GRANBY

Location: 95 miles northwest of Denver

Contact info: Arapaho and Roosevelt National Forest Sulphur Ranger District, (970) 887-4100

Heads up: The elevation is about 9,000′ and the water is *cold!*

TWIN LAKES

Location: 120 miles southwest of Denver

Contact: San Isabel National Forest; Mount Massive Wilderness

Heads up: Ice diving, beautiful ice crystal formations. Call Underwater Phantaseas in Lakewood for tours.

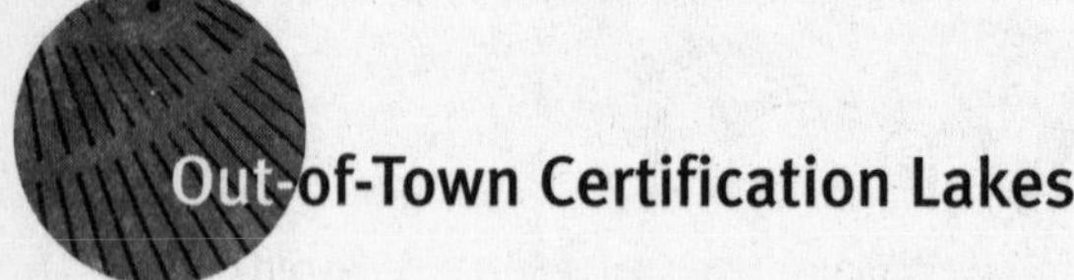

Out-of-Town Certification Lakes

BLUE HOLE

Location: Santa Rosa, New Mexico,

Heads up: About 61°F year-round. On old Route 66.

HOMESTEAD CRATER

Location: Park City, Utah

Heads up: The water temperature is a constant 91–94°F.

Grit

On November 17, 1991, Mike Utley lined up as an offensive guard for the Detroit Lions. They were playing the Los Angeles Rams; it was the first play of the fourth quarter. At the snap and Utley surged forward. It was a pass play, and though he couldn't see the quarterback, Utley knew he was about to let fly because the defender in front of him raised his hands. "No defender likes to get hit in the knees. That was my job. You knock their legs out and they drop their hands." Mike hit him and the defender reacted. He chopped his hands down, caught Utley on the shoulders and drove him into the turf. "I shrugged," Utley said, "and there was no place for the force to go. It crushed three of my vertebrae, C-5, -6, and -7."

Utley is now a C-6/7 incomplete quadriplegic. He's wheelchair-bound, but he was lucky, because he could still feel his hands and recovered use of them. He was determined not to let his injury slow him down. "A spinal cord injury cannot change you unless you allow it. . . . If you want something bad enough you go get it. You've got to have the desire." Utley wanted to learn to scuba dive. He met Scott Taylor, of A-1 Diving in Englewood, and Taylor taught him how. He took Utley to Stewart's Cove in the Bahamas for his open-water dive certification. Utley's first dive after certification was a night dive. "It was 9:30. There was a three-and-a-half-foot chop. I was the last guy in. The boat was surging up and down and the ladder knocked my regulator off and pushed down my mask. My two buddies turned me upside down and began to pull me down. The one rule Scott always told me: Do not panic. I found the regulator and cleared my mask. They were wearing red light sticks stuck in their masks so I could keep track of them. When we got down to thirty-five feet they let me go." A wild initiation. Utley loved it. He wears webbed gloves so he can maneuver, and because he's still close to only ten percent body fat, he "sinks like a stone. I don't need much weight to neutralize." I asked him if weightlessness was a relief. "Not really," he said. "I scuba dive because I like the sights. The colors of the fish, the blues, the yellows. On my first night dive I saw two huge sea turtles. I've been on those James Bond scooters. I've fed moray eels. It's the colors. It's so cool."

Utley also sky dives, kayaks, and drives his jet ski over seventy mph. "I believe in living life to the fullest," he said. "Because when it's over it's over." He is dedicated to helping others with spinal cord injuries. He speaks around the country and has established the Mike Utley Foundation, which raises money for research and helps the injured and their families. He says, "Everybody needs help sooner or later. Those guys who help themselves first, I'll be the first in line to help you out."

For info on scuba diving for the disabled, call Scott Taylor at A-1 Diving, (303) 789-2450. For more info on the Mike Utley Foundation, call (800) 294-4683.

Where to Connect

Shops and Instruction

Denver

A-1 Diving
1800 West Oxford Avenue
Englewood, CO 80110
(303) 789-2450
www.a1scuba.com

Open-water and high-altitude diving (including trips to Jefferson Lake in Leadville), instruction and certification, trips to Aurora, Chatfield, and Granby Reservoirs, rentals, travel, and disabled diving instruction.

Rocky Mountain Diving Center
1920 North Wadsworth Boulevard
Lakewood, CO 80215
(303) 232-2400
www.diveRMDC.com

Open for over 30 years, offering open-water and high-

altitude instruction and certification (including Homestead Crater trips), on-site pool, free 1-hour instruction/orientation, rentals, travel, and repairs.

Underwater Phantaseas
6869 C. Clinton Court
Englewood, CO 80237
(303) 220-8282

and

160 Union Boulevard
Lakewood, CO 80228
(303) 988-6725
www.underwaterphantaseas.com

Open-water and high-altitude diving, instruction and certification, rentals, repairs, and travel.

Denver Divers
557 Milwaukee Street
Denver, CO 80206
(303) 399-2877
www.denver-divers.com

Open-water and high-altitude diving, certification and instruction, on-site pool, rentals, travel, and repairs.

Scuba Den
6729 West 44th Avenue
Wheat Ridge, CO 80033
(303) 431-1088
www.scubaden.com

Open-water and high-altitude diving, certification and instruction, travel, rentals, and repairs.

Boulder

Scuba Joe's Dive and Travel
3054 28th Street
Boulder, CO 80301
(303) 444-9286
www.scubajoe.com

Open-water and high-altitude diving, certification and instruction, travel, rentals, and repairs.

Winter Sports Overview

ALL YOU HAVE to do is look west in any cold month to see the first swell of the Rockies rising in a muscular wall of snowy ridges, plateaus, and peaks. To squint at the clean, almost painfully bright sweep of snowfields running above hills bristling with black timber. All of it cut and folded with ravines and the canyons. You can't help but be moved. And if you get a kick out of winter, you begin to imagine the scores of secluded draws and basins that beckon a skier or snowshoer.

For those who thoroughly enjoy the advantages of a big town and love, or would like to try, strapping on a pair of teardrop snowshoes or waxing up and clicking into a pair of cross-country skis or stretching a pair of climbing skins onto a metal-edged telemark ski, this is a winter paradise. Within an hour and a half of Denver and Boulder are hundreds of wildly beautiful winter trails. Some head straight into challenging backcountry bowls, others meander gently along a creekbed. And there are miles and miles of groomed trails for those who want a smooth classic or skate ski workout.

In the next few chapters are a selection of some favorite routes that are easily accessible from Denver and Boulder. For the snowshoer or cross-country skier, most of the routes in all of the chapters can be happily explored.

After safety, courtesy may be the most valued consideration on a backcountry trail. If you're a snowshoer, don't mash over skiers' tracks. If you're a skier swooping down a fast, well-earned descent, stay under control and keep an eye out for ascending skiers and hikers. Be aware of avalanche danger. Take an avalanche safety class. Call for snow conditions the morning you set out, *not* any earlier, as conditions can change quickly. And carry a few crucial items in your daypack in case you get lost. Several friends, all very experienced outdoorspeople, have gotten lost just heading out for an afternoon ski, and spent the night out above nine thousand feet. What saved all of them was a tube of fire paste and matches.

Winter Safety Tips

By Wesley Massey, Outdoor Recreation Information Specialist with the U.S Forest Service in Denver, Colorado

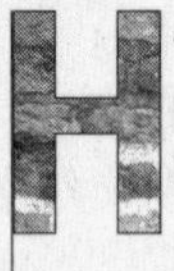

ARSH CONDITIONS OF wind, cold, snow, or whiteout can turn an outing into a tragedy. Knowledge of the terrain, weather, avalanche conditions, route, equipment, and personal limitations can ensure a safe and enjoyable outing.

Here are some tips for your winter outdoor trip:

- Let someone know where you are going and an approximate time of return. This point is easy to leave and crucial to rescuers if you need to be found.
- If recreating on national forests or parks, call the ranger station the day of your travel for an avalanche report and road conditions (some roads are not plowed in the winter). Yesterday's report may not help you today.
- Be courteous and cautious. Watch for snowmobilers, skiers, snowshoers, and dogs all enjoying the same areas.
- Layer your clothes. Begin with a noncotton base layer, followed by fleece or wool, and a water-resistant jacket.
- Sweat can make you wet if you are wearing cotton. Wear quick-drying, synthetic-fabric base layers.
- Cold kills in two ways: exposure and exhaustion.

"Just In Case" list:

- Matches
- Fire paste
- Extra gloves, socks, and hat
- Flashlight with good batteries
- Food (gorp, energy bars)
- Extra water
- Map
- Cell phone

Hot Spots

There are a few very active trailheads and nordic centers worth mentioning. They're within easy shot for a day trip in the winter woods and they serve as gateways to large trail systems, or, in the case of the nordic centers, they're fantastic resources for those who want to learn more and hone their skills.

ELDORA TRAILHEAD AND ELDORA NORDIC CENTER

Location: 21 miles north of Boulder

Contact: Call the center at (303) 440-8700, ext. 267, or 888-2-Eldora, or visit the Web site: www.eldora.com/nordic.html

Description: This superb nordic center has 45 kilometers of well-designed trails that run through woods and alpine clearings. There are classic and skate cross-country trails and a couple of designated snowshoe routes. Cross-country lessons are offered twice a day; skate and telemark lessons are offered on the weekends. The daily pass rates are pretty reasonable, but friends in Boulder and Nederland who are avid cross-country skiers, especially those without 9-to-5 jobs who can get a ski in before trails close at 4:00, find the season pass a good deal. There's a popular Women's Wednesday program, now offered on Tuesdays too, that includes six weeks of breakfasts, lunches, and cross-country or telemark skiing with instructors and other women of the same ability. Also some fun annual races, such as the Nighthawks Race Series (6 weeks of classic and freestyle night races), and the Rising Sun Classic, in which you have to stop, dig a snow pit, and boil an egg. State-of-the-art rental equipment includes snowshoes, telemark gear, and skate and touring skis.

The Eldora trailhead is the take-off point for a number of favorite trails, both shorter out-and-backs and miles and miles of backcountry in the Indian Peaks Wilderness. For anybody in the area who likes to cross-country ski or snowshoe it's worth exploring.

Directions: To get to the ski area and trailhead, drive up Boulder Canyon on Canyon Boulevard (CO 119) to Nederland, bear left at the traffic circle, and continue on 119. Follow the signs for Eldora, which will take you onto 130 RD. The Mountain Resort and Nordic Center access forks left in 1.4 miles. To get to the Eldora trailhead, bear right at this fork and drive straight through the hamlet of Eldora to the end of the plowed road.

VAIL PASS

Location: 70 miles west of Denver

Fee: Weekday passes are $2 per person; $5 on weekends.

Contact: For further information about the Vail Pass Winter Recreation Fee Demonstration Area, call the USFS Holy Cross Ranger District at (970) 827-5715

Description: If you dream of driving into the Rockies, up to a trailhead above 10,000 feet surrounded by meadows and glades covered with powder, rolling ridges, old unplowed roads, dark stands of spruce and fir, and ranks of rugged receding mountains in every direction, all you have to do is drive 1¼ hours up I-70 to Vail Pass.

There's now a U.S. Forest Service hut with a good map of the trail system on the pass, and a nice ranger to take your fee. Heated trail-rage conflicts between snowmachine riders and nonmotorized travelers have been minimized by a system of trails that attempts to separate the two as much as possible.

Directions: Drive west on I-70 to exit 190, Vail Pass. Drive west to the overnight parking area above the rest stop buildings. The trailhead is at the north end.

Avalanche Awareness

by Wesley Massey, Outdoor Recreation Information Specialist for the U.S. Forest Service in Denver, Colorado

AVALANCHE PATHS MAY appear to be the best places to ski, board, or snowshoe because they look like big open, steep chutes. Take note that avalanches usually occur in the same paths again and again and create those open areas by destroying everything in their path.

- Avalanches are most common on slopes of 30–45 degrees. Know the steepness of the mountain and call the ranger station for avalanche-prone areas.
- South-facing slopes are especially dangerous in the spring because of solar heating.
- Leeward slopes can be dangerous when wind-deposited snow adds depth and unstable layers.
- Never try to outrun an avalanche; attempt to take cover off to the side.
- If everyone wears an avalanche transceiver beacon, it improves your chances of being found by 100 percent, but only if everyone knows how to use them.
- Look for snow fracture lines and study the snow layers.
- Scout your route.

Basic avalanche equipment includes:

- Beacon
- Shovel
- Probe pole
- Slope meter

For Colorado Weather and avalanche information, contact the Colorado Avalanche Information Center. It lists daily reports, offers classes around the state, and publishes a great booklet: *Avalanche Wise* by Knox Williams and Dale Atkins.

Colorado Avalanche Information Center
325 Broadway, WS1
Boulder, CO 80303
www.caic.state.co.us
Denver/Boulder (303) 275-5360 (Avalanche Hotline)
Summit County (970) 668-0600

MONTEZUMA

Location: 70 miles west of Denver

Description: In 1863 the first silver strike in Colorado was launched by John Coley, just above Montezuma, near what is now the ghost town of Saints John. At one time Montezuma contained the only silver smelter in the district, along with its share of brothels and bars. Today the quiet, ramshackle collection of buildings that sit above 10,000 feet seems a little shocked by the boom and bust rollercoaster of its history. Montezuma residents have always been, well, independent. For a while, in the 1980s, Rob Ilves ran the Montezuma Inn, a well-loved stopover for skiers. Ilves was a little wild. He was a superb mountaineer. I remember when he skied the crazily steep avalanche chute you can see from town if you look up. He put a parachute on his back and skied straight down it, pulled the chute near the bottom. He still broke something—I think it was his thumb. After one of his lungs collapsed in an airline fire drill (Ilves and his wife Donna worked as flight attendants, among other things) the doctors told him that he had to move down to sea level or he'd die. So he and Donna moved *up* 500 more feet, to the ghost town of Sts. John. They dropped a section of 30-foot silo onto the old mining site, insulated it, put in a triple-glazed bay window, a sleeping loft with a fire pole, a swinging dining room table suspended from ropes, with swing seats, a big woodstove, and happily lived there for years. When they had to fly, they'd drive an hour and a half down to the airport. Next time you're flying and someone says, "Beer, wine, pop?" and blinks down at you with a clear smile, don't assume anything.

Oh, the point of all this is that Montezuma is home to several trailheads, including Peru Creek (a little before you get to town), Deer Creek, and the Sts. John Road. There's a huge amount of beautiful skiable country up here, just at timberline.

Directions: Take I-70 west to Dillon and Silverthorne, exit 205. Drive east on US 6 for 7.7 miles to the second Keystone Resort entrance—River Run. Go past the River Run parking lots and continue on to Montezuma on FR 5.

DEVILS THUMB RANCH NORDIC CENTER

Location: 65 miles northwest of Denver

Contact: Main office (970) 726-5632. Reservation desk, (800) 933-4339. The Ranch House Restaurant, (970) 726-5633. Activities center, (970) 726-8231. Fax: (970) 726-9038. E-mail: devthumb@rkymtnhi.com

Description: Just past Winter Park, in Fraser, is one of the premier cross-country ski centers in North America. Over 100 kilometers of trails run through lodgepole woods, aspen groves, and little meadows beneath the rugged flanks of the Continental Divide. There are dedicated snowshoe trails, lodging, lessons, rentals, and flat-out breathtaking country. The area is full of elk, and a moose or two.

Directions: Take I-70 west to US 40 (exit 232) and drive through Empire, over Berthoud Pass, and down into Winter Park. Drive through Winter Park and then Fraser. Turn right onto 83 RD, which is 2.5 miles past Fraser. In about 3 miles 83 RD dead-ends at the Devils Thumb parking lot.

YMCA'S SNOW MOUNTAIN RANCH

Location: 70 miles northwest of Denver

Contact: Call the nordic center at (970) 887-2152, ext. 4173, for more information

Description: A few miles past Devils Thumb is this huge winter sports enclave with 85 kilometers of groomed classic and skate cross-country trails and 15 more kilometers of dedicated snowshoe trails. It's rolling and beautiful, in lodgepole woods and meadows. The facility includes lodging and pool, sauna, gym, and skating rink for school and church groups. Many nordic teams have trained here, including the U.S. Biathlon and Cross-Country teams. There are daily lessons in classic and skate skiing at 10:30 and 1:30 and a free kids program, for all kids ages 5 to 15, on Fridays and Sundays between 1 and 3, that includes instruction and skiing.

Directions: Take I-70 west to US 40 (exit 232) and drive through Empire, over Berthoud Pass, and down into Winter Park. Drive through Winter Park and then Fraser. Continue on to Tabernash. Drive through town and up the hill. Look for the sign.

BEAVER CREEK NORDIC CENTER

Location: 94 miles west of Denver

Contact: Call (970) 845-5313 for more information, or log on to www.snow.com/beaver-creek/index.shtml

Description: I have to include this state-of-the-art nordic center, which is exuberantly encouraging snowshoeing. It sponsors one of the nation's biggest and fun-est snowshoe events—the North American Snowshoe Championships—which in 2001 had the biggest purse in snowshoe history—$4,000. It's a blast for snowshoers of all levels, with many kinds of races. The center also offers all sorts of telemark and skate-ski programs, all-women skis, children's instruction, day care, and the latest in rental gear. There are other fun amenities associated with being part of a big ski area, such as sleigh ride dinners and ice skating—but the best thing of all is that the nordic trails are *on top* of the mountain at 10,100 feet (you buy a special lift ticket to get there). The views are fabulous.

Directions: Take I-70 west to Avon, exit 167. Follow the signs.

OTHER NORDIC CENTERS

Every ski area today has a well-developed nordic center. If you hanker for groomed trails over different terrain and country, here's a list of places to contact, including a few more independent nordic centers.

Breckenridge Nordic Center
1200 Ski Hill Road
P.O. Box 1776
Breckenridge, CO 80424
(970) 453-6855; fax: (970) 453-4292
E-mail: nord@colorado.net
www.colorado.net/~nord/

Copper Mountain Cross Country Center
P.O. Box 3001
Copper Mountain, CO 80443
(970) 968-2318, ext. 6342; fax: Attn.: Cross Country Center
(970) 968-2308
E-mail: jarosp@ski-copper.com
www.ski-copper.com

Frisco Nordic Center
P.O. Box 532
Colorado Hwy 9
Frisco, CO 80443
(970) 668-0866; fax: (970) 453-4292
E-mail: nord@colorado.net
www.colorado.net/~nord/

Keystone Cross Country Center
P.O. Box 38
Keystone, CO 80435
(970) 496-4275 or (800) 451-5930, ext. 4275
www.snow.com, look under *Keystone, Activities*

Piney Creek Nordic Center and Cookhouse
1520 Mount Elbert Drive
Leadville, CO 80461
(719) 486-1750

Beaver Meadows
P.O. Box 178
Red Feather Lakes, CO 80543
(970) 881-2450, (800) 462-5870

Grand Lake Touring Center
P.O. Box 590
Grand Lake, CO 80447
(970) 627-8008
www.grandlakecolorado.com/touringcenter

SolVista Golf & Ski Ranch
P.O. Box 1110
Silver Creek, CO 80446
(800) 754-7458
E-mail: staff@silvercreek-resort.com
www.silvercreek-resort.com

Steamboat Springs Ski Touring Center
P.O. Box 775401
Steamboat Springs, CO 80477
(970) 879-8180
E-mail xcski@cmn.net
www.nordicski.net

10TH MOUNTAIN DIVISION HUT SYSTEM

Between Aspen, Leadville, and Vail is an extraordinary system of backcountry huts that allows skiers and snowshoers in winter, and hikers and mountain bikers in summer, to travel Colorado high country by day and spend the nights in comfortable cabins. The most basic huts are wildly more luxurious than a breath-frosted tent, with woodstoves and wood, propane stoves, beds and mattresses, pots and pans, and usually a great deck with great views. Some are downright posh, with saunas, electric lights, and bedrooms.

The twenty-four 10th Mountain huts are strung along over 300 miles of trails, are well situated for backcountry trips of all lengths and difficulty, and are usually near-fantastic bowl or glade skiing for telemarkers. The popularity of the huts has skyrocketed, so make the required reservations early—like a year early. Sometimes, however, you can plan a spontaneous trip and get lucky by checking the vacancy status on the Web site. The huts are open for winter use from Thanksgiving to April 30, and for summer use from July 1 until September 30. Prices vary, but tend to be in the $30 per person per night range.

The very best way to check out the hut system and reservation status for each hut is to log on to www.huts.org.

The site includes information and status of the Braun and Summit hut systems as well. Or contact:

10th Mountain Division Hut Association
1280 Ute Avenue
Aspen, CO 81611
(970) 925-5775

The comprehensive guidebook *Colorado Hut to Hut: A Guide to Skiing, Hiking, and Biking Colorado's Backcountry,* 2nd ed., by Brian Litz (Englewood, Colo.: Westcliffe Publishing, 1995), is full of information.

Where to Connect

Shops

Denver

REI
1416 Platte Street
Denver, CO 80202
(303) 756-3100

Mountain Miser
209 West Hampden Avenue
Englewood, CO 80110
(303) 761-7070

Grand West
801 West Broadway
Denver, CO 80202
(303) 825-0300

Confluence Kayaks and Telemark
1537 Platte Street
Denver, CO 80202
(303) 433-3676
Telemark gear only.

Boulder

Mountain Sports
821 Pearl Street
Boulder, CO 80302
(303) 443-6770

EMS
2550 Arapahoe Avenue
Boulder, CO 80302
(303) 442-7566

Boulder Outdoor Center
2510 North 47th Street
Boulder, CO 80301
(303) 444-8420

Neptune Mountaineering
633 South Broadway, Unit A
Boulder, CO 80303
(303) 499-8866
www.neptunemountaineering.com

GOLDEN

Alpenglow Mountainsport
885 Lupine Boulevard
Golden, CO 80401
(303) 277-0133

FARTHER AFIELD

Eldora Nordic Center
P.O. Box 1697
Nederland, CO 80466
(303) 440-8700, ext. 212

Ski Depot Sports
Park Plaza
Winter Park, CO 80482
(970) 726-8055

Estes Park Mountain Shop
358 East Elkhorn Avenue
Estes Park, CO 80517
(970) 586-6548

GUIDE SERVICES

Alpine World Ascents
4224 Corriente Place
Boulder, CO 80301
(303) 247-0668
www.alpineworldascents.com

Complete certified guide services, including ice climbing, mountaineering, backcountry skiing, snowshoe tours, and some of the best avalanche courses around.

Colorado Mountain School
351 Moraine Avenue
Estes Park, CO 80517
(970) 586-5758
www.cmschool.com

Complete guide services and instruction in all winter adventure sports.

Adventures to the Edge
P.O. Box 2636
Crested Butte, CO 81224-2636
(970) 349-1432, (888) 754-2201

Paragon Guides
P.O. Box 130
Vail, CO 81658
(970) 926-5299; fax: (970) 926-5298
E-mail: ParagonGuides@compuserve.com
www.vail.net/paragonguides

Hut-to-hut tours.

Snowshoeing

THERE IS SOMETHING the universe loves about a simple sport, a sport that requires only snow, a pair of snowshoes, and the ability to walk. For once, what makes a sport so appealing to people is the raw, unmediated experience of the thing—it's the woods themselves, and the mountains, and the entranced hush of moving through a country muted by snow. People who do it are passionate about it. They describe the quiet and the peace, the ability to go anywhere, on-trail or off, the rigor of the workout, the sheer fun. One enthusiast who runs, hikes, and bikes describes it as the best cross-training he's ever done, and says that he can get more endorphins in two miles of snowshoeing than in six of running. Famed mountain bike coach Skip Hamilton recommends it as one of the best forms of cross-training for bikers. All of which is probably the reason the sport is the fastest growing winter activity. And snowshoes have changed. They're no longer the quaint cabin ornaments of steamed ash and rawhide that people nail up over the door. They're lightweight and easy to put on; they're made of aluminum frames and tough synthetic decking, with elegant and comfortable binding systems and cleats for traction. And they've become anatomically correct, so a hiker or runner doesn't have to widen her gait or alter her natural stride.

Included here is a sampling of some great trails near Denver and Boulder, and a few farther afield—in Winter Park, Rocky Mountain National Park, and on Guanella Pass—all a day trip. For an activity like snowshoeing, the selection has to be a mere sampling: there are hundreds and hundreds of routes. Any hiking trail that is beautiful in summer can be magical on snowshoes. Any Forest Service road that is closed to vehicles or simply left unplowed in winter can make a delightful trek on snowshoes. Any ridge or basin or valley. Also, snowshoes make a great combination with a snowboard: strap the board on your daypack and snowshoe in to an otherwise inaccessible backcountry slope, then snowboard home. Keep in mind that in the backcountry, awareness and precautions about avalanche dangers and winter mountain weather should be paramount. For daily snowpack conditions around the state call the Avalanche Hotline at (303) 275-5360; check skicountryusa.com for snow and avalanche reports from all the ski areas in Colorado. For regular course offerings on avalanche and mountain safety in Boulder, check with the Boulder Outdoor Center (303-444-8420) and EMS (303-442-7566); in Denver call REI (303-756-3100) and Confluence Kayaks and Telemark (303-433-3676). The Colorado Avalanche Information Center (www.caic.state.co.us) provides courses statewide.

Many thanks to Claire Walter and her magnificent guide, *Snowshoeing Colorado.*

Boulder Backyard

JENNY CREEK TRAIL

Location: 29 miles west of Boulder

Length: 10 miles out and back

Difficulty: Advanced

Elevation gain: 1,380′

Highest elevation: 10,720′

Avalanche hazard: Low

Maps and book: USGS Nederland (7.5 minute); Trails Illustrated 102; USFS Roosevelt National Forest map; *Snowshoeing Colorado*

Snowmobiles: No

Dogs: No

Heads up: Backyard backcountry.

Description: A popular and beautiful out-and-back close to town that culminates in a cirque and Yankee Doodle Lake. On the weekends, watch for skiers flying by on the descent.

Route: Follow the blue diamond trail markers, and all trail signs that say JENNY CREEK. From the parking area, climb along the left side of the beginner ski slope. Enter the trees behind the chairlift at the blue-and-white Forest Access sign. Continue to an intersection with a wide road and follow the Jenny Creek signs to the left. Stay on the Jenny Creek Trail as it passes spur trails and contours around the south side of Guinn Mountain. After about 3 miles, fork left at two small trail junctions. The trail steepens, crosses the creek, and continues almost 2 more miles

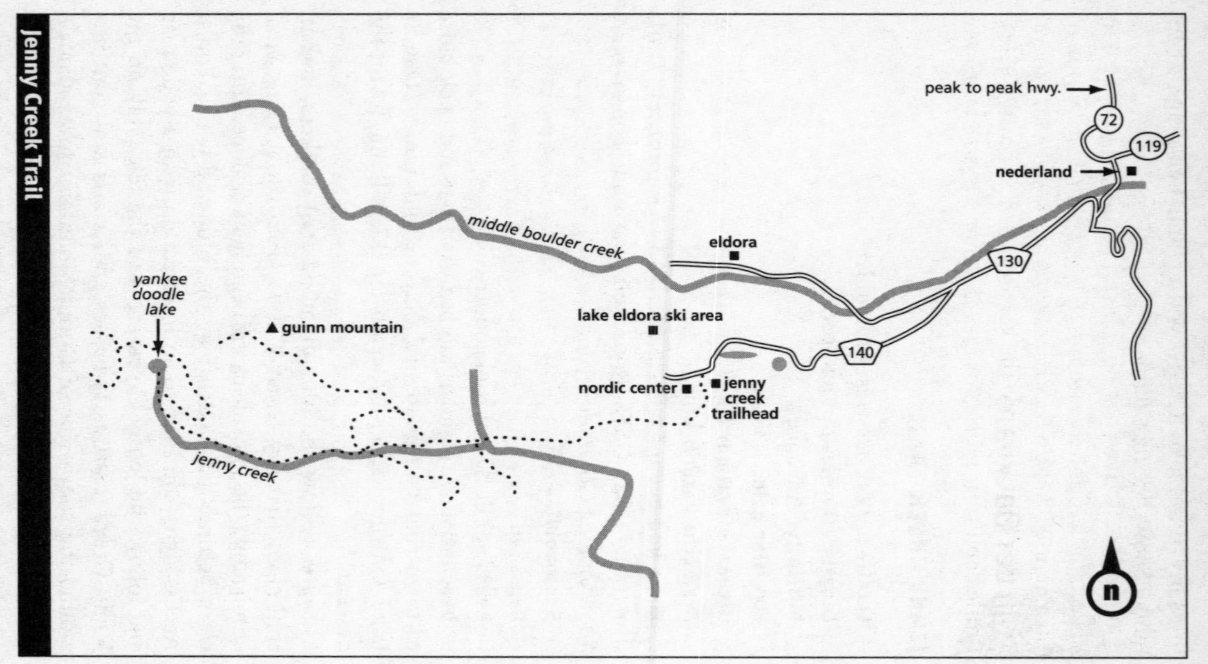
Jenny Creek Trail
peak to peak hwy.
72
119
nederland
130
eldora
middle boulder creek
lake eldora ski area
140
nordic center
jenny creek trailhead
yankee doodle lake
guinn mountain
jenny creek
n

along the north side of the creek, ending at Yankee Doodle Lake. Return the way you came.

Directions: Drive west up Canyon Boulevard (CO 119) to Nederland. Go left (south) at the rotary and drive out of town on the Peak to Peak Highway. Follow signs for Eldora. At the fork turn left onto the ski area road. Continue about 4 miles and turn left again into the first parking area—the tour starts near the Nordic Center office.

The Little VW That Could

BILL DEMAREST WAS a Boulder-based aeronautical engineer with an idea. It came to him in a bar, where some of the best and worst ideas occur. He started drawing on a napkin and then he went home and eyed the old VW put out to pasture in his backyard. The car trembled. It was about to give itself to science. Demarest cut the timing belt out of the engine and swaths of vinyl from the back of the seats. He got some old tent poles, bent them into a tear-drop shape, and stretched the vinyl over them. The timing belt became a support strap—the crucial link between the binding and the rest. Then he strapped on his homemade snowshoes and went for a walk up in the hills. What Demarest created was an innovation in the shape of the modern snowshoe, and the beginning of Crescent Moon Snowshoes. The Boulder company has taken his basic idea and turned it into one of the sport's best products. The tear-drop design is unique and allows for a completely natural gait, because the lifting shoe naturally clears the one being set down. That, combined with other features, such as a binding system that has no pressure points and will not come out of adjustment, make the shoe popular. Bravo to a local.

HESSIE ROAD

Location: 29 miles west of Boulder

Length: 3 miles out and back

Difficulty: Easy

Elevation gain: 210′

Highest elevation: 9,030′

Avalanche hazard: None

Maps and book: USGS Nederland (7.5 minute); Trails Illustrated 102; USFS Roosevelt National Forest map; *Snowshoeing Colorado*

Snowmobiles: No

Dogs: Yes

Heads up: Local favorite, with woods, meadows, hills, and creeks.

Description: Jake Thamm of Crescent Moon Snowshoes says, "This is one of my favorites. You can continue on to Skyline Reservoir, Jasper Lake, and Diamond Lake." These lakes are quite far—strenuous treks that can be dangerous due to avalanche hazard. But the route mentioned here is easy and relatively short. For a slightly longer, more challenging trek, continue on to Lost Lake, described next.

Route: Head up the unplowed road to the junction with Fourth of July Road. Continue straight through (west) to the old Hessie town site. Cross the clearing and enter the woods, continuing to the footbridge over the North Fork of Middle Boulder Creek. Turn back here, or, if you're still energetic, cross the bridge and go on to Lost Lake.

Directions: Drive west up Canyon Boulevard (CO 119) to Nederland. Go left (south) at the rotary and drive out of town on the Peak to Peak Highway. Follow signs for Eldora. At the fork, instead of taking the left fork to the ski area, bear right and drive to the center of Eldora (RD 130). Continue a couple of miles to the end of the plowed road and park.

Hessie Road & Lost Lake

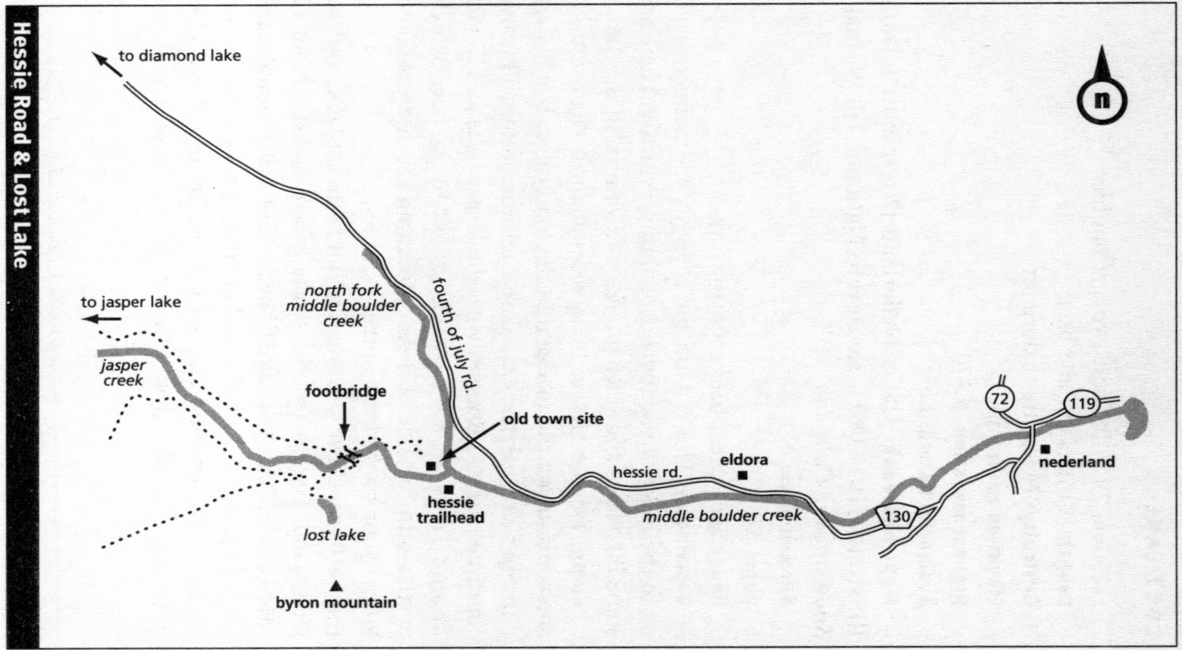

LOST LAKE

Location: 29 miles northwest of Boulder

Length: 6 miles out and back

Difficulty: Moderate to difficult

Elevation gain: 950′

Highest elevation: 9,770′

Avalanche hazard: Low

Maps and book: USGS Nederland (7.5 minute); Trails Illustrated 102; USFS Roosevelt National Forest map; *Snowshoeing Colorado*

Snowmobiles: No

Dogs: Yes

Heads up: Perfect backcountry workout.

Description: This is a fun, picturesque, and energetic add-on to the Hessie Road route described previously. There are some big views and steep pitches and you finish at a lake.

Route: Do the Hessie Road route described previously, and continue on the road across the footbridge. You'll start climbing through aspens. Cross another footbridge and continue past the junction with the Jasper Lake and Devils Thumb Trails. At the next fork go left to the lake, which nestles into the side of Bryan Mountain. Turn around and follow your tracks back home.

Directions: Drive west up Canyon Boulevard (CO 119) to Nederland. Go left (south) at the rotary and drive out of town on the Peak to Peak Highway (CO 119). Follow signs for Eldora. At the fork, instead of taking the left fork to the ski area, bear right and drive to the center of Eldora. Continue a couple of miles to the end of the plowed road and park.

LEFT HAND RESERVOIR ROAD—INDIAN PEAKS

Location: 29 miles northwest of Boulder

Length: 4 miles out and back

Difficulty: Moderate

Elevation gain: 580′

Highest elevation: 10,640′

Avalanche hazard: None

Maps and book: USGS Ward (7.5 minute); Trails Illustrated 102; USFS Roosevelt National Forest map; *Snowshoeing Colorado*

Snowmobiles: No

Dogs: Yes

Heads up: Moonlight hike.

Description: A very popular and lovely trek for both skiers and snowshoers with plenty of room for everybody.

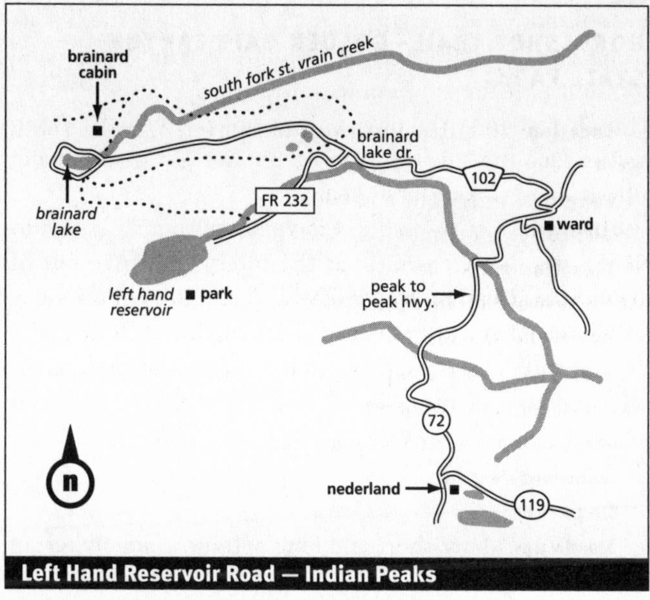

Left Hand Reservoir Road — Indian Peaks

Steady climb most of the way, with magnificent views of the Indian Peaks. Claire Walter, author of the indispensable *Snowshoeing Colorado*, recommends it for a full moon jaunt.

Route: One hundred yards before the barrier gate at the end of the plowed section of Brainard Lake Drive, on the left (south), is another barrier gate blocking the Left Hand Reservoir Road (FR 232). Follow it generally southwest to the reservoir. Return the way you came.

Directions: Drive west up Canyon Boulevard (CO 119) to Nederland. Turn right (north) onto the Peak to Peak Highway (CO 72). Just north of Ward turn left (west) on Brainard Lake Drive (102 RD) and continue to the parking lots.

HORSESHOE TRAIL—GOLDEN GATE CANYON STATE PARK

Location: 29 miles northwest of Denver, 32 miles southwest of Boulder

Length: 4 miles out and back

Difficulty: Moderate

Elevation gain: 940′

Highest elevation: 9,080′

Avalanche hazard: None

Fee: This is a state park, so pull out the wallet: $4 per day, $40 for a season pass.

Map: Golden Gate Canyon State Park brochure

Snowmobiles: No

Dogs: Yes

Heads up: Many short and long options in lovely terrain close to town.

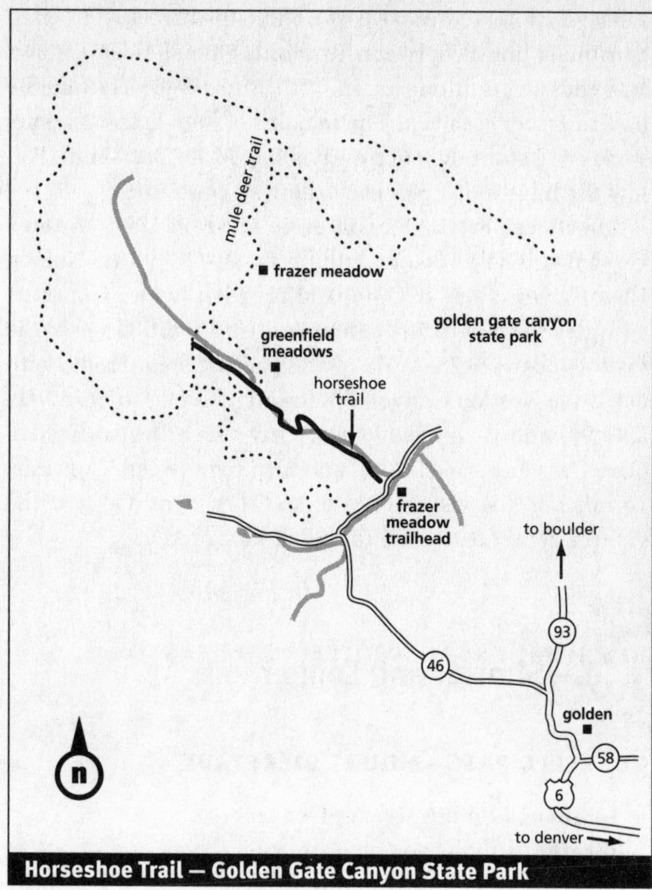

Horseshoe Trail — Golden Gate Canyon State Park

Description: When there's enough snow, Golden Gate is as fine a place to snowshoe as you could ask for. Forty-five minutes from Denver, the steep, pine-swathed hills, the aspen groves and meadows and creeks make it a backcountry Eden close to town. It's quiet and the terrain is diverse. Plenty of options for longer and shorter treks and off-trail exploration.

Route: From the Frazer Meadow trailhead, climb through

a heavily forested draw east of Ralston Creek. The trail continues uphill between Rim and Greenfield Meadows and ends at its intersection with Mule Deer Trail at the base of Frazer Meadow. The remains of John Frazer's homestead are a short distance away along Mule Deer Trail. Follow the huge footprints back the way you came.

Directions: From Denver, drive west on US 6 through Golden to CO 93. Continue north on CO 93 to Golden Gate Canyon Road (CO 46) and turn left (west). Continue 14 miles to the visitors center and turn right. Go past the visitors center 0.25s mile to the parking area. From Boulder, drive west on Canyon Boulevard (CO 119) to Broadway (CO 93) and turn left (south). Drive 19 miles to Golden Gate Canyon Road (CO 46) and turn right (west). Continue 14 miles to the visitors center and turn right. Go past the visitors center 0.25 mile to the parking area.

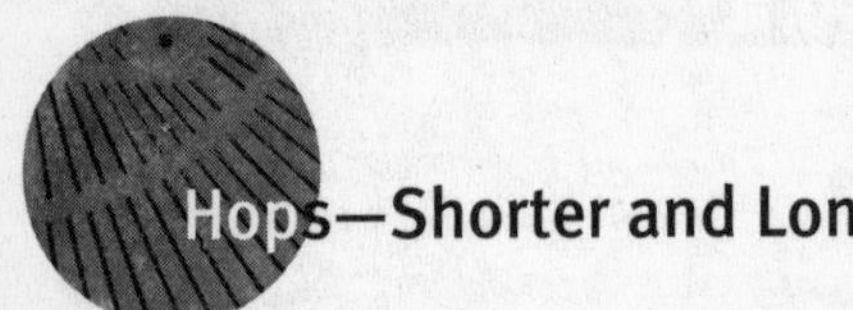

Hops—Shorter and Longer

GUANELLA PASS—MOUNT BIERSTADT

Location: 40 miles west of Denver
Length: As far as you want to go
Difficulty: Moderate to difficult
Elevation gain: Varies
Highest elevation: 14,060′
Avalanche hazard: Moderate
Map and book: USGS Mount Evans (7.5 minute); *Snowshoeing Colorado*
Snowmobiles: No
Dogs: Yes
Heads up: High-altitude springtime fun.
Description: The road to Guanella Pass is plowed in win-

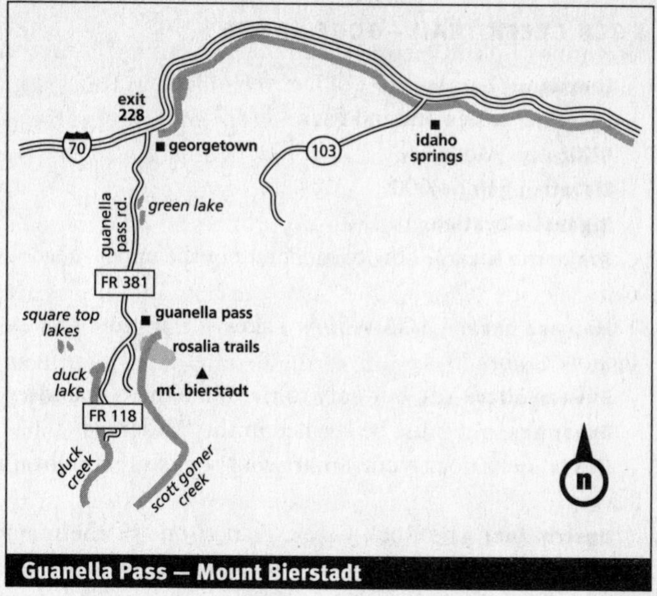

Guanella Pass — Mount Bierstadt

ter, so you can drive right up to the Mt. Bierstadt trailhead and access the wild, above-timberline terrain on the flank of the mountain. Recommended as a spring jaunt, when the snowpack has stabilized. You can run through and over the willow marsh that is such a slog in summer.

Route: Start at the "To Mt. Bierstadt" sign on the east side of the road. Head east and a bit south up onto the slopes of the mountain. Go as far as you want and return.

Directions: Take I-70 west to Georgetown (exit 228). Once in downtown Georgetown, take Guanella Pass Road (FR 381). At the top of the pass (10.7 miles) there is a parking area on the east side of the road.

ROCK CREEK TRAIL—GORE RANGE

Location: 72 miles west of Denver

Length: 7 miles out and back

Difficulty: Moderate

Elevation gain: 1,000′

Highest elevation: 10,180′

Avalanche hazard: Low to moderate in the upper meadow areas

Map and book: USGS Willow Lakes (7.5 minute); *Snowshoeing Colorado*

Snowmobiles: Yes, but only to the Wilderness boundary

Dogs: Yes, but must be leashed in the Wilderness

Heads up: Knock-your-Smartwool-socks-off mountain beauty.

Description: The Rock Creek Trail is one of the major access points for the Eagles Nest Wilderness Area. The stream is lovely, and you'll pass beaver ponds, get views of the Gore Range, and enter the Alfred Bailey Bird Nesting Area, one of the most biologically diverse bird sanctuaries in Colorado. Thanks to Claire Walter and Melissa Hunter, of the USFS Dillon Ranges District in Silverthorne. You can contact them at (970) 468-5400 for information on the trail.

Route: Follow the unplowed road southwest about 1.7 miles. Go through the gate, past the trail register, and continue up the Boss Mine Road. In about 0.3 mile you'll pass a junction with the Gore Range Trail. Continue up Boss Mine Road to the nesting sanctuary. Finish at the mounded tailings piles of the old Boss, Josie, and Thunderbolt Mines.

Directions: Drive west on I-70 to Silverthorne (CO 9, exit 205) and turn right (north). Drive north on CO 9 for 7.3 miles. Turn left onto Rock Creek Road (1350 RD), just across from the Blue River Campground. Drive southwest for 1.3 miles and park.

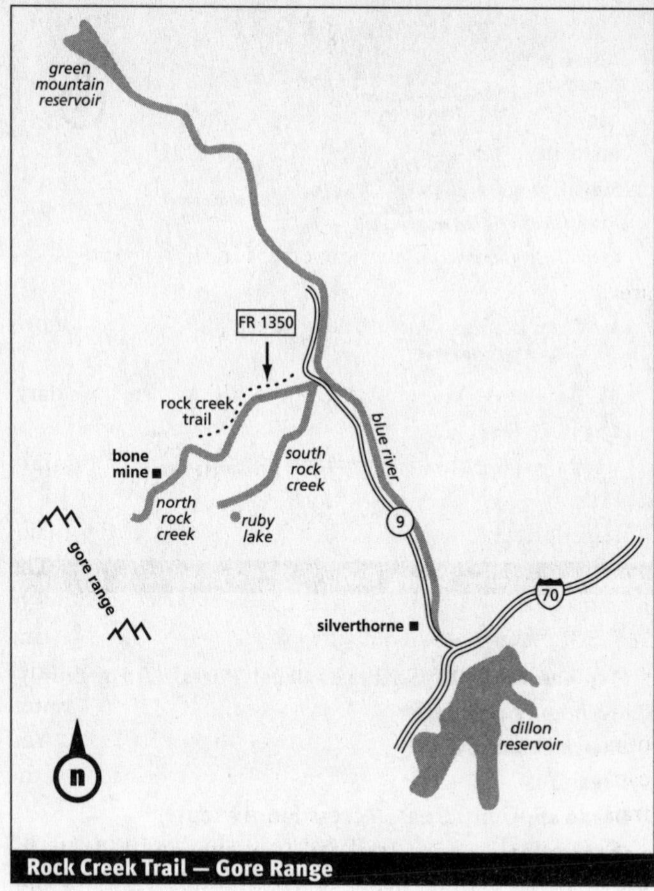

Rock Creek Trail — Gore Range

CHALLENGER TRAIL—WINTER PARK

Location: 60 miles northwest of Denver
Length: 2-mile loop
Difficulty: Easy
Elevation gain: 60′
Highest elevation: 9,280′
Avalanche hazard: None

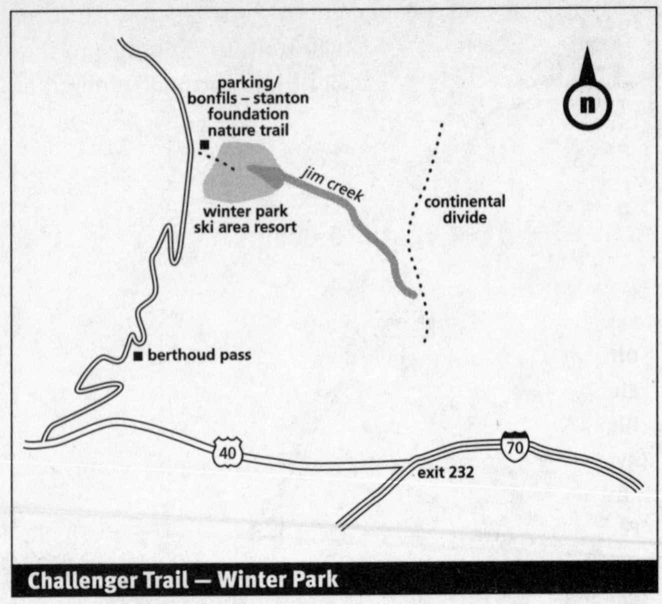

Challenger Trail — Winter Park

Map and book: USGS Fraser, East Portal (7.5 minute); *Snowshoeing Colorado*

Snowmobiles: No

Dogs: Yes

Heads up: Gentle, easy-access family route.

Description: A great trail for beginners and kids, with very little elevation change and lots of big views of the Continental Divide and the ski area. It's a loop with a couple of side trails to a lake and a camping area.

Route: At the trailhead sign check out the map and link the Discovery Trail, the Picnic Spur, and the Challenger Trail for the loop. If you live in Denver, don't gripe about the big ugly beige pipe—it's carrying part of our water supply.

Directions: Take I-70 west from Denver to Empire, Granby, and US 40, exit 232. Drive through Empire and over Berthoud Pass to the Winter Park Ski Resort. The trailhead is directly across US 40 from the entrance to the resort and is well marked: Bonfils–Stanton Foundation Nature Trail.

COLORADO RIVER TRAIL TO LULU CITY

Location: 102 miles northwest of Denver

Length: 6 miles out and back

Difficulty: Easy to moderate

Elevation gain: 320′

Highest elevation: 9,400′

Avalanche hazard: Low, except one avalanche-prone area 1.2 miles from the trailhead

Fee: $15 per vehicle for a 7-day pass or $30 per vehicle per year from date-of-purchase

Contact: Call the Rocky Mountain National Park office (970-586-1399) for more information

Maps and book: USGS Grand Lake (7.5 minute); Trails Illustrated 200; USFS Arapaho National Forest map; *Snowshoeing Colorado*

Snowmobiles: No

Dogs: No

Heads up: Gentle route. Wonderful to hoof it along this remote stretch of the Colorado River.

Description: It's glorious to follow the Colorado River through woods, past meadows and rock-walled bends. This is an easy route, with good chances of seeing elk or moose. And how can anyone miss seeing the site of a town with a name like this. Lulu City boomed for about 4 years around 1880, and there are still some remains of cabins. Excellent views of the Never Summer Range west of the trail. The trail does not follow a road—truly God's country.

Route: Look for the Colorado River trailhead sign. Snow-

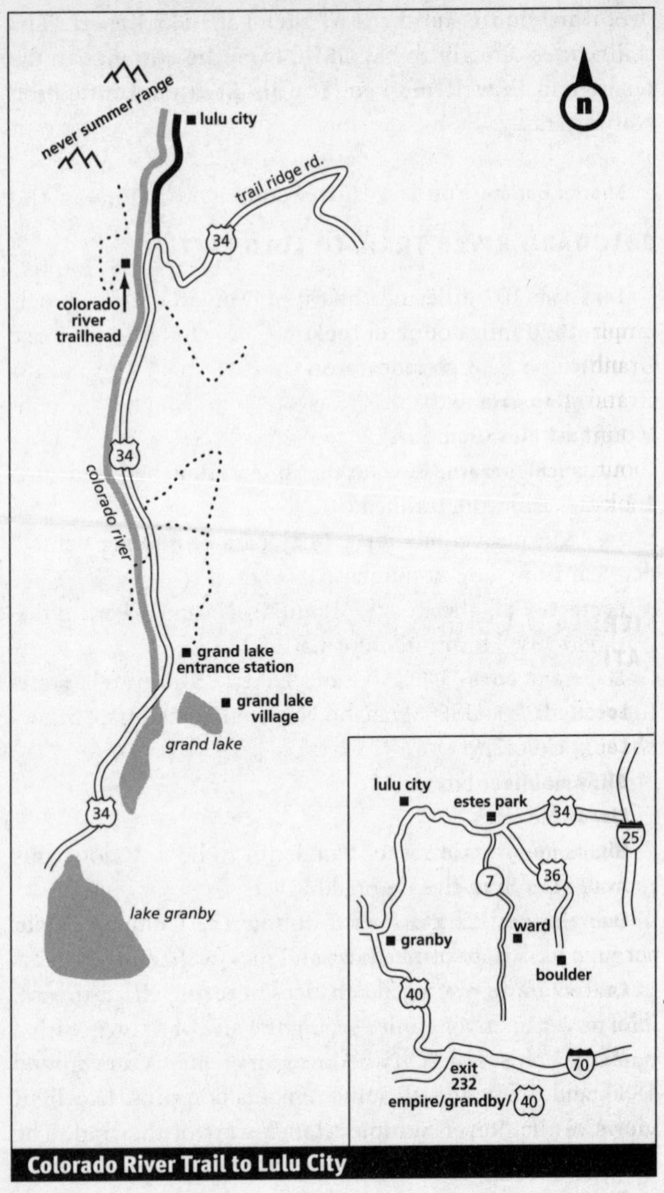

Colorado River Trail to Lulu City

shoe through the summer parking lot to the summer trailhead. Cross four bridges and follow the river. About 1.4 miles from the trailhead and 0.5 mile before Shipler Park you'll pass a west-facing slope with avalanche potential. Turn around here if danger is reported.

Shorter option: You can turn around at the ruins of the Shipler cabins, 1.8 miles in.

Directions: Take I-70 west from Denver to Empire, Granby, and US 40, exit 232. Drive on US 40 north through Empire, Winter Park, and Tabernash. A couple miles past Granby turn right (northeast) on US 34. Drive 14 miles into Grand Lake Village and the western entrance to Rocky Mountain National Park. The Colorado River trailhead is about 8 miles past the gate on the west side of the road. Look for the sign at the parking lot.

BIERSTADT LAKE—ROCKY MOUNTAIN NATIONAL PARK

Location: 37 miles northwest of Boulder

Length: 4 miles out and back

Difficulty: Moderate

Elevation gain: 240′

Highest elevation: 9,770′

Avalanche hazard: Low

Fee: $15 per vehicle for a 7-day pass or $30 per vehicle per year from date-of-purchase

Contact: Call the park office (970-586-1399) for more information

Maps and book: USGS Allenspark, Longs Peak, and McHenry's Peak (7.5 minute); Trails Illustrated 200; USFS Roosevelt National Forest map; *Snowshoeing Colorado*

Snowmobiles: No

Dogs: No

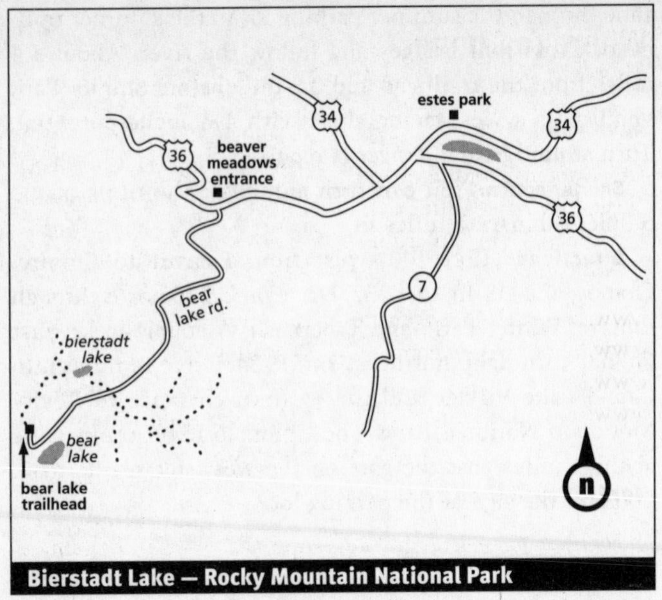

Bierstadt Lake — Rocky Mountain National Park

Heads up: Spectacular alpine route.

Description: Lots of snow makes this an ideal snowshoe. The trail mostly rolls through dense pine woods, but opens on some incredible views of the Divide and some of the peaks in the park. It's a little off the beaten path, so it's likely to be quieter than other trails out of Bear Lake.

Route: From the parking lot, skirt the east shore of Bear Lake and follow the trail that climbs to the northeast. The first section up the Bierstadt Moraine is the only tough part of the trail. Then it's rolling to the lake.

Directions: From Boulder, drive north on US 36 to Estes Park. Enter the Rocky Mountain National Park and take the first left (south) onto Bear Lake Road. Go 9 miles to Bear Lake and park.

Where to Connect

Book and Links

Snowshoeing Colorado, 2nd ed., by Claire Walter (Golden, Colo.: Fulcrum Publishing, 2000).

www.atlassnowshoe.com
www.tubbs-trailnet.com
www.active.com
www.snowlink.com

Nordic Centers and Shops

For a complete list of all the great nordic centers in the area, including Eldora and Devils Thumb, that encourage snowshoeing, and shops that carry snowshoeing gear, see "Winter Sports Overview."

Events

Beaver Creek Snowshoe Adventure Series

This race series features four individual competitions throughout the season in scenic McCoy Park and on the Beaver Creek golf course. Beginners and walkers can enjoy a leisurely 5K or one-mile stroll, while dedicated racers battle for a prize purse in the competitive 10K race.

Call (970) 476-6797 or visit their Web site: www.bcsnowshoe.com.

Eldora's Screamin' Snowman 5K/10K

A great February race in the hills above Eldora. Includes free demo snowshoes from Alchemy, Atlas, Redfeather, and Tubbs. Event information (303) 440-8700, ext. 212.

Estes Park Winter Trails

A huge snowshoe event in February. Races, demos, and a lot of other snowhoeing fanatics! Contact Estes Park Chamber Resort Association, (800) 443-7837, for more details.

Cross-Country Skiing

THERE MAY NOT be a better place on earth to cross-country ski than in the high mountains just above Denver and Boulder. The reasons have to do with relatively easy access to scores of trails that thread over a huge variety of terrain, from dense rolling woods and gladed basins, to cirques and lakes and wind-packed tundra above timberline. There are short routes through gentle country, such as the Brainard Lake Road, that are perfect for families, and tough all-day or overnight traverses of the Continental Divide that give the alpine satisfaction of skiing from one town to another. Combine the routes in this chapter with those in the Snowshoeing and Telemarking chapters, all of which make fine cross-country ski runs, and there are a score of trails that are easy to get to from Denver and Boulder. Wax up and have a blast.

Note: Keep in mind that in the backcountry, awareness of avalanche dangers and winter mountain weather should be paramount. For daily snowpack conditions around the state call the Avalanche Hotline at (303) 275-5360. Also, check skicountryusa.com for snow and avalanche reports from all the ski areas in Colorado. For regular course offerings on avalanche and mountain safety in Boulder, check with the Boulder Outdoor Center (303-444-8420) and EMS (303-442-7566); in Denver call REI (303-756-3100) and Confluence Kayaks and Telemark (303-433-3676). The Colorado Avalanche Information Center (www.caic.state.co.us) provides courses statewide.

This chapter could not have been written without the information found in the superb *Skiing Colorado's Backcountry: Northern Mountains—Trails and Tours,* by Brian Litz and Kurt Lankford, and the indispensable *Snowshoeing Colorado,* by Claire Walter. Thanks.

Boulder Backyard

DEVILS THUMB LAKE

Location: 29 miles west of Boulder

Length: 13 miles out and back

Difficulty: Moderate

Elevation gain: 2,300′

Highest elevation: 11,120′

Avalanche hazard: Some avalanche terrain, easily avoided

Map and book: USGS Nederland, East Portal (7.5 minute); *Skiing Colorado's Backcountry*

Snowmobiles: No

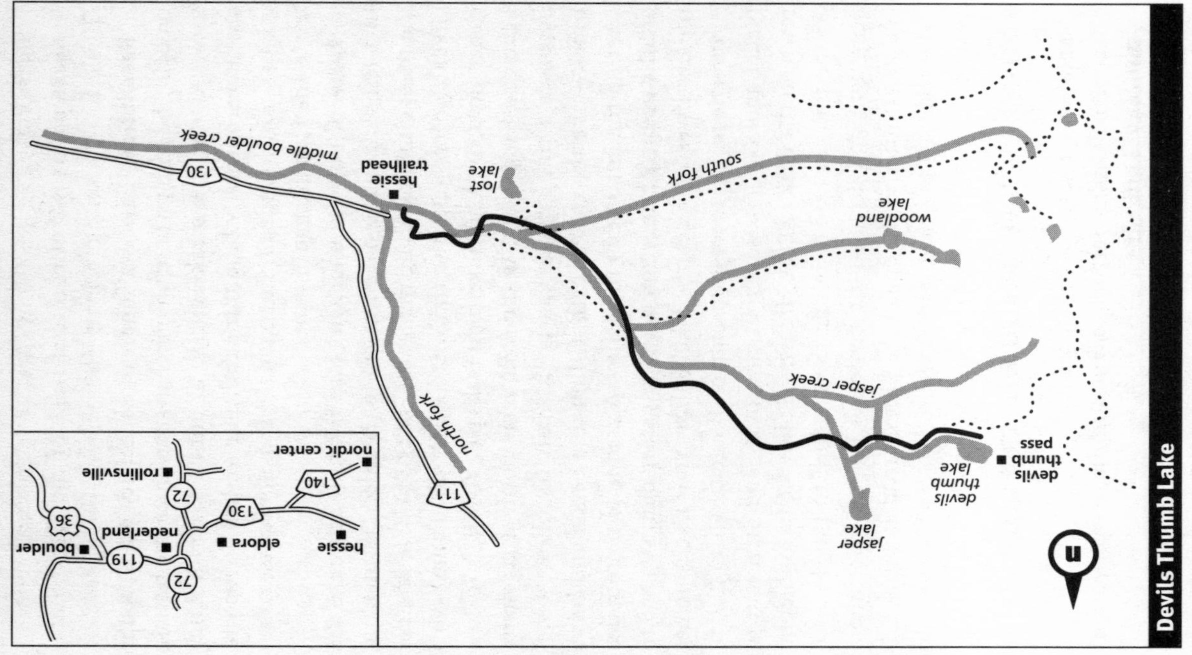
Devils Thumb Lake
n
middle boulder creek
130
hessie trailhead
lost lake
south fork
woodland lake
north fork
jasper creek
devils thumb pass
devils thumb lake
jasper lake
111
nordic center
rollinsville
140
72
130
36
nederland
eldora
hessie
boulder
119
72

Dogs: Yes

Heads up: Views of corniced ridge of the Continental Divide and the spire of Devils Thumb.

Description: This is a long ski, especially since you'll probably be going where no man has gone since the last big snow, so you'll be breaking trail. Count on a very full day and on being totally beat at the end. The reward is that you get to ski into some of the remotest, most beautiful country in the Front Range.

Route: Ski up the unplowed road 0.7 mile and take the first left fork to the old town site of Hessie. Continue on the road, climbing along the South Fork of Middle Boulder Creek. Do *not* take the trail marked Devils Thumb—it's easier along the road. Take right forks past the trails to Lost Lake and King Lake. As the road veers north it gradually becomes a trail, which can be difficult to follow sometimes—take the easiest path. Climb to a bench and curve west up the left side of the valley. A couple of more miles of hilly country brings you to the last steep climb up and to the northwest to reach the lake. Follow your tracks home.

Directions: Drive west up Canyon Boulevard (CO 119) to Nederland. Go left (south) at the rotary and drive out of town on the Peak to Peak Highway. Follow signs for Eldora. At the fork, instead of taking the left fork to the ski area, bear right and drive to the center of Eldora. Continue a couple of miles to the end of the plowed road and park.

ROLLINS PASS, ELDORA TO WINTER PARK

Location: 18 miles west of Boulder

Length: 13 miles out and back minimum, longer options

Difficulty: Difficult

Elevation gain: 2,450′

Highest elevation: 11,810′

Rollins Pass, Eldora to Winter Park

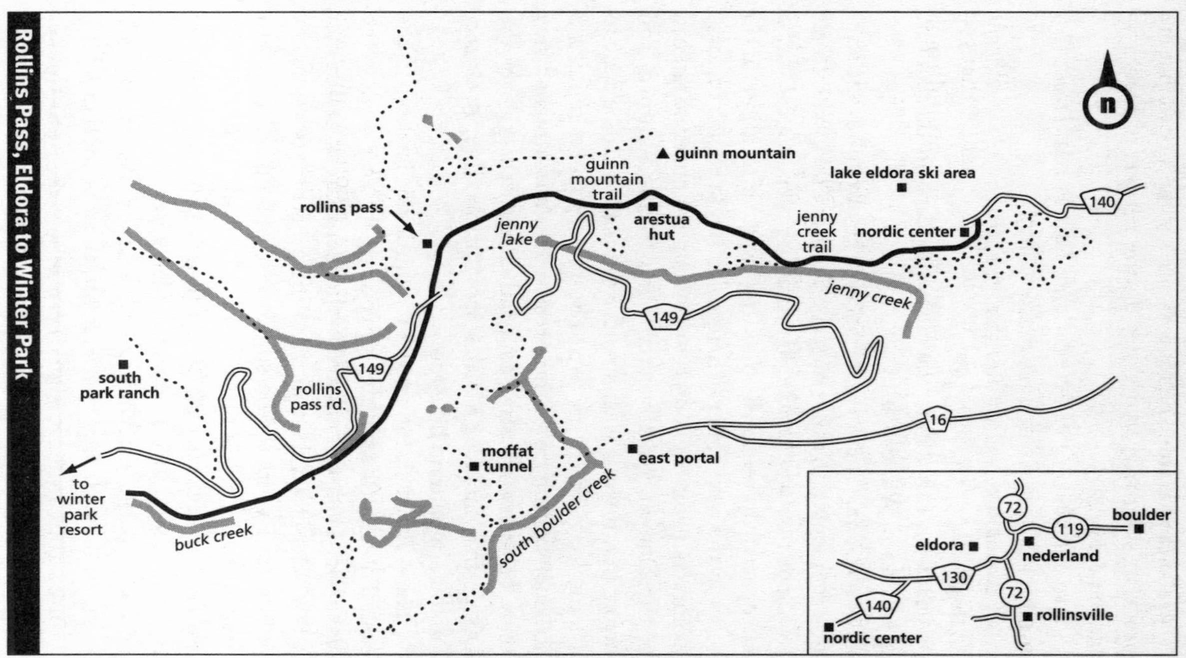

Avalanche hazard: The route crosses some slopes that are prone to skier-triggered slides during periods of high avalanche danger

Map and book: USGS Nederland, East Portal, Fraser (7.5 minute); *Skiing Colorado's Backcountry*

Snowmobiles: Yes, on Rollins Pass Road

Dogs: Yes

Heads up: Exposed to the elements; car shuttle required if you ski to Winter Park.

Description: There's a special, as-the-crow-flies satisfaction in hopping 15 miles over the Continental Divide to get to a spot that would take 70 grinding miles in a car, and a European, alpine thrill in skiing down into a mountain town in the next valley. There's also fun in taking in some Colorado history as you ski over what was once the rail bed of the Denver, Northwestern, and Pacific Railroad; and before that it was a wagon road. Rollins Pass can be done in a long, long day, or in two. The most popular route is a strenuous climb up to the Arestua Hut and a night's stay there before committing to a rather exposed ski over the Divide that includes 5 miles above timberline. A classic. Fun on a mountain bike too.

Route: Begin skiing up the downhill run farthest to the east. The chairlift will be on your right, west. Follow the signs—it's very well marked to the Jenny Creek Trail. After a few hills and a descent you'll be at an intersection; the public trail veers to the southwest, making a long swift descent to the bottom. Ski west up the road about 0.25 mile sto an intersection with a jeep trail. Turn right, climbing into the trees beside a white wooden post. You are going to climb! This is the beginning of the Guinn Mountain Trail. In about 0.5 mile, as it flattens out, there is another white-painted trail mileage sign. Turn left, west, into thicker woods. Begin climbing again on a narrow trail until you are on a large, treeless slope. Ski past the cabin on your right, west into the trees and a small gully. Switchback up the right side of this gully into the trees near the top. Eventually the trail crests and you will continue through thick forest with an occasional clearing. Watch for trail markers! Ski west and a little north into a clearing. Start searching to the left, south. The Arestua Hut sits to the left on a small hill, facing east. It is brown with evergreens behind it. Eat lunch here, then enjoy the fun descent back to the ski area, for a 13-mile round-trip.

Options: You can spend the night at the Arestua Hut—call the Boulder Chapter of the Colorado Mountain Club for information and reservations (303-554-7688)—or continue to Winter Park. If the weather is threatening at all, do not continue over the Divide! Spend the night or return to your car.

If you do continue to Winter Park, ski west over the summit of Guinn Mountain. Descend to the western saddle that separates the Continental Divide and Guinn. Ascend west over easy to moderate terrain, heading for the railroad grade that cuts north to south across the tundra. No trail here. Ski north on the old road. You'll be skiing on the edge of steep north slopes. Crossing several old trestles, ski or walk up to the top of the pass. *Be careful!* Climb over the rocky tundra and cross the pass. Descend past the Corona Range Study Plot. In 2.5 miles you'll approach treeline and get better snow. Ski over the trestle, turn south, and leave the road, skiing through the trees of the South Fork of Ranch Creek. Veer west when the drainage reaches the meadow and ski over flat terrain before regaining the roadbed. Follow the road about 0.5 mile to a small forested knoll on the right, north; the slopes on the left drop steeply into the head of Buck Creek. Turn into the drainage and ski to a meadow. Continue down the creek, then climb up the east side of the drainage to reach an old roadbed. Ski down to the aqueduct, then turn left. Double pole along the aqueduct for several hundred feet to a large cut in the trees that drops down to the right, southwest to the base of the Winter Park Ski Resort. Follow the cut to the highway and cross to reach the resort.

Directions: Drive west up Canyon Boulevard (CO 119) west to Nederland. Go left (south) at the rotary and drive out of town on the Peak to Peak Highway. Follow the signs for Eldora. At the fork turn left onto the ski area road. Continue about 4 miles and turn left again into the first parking area. The tour starts near the Nordic Center office.

BRAINARD LAKE LOOP—CMC TRAILS

Location: 29 miles west of Boulder

Length: 7-mile loop

Difficulty: Easy

Elevation gain: 390′

Highest elevation: 10,450′

Avalanche hazard: None

Map and book: USGS Ward (7.5 minute); *Snowshoeing Colorado*

Snowmobiles: No

Dogs: No

Heads up: Great for families, busy on weekends.

Description: This has got to be the most popular ski touring spot on the Front Range. It's not far from town, the Indian Peaks are glorious, and over the years the Colorado Mountain Club (CMC) has built some very fine trails for cross-country skiing and snowshoeing. They also have a cabin at Brainard Lake that is staffed by volunteers most weekends, so you can ski in and warm up with a crackling fire and a cup of hot chocolate before you ski back. The cabin is available for the night to CMC members (one per group) and can be reserved by calling (303) 441-2436.

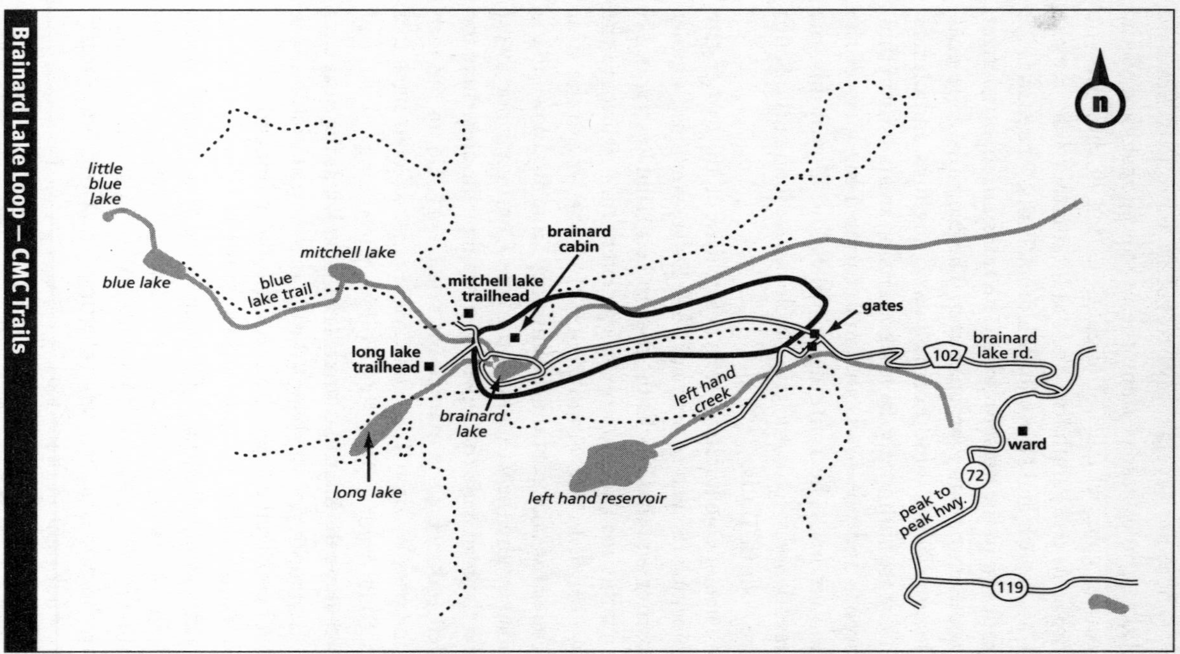

Brainard Lake Loop — CMC Trails

There are several ways to get in and out of Brainard Lake. The easiest is along the unplowed road behind the barrier gate, which is the continuation of the road you drove in on. Paralleling the road, on either side, are the CMC South and North (or Waldrop) Trails. The road is 2.2 miles in to the outlet bridge. The trails are slightly longer, and each has its own character. The North is more challenging, with some exciting swooping dips and climbs. They are both lovely, have a good rising and falling rhythm, woods and meadows, and an occasional big view of the mountains. The route described below is probably the favorite way to do the trip—a clockwise loop of the South and North Trails.

Route: One hundred yards before (east of) the barrier gate blocking the end of Brainard Lake Drive, you'll see another barrier gate that blocks the road to Left Hand Reservoir. Ski out this road, and almost immediately turn right onto the well-signed CMC South Trail. Ski all the way to the west end of the lake, past the old chimneys, and drop down to the road around the west end of the lake. Continuing northwest on the road, pass the Niwot Mountain picnic area. Take the left fork, which is marked MITCHELL LAKE. Go up the road and pass Waldrop Trail and CMC Brainard Cabin signs to a second Waldrop Trail sign. Follow it to the right (east) and ski along the South St. Vrain Trail. Stay left at the next couple of forks, and in about 0.7 mile take a right to follow the Waldrop Trail eastward. Ski back to the parking lot.

Options: For the easy road ski to the cabin simply ski west on Brainard Lake Drive past the winter gate to the lake. To reach the cabin, ski to the west side of the lake to the turnoff for Blue and Mitchell Lakes. Take this spur road to the east edge of a large clearing. The cabin lies directly to your right in the woods.

Directions: Drive up Canyon Boulevard (CO 119) to Nederland. Turn right onto the Peak to Peak Highway (CO 72).

Turn left (west) onto Brainard Lake Drive (102 RD) just north of Ward, and continue to the parking lots.

Short Hops

PERU CREEK—MONTEZUMA

Location: 78 miles west of Denver

Length: 7 miles out and back

Difficulty: Easy to moderate

Elevation gain: 940′

Highest elevation: 10,900′

Avalanche hazard: Low to moderate. High beyond Pennsylvania Mine. Crosses avalanche runout zones, which can be dangerous during the high-hazard periods.

Maps and book: USGS Montezuma (7.5 minute); Trails Illustrated 104; *Snowshoeing Colorado*

Snowmobiles: Yes

Dogs: Yes

Heads up: The Soul House Café at the Montezuma Run—only business in town! Open 7 days for breakfast and lunch. Woodburning stove, backcountry hospitality. Contact (970) 468-1716.

Description: Maybe the first cross-country ski trips you take in Colorado high country will always remain your favorites. This, and Deer Creek, described next, are to my mind two of the finest moderate skis in Colorado. Peru Creek climbs through the woods and breaks out into a basin ringed with mountains. When you finish, head up into Montezuma to the Soul House and have a cup of hot chocolate and a bowl of soup.

Route: From the parking area, ski north along Peru Creek Road (FR 260) which soon curves east. In 1 mile you'll pass

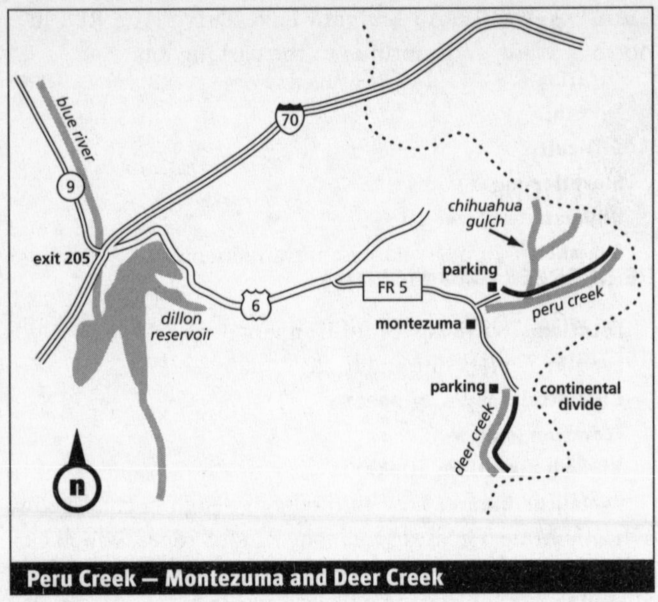

Peru Creek — Montezuma and Deer Creek

below a slide area, so heads up. Bear left and cross Peru Creek. At the fork resist Chihuahua Gulch, which heads to the left, and stay straight on into the valley. Climb to an old mine and continue past intersections with Lenawee Trail and then Warden Road. At about mile 3 is another fork. Left goes to Decatur Gulch. Bear right, cross the creek into Cinnamon Gulch, and climb to the Pennsylvania Mine. Turn around here, as the terrain beyond is very avalanche prone.

Directions: Take I-70 west to Silverthorne, exit 205. Take US 6 east 7.7 miles to the second Keystone Resort entrance at River Run. Pass the River Run parking lots to the well-marked Montezuma Road (FR 5). Go 4.9 miles to the plowed parking area on the left.

DEER CREEK

Location: 78 miles west of Denver

Length: 6 miles out and back

Difficulty: Easy to moderate

Elevation gain: 950′

Highest elevation: 10,900′

Avalanche: Some avalanche terrain encountered, but easily avoided

Maps and book: USGS Montezuma (7.5 minute); Trails Illustrated 104; *Skiing Colorado's Backcountry*

Snowmobiles: Yes

Dogs: Yes

Heads up: Moderately steep terrain, good telemark glades.

Description: This is a fun, pretty, gentle ski up through some large meadows. At the top you can carve some turns in the glades.

Route: From the end of the plowed road, ski onto the unplowed road. Cross Deer Creek and ski up the right side of the valley. You will cross two large meadows to the final steep section below treeline. Some fun telemarking here. Return via the same route.

Directions: Take I-70 west to Silverthorne, exit 205. Take US 6 east 7.7 miles to the second Keystone Resort entrance at River Run. Pass the River Run parking lots to the well-marked Montezuma Road (FR 5). Go 4.9 miles to the plowed parking area on the left.

SHRINE PASS ROAD TO VAIL PASS

Location: 110 miles west of Denver

Length: 12 miles one-way

Difficulty: Moderate

Elevation gain: 509′gain, 2,429′ loss

Highest elevation: 11,020′

Avalanche: Some avalanche terrain encountered, easily avoided

Maps and book: USGS Vail Pass, Redcliff (7.5 minute); Trails Illustrated 108; *Skiing Colorado's Backcountry*

Snowmobiles: Yes

Dogs: Yes

Heads up: Ten-mile ski down! One of the most popular ski tours in Colorado, busy on the weekends. Snowmobilers like it too. Car shuttle is required.

Description: Top of the world. A 2-mile ski up through open meadows and glades while God's country unfurls all around you, then get into a tuck. Ten miles of continuous, hysterical downhill glide through woods and clearings, down into the hamlet of Red Cliff. The trail can get pretty fast when it's packed, and it's lovely, with Mount of the Holy Cross off to the west. This is a flat-out hoot of a ski to do with a group. In Red Cliff you can ski the frozen road into the center of town, and everyone but the designated drivers can get hammered on margaritas at the Mexican restaurant. Good enchiladas too. Remember to set a car shuttle, or you could find yourself in a bleary quandary when the folks at the restaurant dim the lights and kick you out. It's about a 45-minute drive from the trailhead on Vail Pass to the finish at Red Cliff, so plan shuttle time accordingly.

Route: Climb out of the parking area and contour along the side of Black Lakes Ridge for 2.5 miles to the top. Drop into a saddle and take in the Gore Range to the north and east and the Tenmile Range to the southeast. Then—heck, just point your skis down and follow the road.

Directions: To Vail Pass, take I-70 west out of Denver to Vail Pass, exit 190. The trailhead is on the top of Vail Pass and lies on the west side of the overpass north of the large parking area and the modern facilities. To Red Cliff, con-

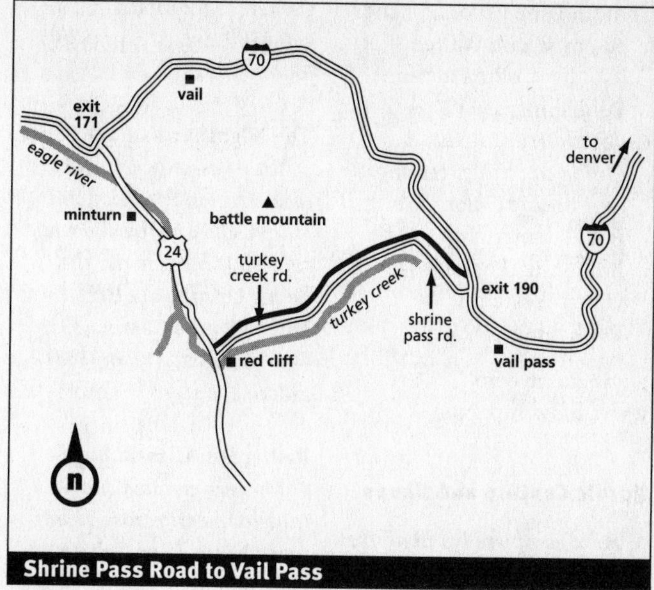

Shrine Pass Road to Vail Pass

tinue west on I-70 to Minturn (US 24, exit 171). Go south on US 24 for 10.3 miles to the north end of the Eagle River bridge and turn left onto Turkey Creek Road (FR 709). The road hugs the canyon wall as you descend into Red Cliff. Turn right onto Shrine Pass Road, and drive as far as you can before parking along the side of the road. If there are lots of cars, you might have to park in town.

Where to Connect

Books and Links

Skiing Colorado's Backcountry: Northern Mountains—Trails and Tours, by Brian Litz and Kurt Lankford (Golden, Colo.: Fulcrum Publishing, 1989).

Snowshoeing Colorado, 2nd ed., by Claire Walter (Golden Colo.: Fulcrum Publishing, 1989).

Colorado Hut to Hut: A Guide to Skiing, Hiking, and Biking Colorado's Backcountry, 2nd ed., by Brian Litz (Englewood, Colo.: Westcliffe Publishing, 1995).

www.active.com
www.snow-link.com

Nordic Centers and Shops

For a complete list of all the great nordic centers in the area, including Eldora and Devils Thumb, and shops that carry cross-country ski gear, see "Winter Sports Overview."

Events

New Year's Day Boulder Nordic Club Race

5K classic and 10K skate race. Call the Eldora Nordic Center for information, (303) 440-8700, ext. 212, or (888) 2-Eldora.

The Nighthawks Race Series

Total gas—6-week night race series in February and March. Classic, freestyle, and snowshoe races under the lights. Open to all. Call the Eldora Nordic Center, (303) 440-8700, ext. 212, or (888) 2-Eldora.

Rising Sun Classic

My personal favorite—a 5-mile round-trip cross-country race to Tennessee Cabin and back in March. Along the way you have to dig a snow pit, get into and out of your sleeping bag, boil water, cook and eat an egg, and finish with a pretty turn. Call the Eldora Nordic Center, (303) 440-8700, ext. 212, or (888) 2-Eldora.

Backcountry Skiing & Snowboarding

THIS CHAPTER WOULD feel at home in the cross-country skiing chapter. There's a gradual segue from cross-country ski tours with some fun slopes for telemarking along the way to trips to destinations with bowls, ridgetops, and mountain faces that people ski into primarily for the turns they'll carve on the descents. All the places mentioned here are beautiful and pretty easy to get to from Denver and Boulder. The verb "ski" is used throughout for simplicity, but the routes below can be snowshoed and then boarded.

Note: Keep in mind that in the backcountry, awareness of avalanche dangers and winter mountain weather should be paramount. For daily snowpack conditions around the state call the

Avalanche Hotline at (303) 275-5360. Also check skicountryusa.com for snow and avalanche reports from all the ski areas in Colorado. For regular course offerings on avalanche and mountain safety in Boulder, check with the Boulder Outdoor Center (303-444-8420) and EMS (303-442-7566); in Denver call REI (303-756-3100) and Confluence Kayaks and Telemark (303-433-3676).

This chapter could not have been written without the information found in the superb *Skiing Colorado's Backcountry: Northern Mountains—Trails and Tours,* by Brian Litz and Kurt Lankford.

Boulder Backyard

MOUNT TOLL

Location: 29 miles west of Boulder

Length: 12 miles out and back

Difficulty: Difficult

Elevation gain: 2,900′

Highest elevation: 12,979′

Avalanche hazard: Avalanche terrain—wait for spring consolidation

Map and book: USGS Ward, Monarch Lake (7.5 minute); *Skiing Colorado's Backcountry*

Snowmobiles: Yes

Dogs: Yes

Heads up: Excellent ski mountaineering descent. Try it in spring!

Description: Mount Toll is what expert telemarkers dream of: a spectacularly beautiful mountain with a tough climb up and then 1,600 feet of vertical drop down a steep southeast face into a hanging bowl, and then down another

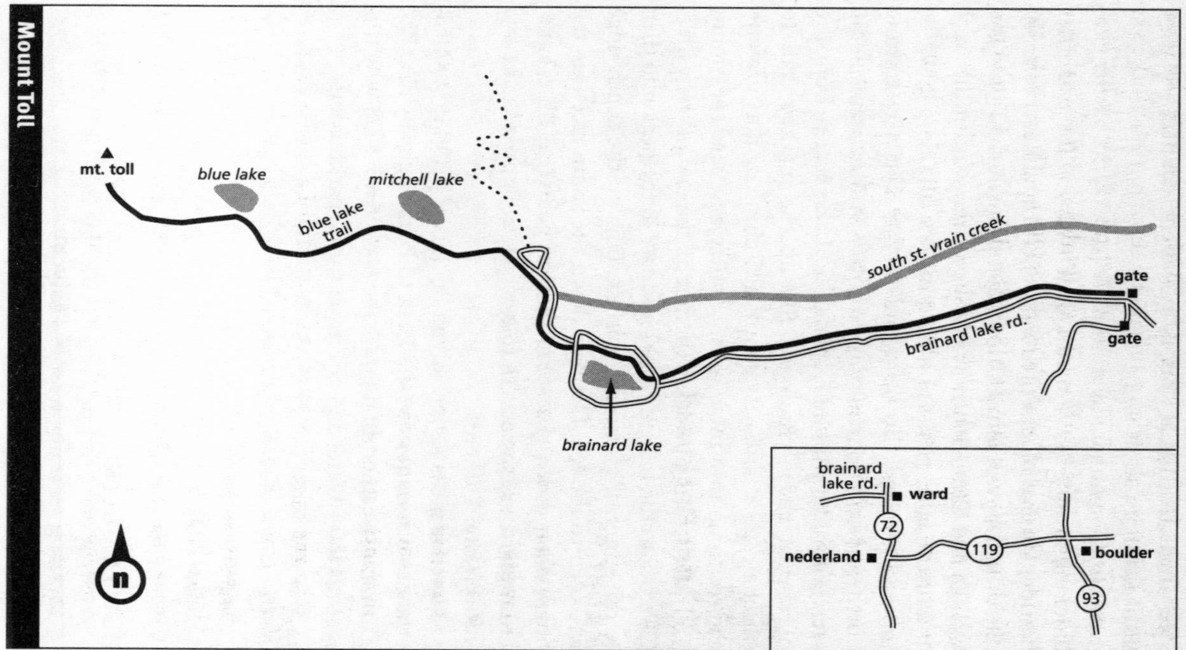
Mount Toll
mt. toll
blue lake
mitchell lake
blue lake trail
south st. vrain creek
gate
brainard lake rd.
gate
brainard lake
brainard lake rd.
ward
72
nederland
119
boulder
93
n

steep run-out. Again, this is avalanche country, so wait until spring to ski it.

Route: One hundred yards before (east of) the barrier gate blocking the end of Brainard Lake Drive, you'll see another barrier gate that blocks the road to Left Hand Reservoir. Ski out this road, and almost immediately turn right onto the well-signed CMC South Trail. Ski all the way to the west end of the lake, past the old chimneys, and drop down to the road around the west end of the lake. Continuing northwest on the road, pass the Niwot Mountain picnic area. Take the Mitchell Lake–Blue Lake access from the northwest end of Brainard. Ski up the marked trail to Mitchell Lake. From its south side climb a short draw to the south up into more open country and head for Mount Toll, the striking peak on the left at the end of the valley. Climb into the hanging bowl just east of the peak and then to the summit, or ascend from the bowl to the south ridge and then to the top. Descend down the south face into the bowl, then down the steep section below to Blue Lake. From there, ski the access route back to Brainard Lake and out.

Directions: Drive up Canyon Boulevard (CO 119) to Nederland. Turn right onto the Peak to Peak Highway (CO 72). Turn left (west) on Brainard Lake Drive (102 RD), which is just north of Ward, and continue to the parking lots.

Short Hops

BUTLER GULCH

Location: 48 miles west of Denver
Length: 4 miles out and back
Difficulty: Moderate

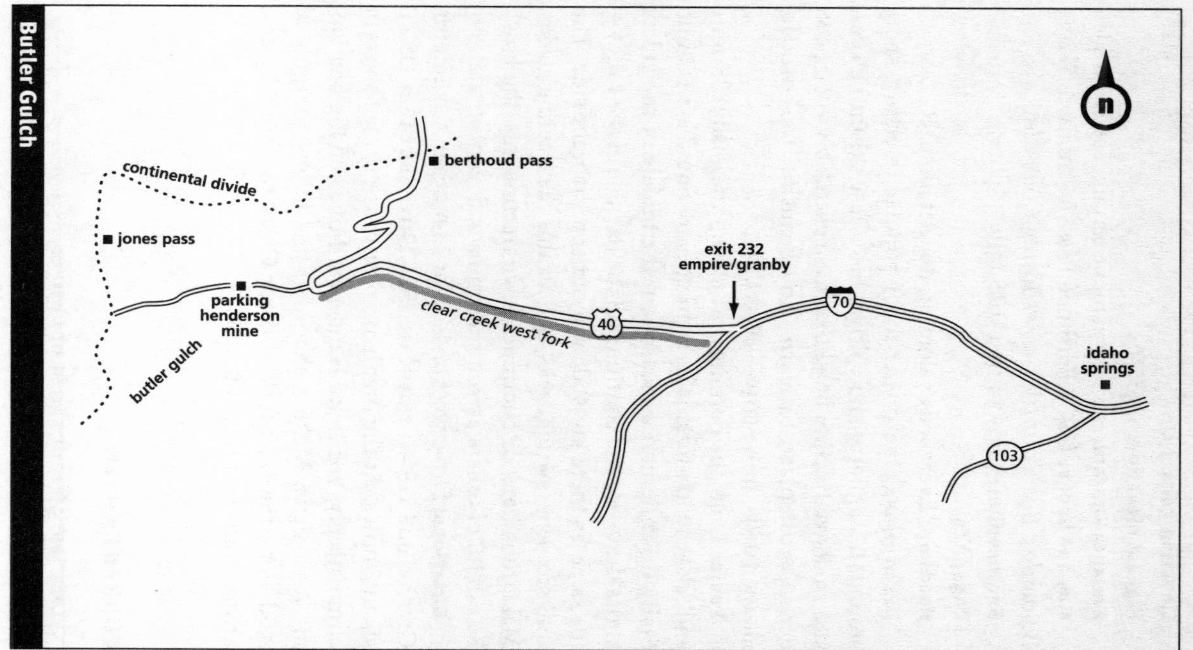
Butler Gulch
n
berthoud pass
continental divide
jones pass
parking
henderson
mine
butler gulch
clear creek west fork
40
exit 232
empire/granby
70
idaho
springs
103

Elevation gain: 1,030′

Highest elevation: 11,350′

Avalanche hazard: Some avalanche terrain, easily avoided

Map and books: USGS Berthoud Pass (7.5 minute); *Skiing Colorado's Backcountry; Snowshoeing Colorado*

Snowmobiles: Only in first 0.25 mile

Dogs: Yes

Heads up: Everybody's doin' it, doin' it, doin' it . . .

Description: One of the most popular telemark spots around. It's a pretty short drive, has a fast ski into glades, and an above-treeline bowl that has dependably good powder. A great place to learn. And beautiful too—woods, glades, bowls, mountains—everything.

Route: From the parking area ski up the road 0.25 mile and take the left fork. (The right goes to Jones Pass.) Climb easily 0.5 mile into a meadow in the middle of the gulch. Cross the creek and continue up the left side of the valley—it's safer, as there are slide run-outs on the right side. The trail steepens, switchbacks, and attains the treeline glades. Make runs here, or continue above treeline into the bowl. Be careful of others as you scream back down the trail.

Directions: Drive west on I-70 for 28 miles to the Empire, Granby, and US 40 exit (exit 232). Drive north on US 40 about 7 miles. At the first hairpin turn, as the road starts to climb steeply, you'll see Henderson Mine and Big Ben Picnic Area signs. Make a sharp left and follow the plowed road along the west fork of Clear Creek to a parking area across from the mine complex.

CURRENT CREEK

Location: 56 miles west of Denver

Length: 1.8 miles out and back

Difficulty: Moderate to difficult

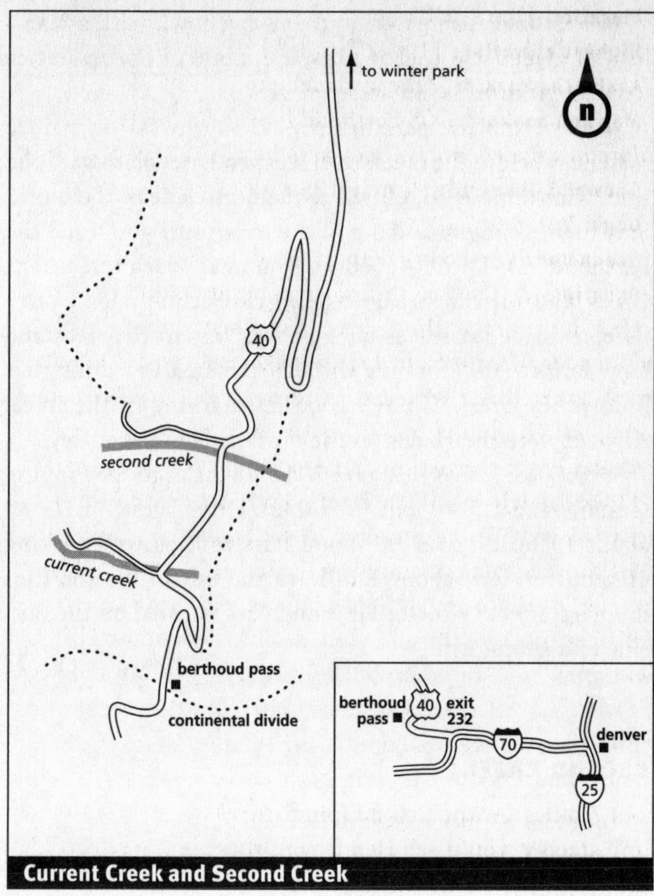

Current Creek and Second Creek

Elevation gain: 800′

Highest elevation: 11,600′

Avalanche hazard: Some avalanche terrain, easily avoided

Map and book: USGS Berthoud Pass (7.5 minute); *Skiing Colorado's Backcountry*

Snowmobiles: No

Dogs: Yes

Heads up: Watch for loaded cornices above you.

Description: A short ski in to one big bowl, with a %#$!-load of glades and rolling hills and a pile of opportunities for telemarking. Ski in and explore.

Route: From the parking area ski southwest on a little road. Just before the creek turn west and ascend toward the trees. Continue west, climbing the north side of the creek. Stay high, skiing in and out of the trees until you reach the Berthoud Pass Ditch Aqueduct. Follow it south to Current Creek and turn upstream toward timberline. Don't tarry here, as loaded cornices hang above. Stay in the trees and loop southward, climbing through the small clearing that follows the creek. There's good telemarking in the trees. Also, explore the glades on the north side of the valley.

Directions: Drive west on I-70 for 28 miles to the Empire, Granby, and US 40 exit (exit 232). Drive west on US 40 about 15 miles, over Berthoud Pass to a plowed parking area on the left, about 1 mile to the north. It's the first drainage after the top of Berthoud Pass, located on the outside of a sharp turn.

SECOND CREEK

Location: 57 miles west of Denver

Length: 1 mile to the cabin, another 0.75 mile to the end of the valley

Difficulty: Moderate to difficult

Elevation gain: 750′ to cabin

Highest elevation: 11,330

Avalanche hazard: Some avalanche terrain, easily avoided.

Map and book: USGS Berthoud Pass (7.5 minute); *Skiing Colorado's Backcountry*

Snowmobiles: No

Dogs: Yes

Heads up: Great telemarking. A steep, challenging descent back down the trail.

Description: A short ski into a bowl and a cabin surrounded by tremendous skiing. Above the cabin, you can ski to the top of the valley and up onto the main ridge, which is windblown, but can have great skiing if the snow's good. This is a wonderful short-day tour.

Route: From the plowed parking area ski up the right side of the creek. At 0.5 mile, switchback up a steep section and around bald knob to the left. From the bowl below the steep face to the west, ski to the cabin—it's in the trees, on the knoll to the right between the First and Second Creek drainages. Continue up the valley and onto the main ridge for challenging telemarking.

Directions: Drive west on I-70 for 28 miles to the Empire, Granby, and US 40 exit (exit 232). Drive west on US 40 about 15 miles, over Berthoud Pass to a plowed parking area on the left, about 2 miles to the north. Second Creek is the second drainage after the top of Berthoud Pass. There are plowed pullouts on both sides of the road.

LOVELAND PASS

Location: 57 miles west of Denver

Length: How much do you want to ski?

Difficulty: Intermediate to advanced

Elevation gain: In your car

Highest elevation: 11,990′

Avalanche hazard: Yes, some avalanche danger—check avalanche report

Map: USGS Loveland Pass, Grays Peak (7.5 minute)

Snowmobiles: Not advised

Dogs: Not advised

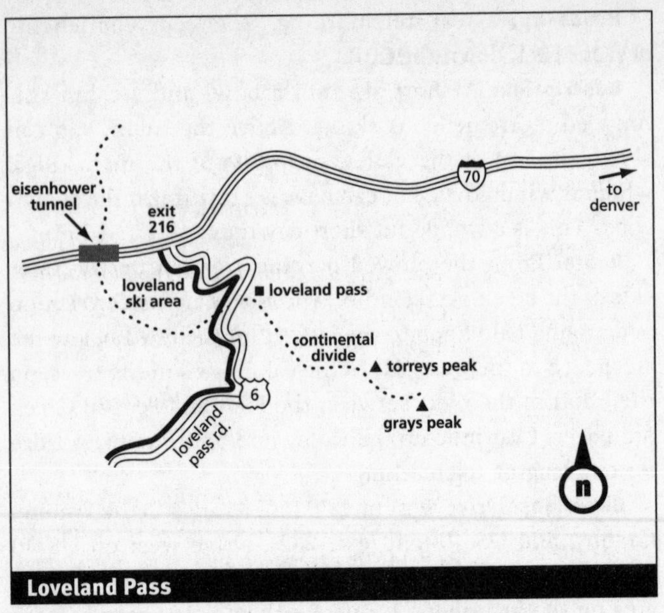

Loveland Pass

Heads up: For those who will fight gravity no more, forever: car shuttle.

Description: Loveland Pass has to be mentioned. It's arguable as to whether this is backcountry skiing, but who cares. Very popular with snowboarders and alpine skiers as well. Essentially, you park a car at the bottom of the pass, drive to the top, and ski or board down. The routes are obvious. It's a leeward slope and can be dangerous. Check avalanche conditions before skiing.

Directions: Drive west on I-70. Just before Eisenhower tunnel look for US 6, exit 216. Take it southeast to the top of the pass.

Where to Connect

Books and Link

Skiing Colorado's Backcountry, Northern Mountains—Trails and Tours, by Brian Litz and Kurt Lankford (Golden, Colo.: Fulcrum Publishing, 1989).

Snowshoeing Colorado, 2nd ed., by Claire Walter (Golden, Colo.: Fulcrum Publishing, 2000).

www.arapahoebasin.com/inside.php3

Arapahoe Basin Ski area is a very active telemark center. Check out their Web site and click on "Events" and "High Adventure Series" for information on "Steep Clinics," lessons, races, and Avalanche School.

Nordic Centers and Shops

For a complete list of all the great nordic centers in the area, including Eldora and Devils Thumb, and shops that carry telemark gear, see "Winter Sports Overview."

Events

Telemark Fest

Demos, classes, and clinics. March. Call the Eldora Nordic Center, (303) 440-8700, ext. 212, or (888) 2-Eldora.

The Three Pin Grin

Loveland Ski Area. March. Popular tele race down a fun obstacle course. Call Loveland at (800) 736-3SKI for info, or check their Web site: skiloveland.com

Tele Freeskiing Championships

Arapahoe Basin Ski Area. March. Exciting three-day race on the double black diamond terrain of the Upper East Wall. Contact A-Basin at (888) 272-7246 for more information.

Tele Dual Bump Competition and Giant Slalom Race

Arapahoe Basin Ski Area. April. The name of this popular event speaks for itself. Call A-Basin at (888) 272-7246 for details.

Ice Climbing

THIS MAY BE the most out-there sport on the planet. Take one of the slickest natural surfaces known to man, tilt it up to something approaching or passing vertical, then climb up it. Oh, and ice is ice-cold, so if your feet go numb, oh well. And the protection—an ice screw twisted in with a hammer—is often iffy. The dinner-plate-size chunks you knock off with every swing of your tool—they're way too big for a cocktail . . .

I guess the outlandishness is part of the exhilaration. It was for me—that and the juice of sheer terror. Ice climbing is growing in popularity, so folks must have their reasons. Below are three areas near Denver and Boulder that have excellent ice. Thanks to Jack Roberts and his indispensable

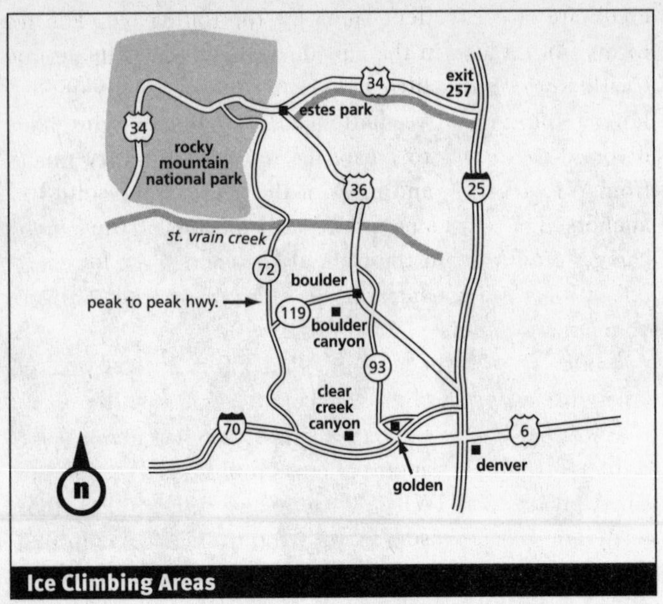

Ice Climbing Areas

guide, *Colorado Ice,* from which most of the information below comes. *Note:* I've used Roberts' difficulty ratings. It's important to remember that the ratings are subjective, can vary from year to year on any given climb, and should in no way be used in decisions concerning safety.

Boulder Backyard

BOULDER CANYON

Location: West of Boulder

Book: *Colorado Ice*

Description: Thanks again to Boulder Canyon for having what we love to do so close at hand. Thirteen miles up the creek are two excellent spots for top-roping ice. The ice forms from a leak in the aqueduct above the cliffs around Castle Rock, with a little help from some vertically unchallenged (horizontally challenged?) engineers who have diverted the water to create ice routes. Difficulty ranges from WI2 to WI5, and most of the routes have solid tree anchors. The sport's popularity can mean that the canyon can get crowded, but there should be enough ice for everyone if folks are considerate. Be safety conscious, both for yourself and others.

Route: The Lower Ice Fall (WI2-4 I) is a great practice area with a 2-pitch climb on the left, an easy gully on the right, and numerous variations in between. Farther to the right are usually a handful of new climbs. Lead or top-rope. The Upper Ice Fall (WI3-5 I) has steeper routes that usually form later in the season. In midwinter, a vertical column—the Pencil—forms in the middle of the rock buttress. Fun mixed climbing in early season.

Directions: For the Lower Ice Fall, drive west up Canyon Boulevard (CO 119) 13 miles from its intersection with Broadway and park at the entrance to Castle Rock. Don't park on CO 119. Walk upstream (west) to the climbs. A little farther west up CO 119 are the Upper Ice Falls. You can walk, or drive up and park in the pullout on the right.

Golden

CLEAR CREEK CANYON

Location: 13 miles west of Denver, 17 miles south of Boulder

Book: *Colorado Ice*

Description: Three drainages within 4.5 miles of the bottom of Clear Creek Canyon, just west of Golden, offer great, short, technically easy ice 25 minutes from Denver. The ice is usually in shape by mid-December, continues to thicken until February, and is gone by April. All climbs can be led or top-roped easily. The proximity and friendliness of the ice make it very popular, so get there early.

Route: Ice 1 (WI2 I) is approximately 2.8 miles up from the intersection of US 6 and CO 58, on the left. Park in the pullout. Ice 2 (WI2/3 I) is 3.9 miles upcanyon. Park at the first bridge, cross the highway, and walk down an old path on the opposite side of the creek from the road. You should see the ice ahead. Ice 3 (WI2/3 I) is approximately 4.3 miles upcanyon. Park at the first bridge and walk 0.25 mile up the highway to the ice. Can't miss it.

Directions: From Denver, take 6th Avenue (US 6) west to the intersection with CO 58 just outside Golden. Continue on US 6 west into the canyon. From Boulder, drive to Broadway (CO 93) and turn south. Take CO 93 to the intersection with US 6 and CO 58. Turn left (west) on US 6 and head into the canyon.

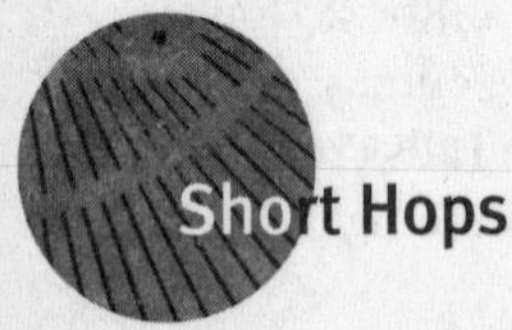

Short Hops

ALEXANDER'S CHIMNEY—ROCKY MOUNTAIN NATIONAL PARK

Location: 72 miles northwest of Denver, 37 miles northwest of Boulder

Fee: $15 per vehicle for a 7-day pass or $30 per year from date of purchase

Book: *Colorado Ice*

Description: Alexander's Chimney (200m AI4 M4 V) is a serious, committing climb on Longs Peak that involves appealing ice, moderate mixed climbing, and breathtaking country. It's an all-day affair, with an approach of 4 miles and 2,500′ of vertical gain. The season is early fall into November, and late spring through early summer.

Route: For detailed descriptions of the climb, the approach, descent, equipment needed, and so forth, see *Colorado Ice.*

Directions: From Denver, take I-25 to the Loveland and US 34 exit (exit 257). Go left (west) on US 34 to Estes Park and turn left (south) on the Peak to Peak Highway Continue about 9 miles to the well-marked Longs Peak trailhead. From Boulder, drive north on 28th Street (US 36) 35 miles to Estes Park. Turn left (south) on the Peak to Peak Highway and continue about 9 miles to the well-marked Longs Peak trailhead.

LOCK VALE GORGE—ROCKY MOUNTAIN NATIONAL PARK

Location: 72 miles northwest of Denver, 37 miles northwest of Boulder

Fee: $15 per vehicle for a 7-day pass or $30 per year from date of purchase

Book: *Colorado Ice*

Description: The gorge has a relatively easy, 2.3-mile approach and routes that range from easy to cutting-edge mixed climbs. They're consistently well formed-up and all can be top-roped. The season is December through late March. The gorge is an excellent place to expose novices to all grades of ice, and very popular, so go early on the weekends.

Route: For detailed descriptions of the climbs, approach, and so forth, as well as descriptions of the Loch Vale routes on Thatchtop, farther up the trail, see *Colorado Ice.*

Directions: From Denver, travel north on I-25 to the Loveland and US 34 exit (exit 257). Go left (west) on US 34 through Estes Park to the Beaver Meadows entrance of Rocky Mountain National Park. From Boulder go north on 28th Street (US 36) north and west 37 miles, through Estes Park, to the Beaver Meadows entrance.

Once in the park, turn left onto Bear Lake Road. Pass the turnoff for the Moraine Park Campground and continue to the Glacier Gorge trailhead parking lot. If you get to the Bear Lake parking lot you've gone too far.

Where to Connect

Book

Colorado Ice, by Jack Roberts (Boulder, Colo.: Polar Star, 1998).

Nordics Shops and Centers

See "Winter Sports Overview" for a list of shops and guide services.

Resources for the Disabled

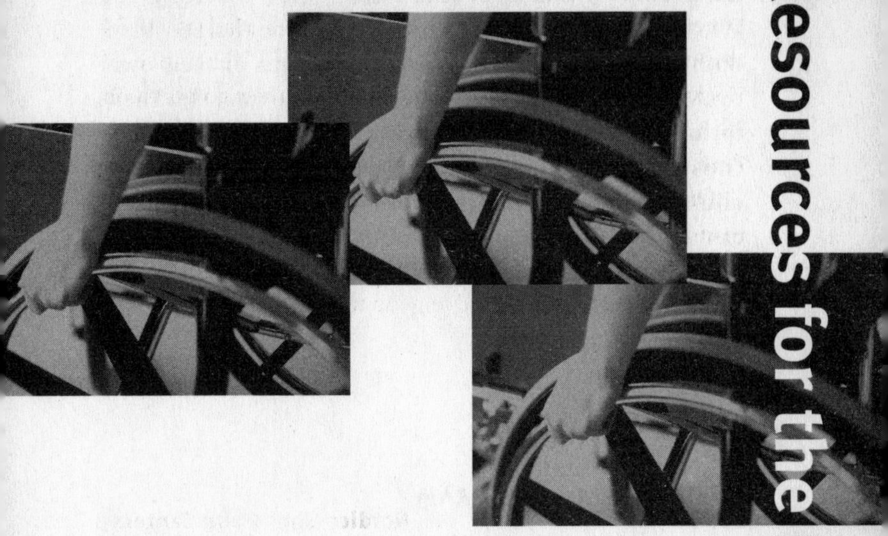

MY YOUNGER SISTER has cerebral palsy. Many years ago we participated in the Breckenridge Outdoor Education Center's (BOEC) adaptive ski program and had one of the funnest weeks in either of our lives. It began a tradition: every few years Les and I take a week or two and go on an adventure together. We've sea kayaked in Baja and paddled down the Grand Canyon. None of this would have happened if we hadn't initially taken part in a superbly designed program run by warm, enthusiastic, skilled professionals, that allowed able-bodied and disabled people alike to share in an outdoor activity.

Residents of Denver and Boulder are lucky to have two of the world's best outdoor centers for

the disabled within an hour and a half drive: the BOEC and Winter Park's National Sports Center for the Disabled. Both cities also have large, active programs of their own, run through their Parks and Rec departments. These include widely hailed water-ski programs, and courses and trips that involve camping, skiing, canoeing, and rock climbing. There are also several beautiful mountain, canyon, and lake areas close to Denver that are wheelchair accessible and have good terrain for the disabled.

Denver

SPECIAL NEEDS PROGRAM

Denver Parks and Recreation offers a bunch of year-round outdoor activities and trips for the disabled through their Special Needs Program. These include skiing, adaptive waterskiing, hiking, camping, horseback riding, and sailing. They also maintain the Stapleton Nature Trail at the Chief Hosa exit on I-70 (exit 253), an interpretive, 1-mile nature trail set up with braille and print signs (not wheelchair accessible). Echo Lake has accessible facilities and paths. For info contact:

Special Needs Program
1849 Emerson Street
Denver, CO 80218
(303) 839-4800 (voice); (303) 839-4820 (TTY)

SCUBA DIVING

Adaptive scuba instruction is available from A-1 Diving. (See *Grit* in "Scuba.") Scott Taylor, the owner of A-1, has had many years of experience teaching the disabled to dive.

A-1 Diving
1800 West Oxford Avenue
Englewood, CO 80110
(303) 789-2450
www.a1scuba.com

WATERTON CANYON

Location: 14 miles southwest of Denver

Length: 12 miles out and back

Terrain: Hardpack gravel road

Elevation gain: 1,500′

Map: Trails Illustrated map 135—Deckers/Rampart Range

Dogs: No

Heads up: Bighorn sheep, gorgeous secluded river canyon.

Description: The charm of a canyon that has been allowed to keep any of its wildness is that once you enter it the rest of the world seems to fall away. As you climb the smooth dirt road up into Waterton, following the South Platte, which spills through rocky drops and black pools, it's hard to believe that Denver swarms a few miles to the north. Big ponderosas lean over the bends, glossy oak brush crowds the shoulder of the road, and steep grassy slopes climb to broken rimrock. If you bring your rod, there's excellent trout fishing. A herd of bighorn sheep lives along

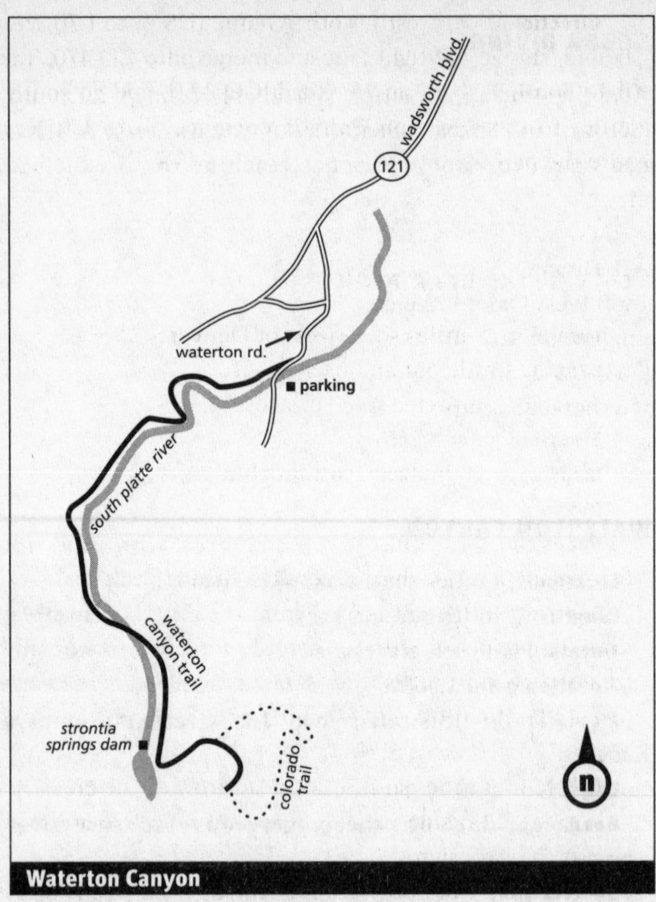

Waterton Canyon

the river—in the heat of summer they hang out in the cool spray below Strontia Dam. The beautiful 6-mile climb can be shortened at any point by turning around and heading back downhill. Watch for mountain bikers.

Route: From the parking lot head across the road to the Waterton Canyon trailhead and stay on the smooth main road. Climb 6.2 miles up the dirt road to where the Colorado Trail comes in from the left and return.

Directions: Go west on 6th Avenue (US 6) to I-70 westbound, stay in the right lane and merge onto CO 470. Take it to South Platte Canyon Road (CO 121), and go south 4 miles to the Waterton Canyon entrance. Turn left (east) into the parking lot.

LAIR O' THE BEAR PARK

Location: 19 miles southwest of Denver

Length: 1 mile out and back

Terrain: Compacted fine surface

Elevation gain: Minimal

Map: Lair O' the Bear Park brochure

Dogs: Yes

Heads up: Beautiful canyon and creek with good trout fishing and a wheelchair-accessible fishing deck.

Description: Instant respite from the city. Lovely stream in a steep canyon with a 1/2-mile wheelchair-accessible trail and good trout fishing. A fantastic place near Denver to get quiet and toss a fly. Picnic tables along the creek are also wheelchair accessible.

Route: From the parking lot head toward the creek and follow the creekside path. A map and brochure are available at the trail sign.

Directions: Take 6th Avenue (US 6) west to I-70 west; bear right on I-70 and pick up CO 470. Take CO 470 south to the Morrison exit. Head west into Morrison and continue west on CO 74 for 4.3 miles to the park entrance on the left.

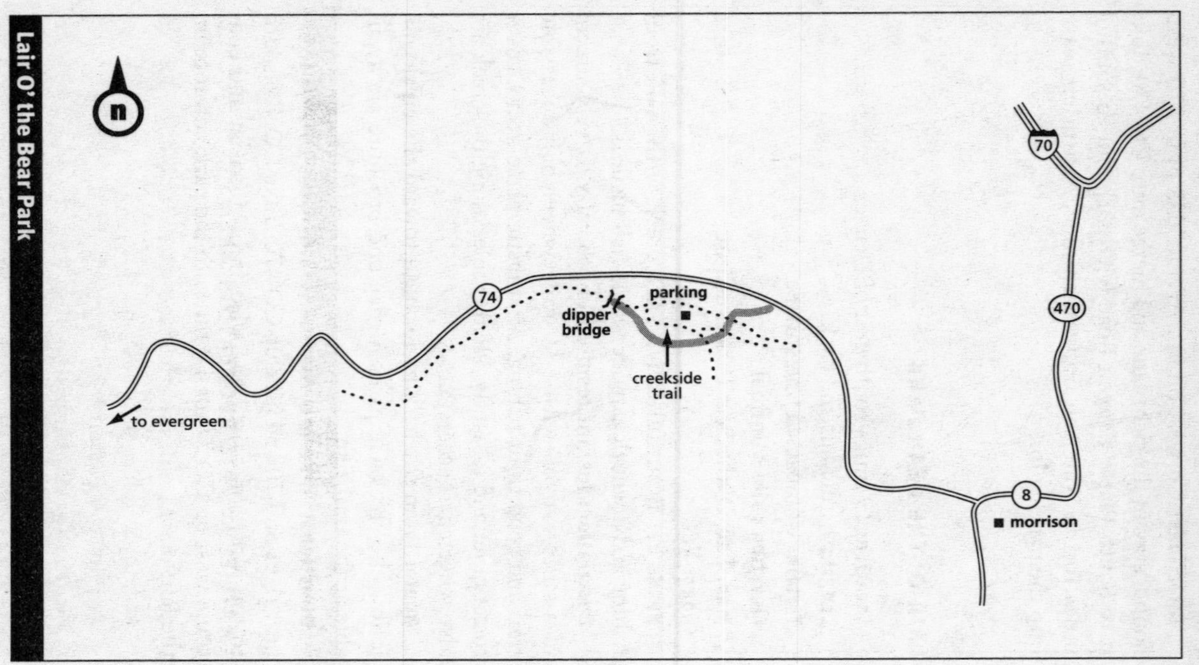
Lair O' the Bear Park
n
70
470
8
morrison
74
parking
dipper bridge
creekside trail
to evergreen

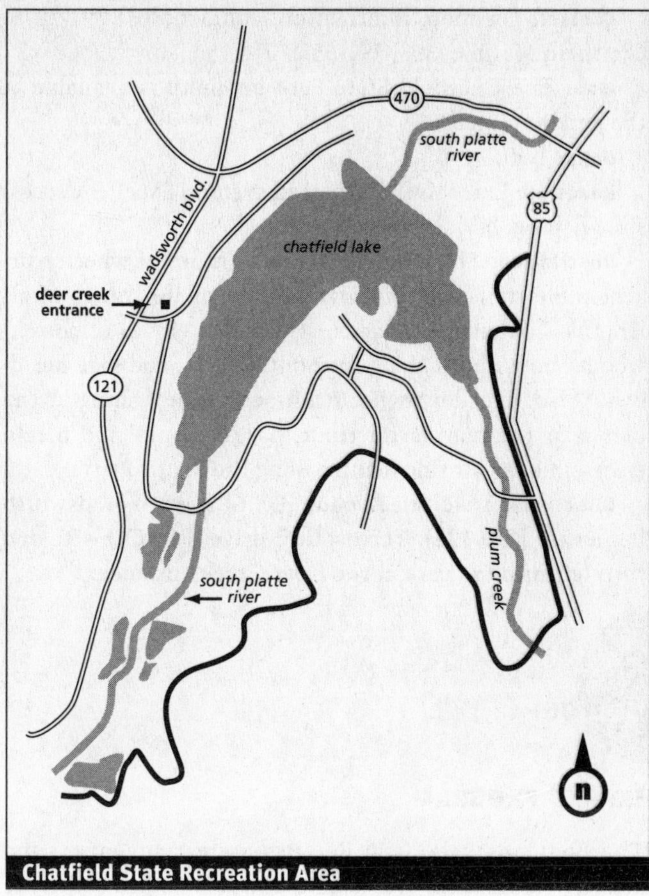

Chatfield State Recreation Area

CHATFIELD STATE RECREATION AREA

Location: 17 miles southwest of Denver

Length: 25 miles of trails

Terrain: Wheelchair-friendly paved trails

Elevation gain: Minimal

Fee: A state parks pass is $4 per vehicle per day or $40 per vehicle per year.

Contact: For more information, contact (303) 791-7275; Chatfield Marina, (303) 791-5555

Map: The Chatfield State Park brochure is available at the park entrance.

Dogs: Yes

Heads up: Extensive, pretty trail system. Excellent accessible fishing, both lake and stream.

Description: This huge park has 25 miles of wheelchair-accessible trails offering myriad options for routes of all lengths. Lakeside grasslands, streamside groves of cottonwoods and willows along the South Platte, and sage meadows. Also, excellent wheelchair-accessible fishing at the pier near the marina for trout, bass, crappie, and perch. Accessible streamside fishing along the South Platte.

Directions: Take 6th Avenue (US 6) west to Wadsworth Boulevard (CO 121). Turn south, drive past CO 470, and turn left into the park at the Deer Creek entrance.

Boulder

EXPAND PROGRAM

The Boulder's Parks and Rec has a great adventure and activity program for the disabled and able-bodied called the Expand Program. Activities include skiing, snowshoeing, camping, rock climbing for children, a hut trip for adults with developmental disabilities, kayaking, canoeing, and a popular adaptive water-ski program.

Expand Program
3198 North Broadway
Boulder, CO 80304
(303) 413-7216

www.ci.boulder.co.us/parks-recreation; click on the Expand Program icon.

TRAIL ACCESSIBILITY PROGRAM (TAP)

Under the aegis of the Expand Program, and with the help of dozens of disabled and able-bodied folks, the Boulder Trail Accessibility Program has published a remarkable guidebook: *Accessibility Guide to Eastern Boulder Country Trails and Natural Sites.* The book assesses scores of trails and natural sites in East Boulder for disability access. It grades sites for a full range of disabilities, not just for wheelchair access. Packed with clear maps and symbols, the guide includes narrative descriptions that detail trail grades, surface materials, trail width, obstacles, and picnic and restroom facilities. The guide is available at the Iris Center, the East Boulder Community Center, and the North and South Boulder Rec Centers. Or call the Expand Program (303-413-7216).

Short Hops

WILDERNESS ON WHEELS—KENOSHA PASS

Sixty miles southwest of Denver, near Kenosha Pass, is the Wilderness on Wheels project. Located mostly on U.S. Forest Service land, this breathtaking area includes over a mile of 8-foot-wide boardwalk that begins at a mountain stream and wends gently to a ridgetop overlook at 9,300 feet. Trout fishing along the stream, picnicking and cookouts, and camping on decks specially elevated to the height of a wheelchair are all possibilities. Open April to mid-October, weather permitting. There is no charge, but donations are requested. Reservations are required for all visits.

Wilderness on Wheels
3131 South Vaughn Way, Suite 222
Aurura, CO 80014
(303) 751-3959
www.wildernessonwheels.org

THE NATIONAL SPORTS CENTER FOR THE DISABLED (NSCD)—WINTER PARK

This incredible nonprofit began in 1970 as a one-time ski lesson for 23 amputee children and has evolved into the largest and most successful program of its kind in the world. Children and adults, with disabilities ranging from blindness and severe diabetes and asthma to amputation and progressive illnesses, engage in a vast program of outdoor adventure activities. In addition to recreational downhill and cross-country skiing, snowboarding, and snowshoeing lessons, NSCD provides year-round competition training to ski racers with disabilities. Summer recreation opportunities include biking, hiking, in-line skating, sailing, therapeutic horseback riding, whitewater rafting, baseball, fishing, rock climbing for the blind, and camping. One thousand trained volunteers participate! The center provides training for outdoor recreation specialists from around the world and hosts learn-to-race ski camps for teens and young adults around the country.

National Sports Center for the Disabled
P.O. Box 1290
Winter Park, CO 80482
(970) 726-1540 or (303) 316-1540; fax: (970) 726-4112

Denver Office: 633 17th Street, Suite 24
Denver, CO 80202
(303) 293-5711; fax: (303) 293-5446
E-mail: info@nscd.org
www.nscd.org

THE BRECKENRIDGE OUTDOOR EDUCATION CENTER (BOEC)

An awesome mountain center that includes a state-of-the-art adaptive ski program for all disabilities, a mountain campus, and log cabin lodge with wheelchair-accessible ropes courses and fishing. A full program of exciting adventure courses for the disabled and able-bodied. These include multiday whitewater trips, hiking, fishing, canoeing, backpacking, snowshoeing, and rock climbing. A philosophy of challenge by choice and a leave-no-trace environmental ethic is fundamental to all programs.

Breckenridge Outdoor Education Center
P.O. Box 697
Breckenridge, CO 80424
(970) 453-6422 or (800) 383-2632; fax: (970) 453-4676
E-mail boec@boec.org
www.boec.org

More Books

Andrews, Robert, and Robert Righter. *Colorado Birds*. Denver, Colo.: Denver Museum of Natural History, 1992.

Banks, Gordon, and Dave Eckardt. *Colorado Rivers and Creeks*. 2nd ed. Woody Creek, Colo.: Published by the authors, 1999.

Barnhart, Tom. *Front Range Single Tracks: The Best-Single Track Trails Near Denver and Boulder*. Littleton, Colo.: Fat Tire Press, 1999.

Bartholomew, Marty. *Flyfisher's Guide to Colorado*. Belgrade, Mont.: Wilderness Adventure Press, 1998.

Barton, Harlan N. *Peak to Peak: Colorado Front Range Ski Trails*. Boulder, Colo.: Front Range Publishing, 1995.

Benningfield, Phillip. *Colorado Bouldering*. Boulder, Colo.: Sharp End Publishing, 1999.

Boddie, Caryn, and Peter Boddie. *Hiking Colorado II.* Helena, Mont.: Falcon Publishing. 1999.

D'Antonio, Bob. *Mountain Biking Denver and Boulder.* Helena, Mont.: Falcon Publishing, 1997.

DeLeon, Fernan. *Dirt: The Very Best of Winter Park and East Grand County, Colorado.* Hood River, Ore.: Hood River Publishing, 1999.

Fielder, John, and Mark Pearson. *The Complete Guide to Colorado's Wilderness Areas.* Englewood, Colo.: Westcliffe Publishing, 1994.

Fisher, Chris C., and Greg Butcher. *Birds of Denver and the Front Range.* Edmonton, Canada: Lone Pine Publishing, 1997.

Fishing Close to Home: Fishing Spots and Information for All Age Groups, Metro Denver, Boulder and Nearby Lakes and Streams. Hudson, Colo.: Outdoor Books & Maps, 1999.

Gray, Mary Taylor. *The Guide to Colorado Birds.* Englewood, Colo.: Westcliffe Publishers, 1988.

Green, Stewart M. *Rock Climbing Colorado.* Helena, Mont.: Falcon Publishing, 1995.

Guide to the High Line Canal. Denver, Colo.: Denver Water Community Relations Office, 1999.

Holt, Harold R. *A Birder's Guide to Colorado.* Colorado Springs, Colo.: American Birding, 1997.

Hosman, Todd. *Fly Fishing Colorado's Front Range: An Angler's Guide.* Boulder, Colo.: Pruett Publishing, 1999.

Hubbel, Peter, and Deaun Schovajsa. *Classic Rock Climbs: Golden Cliffs, Colorado.* Helena, Mont.: Falcon Publishing, 1998.

Kingery, Hugh E., ed. *Colorado Breeding Bird Atlas.* Denver, Colo.: Colorado Bird Atlas Partnership, 1998.

Litz, Brian. *Colorado Hut to Hut: A Guide to Skiing, Hiking, and Biking Colorado's Backcountry.* 2nd ed. Englewood, Colo.: Westcliffe Publishing, 1995.

Litz, Brian, and Kurt Lankford. *Skiing Colorado's Backcountry: Northern Mountains—Trails and Tours.* Golden, Colo.: Fulcrum Publishing, 1989.

National Geographic Society. *Field Guide to the Birds of North America.* 2nd ed. Washington, D.C.: National Geographic Society, 1987.

Rathburn, Linda McComb, and Linda Wells Ringrose. *Foothills to Mount Evans, West-of-Denver Trail Guide.* Evergreen, Colo.: The Wordsmiths, 1980.

Rich, Dave. *Denver Hiking Guide: 45 Hikes within 45 Minutes of Denver.* 2nd ed. Boulder, Colo.: Books West, 1999.

Roberts, Jack. *Colorado Ice.* Boulder, Colo.: Polar Star, 1998.

Rolofson, Mark. *Clear Creek Canyon Sport Climbers Guide.* Boulder, Colo.: Free West Rock Guides, 1999.

Rossiter, Richard. *Rock Climbing Boulder Canyon.* Helena, Mont.: Falcon Publishing, 1999.

Rossiter, Richard. *Rock Climbing El Dorado.* Helena, Mont.: Falcon Publishing, 2000.

Rossiter, Richard. *Rock Climbing the Flatirons.* Helena, Mont.: Falcon Publishing, 1999.

Ryter, Derek, and Jarral Ryter. *Mountain Biking Colorado's Front Range.* Boulder, Colo.: Pruett Publishing, 1998.

Salcedo, Tracy. *Best Easy Day Hikes: Boulder.* Helena, Mont.: Falcon Publishing, 2000.

Salcedo, Tracy. *Best Easy Day Hikes: Denver.* Helena, Mont.: Falcon Publishing, 2000.

Salcedo, Tracy. *12 Short Hikes in the Boulder Foothills.* Evergreen, Colo.: Chockstone Press, 1995.

Salcedo, Tracy. *12 Short Hikes in the Denver Foothills: Central.* Evergreen, Colo.: Chockstone Press, 1995.

Salcedo, Tracy. *12 Short Hikes in the Denver Foothills: North.* Evergreen, Colo.: Chockstone Press, 1995.

Struthers, Burt, and Terry Struthers. *The Guide to Bicycling the Roads Out of Boulder.* 3rd ed. Boulder, Colo.: Published by the authors, 1998.

Walter, Claire. *Snowshoeing Colorado.* 2nd ed. Golden, Colo.: Fulcrum Publishing, 2000.

Where to Connect

A-1 Diving
1800 West Oxford Avenue
Englewood, CO 80110
(303) 789-2450
www.a1scuba.com
Dive Shop

Adventures to the Edge
P.O. Box 2636
Crested Butte, CO 81224
(970) 349-1432
(888) 754-2201
Guiding

Airtime Above Hang Gliding
1372 Sinton Road
Evergreen, CO 80439
(303) 674-2451
Instruction, Shop

Alpenglow Mountainsport
885 Lupine, Suite B
Golden, CO 80401
(303) 277-0133
Shop

Alpine World Ascents
4224 Corriente Place
Boulder, CO 80301
(303) 247-0668
www.alpineworldascents.com
Guiding

American Canoe Association
7432 Alban Station Boulevard
Suite B-232
Springfield, VA 22150
(703) 451-0141
www.aca-paddler.org
Kayaking

American Whitewater Association
1430 Fenwick Lane
Silver Spring, MD 20910
(301) 589-9453
www.awa.org
Kayaking

The Anchorage
(303) 833-6601
www.theanchorage.com

Audubon Society of Greater Denver
9308 South Platte Canyon Road
Littleton, CO 80128
(303) 973-9530
Organization

B&B Livery
Chatfield State Park
11500 North Roxborough Park Road
Littleton, CO 80125
(303) 933-3636
Stable

Bear Creek Lake Stables
14600 West Hampden Avenue
Morrison, CO 80465
(303) 697-9666
Stable

Beaver Meadows
P.O. Box 178
Red Feather Lake, CO 80543
(970) 881-2450
(800) 462-5870
Cross-Country Skiing, Snowshoeing

Bent Gate Mountaineering
1300 Washington Street
Golden, CO 80401
(303) 271-9382
Shop

The Bolder Bicycle Commuters
3239 9th Street
Boulder, CO 80304
(303) 499-7466
(303) 449-7439
Club

Bolder Flight
(303) 444-5455
E-mail: thermals1@aol.com
Hang Gliding Shop

Boulder Bird Club
(303) 666-9827

Boulder Outdoor Center
2510 North 47th Street
Boulder, CO 80301

(303) 444-8420
Shop

Boulder Road Runners
(303) 492-8776
www.boulderroadrunners.org
Organization

Boulder Rock Club
2829 Mapleton Avenue
Boulder, CO 80301
(303) 447-2804
www.boulderrock.com
Rock Climbing Gym

Boulder Running Company
2775 Pearl Street
Boulder, CO 80302
(303) 786-9255
Shop

Boulder Running Company
8116 West Bowles Avenue
Littleton, CO 80123
(303) 932-6000
Shop

Boulder Seniors on Bikes
2431 Mapleton Avenue
Boulder, CO 80304
(303) 443-7623
Club

Boulder Women's Cycling Team
(3030) 497-8427
Club

Bradley Stables
1375 North 111th Street
Lafayette, CO 80026
(303) 665-4637
www.bbcyber.com/bbstbles
Stable

Breckenridge Nordic Center
1200 Ski Hill Road
P.O. Box 1776
Breckenridge, CO 80424
(970) 453-6855
www.colorado.net/~nord/
Cross-Country Skiing, Snowshoeing

Breckenridge Outdoor Education Center
P.O. Box 697
Breckenridge, CO 80424
(970) 453-5422
(800) 383-2632
www.boec.org
Programs for People with Disabilities

Campus Cycles
2102 South Washington Street
Denver, CO 80210
(303) 698-2811
www.campuscycles.com
Bike Shop

Carter Lake Sailing Club
www.sailcarter.org

Chip Graham Windsurfing Academy
(303) 426-6503

CloudStreet AirSports
4623 East County Road 54
Ft. Collins, CO 80524
(970) 493-5339
Hang Gliding Instruction, Shop

CoBirds List Serve
E-mail: listproc@lists.co.edu

Colorado Athletic Training School
2400 30th Street
Boulder, CO 80301
(303) 939-9699
Rock Climbing Gym

Colorado Avalanche Information Center
325 Broadway, WS1
Boulder, CO 80303
(303) 275-5360
(970) 668-0600
www.caic.state.co.us

Colorado Bicycle Racing Association for Seniors, Inc. (COBRAS)
621 17th Street, Suite 1550
Denver, CO 80293
(303) 320-4413
Organization

Colorado Bird Observatory
13401 Piccadilly Road
Brighton, CO 80601
(303) 659-4348
Organization

Colorado Field Ornithologists
www.cfo-link.org

Colorado Mountain Club
The American Mountaineering Center
710 10th Street, #200
Golden, CO 80401
(303) 279-3080
(800) 633-4417
www.cmc.org
Cross-Country Skiing, Hiking/Backpacking

Colorado Mountain School
351 Moraine Avenue
Estes Park, CO 80517
(970) 586-5758
www.cmschool.com
Instruction, Guides

Colorado Sail and Yacht Club
www.csyc.org

Colorado Whitewater Association (CWWA)
P.O. Box 4315
Englewood, CO 80155
(303) 430-4380
www.coloradowhitewater.org
Kayaking

Columbine Polo Club & Equestrian Center
6900 South Platte Canyon Road
Littleton, CO 80128
(303) 933-7881
www.columbineequestrian.com

Community Sailing of Colorado
(303) 757-7718
www.members.tripod.com/~CommunitySailing/index.html

Confluence Kayaks and Telemar
1537 Platte Street
Denver, CO 80202
(303) 433-3676
www.confluencekayaks.com
Kayaking, Telemarking

Copper Mountain Cross-Country Center
P.O. Box 3001
Copper Mountain, CO 80443
(970) 968-2318
Cross-Country Skiing

Denver Bicycle Touring Club
P.O. Box 260517
Lakewood, CO 80226
(303) 756-7240
Club

Denver Divers
557 Milwaukee Street
Denver, CO 80206
(303) 988-6725
Dive Shop

Denver Field Ornithologists
Rare Bird Alert Hotline:
(303) 424-2144
www.geocities/dfobirders

Denver Museum of Nature and Science
(303) 370-6303

Denver Sailing Association
www.denversailing.org

Devils Thumb Ranch Resort
P.O. Box 750
Tabernash, CO 80543
(970) 726-8231
Cross-Country Skiing, Snowshoeing

Dillon Yacht Club
www.summitnet.com/dyc/dyc/html

Doc's Ski and Sport
627 South Broadway
Boulder, CO 80303
(303) 499-0963
Shop

Eldora Nordic Center
P.O. Box 1697

Nederland, CO 80466
(303) 440-8700, ext. 212
www.eldora.com
Cross-Country Skiing, Snowshoeing

EMS
2550 Arapahoe Avenue
Boulder, CO 80302
(303) 442-7566
Shop

Estes Park Mountain Shop
358 East Elkhorn Avenue
Estes Park, CO 80517
(970) 586-6548
Shop

Expand Program
3198 North Broadway
Boulder, CO 80304
(303) 413-7216
www.ci.boulder.co.us/parks-recreation
Programs for Disabled Individuals

Fleet Feet Sports
1035 Pearl Street
Boulder, CO 80302
(303) 939-8000
Shop

Fly Away Paragliding
30590 Highway 72
Golden, CO 80403
(303) 642-0849
Shop

The Flyfisher, Ltd.
120 Madison Street
Denver, CO 80206
(303) 322-5014
Fly-Fishing

Front Range Mountain Guides
P.O. Box 17294
Boulder, CO 80308
(303) 666-5523
www.mtnguides.com
Rock Climbing

Frisco Nordic Center
P.O. Box 532
Colorado Highway 9
Frisco, CO 80443
(970) 668-0866
Cross-Country Skiing, Snowshoeing

Front Range Anglers
629 South Broadway
Boulder, CO 80302
(303) 442-6204
Fly-Fishing

Galyan's
Flatirons Mall
31 West Flatiron Circle
Broomfield, CO 80020
(720) 887-0900
Shop

Grand Lake Touring Center
P.O. Box 590
Grand Lake, CO 80447
(970) 627-8008

Cross-Country Skiing, Snowshoeing

Grand West Outfitters
801 Broadway
Denver, CO 80203
(303) 825-0300
Shop

The Hatch Fly Shop
28055 Highway 74, #202
Evergreen CO 80439
(303) 674-0482
www.thehatchflyshop.webtv
Fly-Fishing

High Prairie Farms Equestrian Center
7522 South Pinery Parkway
Parker, CO 81034
(303) 841-5550
www.highprairiefarms.com

International Mountain Biking Association
P.O. Box 7578
Boulder, CO 80306
(888) 442-4622
Organization

Keystone Cross-Country Center
P.O. Box 38
Vail, CO 80435
(970) 496-4275
Cross-Country Skiing

Larson's Ski & Sport
4715 Kipling Street
Wheat Ridge, CO 80034
(303) 423-0654
Shop

Leave No Trace
www.lnt.org

Mojo Wheels
5970 West Dartmouth
Denver, CO 80227
(303) 985-4487
Bike Shop

Mountain Miser
209 West Hampden Avenue
Englewood, CO 80110
(303) 761-7070
Shop

Mountain Sports
2835 Pearl Street
Boulder, CO 80301
(303) 442-8355
Shop

National Audubon Colorado
3107 28th Street, Suite B
Boulder, CO 80301
(303) 415-0130

National Sports Center for the Disabled
P.O. Box 1290
Winter Park, CO 80482

(970) 726-1540
(303) 316-1540
Denver Office:
633 17th Street, Suite 24
Denver, CO 80202
(303) 293-5711
www.nscd.org

Neptune Mountaineering
633 South Broadway
Boulder, CO 80303
(303) 499-8866
Shop

Outdoor Recreation Information
1416 Platte Street
Denver, CO 80202
(303) 756-3100

Paradise Rock Gym
6920 North Washington Street, Unit 5
Denver, CO 80216
(303) 286-8168
www.ParadiseRock.com
Rock Climbing Gym

Paragon Guides
P.O. Box 130
Vail, CO 81658
(970) 926-5299
Hut-to-Hut Cross-Country Skiing, Snowshoeing, Biking, Hiking

Peak to Peak Pony Club: Boulder
15 Copperdale Lane
Golden, CO 80403
(303) 642-0401

Phidippedes Track Club
(303) 721-1520

Pine Cliff Stables
21517 West 56th Avenue
Golden, CO 80403
(303) 279-1221
Stable

Piney Creek Nordic Center and Cookhouse
1520 Mount Elbert Drive
Leadville, CO 80461
(719) 486-1750
Cross-Country Skiing, Snowshoeing

Red Rocks Cyclery
300 Bear Creek Avenue
Morrison, CO 80465
(303) 697-8833
Mountain Biking

REI
1416 Platte Street
Denver, CO 80202
(303) 756-3100
Shop

Rock'n & Jam'n
9499 North Washington Street, Unit C

Thornton, CO 80229
(303) 254-6299
belayme@worldnet.att.net
Rock Climbing Gym

Rocky Mountain Back Country Horsemen
P.O. Box 41
Penrose, CO 81240
(719) 372-0317
Club

Rocky Mountain Canoe Club
(303) 989-4833
www.chssolar@quest.net
Club

Rocky Mountain Cycling Club
P.O. Box 101473
Denver, CO 80250
www.rmccrides.com
Club

Rocky Mountain Diving Center
1920 North Wadsworth Boulevard
Lakewood, CO 80215
(303) 232-2400
Dive Shop

Rocky Mountain Hang Gliding Association (RMHGA)
P.O. Box 28181
Lakewood, CO 80228
www.rmhga.org

Rocky Mountain Paragliding School of Colorado
6595 Odell Place, #C
Boulder, CO 80301
(303) 579-9971
www.rmparagliding.com
Instruction, Shop

Rocky Mountain Region Pony Club
www.rockymountainupsc.org

Rocky Mountain Road Runners
(303) 871-8366
www.rmrr.org
Organization

Rocky Mountain Sea Kayak Club
www.dotzen.org/paddler/rmskc
Club

Rocky Mountain Windsurfing Association
P.O. Box 27961
Denver, CO 80227
E-mail: RMWA@windsurfing-co.com

Runner's Choice
2460 Canyon Boulevard
Boulder, CO 80302
(303) 449-8551
Shop

Runner's Roost
1685 South Colorado Boulevard

Littleton, CO 80222
(303) 759-8455
Shop

Schwabb Cycles
1565 Pierce Street
Lakewood, CO 80214
(303) 238-0243
www.schwabbcycles.com
Bike Shop

Scuba Den
6729 West 44th Avenue
Wheat Ridge, CO 80333
(303) 431-1088
Dive Shop

Scuba Joe's Dive and Travel
3054 28th Street
Boulder, CO 80301
(303) 444-9286
www.scubajoe.com
Instruction

Silver Creek Resort
P.O. Box 1110
Silver Creek, CO 80446
(800) 754-7458
Cross-Country Skiing, Snowshoeing

The Single Track Factory
1005 South Gaylord
Denver, CO 80209
(303) 733-3334
Bike Shop

Ski Depot Sports
Park Plaza
Winter Park, CO 80482
(970) 726-8055
Shop

Sombrero Ranches, Inc.
3300 Airport Road
Boulder, CO 80301
(970) 586-4577
(303) 442-0258
www.sombrero.com
Stable

Special Needs Program
1849 Emerson Street
Denver, CO 80218
(303) 839-4800 (voice)
(303) 839-4820 (TTY)

The Sporting Woman
2902 East 3rd Avenue
Denver, CO 80206
(303) 316-8392
Shop

Steamboat Springs Ski Touring Center
P.O. Box 775401
Steamboat Springs, CO 80477
(970) 879-8180
www.nordicski.net
Cross-Country Skiing

Tandem Cycle Works
1084 South Gaylord Street
Denver, CO 80209

(303) 715-9690
Bike Shop

Tattered Cover Book Store
1628 16th Street
Denver, CO 80202
(303) 436-1070
www.tatteredcover.com
Book Shop

Team Evergreen Bicycle Club Inc.
P.O. Box 3804
Evergreen, CO 80437
(303) 674-6048
www.teamevergreen.org
Club

10th Mountain Division Hut System
1280 Ute Avenue
Aspen, CO 81611
(970) 925-5775
www.huts.org

Thrillseekers
1912 South Broadway
Denver, CO 80210
(303) 733-8810
www.thrillseekers.com
Rock Climbing Gym

T'n'T Cafe
408 Bear Creek Avenue
Morrison, CO 80465
(303) 697-1011
Mountain Biking, Running

Turin Bicycles, LTD
700 Lincoln
Denver, CO 80203
(303) 837-1857
www.turinbikes.com
Bike Shop

Underwater Phantasies
6869 Clinton Court
Englewood, CO 80237
(303) 220-8282
Dive Shop

Underwater Phantasies
160 Union Boulevard
Lakewood, CO 80228
(303) 988-6725
Dive Shop

Union Boat Yard
2045 West Union, Bldg. D
Englewood, CO 80110
(303) 783-3661
Kayaking, Telemarking, Rock Climbing Gym

University Cycles
839 Pearl Street
Boulder, CO 80302
(303) 444-4196
Bike Shop

Vail/Beaver Creek Nordic Center
P.O. Box 7
Vail, CO 81658
(970) 845-5313
Cross-Country Skiing

Victoria Sailing School
(303) 697-6601
www.victoriasailingschool.com

Wheat Ridge Cyclery
7085 West 38th Avenue
Wheat Ridge, CO 80033
(303) 424-3221
Bike Shop

Wild Bird Center (Boulder)
1641 28th Street
Boulder, CO
(303) 442-1322

Wild Bird Center (Denver)
1685 South Colorado Boulevard
(303) 758-7575
I-70 and Youngfield
(303) 231-9252
5270 East Arapahoe Road
(303) 694-4616

Wild Birds Unlimited (Denver)
2720 South Wadsworth Boulevard
(303) 987-1965
2677 West 88th Avenue
(303) 467-2644
7400 East Hampden Avenue
(303) 694-1088

Wild West Ranch
8001 Alkire Street
Arvada, CO 80005
(303) 425-8902
Stable

Wilderness on Wheels
3131 South Vaughn Way, Suite 222
Aurora, CO 80014
(303) 751-3959
www.wildernessonwheels.com
Wheelchair-Accessible Trails

Wildwasser Sport
7161 Valtec Court
Boulder, CO 80301
(303) 444-2336
Kayaking

Index